Events at the Court of RANJIT SINGH 1810-1817.

Translated from the Papers
in the Alienation Office, Poona.

EDITED BY

Lt. Col. H. L. O. Garrett, M.A., I.E.S.
Keeper of the Records of the Government of the Punjab,

AND

G. L. Chopra, M.A., Ph. D., P. E. S.,
Deputy Keeper of the Records.

A Note on
MAHARAJA RANJIT SINGH
BY
Ihsan H. Nadiem

SANG-E-MEEL PUBLICATIONS
25, Shahrah-e-Pakistan (Lower Mall) Lahore.

904.7   Events at the court of Ranjit Singh,
        1810-1817 / ed. By H. L. O. Garrett &
        G. L. Chopra.-Lahore: Sang-e-Meel
        ·Publications, 2002.
        278p.
        1. History - India. 2. India - History -
        1810-1817. I. Garrett, H. L. O.
        II. Chopra, G. L.

1st ed. 1935.
2nd ed. 2002.

2002
Published by:
Niaz Ahmad
Sang-e-Meel Publications,
Lahore.

We are grateful to Mr. Muhammad Rafiq Doger
(Deed-o-Shuneed) for Providing us the original Book.

ISBN 969-35-1352-5

SANG-E-MEEL PUBLICATIONS
25 Shahrah-e-Pakistan (Lower Mall), P.O. Box 997 Lahore-54000 PAKISTAN
Phones: 7220100 - 7228143   Fax: 7245101
http://www.sang-e-meel.com e-mail: smp@sang-e-meel.com

Chowk Urdu Bazar Lahore. Pakistan. Phone 7667970
PRINTED AT: ZAHID BASHIR PRINTER, LAHORE.

A Note on
·MAHARAJA RANJIT SINGH

His Ancestry

Maharaja Ranjit Singh, the lion of Punjab, belonged to the Sukerchakia *misl* of the Sikhs, which by far was the smallest though destined to become most important of them all. His ancestors were Hindu Jats and lived peaceful life until one of them named Kalu and his wife were driven by circumstances to live with untouchable nomads, *Sansis* around the third quarter of the 15th century AD. A son was born to them there, who took up the profession of freebooting under the influence of the *Sansis*. One of Kalu's descendants in the third generation got settled in Sukerchak near Wazirabad and led a peaceful life, multiplying his fortunes through marriage and managing his estate. Down the line, around 1692, a certain Buddha was the first to adopt the Sikh religion. He was not as peaceful and had associated himself with the plundering gangs of Sikhs and *Sansis*. His alliance by marriage with the well-off Majithia Sikh family made him richer and more important and was thus looked upon as the chief of Sukerchak. His son, Charat Singh, was the first to lay down the foundations of the greatness of the *misl* as he headed a daring band of Sikhs who became a force to reckon with due to their plundering excursions. With time, his gang grew in power and numbers, which enabled him to take forcible possession of all the villages in the neighbourhood of Gujranwala. He was married to the daughter of another notorious robber, Amir Singh, with whom he also joined in their adventures. They both belonged to the Sikh *misl* of Fyzulpuria but this marriage united the wealth and power of two sardars and thus a separate *misl*, Sukerchakia, came to be known after the name of the place of their residence. After Charat Singh, his son Maha Singh continued with plunders and with his bravery and courageous exploitations extended the area of his influence.

His Life and Time

Maha Singh died young. His only son, Ranjit Singh, who was born on 4th November 1780, is said to be just eight years of age at the time of the death of his father. He was thus left to the charge of his mother, Mai Malwain and his father's mother-in-law, Sada Kaur, assisted by the '*diwan*', minister, of her deceased husband, Lakhpat Rai, who was nominated regent and ruled the confederacy in the name of the minor. However, Sada Kaur had much influence over the conduct of the state affairs. She was an ambitious woman and artfully engaged his daughter, Mahtab Kaur, to the young Ranjit Singh with the hope to get the support of Sukerchakia *misl* in getting for her the fruit of sardari, chief-ship, of her own Kanhi *misl*. It is said that Lakhpat Rai was the suspected lover of Ranjit Singh's mother so when the latter reached of age he got killed the Diwan and gave poison to his mother. During the lifetime of the Diwan, Ranjit Singh could exercise no power over the affairs of the estate of his father. No care had been taken in his bringing up. He was not even formally educated and could not read or write. He spent his early days in hunting and merrymaking. His mother-in-law and wife, Sada Kaur and Mahtab Kaur respectively, are also said to be of redoubtable moral character. While still a minor, he then married second time with Raj Kaur daughter of the Nakai Sardar, Khazan Singh. Jind Kaur, mother of Dalip Singh, became his third wife.

On taking the responsibility of the state he appointed Dal Singh, a maternal uncle of his father's, as his Prime Minister and following the footsteps of his father continued with the courageous adventures. The Sikhs by then though wielding much power, were still not a disciplined force.

3

After the return of the Durrani King, Shah Zaman, to Kabul he started nurturing the idea of holding control over Lahore. His authority by then had gradually increased among the Sikhs and after the recovery of the Durrani guns from the river Jhelum and their despatch to Kabul, he had obtained a formal grant of this city. Lahore at this time had three rulers from the Bhangi *misl* of the Sikhs, who are said to be 'unscrupulous, drunken, profligate and tyrannical'. After their deaths their sons were holding sway over their respective areas. With the active assistance of the local notables of Lahore and combined force of Sikhs Ranjit Singh took over the possession of Lahore through artful tactical manoeuvres in 1799. The citizens were given the assurance of internal order and against external aggression.

His success in occupying Lahore made him the object of envy and hatred among the other Sikh Sardars who formed a coalition against him. They were no match to Ranjit Singh and thus perished before the forces led by him and his mother-in-law in the early part of 1800 AD. The following year, Ranjit Singh assumed the title of 'Maharaja', the greatest of the rajas, and declared that in the public correspondence he should be styled as "Sarkar", signifying power and state. A mint was then established at Lahore and coin struck in his name. He also recognised the hereditary offices of the *Kazis* and *muftis* like his earlier Muslim kings and emperors, in addition to making administrative arrangements for a just society.

He reduced the chiefs of Gujrat and Kasur and subdued, by lure or by power, most of the Sikh Sardars. He led successful excursions to Pindi Bhattian. Dhani and Potohar regions as also the forts of Daska and Chiniot. During his campaigns he reached as far as Afghanistan, which by then had lost its over-awe and power due to the civil war. He humbled the rival Bhangi *misl* at Amritsar and subjugated Multan during the siege of which the famous *zamzama* gun, better known the Bhangi top, was successfully used. He humbled Dera Ismail Khan and the area around it, also going up to Bhakkar in Sindh. He wrested the fort of Shujabad. Later on his march to Peshawar, his confidential agent sent in advance was murdered by the rebellious Khattaks, which event grieved the Maharaja very much and he ordered invasion, which resulted in humbling the Khattak chiefs. He captured Jahangira and Khairabad and pushed on to Peshawar, which he also occupied in 1818. The same year Shah Shuja of Kabul tried his luck on the Indus country but failed. On the other side he was successful in occupying Kashmir.

In 1820, an adventurous traveller from Britain. William Moorcroft, visited the court of the Maharaja. Two years later, two European adventurers, Ventura from Italy and Allard from France, who were army officers, came to the Maharaja for employment. Four years later two more Europeans, Court and Avitable, were made generals in the Sikh Army. In the meanwhile, he had also entered in 1809 into a treaty with the British, who by then held the government adjoining the state of the Sikhs. He also successfully crushed, with the help of Pathans, the *jehad* movement led by the reformer Syad Ahmad. A new treaty was signed between the Maharaja and the British Government of India on 31st October 1831.

After leading a very vigorous life the Maharaja had an attack of paralysis in 1834, assumed to be the result of his insatiable appetite for strong drink. He never recovered fully from this affliction and in spite of all efforts of physicians, *hakims* and *veds* he died on 18th June 1839.

Ihsan H. Nadiem,
Former Director of Archaeology, Pakistan.
01-05-2002.

INTRODUCTORY

The original material, of which the present volume represents an English translation, is in the form of news-letters written in the Persian language. These letters are contained in 193 loose sheets of varying size, and together form only a small part of a larger collection, which exists in the Alienation Branch of the Divisional Commissioner's Office at Poona. The larger collection has not yet been explored for purposes of historical investigation. Out of this heap, however, Dr. Muhammad Nazim, an officer of the Archaeological Survey of India, who happened to be stationed in Poona in 1932-33, made a selection of these letters which relate to Ranjit Singh and his Court. Indeed, it was Dr. Nazim himself who had chanced to discover the existence of this material in Poona earlier in 1932 and had brought this fact to the notice of the Keeper of the Records of the Punjab Government.

Our information regarding this smaller collection before it came into our hands is thus based entirely on the communications which we received from its discoverer and the authorities in Poona by whose courtesy it was sent to Lahore for our examination. We have consulted the files of this correspondence and have had recently a personal discussion with Dr. Nazim at Lahore and we take it that these letters were written or recorded for the benefit of some Maharatta ruler of the period, most probably for the Peshwa at Poona. But this is merely an inference, the soundness of which solely depends on two facts: first, that the collection is lodged in Poona and secondly that in the whole collection as scrutinized by Dr. Nazim there cannot be traced a single letter containing news of the Court of the Peshwa, but that news concerning other notable Indian rulers of the time is forthcoming. It thus seems probable that the Peshwa was the person addressed to by the various news-writers including those of the court of Ranjit Singh.

The present collection—193 sheets—reached our Record Office in January, 1933 and was soon after its receipt subjected to a preliminary examination. It was discovered that two kinds of paper had been used in these letters, namely the Sialkoti and the Kashmiri. The Sialkoti sheets were, as usual, of pale brown colour and contained news of the

court of Ranjit Singh only, each item being separately headed as
اخبار ڈیوڑی سردار رنجیت سنگھ بہادر. The Kashmiri variety, besides being white in
colour, had one general heading, viz., منتخب اخبار ہندوستان. Most papers of
either variety were written on both sides, the writing invariably being in
Persian Shikasta. Some of these letters were not easily decipherable, partly
on account of their "Shikasta" characters and partly because of the
decayed condition of the loose sheets, which, in a few cases, were even
damaged or torn. The large majority of them, however, were free from this
latter defect. Almost all of them were deciphered successfully, though the
process involved extraordinary effort on the part of the Persian translators
who were engaged for this work. This preliminary examination alone took
six months, and mainly consisted of a rapid reading through the whole lot
and sorting it chronologically.

The contents of the Kashmiri sheets indicated, at least, one obvious
uniformity in the order in which the different "Deorhis" (courts) were
mentioned. This is as follows:-

(1)   Deorhi-i-Darbar-i-Muala.
(2)   Do.   Muntazim-ud-Daula Bahadur.
(3)   Do.   Sardar Ranjit Singh Bahadur.
(4)   Do.   Maharaja Jagat Singh Bahadur.
(5)   Do.   Maharaja 'Alijah Daulat Rao Sindhia.
(6)   Do.   Maharaja Malhar Rao Holkar.

The Punjab Record Office, being primarily interested in the new
knowledge which this collection might yield about Ranjit Singh and the
events of his reign, it was decided to prepare a translation into English of
that matter alone on each sheet which related to him or any part of his
dominions, and to omit the rest which concerned other princes. In regard
to this latter kind of material, however, it may generally be mentioned that
the letters concerning the "Deorhi-i-Muala" (The Mughal Court) seldom
contained anything of historical or political importance, that those
concerning the "Deorhi-i-Muntazim-ud-Daula" (Mr., afterwards, Sir
Charles Metcalfe) were only a little more detailed than the former, but that
those relating to the "Deorhi of Sardar Ranjit Singh Bahadur" were
comparatively the most copious of all. Again, we found that the number of
the sheets used for each news-selection was mentioned on the top of the
first page as دو بله (two leaves) or سه بله (three leaves), etc. and yet the actual
leaves in each such selection were, in very many cases, not forthcoming.
Usually, the end sheets were missing. Moreover, from the language used

in these letters one could safely say that the writer was not a man of any very great literary accomplishment and that his style was largely affected by local influences. Mistakes of spellings, as apart from mere slips of pen, which are so common in this text, were also very much in evidence.

The actual translation of the letters has taken as long as eighteen months, owing to the great care which was necessary to make an accurate rendering. Every word and phrase of the original has been translated into equivalent English not excluding those relating to the minutest details of the life of the Sikh ruler, such as would apparently be deemed to be of no great historical worth. English idiom had in many places to be sacrificed to accuracy and therefore no apology is needed for the retention of characteristically oriental constructions and phraseology which often sound odd to English ears. In this connection, it may also be mentioned that one peculiar phrase touching upon the most personal and private habit of the Sikh ruler and reading in the original as از امورات ضروری فراغت کرده, occurs twice in each letter but has been for obvious reasons omitted in the translation. This omission provides the only exception of its kind in a text in which everything else has been faithfully included. Each news-letter, as already mentioned, had a separate heading or title which invariably mentioned the name of the court or the ruler—in this case; "The Deorhi of Sardar Ranjit Singh Bahadur," the date of writing or recording the events together with the corresponding day of the week, and the place of despatch of the letter. This last seems to have been the same at which the account was completed—a Mauza, a Taaluqa, a Parganna, or a town, or, as in a very large number of cases, the place of Ranjit Singh's normal residence, namely, the fort at Lahore. The date includes the name of the month and year which are given in most cases both in the Hijri and the Christian eras. Such variations in headings definitely indicate that the news-writer or his agent, openly or otherwise, moved with the Sikh ruler on his tours through his kingdom. The comprehensive nature of these headings is, indeed, a very significant feature of this collection as they suggest the movements and many new aspects of the life and ways of Ranjit Singh, which are seldom brought out in other contemporary works. These headings are all the more important in the absence of other definite internal evidence regarding many points on which students of Sikh history should have welcomed direct information.

The collection suffers from various omissions, the most striking being the complete absence of the name and identity of the writer of these letters or of the circumstances of his appointment. This is generally true in all cases except with regard to three letters at the end of which is written the word عرضی (sender) followed by a seal inscribed "Azim Ullah 1236 A.H." Each of these three letters belongs to the year 1817 which is particularly the last year of this collection. Besides, at the end of ten other letters—all relating to the first two years of this collection (1810-12)—Khushal Singh is mentioned as خبردار (informant), thus, زبانی خوشحال سنگھ خبردار نوشته شد (This news is based on verbal statements of Khushal Singh, the informant). Nothing is said as to who this man was or what position he occupied at the Court, nor is it stated whether he acted clandestinely in lending information to the sender of the news. It is not possible to establish the identity of Azim Ullah either. Another serious gap is the absence throughout this lengthy record of the name of the ruler or of the place to which the letters were sent, nor is there any trace of the agency through which they were transmitted. Again, the abrupt beginning of this series on 1st November, 1810 and its equally abrupt ending towards the close of the year 1817 (except in one single instance of a letter which bears the date 1822 but is otherwise without any proper heading) do not admit of any explanation based on textual evidence. Lastly, presuming that the letter-writer was bound to have attended to his task with some regularity, the irregular chronology of the available letters shows gaps which can only be explained by assuming that part of the material has not yet come to hand. Several months are missing in every single year.

These shortcomings in the text, however, do not imply that the available material is historically deficient. On the other hand some omissions serve as an impetus to a close study of other contemporary works on Ranjit Singh and lead to the elucidation of interesting problems. For example Khushal Singh خبردار so far as these letters are concerned, is a mere name without any further clue to his identity. But we know from other sources (such for example as Sohan Lal's *Umdut-ut-Tawarikh*) that—

   (1)   A Jamadar Khushal Singh was put in charge of the "Deorhi" of the Sikh Chief;

   (2)   And that he was the chief "Deorhiwala", *i.e.*, the man in charge of the main entrance of the residence of Ranjit Singh in the fort at Lahore from 1810 to 1817. Keeping this in mind and turning to the letters we find that—

   (1)   every letter is headed as "news from the Deorhi of Sirdar Ranjit Singh Bahadur;"

(2)   the informant bears the same name as the officer carrying on the duties of the Chief Deorhiwala;

(3)   most important still, the letters are full of information of what went on inside the private apartments of Ranjit Singh and his zenana and therefore are obviously written by a person who had free access to the royal residence; and

(4)   lastly, that the collection begins and ends with the years 1810 and 1817 respectively.

Such comparative study may safely be taken as providing a very strong case for the suggestion that the two persons were identical.

It is also worthy of note that, with one exception, the letters cease after 1817. Apart from the fact that Khushal Singh was no longer there to supply information. 1817 is the year in which the last war between the Peshwa and the British broke out which resulted in the surrender of Baji Rao to the British in June, 1818 and the abolition of the office of Peshwa. There was then no independent court at Poona to which foreign intelligence would be welcome or which would be prepared to pay for it.

The real worth and interest of these papers are to be found in their substance, variety, authenticity and richness of detail. They are full of information on all kinds of matters—personal, administrative, financial, military and judicial, concerning Ranjit Singh and his dominions. The news is most authentic both with regard to the facts and the dates. Certain matters, though of no marked worth individually, are narrated in such minute detail that cumulatively, they provide numerous and illuminating sidelights on the life, policy and character of the Sikh potentate. They afford vivid glimpses into his daily routine, his engagements in the forenoons, afternoons and evenings, his private and personal habits, his associates, the political and administrative problems that engaged his individual attention, the treatment he meted out to his vassals and other princes who sought shelter at his Court and the pastimes and sports which generally amused him. The care which he bestowed on the building up of his military resources is revealed in all its intensity. The extent to which he succeeded in reorganizing his forces after the European style, even before the arrival of the French officers at his Court, can be fully gauged from the names of the commandants of the battalions, which are mentioned in this text. The instructions which he issued to his 'Adaltis' (Justices) in regard to the proper discharge of their duties are being quoted in original, as they lead us definitely to reject the contemporary English testimony that the

9

Sikh ruler paid no heed to this matter. Certain notable incidents of his career such, for example, as his dealings with Shah Shuja-ul-Mulk and his family are treated more exhaustively than elsewhere in the chronicles of his reign. Ample material is provided for studying his attitude towards other rulers whose territories were contiguous to his own—the Barakazais of Peshawar, the Daudputras of Bahawalpur, the Sadozais of Multan, the Nazims of Kashmir, and last but not least the British power on the eastern frontier of his kingdom.

It is not, however, possible within this preface to enumerate all the various points of definite historical value on which this record throws fresh light. They are scattered all over this copious mass and relate to so many different episodes of Sikh rule that they are best studied as a whole and in close association with the dates and contexts of the letters in which they occur. In all such cases explanatory notes and other relevant references have been offered at the end of the text. Some statements of outstanding historical significance are retained in original Persian side by side with the English translation.

One peculiar feature of these letters is the remarkable detachment with which the writer has presented us with bald narratives of facts as they were seen or noticed by him, without in the least attempting to intrude his own views. No opinions are expressed either in the language or in the substance. The writer draws graphic pictures and yet manages to keep himself completely out of them. This entire absence of the personal factor, which creates difficult problems of interpretation in most historical materials, gives this record a rare position among the sources from which to reconstruct or elucidate the events of this period.

In the end, we might say that, apart from their undoubted usefulness to scholars of Sikh history, we regard this material as a valuable addition to the collection in the Punjab Record Office. Here we already possess a fine storehouse of English correspondence regarding the Sikhs and their administration. But whereas the English record is more complete with regard to the latter half of Ranjit Singh's reign and the subsequent years, there is an obvious paucity of evidence about the earlier period. This Persian intelligence deals with an earlier decade and thus forms a welcome addition to our existing resources.

H. L. O. GARRETT
G. L. CHOPRA

1810 (1)

News of the Deorhi[1] of Sardar Ranjit Singh Bahadur. Thursday, dated 1ˢᵗ November 1810 (3ʳᵈ Shawwal 1225 A.H.), the Village of Jadarsai, situated at a distance of one kos[2] from the Fort of Dal Singh in the Division of Nadhan Singh Ayu.

Yesterday, the Noble Sarkar remained in bed until noon and came out walking to the tent set apart for audience at about the third quarter[3] of the day. Khalsa Kharak Singh, the prince, Diwan Muhkam Chand, Harbajh Rai Mustaufi, Mathra Dass, Dewan Bhawani Dass of the low stature, Munshi Devi Dass, Buland Khan, Jahan Khan Bareech, Hakim Aziz-ud-Din Khan and several other sirdars presented themselves and made obeisance. The Noble Sarkar talked for a while to every one of them. The messengers (Jauri)[4] brought the news that Zaman Shah continued to be in Rawalpindi, that Shahzadas Abdul Wadud and Mansur, the sons of Zaman Shah, had left Rawalpindi and gone over to the fort of Attock in response to an invitation from Jahandad Khan, the brother of Muhammad Khan, the Subedar of Kashmir and Ghulam Muhammad Khan, and that it was rumoured in Rawalpindi that Jahandad Khan had made Shahzada Abdul Wadud Khan succeed to the throne of Kingship, according to a note from Ata Muhammad Khan, the said Subedar, and that he had marched to a distance of two or three kos in the direction of Peshawar together with the said Shahzada, some other sirdars and his own troops, in order to punish Muhammad Azim Khan, the brother of Sirdar Fateh Khan who together with Shahzada Lus was staying at Peshawar at that time. They further stated that sixty thousand horse and foot, two lakhs of rupees in cash and some rolls of Pashmina, sent from Kashmir by Ata Muhammad Khan, the Subedar of that Province, had also reached the fort of Attock. They also reported that His Highness Shah Shuja-ul-Mulk Badshah Ghazi was encamped near Pind Dadan Khan as previously. The Noble Sarkar heard all this news and despatched some written order to Jamiat Singh Karohi and Bahadur Singh Man. Later Nihal Singh Atariwala, who had gone to plunder the village of the refractory zamindars of the riverain district of Jehlum, returned from there and humbly stated that he had brought as captives some of the notorious ringleaders-mischief-makers and bastards. The Noble Sarkar replied that he must keep them in his own custody. Then the Noble Sarkar had letters despatched to Sardar Jodh Singh of Ramgarh (who was in Lahore at that time), Raja

Fateh Singh Ahluwalia, Sirdar Desa Singh Majithia and to several others. The messengers came and presented a written answer from Jamiat Singh Karohi and Bahadur Singh Man, to the above-mentioned order of the Noble Sarkar to them. It became known that Nadhan Singh Ayu would present himself to the Noble Sarkar on the morning of the following day and could not do so immediately, being busy in removing his property and effects out of the fort. When the night had passed four hours the Noble Sarkar went to sleep. The night passed away uneventfully.

To-day the Noble Sarkar woke up early in the morning and came to the tent set apart for audience where the officers and sirdars presented themselves and made obeisance. The courier came to inform him about the satisfactory progress of the siege and retired. It was stated that the men of Diwan Muhkam Chand had entered the fort, that Dal Singh had established at that place a Thana[5] on behalf of the Noble Sarkar, and that Nadhan Singh personally was coming to the Noble Sarkar. Soon after, Jamiat Singh Karohi, Bahadur Singh Man, Pardhan Singh and Nadhan Singh came in and presented themselves. The Noble Sarkar stood up to show respect to Nadhan Singh Ayu, and embraced him, whereupon the latter presented a bow by way of Nazar and showed contrition. The Noble Sarkar re-assured him by promising award of an estate worth thirty thousand rupees, and gave him a fine woolen shawl and a turban by way of kindness. Nadhan Singh then retired to his own camp which had been pitched near the army of the Noble Sarkar. In the meantime the messengers (Jauri) came and stated that Raja Fateh Singh Ahluwalia, marching from Bhirowal, which is at a distance of seventeen kos from Amritsar, had reached Amritsar, and was expected soon to present himself to the Noble Sarkar. Then the Noble Sarkar went into the zenana. All else went on well until noon. This is written according to the verbal statements made by Khushal Singh, the informant.

1810 (2)

News of the Deorhi of Sirdar Ranjit Singh Bahadur. Thursday, dated 22nd November, 1810 (24th Shawwal, 1225 A.H.); the Royal Fort, Lahore.

Yesterday the Noble Sarkar remained in bed until noon, and came out to the Saman Burj at about the third quarter of the day. Sirdar Dal Singh Bharania, Sardar Lodhi Singh Ramgharia, Ghaus Muhammad Khan, Munshi Devi Dass, and several other sirdars, high and low, presented themselves and made obeisance. Chaudhri Qadir Bakhsh from Raja Fateh Singh Ahluwalia made obeisance and represented that the said Raja had gone to make Sahib Singh of Gujrat understand his real situation, had taken upon himself the whole responsibility, and that he (the Raja), taking him (Sahib Singh) out of the fort of Mangalanpur, and proceeding forward from Deva Miana up to three kos in the company of the Chaudhri himself, was at the time marching on his way to Amritsar, because the Noble Sarkar was also to go there to witness the taking of the oath. He told the Noble Sarkar something more in privacy about the conditions of that place. The Noble Sarkar ordered Bhai Gurmukh Singh to get ready to depart soon. He replied that he was ready to undertake whatever he was ordered. It was stated that Budh Singh of Faizullapur had gone over to Amritsar after marching from this place, as ordered by the Noble Sarkar. The Noble Sarkar said to the representatives of the rajas of the mountainous regions that several loaded camels had been robbed in their divisions and ordered them to write to their masters to procure those camels with their loads and send them to the Noble Sarkar, otherwise it would not be good for them. Misar Devi Dass was ordered to send a Hundi[6] of five thousand rupees towards Patiala for the purchase of oxen and "Shatranji" (carpet matting). He replied that he would do so. The messengers (Jauri) arrived and reported that Jaimal Singh of Kalanaur had come from there to Amritsar for purchasing articles on the occasion of the marriage of his daughter who had been betrothed to Khalsa Kharak Singh, the prince. The Noble Sarkar heard it and had letters despatched to Diwan Muhkam Chand, Raja Chet Singh of Jammu, the Raja of Jasrota and many others. Then the news came that Colonel Nasir-ud-Dawla Bahadur[7] had gone to Sirhind and Shahdara on a pleasure trip and was expected to return soon to his cantonment in the town of Ludhiana. It was reported further that Rani Rattan Kaur was busily engaged in the matrimonial ceremonies of her son, Khalsa Karam Singh, in Patiala. The Noble Sarkar, then, went into the zenana and the sirdars and others who were present, retired. He took the prescribed food when the night had passed one quarter and went to sleep. The night passed away uneventfully.

To-day the Noble Sarkar awoke early in the morning and came out to the Saman Burj where his staff of officials presented themselves and made obeisance. He showed his pulse to Hakim Muhammad Ali Khan who administered an aperient to him. The Noble Sarkar issued an order that no one might go inside his apartments without his permission. All else is well until early in the afternoon. This is written according to the verbal statements of Khushal Singh, the informant.

Deorhi of Sirdar Ranjit Singh Bahadur. Friday, dated 8th December, 1810 (10th Ziqaad 1255 A.H.); the Royal Fort, Lahore.

Yesterday the Noble Sarkar came to the Saman Burj at about the third quarter of the day and said to Hashim Khan Satul Bashi, Badal Khan, and other representatives of Hazrat Shuja-ul-Mulk that Mian Khairata, the Darogha[8] of the Topkhana at the head of his Topkhana, Sarbuland Khan and other Afghans and Nawab Kutub-ud-Din Khan Afghan of Kasur, with three or four battalions, would be made to accompany them, as also the representative of Nawab Muhammad Ali Khan of Thatha Bhakhar. The Noble Sarkar further said that if Nawab Muzaffar Khan would evacuate and surrender the fort of Multan out of the fear of his troops, well and good, otherwise he himself would march there. Of this they all approved. The Noble Sarkar made Munshi Devi Dass despatch a letter to Mian Khairata, the Darogha of Topkhana, towards Jammu, calling him back to his presence. When the night had passed two hours he retired into the zenana.

To-day he came out to the Saman Burj early in the morning and Munshi Devi Dass presented him the news about Afghanistan. It became known that Mirza Mahmud Shah and Sirdar Fateh Khan were still in Peshawar and had pitched their advance camp and their banner on the bank of the river Attock. It further became known that the money-lenders of Shikarpur who resided in Peshawar had hidden themselves out of fear of Mirza Mahmud Shah who was reported to have seized ten thousand rupees from the money-lenders and traders of Kabul but was still short of funds. They were reported to have hidden themselves for fear lest he should demand money from them also. The shops of better class of tradesmen were all reported to be closed. The messenger (Jauri) brought the news that Korin Sahib Bahadur, the collector, had reached a place at a distance of five kos from Fatehabad with English troops in order to punish the Bhattis and other inhabitants by establishing his camp there. He was further reported to have established his "Thana" in the "Garhi."[9] it was also reported that the troops of Raja Jaswant Singh of Nabha had reached the spot and had collected sixteen hundred oxen out of the cattle which the Bhattis had concealed at various places in the desert. The Raja had distributed them among his horsemen, giving ten oxen to each. The messengers also stated that the above-mentioned Sahib had proceeded towards Fatehabad and had established there also a "Thana" of the English. On hearing this the Noble Sarkar remarked that the active hostility of the English was a serious matter, for nobody had the power to oppose them. At noon he went into the zenana. All's well otherwise.

1810 (4)

Deorhi of Sirdar Ranjit Singh Bahadur. Tuesday, dated 11th December, 1810 (13th Ziqaad 1225 A.H.); the Royal Fort, Lahore.

Yesterday the Noble Sarkar came over to the Saman Burj at about the third quarter of the day and the messengers (Jauri) came in and said, "The Mughals of Afghanistan some time ago killed Nihal Singh, a broker of Amritsar. They are in prison since that time under Sirdar Dal Singh Majithia in the fort of Bhangian there. This sirdar had confiscated all their property and has handed it over to the traders of Amritsar. He now wants to know the order of the Noble Sarkar as to the punishment for the murderers. Sirdar Jodh Singh of Ramgarh continues to be in Amritsar and Raja Fateh Singh Ahluwalia in Kapurthala. Rani Sada Kaur, the mother-in-law of the Noble Sarkar, is in the town of Mukerian." After hearing all this the Noble Sarkar had a letter despatched to Mian Khairata, the Darogha of the Topkhana, who was in the district of Jammu at that time, ordering him to march towards Multan with his Topkhana *via* the river Ravi. Diwan Bhawani Dass was also sent towards that place with the "Sikhi" troops. The said Darogha was ordered to obey loyally the said Diwan. When the night had passed by two hours the Noble Sarkar went into the zenana.

To-day he came out of the royal sleeping chamber early in the morning. The messengers (Jauri) brought the news that Mirza Mahmud Shah and Sirdar Fateh Khan continued to be in Peshawar and that the money-lenders of the place were still in hiding. They also reported that Mirza Mahmud Shah and Fateh Khan had issued strict orders that none of the soldiers, messengers or the like be allowed to cross over the river Attock to their side, and that Jahandad Khan, the brother of Muhammad Khan, the Subedar of Kashmir, was still staying in the fort after having established his firm control over the "Ghat"[10] of that river which nobody could now cross without his permission; that Zaman Shah was still in Rawalpindi but was contemplating leaving it for some other direction; that Shahzada Kamran, the son of Mirza Mahmud Shah, was reported to be in the town of Qandahar where grain had become very dear and was being sold at the rate of ten seers of the "Pukhta Wazan" (1¼ English seers=1 Pukhta Seer); and that scarcity of grain also prevailed in Afghanistan.

14

After listening to all this, the Noble Sarkar talked with Pindi Dass, a representative of Nawab Muhammad Ali Khan of Thatha Bhakhar and gave him a "Hundi" worth two hundred rupees in continuation of the old favours, to be realized by him from Nawab Muzaffar Khan of Multan out of his liability for the tax. Pindi Dass then took leave and crossed over to the other side of the river Ravi. The Noble Sarkar went into the zenana and it went on well otherwise up till noon.

1810 (5)

News of the Deohri of Sirdar Ranjit Singh Bahadur. Thursday, dated 20th December, 1810 (22nd Ziqaad 1225 A.H.); the Royal Fort, Lahore.

Yesterday the Noble Sarkar remained inside in the zenana until the day advanced one quarter and a half, and continued merry-making, drinking wine and enjoying the dance of the dancing girls. At noon he took his meals and went to rest. He awoke at about the third quarter of the day and came out to the Saman Burj. The sirdars usually present at the court came in and made obeisance. Duni Chand, the Vakil of Raja Bagh Singh of Jind, sought permission to depart. The Noble Sarkar said that it would be given, and ordered Munshi Devi Dass to write out and address a letter on his behalf to the said Raja acknowledging the receipt of the "Khass" tent sent by him through his representative and explaining the latter's departure. The Noble Sarkar granted Duni Chand one fine woolen shawl, one turban, one roll of "Gulbadan"[11] and rupees one hundred and twenty-five in cash, and entrusting him the letter, allowed him to depart. Rama Nand Sahu, the agent, was ordered to deliver to Duni Chand a letter for two thousand rupees for the purchase of oxen from the district of Banker in Jind to be made by his master for the Noble Sarkar. Munshi Devi Dass presented the letter of authority regarding the forts of Kota, of Sobha Singh, and several other places which had been granted to Jamna Dass, the agent, Rama Nand Sahu and Mathra Dass, the Noble Sarkar's accountants, according to his (Sarkar's) orders against two lakhs and five thousand rupees. The Noble Sarkar said that it would be given to the aforesaid person on the following day and that it must remain for the time being with Devi Dass himself. It was stated that Diwan Bhawani Dass of the low stature, Nawab Kutub-ud-Din Khan of Kasur, Sarbuland Khan Bareech and several others had proceeded towards Multan from the village of Saidpur which was situated at a distance of six kos from Lahore and three kos from Shahdara. Munshi Devi Dass was ordered to purchase flint for the guns to the value of two hundred and fifty rupees. When the night had passed by two hours the sirdars and others, who were present, walked out. The Noble Sarkar went into the zenana and engaged himself in enjoying the music of the dancing girls after taking his meals. When the night had passed by one quarter, he retired to rest. The night passed away uneventfully.

To-day he woke up early in the morning and came out when the day had advanced two hours. The sirdars, who are usually at his court, presented themselves, making obeisance. It was stated that during the night the dacoits had raided the quarter of the goldsmiths and had carried away property worth two hundred and seventy-five rupees. The Noble Sarkar summoned Bahadur Singh incharge of the police station of the city, showed his annoyance, peremptorily ordered him to start investigation and produce in his presence all the robbers, warning him at the same time that failure to do so would not be to his credit. Munshi Devi Dass presented news of the various parts. It became known that Mirza Mahmud Shah and Sardar Fateh Khan were still in the town of Peshawar; that negotiations for peaceful settlement continued between Ata Muhammad Khan, the Subedar of Kashmir and Mirza Mahmud Shah through Muhammad Azim Khan, the brother of Fateh Khan and the representatives of the Province of Kashmir; and that it was hoped that some settlement might speedily be reached. It was also reported that Mahmud Shah had distributed twenty rupees to each horseman in his army, and Zaman Shah had shifted his camp from Rawalpindi to Pind Dadan Khan. Raja Sahib Singh was still reported to be at Patiala, and was engaged in making arrangements for the marriage of Khalsa Karam Singh and in insisting on his officials discharging their duties in that matter very carefully. It was also stated that his officials had reported that there was great dearth of money and that he must procure some from the villages of Afghans. Tej Singh, the brother of Raja Chain Sukh, had been sent to fetch Raja Bhagh Singh and Mai Khem Kaur from Jind; and Budh Singh Nami, a reliable person of Raja Bhagh Singh, had also been allowed to depart for Jind in the company of Tej Singh, with a farewell gift of twenty rupees. The Noble Sarkar heard all this and then went into the zenana and the sirdar and others present, walked out. He took his meals and went to bed. All else went on well until noon. This is written according to the verbal statement of Khushal Singh, the news agent or the informant.

News of the Deorhi of Sirdar Ranjit Singh Bahadur. Saturday, dated 22nd December, 1810 (25th Ziqaad, 1225 A.H.)

Yesterday the Noble Sarkar remained in bed until noon, and leaving it at about the third quarter of the day, came out to the Saman Burj when four hours of the day were left. The sirdars, usually present at the court, came in and made obeisance. A messenger came and presented letters from Hakim Aziz-ud-Din Khan and Bhai Gurbakhsh Singh. It was written in them that they had seen Raja Fateh Singh Ahluwalia near Phagwara, and had explained to him that he must hand over Amar Dass Singh to them and also agree to the establishment of the "Thanas" of the Noble Sarkar in the places belonging to him. They had further told him that Amar Dass Singh's possessions could not revert to him (Fateh Singh Ahluwalia). It seemed that the Raja did not heed their communication, but became displeased with them. Further, it was stated that they had returned and were hoping soon to reach the presence of the Noble Sarkar and explain matter fully. Mehr Singh, the garrison-master, stated that twenty-nine carts laden with iron balls had reached the other side of the river Ravi from Ramgarh and certain other places. The Noble Sarkar ordered that he must look after them carefully. Munshi Devi Dass presented the news of various directions. It was reported that Mirza Mahmud Shah and Sirdar Fateh Khan were still in the town of Peshawar. Further it had become known concerning the negotiations for peace between Ata Muhammad Khan, the Subedar of Kashmir, and Muhammad Azim Khan through their representatives, that these latter had accepted to pay the revenue tax and had also agreed that some horse and foot of the Subedar of Kashmir would always remain in the service of Mahmud Shah Mirza. It was further stated that a representative of the ruler of Sind had paid thirty thousand rupees as part of the revenue tax on behalf of his master to Mirza Mahmud Shah and Sirdar Fateh Khan; that Zaman Shah was still in Rawalpindi though his camp had moved to Pind Dadan Khan; and that Raja Sahib Singh was still in Patiala and had issued letters of invitation to all the sirdars of his brotherhood to join the marriage of Kanwar Karam Singh, for which he was purchasing fine woolen shawls and rolls of brocade, etc., and that Khan Bahadur Bhatti had fled away from Sirsa where the Government of the English had been established. When the night had passed two hours the Noble Sarkar went into the zenana, the sirdars and others present having walked out. He took his meals and retired to bed when the night had passed one quarter. The night passed away uneventfully.

To-day he awoke early in the morning and came out when the day had advanced two hours. The sirdars made obeisance. The Noble Sarkar rode out on a horse to hunt towards the open country. The time passed away uneventfully until the forenoon. It became known that some Shahzadas from Afghanistan had gone over to Ludhiana to Ochterlony Sahib Bahadur.

Yesterday the Noble Sarkar came out to the Saman Burj at about the third quarter of the day after spending the time inside the zenana up-till noon. Sirdar Jodh Singh of Surian, Munshi Devi Dass, Karam Singh Jahal and several other sirdars presented themselves and made obeisance. Munshi Devi Dass stated that two Mughals of Afghanistan, who some time ago had killed Nihal Singh, a broker in Amritsar, and were in prison there according to the order of the Noble Sarkar, had reached Lahore, having been sent by Desa Singh Majithia. He further stated that a brother of this Nihal Singh had also come from Amritsar seeking justice and compensation for the murder of his brother. The Noble Sarkar ordered these Mughals to be made over to the Thanadar and the brother of the victim to be re-assured. Gopal Singh Jamadar stated that two more cannons driven by horses had been completed, and the Noble Sarkar replied that he would inspect them on the following day. Bahadur Singh Thanadar came in and stated that he had carefully investigated the theft that had been committed in the house of a goldsmith in the street of the goldsmiths, had found that it had been planned and committed by someone previously acquainted with the situation, and had arrested and brought two or three persons along with him. The Noble Sarkar answered that he was not satisfied with what he had done, but that he must produce the thieves together with stolen property or else his credit would suffer. Bahadur Singh represented that he was still engaged in search and would strive his utmost to produce them. Hakikat Rae, the Diwan of Sirdar Sahib Singh of Gujrat, presented himself to the Noble Sarkar and requested permission for his master to leave for the new estates which the Noble Sarkar had granted him. The Noble Sarkar replied that he must wait for a few days after which his request would be allowed. The night having elapsed two hours the sirdars and other walked out and the Noble Sarkar retired to the zenana. He went to bed when the night had passed one quarter, having taken his meals earlier. The night passed away uneventfully.

To-day he woke up early in the morning and came to the Saman Burj when the day had advanced two hours. The sirdars presented themselves and made obeisance. He kept on talking to all of them for some time. Later, he granted one horse as a token of his kindness to Sirdar Sahib Singh of Gujrat, saying that he was free to enter upon the Taaluqas of Baigwat and Kallowal and other places which had been granted to him by the Noble Sarkar, who would suitably concede to his requests also in the future. He was again re-assured and comforted by the Noble Sarkar. (The text of half a line is unreadable) from his places in the mountainous regions because some place would be granted to him by the Noble Sarkar to defray their expenses. The aforesaid person kept quiet and said nothing. Then the Noble Sarkar came out into the courtyard, set apart for public audience, and inspected the two cannons driven by horses which Gopal Singh Jamadar had got ready. The Noble Sarkar had them fired, feeling greatly pleased with the result and granting one fine woolen garment ... (a part of a line in the end cannot be deciphered.)

1810 (7)

News of the Deohri of Sirdar Ranjit Singh Bahadar. Monday, dated 24th December, 1810 (26th Ziqaad, 1225 A.H.); the Royal Fort, Lahore.

Yesterday the Noble Sarkar remained in bed inside the zenana until noon and came out of the royal sleeping chamber at about the third quarter of the day. The sirdars came in and made obeisance. The messenger brought the news that Hakim Aziz-ud-Din Khan and Bhai Gurbaksh Singh had come away from the district of Phagwara, spent one night at Amritsar and left on the following day for Lahore, and that Sirdar Jodh Singh Ramgarhia, and Akram Shah, the Raja of Srinagar, were still staying in Amritsar. He further reported that Rani Sada Kaur was in the town of Mukerian, Jaimal Singh in Kalanaur and Fateh Singh Ahluwalia in the district of Phagwara, as previously. He further said that he (Fateh Singh) was carrying on battle from within the fort of Amar Dass Singh who was formerly a companion of the late Sukhbal Singh and was at that time in the custody of the above-mentioned Raja. After this the Noble Sarkar said to Sirdar Sahib Singh of Gujrat that he regarded him (Sahib Singh) like his own father Maha Singh, that he would always look after and protect him and his dignity and that he should go thoroughly re-assured to Baigwat and Kallowal which had been granted to him and take their possession. Sahib Singh replied that he certainly would. Sher Muhammad Khan, the representative of Mir Sohrab Khan of Malpur, presented himself and spoke to the Noble Sarkar in privacy, and the latter continued talking with the former about various sides. The latter remarked that the Noble Sarkar had devoted his whole attention during the previous year to the fort of Multan yet it could not be conquered, and observed that the only reason for the failure was that Munshi Devi Dass, Hakim Aziz-ud-Din Khan, Bhai Gurbakhsh Singh and several other sirdars were friendly with the Nawab of Multan. The Noble Sarkar said that he knew all about it. A letter from Diwan Muhkam Chand intimated that he had allowed a jagir worth thirty thousand rupees near Chenab to Sirdar Nadhan Singh Ayu, the son of Dia (or Dal) Singh. When the night had passed two hours, the sirdars and other who were present walked out and the Noble Sarkar went into the zenana, took his meals and retired to rest. The night passed away uneventfully.

To-day the Noble Sarkar awoke early in the morning and came out to the Saman Burj when the day had advanced two hours. The sirdars presented themselves and made obeisance. It was stated that Hakim Aziz-ud-Din Khan and Bhai Gurbakhsh Singh had arrived and entered the city. Munshi Devi Dass presented the news of various sides. It had become known that Mirza Mahmud Shah and Fateh Khan were still at Peshawar; that Jamiat Rai, a Vakil of Muhammad Khan of Mankera, who was present there, had offered them another sum of rupees sixty thousand out of his wisdom, for use by them in time of emergency; that grain was still being collected from the Hindu residents of Peshawar, according to the old custom, that the money-lenders and respectable traders residing in Peshawar, had hidden themselves out of fear; that Jahandad Khan, the brother of the Subedar of Kashmir, was reported to be still in the fort of Attock, but Zaman Shah was on the point of leaving Rawalpindi on his march towards Pind Dadan Khan which he might have already reached; that Hazrat Shah Shuja-ul-Mulk Badshah was still encamped at a distance of ten to twelve kos from Multan, that Nawab Muzaffar Khan of Multan had granted Rangpur Kara and several other places to him to meet his expenses and that he (Shah Shuja) had sent his Afghans there and established his control over them. Later the Noble Sarkar went out for recreation and enjoyed the sight of the flood in the river Ravi. In the meantime Hakim Aziz-ud-Din Khan and Bhai Gurbakhsh Singh had arrived and presented a "Hundi" of ten thousand rupees from Raja Fateh Singh Ahluwalia, saying "We went to him under your orders to make him understand various things, namely, that he must release Amar Dass Singh, stop interfering with his buildings and supporting him against Karam Singh of Kachhar or molesting him with a view to extort from him the arrears of revenue of Jagraon and other places. The Raja (Fateh Singh Ahluwalia) gave us this "Hundi" of ten thousand rupees in part payment of that revenue. Promised to present himself shortly to you together with Amar Dass Singh, and assured us that he would abide by your orders. And yet he has not done anything to show that he intends keeping his promises". The Noble Sarkar replied that it did not matter much. At noon he went into the zenana after the sirdars and others who were present had walked out. He took his meals and retired to take rest. There is nothing to record about the time until now when one quarter of the day is left. This is written according to the verbal statements of Khushal Singh, the informant.

1811 (1)

News of the Deorhi of Sirdar Ranjit Singh Bahadur. Tuesday, dated 1st
January, 1811 (5th Zilhaj, 1225 A.H.); the Royal Fort, Lahore.

Yesterday the Noble Sarkar remained inside the zenana until noon and had a talk with Shiam Kaur, a specially reliable attendant of Rani Sada Kaur, his mother-in-Law. Shiam Kaur had brought with her the keys of various houses which formed the property of Rani Sada Kaur for a very long time, and, putting them before the Noble Sarkar stated that the Rani would in future have nothing to do with them and that either the Noble Sarkar should himself take possession of them or should personally make them over to his own sons, Sher Singh and Tara Singh, who were born of the late Rani Mehtab Kaur and were both six years of age. The Noble Sarkar re-assured her in every way, saying that he had no ill-will against the Rani and that if she still harboured any suspicion about him he would take over the houses after making a friendly settlement with her. He also said that she could transfer these houses which belong to Shiv Bakhsh Singh, her husband, to her grandsons by making an application to him and he would not object to the transfer, adding that when he would go to Amritsar he would act according to her (Rani's) wish and that as she (Shiam Kaur) was a wise woman she should remove all feelings of distrust against him from the Rani's mind. Shiam Kaur heartily agreed with the Noble Sarkar's view, and urged that when he should go to Amritsar he might send for the Rani through a reliable person to his own presence and personally reassure her. The Noble Sarkar accepted her request, and granting her suits of clothes consisting of four garments for Sher Singh and Tara Singh respectively, one fine woolen shawl for herself, and returning the keys of the said houses to be kept by her for the time being, made her depart. Shiam Kaur walked out and the Noble Sarkar retired to rest after taking his meals when the day had advanced two quarters and four hours. He woke up again when two hours of the day were left and went into the zenana. Hakim Muhammad Ali Khan, Hakim Aziz-ud-Din Khan, Bhai Gurbakhsh Singh, Bhai Basti Ram, Ghulam Mohy-ud-Din Khan, the surgeon, Munshi Devi Dass, Hukma Singh, the Thanadar of Lahore, Harnath Singh, the garrison-master, Sirdar Nihal Singh, Hukam Singh Atariwala, Sirdar Karam Singh Jahal, and several other sirdars presented themselves at the door of the zenana. The Noble Sarkar had arrangements made for their admission and they entered into his presence.

Munshi Devi Dass presented a letter from Raja Fateh Singh Ahluwalia, stating that it had been brought by the staff-bearer of the Raja. In it was written that he (Fateh Singh Ahluwalia) had already sent Mehr Chand and certain other reliable persons with Hakim Aziz-ud-Din Khan and Bhai Gurbakhsh Singh to the Noble Sarkar to whom they must have explained the situation existing in his country, and that he was ever steadfast in his loyalty and devotion to him. The Noble Sarkar sent him a reply that some of the matters could not be explained to Mehr Chand and other reliable persons, and that he must send Chaudhri Qadir Bakhsh and Pandit Naurang Singh who alone could speak authoritatively on his behalf. Munshi Devi Dass was ordered to award ten rupees to the staff-bearer and to make him depart with the reply. It was reported that Fateh Khan Baloch of Sahiwal and his son's father-in-law who were prisoners in the fort of Gobindgarh at Amritsar had come to the court according to his orders. The Noble Sarkar ordered that they must be made over to the custody of Chanda Singh and Ram Singh who should be warned that they must show great care and vigilance in keeping those persons with the "Haveli"[12] of Sobha Singh. The Noble Sarkar had his pulse examined by the physicians who pronounced him to be quite normal and yet administered some medicines to him. Ghulam Mohy-ud-Din Khan, the surgeon, treated the boil, and, when the night had passed four hours, all the sirdars walked out together. The Noble Sarkar took the prescribed food and retired to bed when the night had passed away uneventfully.

Early in the morning, the Noble Sarkar woke up and came out to Saman Burj when the day had advanced by four hours. The sirdars, high and low, made obeisance. Munshi Mehtab Rae submitted to him a letter from Diwan Muhkam Chand after making a Nazar of a gold ducat on his behalf and of five rupees on his own in honour of the conquest of the fort of Manglanpur, representing at the same time that the said Diwan had made that conquest simply through the blessings and glory of the Noble Sarkar. Then Munshi Devi Dass, Sirdar Nihal Singh, Sirdar Hukma Singh Atariwala, Bhai Basti Ram, Bhai Gurbakhsh Singh, and Karam Singh Jahal, presented a Nazar of five rupees each, while Mehr Singh, the garrison-master, Hukma Singh Thanadar, Bahawalpur[13] Singh Kotwal and Bahadar Chand, the Darogha-i-Adalat[14] presented four rupees each. The representatives of various rajas and the sirdars of the near and the far off places also presented Nazars according to their position and rank in honour of the conquest of Manglanpur. The physicians felt the pulse of the Noble Sarkar who took some medicine and a refreshing drink proposed by them. The Noble Sarkar said that if the physicians liked they could give him an aperient. They replied that by the application of leeches already he had bled considerably, and that there was no need of an aperient because he had no fever. Hukma Singh Thanadar presented the detailed statement فرد about rupees five hundred which he had brought for certification. This was signed in token of acceptance. The Noble Sarkar ordered Munshi Mehtab Rae to write to Diwan Muhkam Chand to send to him from the town of Gujrat two hundred maunds of gunpowder and ammunition, twenty-five maunds of ... (one word undeciphered), and as many iron balls as he could afford. Munshi Devi Dass related some news about Afghanistan for information. It had become known that Mirza Mahmud Shah and Sirdar Fateh Khan were putting up in a tent as before in the garden of Taimur Shah, which was situated at a distance of four kos on this side of Peshawar in the direction of the river Attock; that Jahandad Khan, the brother of Ata Muhammad Khan, the Subedar of Kashmir, was encamped in the fort of Attock together with Kashmir Khan and other sirdars; that some troops of the latter were stationed in the village of Akora on the other side of the river Attock with Sirdar Khan who was also known as Sarfaraz Khan, the owner of that place; and that Zaman Shah was still in Rawalpindi and Hazrat Shah Shuja-ul-Mulk in the district of Multan. After hearing this the Noble Sarkar had his boil treated by Ghulam Mohy-ud-Din, the surgeon, and went into the zenana, took his meals and retired to bed. All the sirdars and others who were present walked out. All else went on well until noon. This is written according to the verbal statements of Khushal Singh, the informant.

1811 (2)

News of the Deorhi of Sirdar Ranjit Singh Bahadur. dated 6th January, 1811 (10th Zilhaj, 1225 A.H.); the Royal Fort, Lahore.

Yesterday the women's apartments remained duly arranged for the admission of men up to the time when they had advanced one quarter and a half. Ghulam Mohy-ud-Din Khan, the surgeon, had been present all the time, and the Noble Sarkar had been quite unwell on account of the boil. The said surgeon walked out after treating the boil, and the Noble Sarkar went to bed at noon after taking the prescribed diet. The arrangements of the women's apartments continued as before. The Noble Sarkar woke up at about the third quarter of the day, but continued to stay inside the zenana. It was reported that Munshi Devi Dass, Munshi Mehtab Rae in the service of Diwan Muhkam Chand, Hakim Muhammad Ali Khan, Hakim Aziz-ud-Din Khan, Ghulam Mohy-ud-Din Khan, the surgeon, and several other high and low sirdars were at the door of the Deorhi. The Noble

24

Sarkar arranged their admission inside the zenana and they were called in when four hours of the day were left. They made their obeisance, and the said physicians discovered on feeling the pulse that there was yet an excess of bile in his disposition and made him drink a cold refreshing syrup after holding a mutual consultation. Munshi Devi Dass ordered to hand over to Ganga Singh commandant one hundred scarlet-coloured uniform coats, a hundred caps, a hundred flint-lock guns, and to tell him to distribute the same among the newly employed soldiers whose drill would be inspected in the near future. Munshi Mehtab Rae presented a letter from Diwan Muhkam Chand which had come from the fort of Manglanpur. It was plainly written in it that Ata Muhammad Khan, the Subedar of Kashmir, showed avoidance in paying revenue tax to the Noble Sarkar, and that Diwan Muhkam Chand, therefore, proposed marching towards Kashmir. He further hoped that some trusted person would soon be deputed as garrison master at the fort of Manglanpur, so that he might make over its charge to him before proceeding further. The Noble Sarkar considered the letter and made Munshi Devi Dass write out a reply, that he must postpone preparations for his departure towards Kashmir for the time being, and that as soon as the Noble Sarkar should completely regain his health he would himself go over to that fort and then decide with his (Mohkam Chand's) consultation as to what was next to be done, adding that the chastisement of the Subedar of Kashmir was not a very difficult matter. It was further written that the Noble Sarkar would soon appoint someone to proceed towards him to act as a garrison-master there. Munshi Mehtab Rae was also ordered to write to the Diwan independently. He replied that he would do so. At nightfall the sirdars and others who were present walked out, and the Noble Sarkar had his boil treated by Ghulam Mohy-ud-Din Khan, the surgeon. The boil was found still to contain pus on account of which the whole foot seemed affected. When the night had advanced four hours, the surgeon walked out and the normal arrangements of the zenana were restored. The Noble Sarkar took a little food and retired to bed when the night had passed one quarter. The night passed uneventfully.

To-day the Noble Sarkar woke up early in the morning and came out to the Saman Burj when the day had advanced four hours. The sirdars presented themselves and made obeisance. The physicians examined his pulse and discovered that there was yet an excess of bile in his disposition, though it had somewhat decreased. He was given a cold refreshing drink. The Noble Sarkar said to Hakim Aziz-ud-Din Khan, who is the paymaster, that he must emphatically order the gunners of the Topkhana and the arsenal to keep ready four hundred and five hundred well cast balls, respectively, because as soon as the Noble Sarkar regained his health they would be ordered to march under him (Noble Sarkar) in some direction, and should tell them further that every one of their soldiers must remain ready with his complete kit. Munshi Devi Dass was ordered to issue letters to Imam-ud-Din Khan and Sirdar Desa Singh Majithia, the garrison-masters of the forts of Gobindgarh and Bhangian respectively, reminding of what they had been told previously several times, that they must get ready the mortars with themselves promptly and send the same without delay to the Noble Sarkar through the nephew of Mian Khairata, the Darogha of the Topkhana. Rattan Chand said that he had enlisted new messengers. The Noble Sarkar directed that they must be despatched towards Kashmir and Northern India to send daily reports to him. He[15] further ordered him to give rupees eight to each of them to meet their expenses. It was reported that Phula Singh Akalia had been staying in Amritsar, but had gone at the time to the sacred place of Tarn Taran, which is seven kos from Amritsar, for the performance of sacred ablution there. Munshi Devi Dass submitted news of various sides for information; that Mirza Mahmud Shah and Sirdar Fateh Khan were still encamped in the garden of Taimur Shah at a distance of four kos on this side of Peshawar; that the representatives of Ata Muhammad Khan, the Subedar of Kashmir, and of Sind, were present and negotiations regarding the revenue tax of the province of Kashmir were being held, though no definite settlement had yet been made; and that these representatives had delivered three lakhs of rupees in part payment of this tax and were about to leave for Dera Ismail Khan and Dera Ghazi Khan. Zaman Shah was reported to be still in Rawalpindi. It was also reported that Raja Sahib Singh of Patiala had completed the nuptials of his son, that the maternal uncle of Kanwar Karam Singh had given a suit of clothes each to Kanwar Sahib and Raja Sahib Singh and suit of clothes to Mai Khem Kaur, with one fine woolen shawl, some silk "lungis"[16] and rupees one thousand and ninety-five in cash. Raja Bhag Singh of Jind gave rupees five hundred, Raja Jaswant Singh of Nabha rupees one hundred, Himmat Singh rupees two hundred and others gave whatever they could according to their rank and position by way of "Tambool"[17] on the occasion of the marriage. It was stated that the "Tambool" amounted in all to rupees four thousand, two hundred and five. The Noble Sarkar then went into a separate apartment and had his boil treated by the surgeon. Pus was still found in it, though the pain had lessened. The Noble Sarkar went into the zenana when the day had advanced one quarter and the sirdars and others who were present, walked out. He took his meals and went to bed. Such is the state of things until noon. This is written on the verbal statement of Khushal Singh, the informant.

1811 (3)

News of the Deorhi of Sirdar Ranjit Singh Bahadur. Thursday, dated 8ᵗʰ January, 1811 (12ᵗʰ Zilhaj, 1225 A.H.); the Royal Fort, Lahore.

Yesterday the Noble Sarkar remained inside the zenana till the day had advanced one quarter and two hours and arrangements continued to be made for his "Tuladan[18]". Later he sat in the scale and said that all those things were to be distributed to the poor and to those who were the sacred thread by way of charity. It was done accordingly. Arrangements were made for men's admission, and Ghulam Mohy-ud-Din, the surgeon, entered. The Noble Sarkar took some medicine and a cool refreshing drink and had his boil treated by him. Pus was still found in the boil, though the pain had lessened a great deal. After the noon the surgeon walked out and the Noble Sarkar went to bed after taking his meals. When four hours of the day were left, he woke up and Munshi Devi Dass presented himself according to his summons. The Noble Sarkar dictated him a reply to the letter of Khan Bahadur Bhatti, and asked him to deliver it to the messengers (Jauri). At nightfall the physicians and the surgeons came in, examined his pulse and declared him to quite normal. Munshi Devi Dass stated that Bahawal Shah, the son of Zaman Shah, had arrived in Amritsar from the cantonment of Ludhiana and, after spending one night there, had left on that day on horse-back and was expected to reach Lahore the very same day or on the following day. The Noble Sarkar ordered him to make him put up in some mansion inside the town. He submitted again that Mangal Singh, the Vakil of Bhai Lal Singh Kaithal, expected to be granted leave to depart. The Noble Sarkar replied that it would be given, adding that he must stay for another day or two. Then all those, who were present, walked out, and the Noble Sarkar had his boil treated by Ghulam Mohy-ud-Din Khan, the surgeon. When the night had passed two hours, the surgeon walked out, and the arrangements were set right again in the zenana. The Noble Sarkar engaged himself in listening to the music of dancing girls, and retired to rest when the night had passed one quarter. He had his meals earlier, when the night had advanced only four hours. The night passed away uneventfully.

To-day the Noble Sarkar woke up early in the morning and came out to the Saman Burj where officers and sirdars made obeisance to him. He showed his pulse to Hakim Aziz-ud-Din Khan and Muhammad Ali

Khan. He was found to be quite hale and hearty, yet he took a cold refreshing drink according to their advice. Munshi Devi Dass stated that the sepoys under Ganga Singh were ready in their uniform shirts, caps and the like, and requested the Noble Sarkar to inspect them. He replied that he would do so. The said Munshi presented the news of various sides for information. It became known that Colonel Nasir-ud-Daula Bahadur had gone to Patiala together with five glorious sahibs from the cantonment of Ludhiana, and that Raja Sahib Singh of Patiala, Raja Jaswant Singh of Nabha, Raja Bhang Singh of Jind and all their sirdars and associates had gone out to receive them up to a distance of four kos from Patiala. It was further stated that they had met together a little beyond the second kos from Patiala and embraced each other, after which they had escorted the glorious *sahibs* to their camps. Raja Sahib Singh had sent rupees one thousand in cash and twenty trays of sweet-meats by way of entertainment for Nasir-ud-Daula Bahadur, and rupees nine hundred and twenty five with several trays of sweet-meats for other *sahibs* through Hamir Singh, his Vakil. All the sirdars of that district and the relations of Raja Sahib Singh Bahadur had attended the marriage of Kanwar Karam Singh. At nightfall the marriage procession was formed with great pomp at the head of which Kanwar Karam Singh had gone to a distance of a quarter of a kos, performed a religious ceremony round a tree and had returned to enter his palace through the "Haveli" of Diwan Singh. The Noble Sarkar heard all this. He then came over to the compound of the courtyard and engaged himself in inspecting the drill of the soldiers under Ganga Singh, commandant. He felt greatly pleased with them and rewarded them with rupees twenty-five. Later he went into the zenana and sirdars and others came away. Arrangements of the zenana being made, Ghulam Mohy-ud-Din Khan, the surgeon, went in and treated the boil. It was reported that Bahawal Singh, the son of Zaman Shah, had entered Lahore and had been accommodated in the "Haveli" of Sobha Singh. This is written according to the verbal statement of Khushal Singh, the informant.

1811 (4)

News of the Deorhi of Sirdar Ranjit Singh Bahadur. dated 9th January, 1811 (13th Zilhaj, 1225 A.H.); the Royal Fort, Lahore.

Yesterday the Noble Sarkar remained inside the zenana until the day had advanced one quarter and a half, and remained lying all this time in bed on account of the pain of the boil known as bubo imposthume, while Ghulam Mohy-ud-Din Khan, the surgeon, kept on treating him. Then the surgeon came out after finishing his treatment, and the Noble

Sarkar went to rest in the afternoon, after taking a little quantity of the prescribed diet. The arrangements of the zenana continued as before. When four hours of the day were left the Noble Sarkar woke up and went into the zenana. At nightfall Munshi Devi Dass presented himself according to his order. The Noble Sarkar had a talk with him for a while in privacy and ordered him thus, "Shahzada Bahawal Shah, *alias* Shahzada Yunas, the son of Zaman Shah, has come today from the cantonment of Ludhiana. Send him rupees two hundred and fifty in cash to meet his expenses together with some essentials of entertainment on my behalf, tell him to stay on here for a day or two and assure him that he would be made to reach Rawalpindi in perfect safety according to the note of Colonel Nasir-ud-Daula Bahadur. He should be thoroughly re-assured". Devi Dass replied that he would do so. He also stated that a man looking like a Fakir was persistently sitting in front of the Deorhi of the Noble Sarkar for some time, and urging the release from prison of Fateh Khan Baloch and his companion, the father-in-law of his son. The Munshi solicited the Noble Sarkar's orders with regard to this matter. He was told to bring that holy person along with himself to the presence of the Noble Sarkar on the following day. When the night had passed two hours the Munshi walked out, and Ghulam Mohy-ud-Din Khan, the surgeon, came in according to summons. He kept on treating the boil for some time and left only when the night had passed six hours. After that the Noble Sarkar took his meal, enjoyed the music of the dancing girls, and went to take rest when the night had passed two quarters. The arrangements of the zenana continued as before, and the night passed away uneventfully.

To-day he rose early in the morning and came out to his Royal sleeping chamber when the day had advanced two hours. Sirdars Mat Singh Bharania, Jodh Singh Soriyanwala, Karam Singh Jahal, Munshi Mehtab Rae, Sirdar Hukma Singh Atariwala, Hakim Aziz-ud-Din Khan, Muhammad Ali Khan, Ghulam Mohy-ud-Din Khan, the surgeon, Ganga Singh commandant, and several other high and low sirdars made obeisance. The Noble Sarkar showed his pulse to the physicians, and took some medicine and cold refreshing drink according to their advice. The physicians said that Qazi Faqirullah proclaimed by drum beat all over the town on the day of Id-uz-zuhah[20] that all the Mussalmans must go to the Royal Mosque[21] to offer their Id prayers, declaring those who would go elsewhere to be sinners; that accordingly all the Mussalmans had gone to that Id-gah; and that the said Qazi was present for reward. The Noble Sarkar called upon Qazi Faqirullah and granted him one fine woolen shawl. He ordered Mushtaq Rae, the accountant, to post men in every

29

street and by-lane of the city of Lahore to watch if anybody behaved improperly or exercised tyranny over anybody else and to inform the same to him at once. He replied that he would do so. Munshi Devi Dass came and reported that he had sent rupees two hundred and fifty in cash with several essentials of entertainment to Bahawal Shah, the son of Zaman Shah, on behalf of the Noble Sarkar, and that he had told him that he would be allowed to proceed further towards Rawalpindi after staying there for a week or ten days. The Munshi asked permission of the Noble Sarkar to call in Fateh Khan Baloch and was told to do so at about the third quarter of the day. The Noble Sarkar went over to a separate room and had his boil treated by Ghulam Mohy-ud-Din Khan, the surgeon. It was found that there was no pain on that day though the pus still appeared. When the day had advanced one quarter the Noble Sarkar went into the zenana and the sirdars and others, who were present walked out. He took his meals and went to take rest. There is nothing else to record until noon.

Thursday, 10th January, 1811 (14th Zilhaj, 1225 A.H.), the Place of Despatch as Before.

·   Yesterday the Noble Sarkar remained in bed inside the zenana until noon, and went in on rising at about the third quarter of the day. When four hours of the day were left, he came out to the Saman Burj where the officers and sirdars presented themselves and made obeisance, and he talked to them for a while. Munshi Devi Dass presented Fateh Khan Baloch of Sahiwal, and the father-in-law of his son, who were prisoners with the Noble Sarkar. The Noble Sarkar re-assured them, granted each a fine woolen shawl and a turban on their release, fixed rupees seven daily as their allowance, and promised grants of estates as well. The Noble Sarkar also ordered that the "Darvesh[22]" from Sahiwal, who was sitting so persistently at his gate, should be informed of the release of the said Khan. The aforesaid person then walked out. Ganga Singh Jamadar was ordered to take to Sirdar Jodh Singh of Kalsia a horse with a saddle, a quiver and various other articles, and to bring him to the presence of the Noble Sarkar. He replied that he would depart whenever permitted to do so. At nightfall the Noble Sarkar went into the zenana, and the sirdars and others who were present walked out. When the night had passed two hours, arrangements for the admission of men into zenana were made, and Ghulam Mohy-ud-Din Khan, the surgeon, entered, and after treating the boil, went out again. He took his meals when the night had passed one quarter. The rest of the night passed away uneventfully.

To-day he awoke in the morning and came out to the Saman Burj when the day had advanced two hours. The officers and sirdars arrived and made obeisance, and the Noble Sarkar showed his pulse to the physicians after a short conversation with the former. Then he took a cold refreshing drink and some medicine proposed by the physicians, and ordered Munshi Devi Dass to keep ready with rupees five thousand which were to be given in charity on the occasion of the "Sankrant[23]" which was to come off within two days. It was stated that Rustam Khan of the Durrani tribe, the younger brother of Muhammad Khan Nami, of the Toorazai tribe, had come to India from his district in Afghanistan in search of employment, and that Rani Sada Kaur, the mother-in-law of the Noble Sarkar, had sent Sher Singh and Tara Singh, the sons of the Noble Sarkar, who were her grandsons, at the head of one hundred and fifty horsemen, from the town of Mukerian towards the Noble Sarkar; that they had reached Amritsar where in her own presence, the Rani had made them sacred baths at the temple. The Noble Sarkar went into a separate apartment and had his boil treated by Ghulam Mohy-ud-Din Khan, the surgeon. It became known that there was pus in the boil that day. Later he went into the zenana and the sirdars and others, who were present, walked out. He took his meals and retired to bed. There is nothing else to record until noon. This is written according to the statements made verbally by Khushal Singh.

1811 (5)

News of the Deorhi of Sirdar Ranjit Singh Bahadur. Friday, dated 12th December, 1811 (25th Ziqaad, 1226 A.H.)

Yesterday the Noble Sarkar rose at about the third quarter of the day and returned to enter his palace at about nightfall after enjoying a hunt in the open land. On the request of Raja Ram Brahman, a written order for the realization of rupees five hundred from the Taaluqa of Jullundur for Gurdial Singh Brahman, the cook of Maharaja Daulat Rao Schindia Bahadur, was sent to the person in charge of the said Taaluqa, and he was also instructed to provide him an estate worth rupees one thousand and a daily allowance of rupees two. Five hundred rupees in cash were granted to Mir Mazhar Ali, the Darogha, as "Tambool" on the occasion of his marriage. It was reported that Duni Chand, the representative of Raja Bhag Singh of Jind had come, and a permit allowing him to enter the gate was needed. The Noble Sarkar granted the same. Munshi Devi Dass informed that Karam Singh, the son of Raja Sahib Singh of Patiala, had entered Patiala after completing his marriage and the ceremony of the first visit after marriage at Thanesar, and that Raja Sahib Singh himself was still encamped in the town of Sarnam. The Noble Sarkar heard it and then returned to the zenana.

Saturday, dated 13th December, (26th Ziqaad)

Yesterday the Noble Sarkar inspected the drill of the battalion of the Sikhs and granted them rupees two hundred for preparation of a gold "Kantha[24]" and twelve mortars. The representative of Ghaus Muhammad Khan Darogha was ordered to set up the camp of the Topkhana on the bank of the river Ravi. Salutes of cannon were heard. During the night a gunner escaped away. The Noble Sarkar gave a letter of authority to Kaida Singh for the purchase of a palanquin (sedan chair). To-day the Noble Sarkar sent a letter to Diwan Muhkam Chand, written out under his own order by Munshi Devi Dass, asking him to present himself after finishing with his business there. Ghaus Muhammad Khan Darogha came and respectfully presented a tray of sweetmeats, and the Noble Sarkar asked him if he had ready with him the felt cloth uniform for the gunners. He replied that they could be made ready but their cost should be granted to him. Debi Sahai was ordered to enquire from Mirza Abdul Hasan Khan, the representative of Hazrat Shah Shuja-ul-Mulk, the whereabouts of Mahmud Shah and Sirdar Fateh Khan Wazir. Later the Noble Sarkar went in. Nothing else to record.

1811 (6)

News of the Deorhi of Sirdar Ranjit Singh Bahadur. Sunday, 15th December, 1811 (28th Ziqaad, 1226 A.H.); the Royal Fort, Lahore.

Yesterday the Noble Sarkar continued taking rest inside the zenana until noon, and came out to the Saman Burj at about the third quarter of the day. The sirdars presented themselves and made obeisance. He held a private conference with Sirdar Mat Singh Bharania and Bhai Gurbakhsh Singh privately for full four hours. He told them that some four lakhs of rupees in cash had to be spent on the occasion of the marriage of Kanwar Kharak Singh, the eldest prince, and asked what arrangements were to be made for that sum. They suggested that the Noble Sarkar must consult Munshi Devi Dass and Hakim Aziz-ud-Din Khan also in the matter as being his officials and resourceful councillors. He called in the said persons, made them join the private consultation, and asked their advice. They replied that they would offer suggestions within two days after mutual consultation as to the best course to be adopted. When the day was left only two hours the Noble Sarkar came out as usual and Munshi Devi Dass reported that Duni Chand, the representative of Raja Bhag Singh of Jind, had come to pay respects. He replied that he must bring him to his presence the next day in the afternoon. The said Munshi presented the news from Shahjahanabad, reporting that the General Sahib Bahadur had entered Delhi. At nightfall the Noble Sarkar returned to the zenana, the sirdars and others, who were present, having walked out. He retired to rest after taking his meals when the night had passed one quarter. The night passed away uneventfully.

To-day he rose early in the morning and came out to the place of the throne, when the day had advanced four hours. The sirdars, who were usually present in the court, came in and made obeisance. It was reported that on the preceding day some four or five Sahibzadas had pierced their thighs with daggers and that the rest were about to do so on that very day. The Noble Sarkar ordered Sirdar Mat Singh Bharania to accompany Munshi Karam Chand and prepared a detailed list of all the various agricultural wells, villages and lands marked out as estates of the said Sahibzadas and recognised by the Sikhs as such since olden times, to mention the localities where these were situated, and to examine and scrutinise the title deeds in each case, because the Noble Sarkar would grant them estates according to those documents. Later he went into the mosque of Wazir Khan and took his seat on a high place to see the performance of the marriage ceremony of the son of a dancing girl. All the dancing girls appeared on elephants dressing in fine garments and began to make dancing movements, as is customary with their class. The Noble Sarkar, inviting all of them, sent for wine. He took wine and asked them to dance which he enjoyed until noon. There is nothing else to record until that time. This is written according to the verbal statements of Khushal Singh, the informant.

1812 (1)

News of the Deorhi of Sirdar Ranjit Singh Bahadur. Friday, dated 7th
February, 1812 (23rd Muharram, 1227 A.H.); the Fort of
Gobindgarh, Amritsar.

The Noble Sarkar inspected papers of the distribution of "bara" (?) from Rama Nand Sahu, wherein something like two lacks of rupees had been spent on the marriage, and remarked that by the grace of God the ceremony of marriage had been celebrated in the best possible manner quite according to his desire, except that Rani Sada Kaur, his mother-in-law, did not take part in it nor did her grand children, because their ideas seemed to quite far-fetched and different. At about the third quarter of the day the Noble Sarkar rode on an elephant and went to the camp of Colonel Sahib Bahadur. The latter advanced from the opposite direction to receive him and they met and went into the tent talking together amidst firing of salutes. The Noble Sarkar sat on a golden chair while Colonel Sahib sat on a chair of silver. The former asked, on hearing the salute, whether it was the report of a single cannon or of a number of them, and was told by Colonel Sahib Bahadur that it was of one cannon. The Noble Sarkar felt greatly pleased. Later he rode together with Colonel Sahib to inspect the drill of the English Company in the style in which they would behave in the field of battle, and, after expressing praise, returned to the camp and sat down. Colonel Sahib Bahadur gave an elephant, a horse, a tray containing gems and a pearl necklace, a turban gem, an under-turban beset with jewels, a plume, an English sword and four trays containing garments as suits of clothes to the Noble Sarkar, and nine trays containing garments as suits of clothes with two pieces of jewellry to Dewan Muhkam Chand, Bhai Gurbakhsh Singh, Munshi Devi Dass and the remaining four associates of the Noble Sarkar, respectively. The Noble Sarkar accepted them and departed from him with great satisfaction and returned to the fort of Gobindgarh. A messenger came in and reported that Kanwar Kharak Singh, the eldest prince, has arrived with his wife and entered the fort of Bhangian at a very suspicious hour. On learning this the Noble Sarkar rode and went to fort of Bhangian. There is nothing else to record.

1812 (2)

News of the Deorhi of Sirdar Ranjit Singh Bahadur of Lahore: Tuesday,
dated 11th February, 1812 (27th Muharram, 1225 A.H.)

Yesterday the Noble Sarkar remained lying in bed until noon inside the zenana in the fort of Gobindgarh at Amritsar. He came out to the audience chamber at about the third quarter of the day and the sirdars presented themselves with obeisance. He sent a word verbally through Nand Singh, his Vakil to Colonel Octerlony Sahib Bahadur that as he intended journeying to Lahore on the following morning and reaching there the same day he did not want to put the said Sahib to the trouble of such a long journey; that he could halt on the way and reach Lahore a day later; and that all the sirdars would be accompanying the said Sahib. Rama Nand Sahu showed ten bejewelled under turbans which were for sale and the Noble Sarkar liked them and took them. It was stated that the "Badfaroshes" قوم بادفروشاں had been at the Deorhi for a few days wanting one Ashrafi by way of charity for each ceremony connected with the marriage of Kanwar Kharak Singh, the eldest prince. The Noble Sarkar ordered Raja Ram Pandit and Sirdar Kesra Singh the special reliable person to satisfy and please the "Badfaroshes" by giving them rupees two thousand and five hundred, and to make them depart satisfied. The Noble Sarkar sent for plumes through Rama Nand Sahu and liked them. The Brahmans said that it was the "Sankarant" of Phagan on that day and asked the Noble Sarkar to make some offering on Harmandar Sahib.[26] Thereupon the Noble Sarkar, mounting on elephant, went to the city, took a bath at the sacred tank of Harmandar, offered about five hundred rupees to its Bungas,[27] and riding from that place returned and entered into the tent made of coarse cloth, and granting one shawl, a roll of brocade, a turban, one roll of Gulbadan, another of Mahmudi,[28] and a horse to the representative of Ahmad of Jhangsialan, allowed him to depart. At night-fall it was stated that the conveyances of the ladies and other luggage and the dancing girls had left for Lahore. The Noble Sarkar granted by way of a farewell gift, a robe of honour consisting of seven garments, two horses and one saddle made of gold and silver in the "Ganga Jamani"[29] style to Raja Fateh Singh Ahluwalia, and a robe of honour consisting of four garments to Chaudhri Qadir Bakhsh, Mehr Chand and the other four companions of the said Raja, respectively. The aforesaid persons walked out and the Noble Sarkar ordered Diwan Bhawani Dass of the low stature to send five hundred rupees daily as entertainment according to the old custom to the camp of Colonel Sahib Bahadur, and two hundred rupees in cash to Raja Bhag Singh of Jind, Bhai Lal Singh and Raja Jaswant Singh, respectively, and repeated that he (Bhawani Dass) would be held personally responsible for carrying out this order. All the high and low sirdars were ordered to accompany the Noble Sarkar on the following day because he was leaving for Lahore in the morning, and to despatch their luggage towards Lahore immediately. Action was taken according to the order. When the night had passed one quarter the sirdars and others who were present, walked out and the Noble Sarkar retired to take rest after his meals. The night passed uneventfully.

The Aforesaid Date of the Aforesaid Year; the Royal Fort, Lahore.

The Noble Sarkar rose early in the morning. He ordered the beating of drums to announce the march. All the royal effects had been sent to Lahore. He mounted an elephant, and, making Dewan Muhkam Chand sit besides himself in the royal seat, marched towards Lahore. While on the way Sirdar Mat Singh Bharania approached him riding, made obeisance and joined the stirrup. It was stated that the other sirdars were coming, marching one after the other. At noon he reached the Tawaifpul where he had permanently set up a charity house, alighted, and took his meals along with his associates. It was stated that Colonel Sahib Bahadur had marched from Amritsar and had reached and encamped in the village of Pateky. When one quarter of the day was left, he rode from that place as before and marched forward and reached Lahore after covering a distance of twenty-five kos and entered the royal fort. A salute of cannons from over the fort was fired on his entry. He went to the Saman Burj and Hukma Singh, the Thanedar of Lahore, presented one tray of sweetmeats as Nazar,[30] submitted papers of income and expenditure regarding the construction or repair of the city wall and was ordered to hand them over to Diwan Muhkam Chand. Later he called in the dancing girls of the town and enjoyed their dance and the drinking of wine. When the night had passed one quarter and a half, the dance came to an end, and he took his meals. At midnight he went into the zenana to take rest. There is nothing else to record.

This is written according to verbal statement of Khushal Singh, the informant.

1812 (3)

News of the Deorhi of Sirdar Ranjit Singh Bahadur. Sunday, dated 23rd February, 1812 (9th Safar, 1227 A.H.); the Royal Fort, Lahore.

The Noble Sarkar rose early in the morning, and came to the Saman Burj when the day had advanced two hours. The sirdars, usually present at his court, presented themselves. He called upon a soldier from the "Jahal" troops and ordered him to go to the village of Lakker which was four kos on this side of Amritsar and bring Raja Sansar Chand riding from there. The aforesaid person walked out according to the order and went away. When the day had advanced four hours the Noble Sarkar mounted his special horse and went out for hunting, accompanied by several sirdars. When the riders reached near Mahmudbooti, Rana Sansar Chand came from the opposite direction, and both went out together for recreation. They searched in all directions for game in the jungle in the neighbourhood of the village of Awan, situated at a distance of seven kos from Lahore but nothing fell into their hands until the third quarter of the day. At last losing all hope of finding any game they sat down under the trees in the jungle, took their meals together and talked about the affairs of the cantonment of Ludhiana. The Noble Sarkar said that it was very well known to him that everything was due to the goodness of the sirdars of the country of Malwa. Raja Sansar Chand said that the Noble Sarkar himself promised at Kot Kangra that the fort of Jauke and Kothas would be given to him after their conquest, and that no action had been taken in that matter. The Noble Sarkar replied that he should rest assured that at the time of his departure all his demands would be satisfactorily conceded. The Raja departed and went to his own camp, and the Noble Sarkar separated from him, crossed the river towards Shahdara and enjoying a ramble from road to road, returned and recrossed the river and entered the fort at nightfall and later went into the garden. The sirdars and those who were present, walked out. Later he sat down to tell beads. When the night had passed four hours he entered the zenana, took his meals and retired to take rest when the night had passed one quarter. There is nothing else to record.

1812 (4)

Deorhi of Sirdar Ranjit Singh Bahadur. Friday, dated 14th March, 1812 (28ᵗʰ Safar, 1227 A.H.); the Royal Fort, Lahore.

A letter from Hari Singh Nalwa from the country of Paghah (?) intimated that he had sent ten thousand rupees from the collections of the said district and would send whatever more he would be able to realize. The Noble Sarkar sat separately with Diwan Muhkam Chand and discussed with him for four hours plans about the management of the district of Gujrat, etc. Fifteen Sikhs, in search of employment, were recruited and enlisted in the battalion of Sheikh Basawan, the commandant. The Noble Sarkar asked Sirdar Mat Singh Bharania about the marriage of his son and granted him two thousand and five hundred rupees as "Tambool". A representative of Raja Sansar Chand stated that the Raja had written to him that his people were again afflicted by fever and smallpox with the change of season, and also felt the strain of their expenses, and so he requested the Noble Sarkar to allow them to depart. The Noble Sarkar replied that he himself was ready and would be marching with him within ten or fifteen days. A letter from Diwan Moti Ram, the son of Diwan Muhkam Chand, containing an account of the Taaluqa of Phillaur, was received. After considering it, Munshi Devi Dass was authorized to write a reply to it. Duni Chand, the Vakil of Raja Bhag Singh, requested for the grant of two horses about which the Noble Sarkar had spoken to his master so that he might send them over to him. The Noble Sarkar said that he would be given the horses within a day or two.

Saturday, dated 15th March, (29th Safar), the place of Despatch as Before.

A note for seven hundred rupees was given to Babu Baj Singh. The sum was to be realized by him from Duni Chand, the banker to meet his own expenses. Dal Singh Majithia presented a horse which the Noble Sarkar kept for himself. Ajodhia Dass Adalatwala stated that he had fined the Mussalmans of the town of Jullundur two thousand rupees for slaughtering a cow and that they were at that time in prison. The Noble Sarkar said that three thousand rupees be taken from them before they are set free. Mohsin Shah, the Vakil of Nawab Muzaffar Khan of Multan, was told that eighty thousand rupees would be charged from him as annual tribute. He replied that rupees seventy thousand had been fixed for him which should be taken in instalments. Kishen Dass, the agent of Bahawalpur, was told to state definitely about his tribute and he replied that he had written to his master and would make a statement on hearing from him. Bishen Dass Khatri was granted the post of acting as a trustee for the division of Dharamkot, and Chhajju Misar was granted a fine woolen shawl and a turban in token of his appointment to the division of Kangra. Bhai Lal Singh and Raja Jaswant Singh of Nabha came in and met the Noble Sarkar who talked to them about many things. The Bhai made the cooks prepare the food at that very place, and dance of the dancing girls began. There is nothing else to record.

1812 (5)
Deorhi of Sirdar Ranjit Singh Bahadur. Saturday, dated 29th March, 1812 (14th Rabi-ul-Awwal, 1227 A.H.); the Royal Fort, Lahore.

The Noble Sarkar applied medicine proposed by Hakim Sharf-ud-Din Khan to his tooth, felt a little relief. He asked him if the English used medicines of Hindustani Hakims. He replied that they used medicines of

English physicians. Raja Sansar Chand came in and enquired after the health of the Noble Sarkar who showed him great respect, made him sit on a chair and talked to him all about the pain in his tooth. Kanwar Kharak Singh, the eldest prince said that if the Noble Sarkar permitted him he would march ahead. The Noble Sarkar replied that he should march ahead on the day following the next, which was considered auspicious. Hukma Singh Attariwala stated that Sabit Khan Afghan wanted to leave for Kashmir, that he might have left already or might do so the next day. On hearing this the Noble Sarkar sent for the Khan at once, tried to persuade him to stay on at his court and not to leave for anywhere else, and assured him of kindly treatment. That dignitary replied that the late Maharaja Jaswant Rao Hulkar Bahadur was a true patron of soldiers like him, and that now the Most High God seemed to have created the Noble Sarkar to act like him. This pleased the Noble Sarkar who, out of his kindness, asked him to show his skill at the sword and the pistol while riding on a horse. It was displayed by him. Later the Noble Sarkar rode out for a ramble on the bank of the river Ravi and afterwards returned to his palace. There is nothing else to record.

1812 (6)
Deorhi of Sirdar Ranjit Singh Bahadur Monday, 7th April, 1812 (23rd Rabi-ul-Awwal, 1227 A.H.)

The Noble Sarkar summoned Ganda Singh Qazi to his court. Two hundred rupees were given to the battalion of Sheikh Basawan towards the arrears of their salary for two months. Bhai Lal Singh came and the Noble Sarkar respectfully seated him on a chair and shared wine with him. On enquiring, Bhai Gurbakhsh Singh was told that if the rain would allow the Noble Sarkar would certainly march towards Amritsar. A letter came from Bahar Singh Man from the districts of Bhimber and Rajauri, mentioning that he at the head of his troops was enthusiastically engaged in establishing control over that country and asked for further reinforcements. It was written to him in reply that Kanwar Kharak Singh, the eldest prince had already left with sufficient numbers, and that their joint efforts would bring about effective settlement of the country. Diwan Muhkam Chand was ordered to gather his troops by going over to Amritsar because Noble Sarkar had in his mind to go to Jawala Mukhi. Sabit Khan Afghan was reassured that a Jagir would be granted to him on Noble Sarkar's reaching Amritsar. Raja Sansar Chand came and met the Noble Sarkar who enquired after his health, granted him fine bungalow and assured him that all his demands would be favourably considered on his (Noble Sarkar's) reaching Amritsar.

Tuesday, dated 8th April (24th Rabi-ul-Awwal.)

Diwan Muhkam Chand was ordered to leave for Amritsar immediately, and was also told that the Noble Sarkar would leave at about the third quarter of the day and would set up his camp in the Shalamar Gardens. Hakim Sharf-ud-Din Khan of Shahjahanabad, Hakim Aziz-ud-Din Khan and others had a conversation with the Noble Sarkar. Chet Singh, Sheikh Basawan, and Mazhar Ali Darogha were ordered to march towards Amritsar. Mohsin Shah, the agent from Multan, was granted a fine woollen shawl, a roll of Gulbadan, a roll of white cloth, rupees four hundred in cash and other gifts for himself, and one turban, one fine woolen shawl, one roll of brocade, four rolls of white cloth for Nawab Muzaffar Khan, and was allowed to depart. When four hours of the day were left the Noble Sarkar rode out and went towards the Shalamar Gardens. There is nothing else to record.

1812 (7)
Deorhi of Sirdar Ranjit Singh Bahadur. Tuesday, dated 15th April, 1812 (1st Rabi-us-Sani, 1227 A.H.); the Fort of Gobindgarh, Amritsar.

The Noble Sarkar rose in the morning, and came out to his Diwankhana. The sirdars presented themselves and made obeisance. When the day had advanced four hours he mounted an elephant and went to enjoy the sacred sight of the famous faqir Ganga Dhar in the company of Bhai Gurbakhsh Singh and Hari Singh Nalwa, and had the privilege of sitting with him and offering him rupees one hundred. That holy person distributed that money among the poor there and then, Mat Singh Nami verbally submitted in the Durbar at Amritsar, that the country of the Noble Sarkar was being indifferently administered, and that great injustice prevailed, e.g., out of the eleven hundred rupees which formed the contributions to Darbar Sahib on the occasion of Baisakhi. Phula Singh Akali was claiming from the Akalis of Darbar Sahib rupees one thousand and one horse was threatening to fight for his claim. The Noble Sarkar said that he would send for him and dismiss him. After four hours he rode from that place and went into the fort. A letter from Nawab Sherkhan Afghan came through Sabit Khan Afghan, representing that for long time two villages in the districts of Sher Garh and Hujra had belonged to Ahmed Shah Pirzada as rent-free estate but that since a little while ago they had been confiscated by the Noble Sarkar, and requesting that for the sake of the sender of the letter the Noble Sarkar should regrant the said two villages to him (Pirzada). The Noble Sarkar gave ten rupees to the messenger, and gave him a written authority indicating the release of those two villages and also a valuable quilt and a gold threaded saddle for Sabit Khan Afghan. Mat Singh Bharania stated that the people of the Paragana of Jullundur had approached him with a complaint that Hari Singh, the son of the contractor of that place, was tyrannizing over them. The Noble Sarkar said that he would be dismissed and replaced by Surat Singh Nami. Ganda Singh Safi was told that the villages in the division of Khunkaranta were to be given to him on contract, provided he would not quarrel or interfere with anybody there, lest the Colonel Sahib Bahadur in Ludhiana might be unnecessarily disturbed. He replied that he could never do anything contrary to the wish of the Noble Sarkar. The Sarkar added that he did not have complete confidence in him, but, in the end, bound Hakim Singh Attariwala as is surety before issuing an authority to indicate the grant of those villages. Baba Naurang Singh, a reliable officer of Raja Fateh Singh Ahluwalia, presented himself and enquired of the Noble Sarkar his orders for his master. The Noble Sarkar replied that at first he had a mind to go towards the hills of Kangra but had given up that idea for the time being, and had decided to send Diwan Muhkam Chand and Mat Singh Bharania with some other persons in that direction and that later he himself will proceed to Pathankot to be there in case his own marching further became necessary, that he should tell Raja Fateh Singh to send his troops on leave to their homes in Doaba and come himself alone to the Noble Sarkar. At noon all those who were present walked out and the Noble Sarkar went to take his meals and later retired to rest. He rose again at about the third quarter of the day and came out to his audience chamber. The sirdars presented themselves, making obeisance. Jiwan Singh of Rawalpindi came in, presented a tray of sweetmeats and paid his respects to the Noble Sarkar who enquired after his health and ordered him to arrange for an inspection of the troops with him. He replied that at that time he had come all alone but would arrange for an inspection if permitted to muster his troops. It was reported that Phula Singh Akali had arrived in Amritsar with his troops, had started fighting with the Akalis of Darbar Sahib with arrows and guns, and that two or three men had been killed and wounded on both sides. The Noble Sarkar heard this and despatched his special horsemen to suppress the disturbance. A letter from Sheikh Budha, the commandant, intimated that he had set up his camp near Taragarh and wanted to know further orders. It was reported that Rani Sada Kaur, the mother-in-law of the Noble Sarkar, arrived in her own

41

"Katra".[31] The Noble Sarkar heard it and kept quiet. When three hours of the day were left he granted the charge of Risala of two hundred horsemen to Jawahar Singh Nami, the son of Raja Ram Bedi. At nightfall the Noble Sarkar rode his horse and went up to the Lohari Gate and later came straight back and entered the fort. Those who were present walked out and the Noble Sarkar retired to take rest when the night had passed one quarter, after taking his meals. There is nothing else to record.

1812 (8)

Deorhi of Sirdar Ranjit Singh Bahadur. Wednesday, 12th August, 1812 (3rd Shaban, 1227 A.H.); the Royal Fort, Lahore.

The Noble Sarkar gave to each …….. (text mutilated) one turban, one Benares shawl, one roll of Gulbadan, two rolls of white cloth and rupees one hundred in cash ….. (text mutilated) were ordered to send to the fort of Gobindgarh. Four Sikhs were newly recruited. Two horses were purchased from a merchant who was rewarded with a pair of gold bangles. The Noble Sarkar sat in privacy with Diwan Muhkam Chand, and ordered Nawab Kutb-ud-Din Khan of Kasur and Gulab Singh Khara to march at the head of their troops from that place and set up their tents at Kasur, and further reinforcements were promised to them. After that he rode a horse, went out on a ramble about the bank of the river Ravi, and returning to the Saman Burj, engaged himself in enjoying the dance of the dancing girls. There is nothing else to record.

1812 (9)

Deorhi of Sirdar Ranjit Singh Bahadur. Thursday, dated 13th August, 1812 (4th Shaban, 1227 A.H.); the Royal Fort, Lahore.

Namdar Khan, the Vakil of Raja of Jasrota, presented two falcons sent by his master, and the Noble Sarkar awarded him one Benarsi shawl. The Noble Sarkar inspected the drill of the battalion of the Sikhs and the firing of guns. Imam-ud-Din Khan, the garrison master of Gobindgarh, was sent an order to prepare a detailed account of the salaries of the persons employed in that fort, and, after checking it, to send it to the Noble Sarkar, so that the necessary amount might be sent to him. Mehr Singh and other attendants upon horses were ordered to bring to the Noble Sarkar the belongings of Baba Mehr Bakhsh, lying in Jagadhri. Raja Fateh Singh Ahluwalia came, paid his respects and presented two trays of sweetmeats. The Noble Sarkar seated him on a chair with great respect and enquired after his health. He told him to stay there for a few days, after which they together would go out into the open country for a hunt. They held a private consultation without the participation of anybody else for about four hours. A reliable person from Rani Sada Kaur said that he had to say something in private, and the Noble Sarkar replied that he would be called in at leisure. Diwan Muhkam Chand was ordered to take the papers of accounts of all the employees of the Noble Sarkar and inspect them. The Noble Sarkar then went out to enjoy a ramble on the bank of the river Ravi. There is nothing else to record.

1812 (10)

News of the Deorhi of Sirdar Ranjit Singh Bahadur. Tuesday, dated 15th September, 1812 (8th Ramzan, 1227 A.H.); the Fort of Bhangian, Amritsar.

The Noble Sarkar rose early in the morning and came out to the Diwankhana when the day had advanced four hours. The sirdars, usually present at the court, presented themselves, making obeisance. Sirdar Jodh Singh Ramgarhia came and met the Noble Sarkar and stated that according to his order he had despatched his two thousand horsemen towards Bhimber and Rajauri. The Noble Sarkar said that he had done well. A camel rider arrived and delivered a letter from Kanwar Kharak Singh, the eldest prince. It was written therein, that he had left Fatehgarh with his troops and would soon be reaching the district of Rajauri, and that he would send a further report after restoring control over that district. It was considered and a reply was written to him, that he had not done well in going there on his own accord and without reference to the Noble Sarkar, and that it was necessary for him now to warn and chastise suitably all offenders and banish some from that district, so that in future no disturbance might recur. Diwan Muhkam Chand was consulted in privacy, and Munshi Devi Dass was called in and four letters were issued in various directions. When the day had advanced one quarter the sirdars and those who were present, walked out, and the Noble Sarkar went into the zenana, took his meals and went to rest at noon. He awoke again at about the third quarter of the day, and came out to his Diwankhana where the sirdars, usually present at the court, appeared and made obeisance. The messengers (Jauri) arrived from Kabul and stated that Hazrat Mahmud Shah was in Kabul as before, and that letters were being issued repeatedly to Sirdar Fateh Khan Wazir and Muhammad Azam Khan to punish speedily Jahandad Khan, the traitor. He also stated that one lakh of rupees, sent by the Nazim of Kandahar, had reached Hazrat Mahmud Shah, that Zaman Shah was in Peshawar as before and that Jahandad Khan had sent his goods to the fort of Attock and was himself proceeding to encamp outside Peshawar, at the head of his troops, to fight those of Hazrat Mahmud Shah. The Noble Sarkar heard it and said to his associates that the said Khan would not succeed against Sirdar Fateh Khan, and ordered the despatch of a letter from himself to Hazrat Mahmud Shah and Fateh Khan Wazir, stating that so long as the king would not punish Nawab Ata Muhammad Khan and reduce the fort of Attock into his own possession, the disturbance would not be suppressed, and made the messengers (Jauri) to depart with it. Later, the representative of Nawab Sadiq Muhammad Khan of Bahawalpur came and presented a letter from his master. It was written therein that Mir Sorab Khan of Malpur was again planning to interfere with him. After hearing this the Noble Sarkar went into the zenana and the sirdars and those who were present walked out. The Noble Sarkar took his meals and went to sleep when the night had passed one quarter. There is nothing else to record.

1812 (11)

News of the Deorhi of Sirdar Ranjit Singh Bahadur. Thursday, dated 17th September, 1812 (10th Ramzan, 1227 A.H.); the Fort of Bhangian, Amritsar.

The Noble Sarkar got up early in the morning and came out to his Diwankhana. Diwan Muhkam Chand, Munshi Devi Dass, Sirdar Karam Singh Jahil (باهل), Bhai Gurbakhsh Singh, Raja Fateh Singh Ahluwalia and several others high and low, came in when the day had advanced six hours and made obeisance. The Noble Sarkar talked for two hours in privacy with Diwan Muhkam Chand and Raja Fateh Singh and instructed the latter to send for his troops speedily. He replied that his troops were coming from various places to gather together near Fategarh which was situated in the district of Doaba, and that he would then act according to the orders of the Noble Sarkar. The messengers (Jauri) brought a letter from Kanwar Kharak Singh, the eldest prince, in which was written, that two hundred zamindars of that district had collected together in a central place, that the troops with him had traced them out and had made an attack upon them, with the result that twenty men had been killed, most of them wounded, and the remaining captured and brought to him alive. He further added that he had put them in prison and has posted his troops and cannons near Rajauri for further attack, and that whatever would follow later, would be reported to the Noble Sarkar. The Noble Sarkar went into the zenana when the day had advanced one and a half quarter, and the sirdars and those who were present, walked out. He took his meals and

44

retired to rest at noon. He woke up again at about the third quarter of the day, and came out and sat down in the house of Sirdar Mahan Singh when four hours of the day were left. The sirdars came in making obeisance. Munshi Devi Dass presented a letter from the Begum of Hazrat Shah Shuja-ul-Mulk at Lahore, in which it was written that she felt very uncomfortable on account of the shortage of funds for her expenses and that the Most High God had made him a big Sirdar. After considering the contents of the letter the Noble Sarkar ordered Hukma Singh, the Thanadar of Lahore, to give every month rupees four thousand to the said Begum Sahiba. The Munshi presented the news about Patiala: it became known that Raja Sahib Singh was staying there as before, and that Misar Budha Mal had sold twenty-seven villages in the district of Sirhind for rupees seventeen thousand to Hanu Mal, and all the parts of Saifabad for rupees nine hundred to Pindi Ram, and that officials of that state were being warned that if they continued in future embezzling and misappropriating state funds, it would not help them, for in the end their gains would be seized and they would be severely punished. If they wanted to maintain their dignity and respect they must acknowledge and confess their wrong and should give in writing that they did not dispute the matter but admitted every thing. They agreed, and a proposal was made that the letters about the army be prepared according to the list and the properties and the revenue taxes of the various Thanas. After listening to this the Noble Sarkar began to talk with his associates, and later went into the zenana. Those who were present, walked out. The Noble Sarkar retired to take rest after his meals when the night had passed one quarter.

Friday, dated 18th September, 1812 (11th Ramzan, 1227 A.H.)

The Noble Sarkar woke up early in the morning and came out to the Diwankhana. The sirdars presented themselves and made obeisance. The messengers (Jauri) came from Rajauri and delivered a letter from Kanwar Kharak Singh, the eldest prince. It was written that he had established entrenchment around Rajauri and was storming the fort with cannons, and that the persons besieged in the fort of Rajauri had sent him a message, namely, "Send some one of yours to us and let your power be established in this place. Spare us our lives and receive us out of the fort with respect." He further added that by the glory of the Noble Sarkar and the Most Powerful God control would very shortly be established over that place. The Noble Sarkar sent to him words of praise and appreciation in reply. Kishen Dass, the brother of Dawani Bhawani Dass, came in and made a request for the grant of rupees one lakh. The Noble Sarkar asked him to submit his acceptance and to take the letter of authority from•the office of the Noble Sarkar. After that the Noble Sarkar rode out on a horse to the Sarai, and having a ramble through it and inspecting the drill of the battalion of the Sikhs, returned to the zenana when the day had advanced one quarter. Those who were present walked out and he laid himself down to take rest at noon after taking his meals. He awoke again at about the third quarter of the day, came out to his audience chamber, and the sirdars made obeisance. The Noble Sarkar said to Munshi Devi Dass that if he wanted to keep the office of Mir Munshi[32] to himself he must give in an acceptance for rupees one lakh. He replied that it would be better if the Noble Sarkar granted to him some concession in that amount. The Noble Sarkar said to him that more places had come into the possession of the Noble Sarkar and therefore he could willingly agree to it or not. He accepted and promised that he would abide by all the orders of the Noble Sarkar. After that Sirdar Karam Singh Jahil said that the horses of the cavalry with him had become very thin and lean on account of insufficient supply of grain and straw. The Noble Sarkar councelled patience to him, adding that he himself was marching out in a day or two. Chaudhri Qadir Bakhsh, the companion of Raja Fateh Singh Ahluwalia, came after taking a bath in celebration of his recovery and presented a tray of sweets by way of Nazar. The Noble Sarkar said that they must get ready ten thousand horse and foot with him, for they had soon to be directed to proceed in some direction. The news came that Debi Sahai had met Raja Jaswant Singh of Nabha, and, after talking with him about the village of Salani, had left for the town of Sarnam, and that Misar Budha Mal had sent a letter of his own to Lal Singh, stating that he was proceeding towards Jawalamukhi and wanted him to send some reliable person to accompany him. The Noble Sarkar heard this and caused a letter to be despatched to Ghaus Muhammad Khan, the Darogha of the Topkhana. The Noble Sarkar went into the zenana and the sirdars who were present walked out. He took his meals and went to rest when the night had passed one quarter. There is nothing else to record.

1812 (12)

News of the Dorthi of Sirdar Ranjit Singh Bahadur. Saturday, dated 10th October, 1812 (3rd Shawwal, 1227 A.H.); the Royal Fort, Lahore.

Yesterday the Noble Sarkar remained inside the fort of Bhangian in Amritsar until nightfall, and the staff and the servants accompanying his procession remained present. After that the procession of the ladies was made to leave for Lahore and the Noble Sarkar himself rode out and went to Harmandar Sahib, enjoyed its sacred sight, made an offering of rupees one hundred and twenty-five to Granth Baba Sahib,[35] caused "Halva"[36] and food to be distributed to every one in his presence, and, taking a little of it himself, returned from that place and came to the fort of Gobindgarh. Hakim Imam-ud-Din Khan, the garrison master of Gobindgarh, and Sirdar Desa Singh Majithia were called in and ordered to exercise great vigilance and alertness with respect to the town and the fort and to be very careful and considerate about the people, so that all may praise them. Then the Noble Sarkar took his meals, and rode out in the palanquin when the night had passed one quarter and a half along with five hundred horsemen and one company of the Sikh Regulars of Lahore, and, reaching a distance of two kos from Amritsar, allowed Hakim Aziz-ud-Din Khan and other sirdars to go back to Amritsar and himself marched onward. Before sunrise he reached Tawaifpul, alighted from his conveyance, and began to talk about the stream, saying that on account of the absence of rains it had no water in it. Later he rode on from that place, and, covering the distance of twenty-two kos, reached the Shalamar Gardens when the day had advanced one quarter and took his seat in its "Baradari."[37] Muhammad Khan, the Superintendent of the garden, came in and presented a Nazar of rupees two and a basket of seasonable fruits. The Noble Sarkar ordered all to proceed forward but laid himself down to take rest after taking his meals when the day had advanced one quarter. When four hours of the day were left he woke up and came out and stood in the "Sihdara."[38] Hukma Singh , the Thanadar of Lahore, came in and made a courteous bow and presented a Nazar of rupees five. The Noble Sarkar mounted an elephant and making Bhai Gurbakhsh Singh sit in the special royal seat, first went to the bank of the river Ravi, enjoyed a pleasure trip and then to the fort. At that time a salute of cannons from over the fort was fired. The Noble Sarkar entered the zenana and those who were present walked out. It all went on well until nightfall.

1812 (13)

News of the Deorhi of Sirdar Ranjit Singh Bahadur. Saturday, dated 10th December, 1812 (12th Ramzan, 1227 A.H.); the Fort of Bhangian, Amritsar.

The Noble Sarkar rose early in the morning and came out to the house of Sirdar Mahan Singh and sat down there. Diwan Muhkam Chand, Munshi Devi Dass, Raja Fateh Singh Ahluwalia, and several other sirdars came in and made obeisance. Munshi Devi Dass was made to write out a letter and send it to Mir Sohrab Khan of Malpur. Rani Sada Kaur, the mother-in-law of the Noble Sarkar, came in and met him and presented a paper containing a list of various things which she had purchased for the marriage of Sher Singh, her grandson, and added that there were some other things which were yet required. After the inspection of the list by the Noble Sarkar, she said that rupees fifty thousand which he had granted her had already been exhausted and that more money was wanted for the preparation of other things. The Noble Sarkar said that she would be given the amount for them. The news came that a certain Sikh had come to the Deorhi of the Noble Sarkar and had ventured to enter it but the sentinels appointed at the Deorhi had checked him, whereupon he had drawn his sword out of his sheath, had killed one sentinel, had wounded the other and had run away. On hearing this the Noble Sarkar ordered the horsemen and the messengers to capture and bring alive the aforesaid murderer. He then talked about the Sikh who had killed and wounded the men at the Deorhi to Raja Fateh Singh who remarked, that although that Sikh has shown fine skill in the art of fighting, yet nothing could be judged without his being produced before them. The Noble Sarkar called upon one company of Sikhs and posted them for watch and ward at the Deorhi, and at the same time gave rupees twenty to the wounded and rupees twenty-five for the burial of the other. When the day had advanced one quarter, he went into the zenana and the sirdars and others who were present walked out. He took his meals and retired to take rest at noon. He rose again at about the third quarter of the day, came out to the audience chamber and the sirdars, who were usually present, entered and made obeisance. The Munshi presented the news of Patiala and it became known that Misars Budha Mal and Dhanpat Rai, the sons of the late Diwan Singh, had been called upon to present the various articles such as Dushalas and the like, which they had made over to their wives at the time of the marriage of Kanwar Karam Singh. They had replied that the articles were not in their houses, and that enquiries regarding them should be made from Kandari Mal. Thereupon the aforesaid person was emphatically ordered to explain the matter. The Noble Sarkar then went over to the audience chamber where the officials came in and showed him the papers of the accounts of the agent Sukh Ram Chand, and stated that rupees fifteen thousand and a few hundred more belonging to the aforesaid person were due to him from the Noble Sarkar, that out of that sum rupees six thousand had been paid into the shop of Mani Dhar, the agent of Sukh Ram Chand and the remaining nine thousand and a few hundred had come out from the aforesaid person himself. It was further added that letter bearing the seal of the Noble Sarkar had been seized from the aforesaid person and burnt. A Hundi, too, had been taken from Mani Dhar. They stated further that henceforth if any new claim appeared from any account book or Hundi it would be treated as null and void. On hearing this the Noble Sarkar said that they had done well. After that Suhel Chand, in charge of the Police Station, came in and presented the sale deed of the stables of Lakhpatari, which, Gujar Singh, the son of Tara Singh, had purchased from the deceased for rupees four hundred, and, after getting the seal of the Noble Sarkar fixed on that paper together with the endorsement of his (Noble Sarkar's) employees according to the old procedure, he left. A representative of Sukh Dayal Sahu presented rolls of brocade and Chinese cloth. The Noble Sarkar purchased rolls of brocade and two Chinese pieces. When the night had passed two hours the sirdars walked out, and the Noble Sarkar went into the zenana and retired to take rest after taking meals, when the night had advanced one quarter. There is nothing else to record.

1812 (14)

Deorhi of Sirdar Ranjit Singh Bahadur. Sunday, dated 13th December, 1812 (8th Zilhaj, 1227 A.H.); the Royal Fort, Lahore.

Yesterday the Noble Sarkar went into the zenana after despatching letters in various directions. To-day a messenger presented a letter from Nawab Kutub-ud-Din Khan of Kasur, which he had brought from Rajauri, and which mentioned that on account of heavy snowfall his men were feeling very uncomfortable, that Sirdar Fateh Khan Wazir had prepared to march ahead from his station towards Kashmir, and that Diwan Muhkam Chand was also proceeding thither on the following day. It was written to him in reply that he must accompany Sirdar Fateh Khan Wazir to help him whole-heartedly together with Diwan Muhkam Chand and that he should rest assured and take whatever he wanted for his expenses from the agent of Rama Nand Sahu, who was present there. The Noble Sarkar felt greatly pleased to listen to the sound of one newly prepared mortar with a ball in it, and granted one fine woolen shawl to Mistri Mir Muhammadi with whose efforts this weapon had been prepared. Gulzara Singh, the horse attendant of the special Risala, was granted by the Noble Sarkar one fine woolen shawl, one turban, two rolls of white cloth, one pair of bangles, and five villages in the district of Gujrat, as a Jagir. The Noble Sarkar kept on talking about the climatic condition of the hilly districts with Raja Sansar Chand.

Monday, dated 14th December, 1812 (8th Zilhaj, 1227 A.H.)

The messengers (Jauri) arrived from Kashmir with the news, that Nawab Ata Muhammad Khan, the Nazim of Kashmir, had sent a large force to oppose Sirdar Fateh Khan Wazir that he intended to dress himself and his associates in a mourning attire on the approach of the "Wazir-i-Azam," and that he would offer him, at least once, a great battle in which victory or defeat would rest with God. It was further stated that Sirdar Fateh Khan Wazir had marched from the village of Thana, Breech to Goshaghat. The Noble Sarkar heard the news and, giving rupees eight to the messengers, made them depart again towards Kashmir. He said to his sirdars and associates that whatever of his forces had gone to Kashmir, would be shown special consideration by him, and that each person among them would receive rewards if Kashmir were conquered in that expedition. Sirdar Jodh Singh of Ramgarh was told in reply to his request that he would be allowed to leave for Amritsar in a day or two. A letter from Hakim Imam-ud-Din Khan, the garrison master of Gobindgarh, intimated that he would shortly present himself to the Noble Sarkar in obedience to his summons. The representative of Nawab Sadiq Muhammad Khan of Bahawalpur presented a letter from his master and walked out. There is nothing else to record.

1812 (15)

Deorhi of Sirdar Rangit Singh Bahadur. Thursday, dated 17th December, 1812 (12th Zilhaj 1227 A.H.); the Royal Fort, Lahore.

Yesterday Abdul Hasan Khan presented himself, whispered something into the ears of the Noble Sarkar as a verbal message from the wife of Hazrat Shuja-ul-Mulk, and went away. It transpired that he had conveyed nothing but a refusal. The Noble Sarkar ordered Hukma Singh Thanadar, that as both the Rajas, namely, Raja Fateh Singh Ahluwalia and Sansar Chand, were expected at the court on the following day, therefore, he must open the gates of the city a little wider. To-day Sansar Chand and Fateh Singh Ahluwalia arrived, met the Noble Sarkar, and represented that God's people are being put to great inconvenience owing to the narrowness of the gates of the city, which must be made wider for all time. They also asked for the appointment of some men who would carefully attend to the needs of the wife of Hazrat Shuja-ul-Mulk. The Noble Sarkar ordered Hukma Singh Thanadar and he must open the gates of the city wider but should also emphatically warn the sentinels not to allow the men of the aforesaid Begum to go out without permission. The Noble Sarkar then had some talk in private with Raja Fateh Singh Ahluwalia, after which the latter sought permission to leave. The Noble Sarkar said that he keenly felt his separation but as his stay was impossible on account of his being called away to attend to important affairs he would not stop his departure. He wished him to return as speedily as he could. That Raja marched away to Kapurthala. A messenger came from Peshawar and informed, that Hazrat Mahmud Shah Badshah continued to be in Peshawar, that fifty thousand horsemen of the Yusafzai tribe had gone over to the bank of the river Attock with his permission to join the army of Sirdar Fateh Khan Wazir, and that the king had also written to the aforesaid Wazir that he must speedily punish Ata Muhammad Khan, the traitor. The Noble Sarkar heard this and awarded rupees forty to the messenger. He attentively listened in private to a letter from Nand Singh, his representative at the cantonment of Ludhiana. There is nothing else to record.

The Noble Sarkar asked Sirdar Mat Singh Bharania what amount of Nazrana had been settled on the Rani of the late Chet Singh. He replied that the widowed Rani was ever steadfast in obedience to the Noble Sarkar, that she would never act against his wishes, and that when she would be free from the cremation ceremonies of her husband she would do whatever the Noble Sarkar would order. Munshi Devi Dass was ordered to ascertain from Gurdial Diwan what answer he had received from Sirdar Fateh Khan Wazir with respect to his intimation to him regarding the jewellery of the Begum of Hazrat Shah Shuja-ul-Mulk. The messengers (Jauri) delivered a letter from Diwan Muhkam Chand, Sirdar Dal Singh Bharania, Sirdar Jodh Singh Kalsia, and the rajas of the mountainous regions, stating, "Sirdar Fateh Khan Wazir and we are encamped as before. The "Wazir-i-Azam" called upon Akbar Khan, Sultan Khan, Alam Khan and other rajas and showed them an authority from Hazrat Mahmud Shah Badshah to his own name in which he had been strongly urged to conquer Kashmir. He (the Wazir) told them that in spite of his repeated messages they had remained idle at a distance of ten kos from Kashmir, while the troops of the enemy were obstructing his way and that the changes of war grew worse every day. So he proposed that war might be actively started against the enemy. They replied that he must wait for another two or three days, for they were making arrangements to march forward from that place down into Kashmir where they might set up their camps adding that a single attack would establish their control over the enemy, and there would be no need for further fighting." It became known verbally from the aforesaid messenger (Jauri) that the representative of Nawab Ata Muhammad Khan had approached Sirdar Fateh Khan Wazir and Diwan Muhkam Chand two or three times, and had diplomatic talks with them but had to return utterly disappointed. After hearing this the Noble Sarkar ordered the Munshi to write words of encouragement and assurance to everyone of his men, and rewarded the messengers (Jauri) with rupees fifty. After that the Noble Sarkar purchased from jewellers one pearl necklace which had very large beads and was valued at rupees five thousand. Raja Sansar Chand introduced Kale Khan Afghan who promptly presented one sword and one horse by way of Nazar. The Raja talked at length of his bravery and blessing him remarked that he was present there to assure success in any undertaking. The Noble Sarkar assured him with regard to his employment, and immediately despatched letters through messengers to Raja Fateh Singh Ahluwalia, Jaswant Singh of Nabha, Bhag Singh of Jind and Bhai Lal Singh. All's well otherwise.

1813 (2)

News of the Deorhi of Sirdar Ranjit Singh Bahadur. Tuesday, dated 9th February, 1813 (7th Safar, 1228 A.H.)
At the time when the March commenced from Amritsar
for the Performance of a Sacred Bath at the
Tank of the Temple of Tarn Taran.

Yesterday the Noble Sarkar remained lying in bed inside the zenana until noon. He got up at about the third quarter of the day and came out to his audience chamber where his attendants and associates presented themselves. Bir Singh, the younger brother of Sirdar Jodh Singh of Ramgarh, came in, offered a tray of sweetmeats by way of Nazar and paid respects to the Noble Sarkar who enquired after his health for a while. Namdar Khan, the representative of the Raja of Jasrota, presented a preparation of pickles and paid his respects. The Noble Sarkar turned his face towards him and asked him where his raja was at that time. He replied that he had sent his troops along with Diwan Muhkam Chand but was himself at the time at Jasrota. The Noble Sarkar gave some pickles to Hukma Singh Attariwala. He ordered Hakim Aziz-ud-Din Khan to go to the camp of Abdul Nabi Khan, the Vakil of Colonel Sahib Bahadur, and tell him that the Noble Sarkar was shortly proceeding towards Lahore and would be pleased to show him the Gardens of Shalamar, the Saman Burj and the fort. Later two Sikhs were granted one gold necklace each. Kangna, the Wazir of the Raja of Nurpur, was allowed to depart with a robe of honour consisting of four garments. Gobind Sahai, the representative of the Raja of Saholi, came in, offered a Nazar of rupees two and paid his respects to the Noble Sarkar, who enquired after his health for a while. The Noble Sarkar gave away to the Brahmans ten cows, one roll of red cloth, some mirrors, one tin of "Ghee"[39] and some "Muradi"[40] cloth, in charity. Ten Sikhs were newly employed and sent over to Lahore. It was remarked by the Noble Sarkar that the tank of Tarn Taran must be strengthened on all its outer sides. The Noble Sarkar inspected the parade of the horsemen of Budh Singh, and allowed them to depart. Khan Singh, the nephew of Raja Sahib Singh Bedi, was called in by the Noble Sarkar and allowed to depart with the grant of a horse, a shawl and turban. Gosayin Gokal was granted one village as Jagir and Nadhan Singh another estate worth rupees five thousand. The latter was ordered to raise five new battalions of the Sikhs. Kanwar Kharak Singh

53

came and presented himself to the Noble Sarkar who turned his face towards him and kept on talking with him regarding the administrative and financial matters of various sides. The representative of Sirdar Jassa Singh was told that it would be good if the fort of Nurpur passed into the possession of the Noble Sarkar. He replied that whatever ideas and proposals occurred to the Noble Sarkar were good. Thereupon it was proposed that fifty thousand rupees be demanded from the Raja of Nurpur or else he should be asked to surrender the fort. When the night passed four "gharis" those who were present walked out, and the Noble Sarkar engaged himself in enjoying the dance of the dancing girls and, after rewarding them one shawl, went into the zenana. He took his meals and when half of the night had passed, laid himself down to take rest. To-day he got up early in the morning and came out to the audience chamber. The sirdars came in and made a courteous bow. The Noble Sarkar ordered the staff in charge of floorings to pitch up a tent and a "kanat"[41] near the tank at Tarn Taran. The Raja of Kotli was granted a robe of honour consisting of five garments and was allowed to depart. Karam Singh, the nephew of Raja Bhag Singh, was given five thousand rupees to meet his expenses and was assured regarding an estate. Raja Ram Pandit was ordered to get ready all articles to be given away in charity at Tarn Taran, while all the associates were told that none was to accompany the Noble Sarkar who was proceeding on that day towards Tarn Taran, and that he would return from there in two or three days. The Noble Sarkar then went into the zenana, took his meals and ordered for the despatch of the necessaries of the kitchen. He made Munshi Devi Dass despatch a letter to Ahmad Khan of Jhang, calling upon him to present himself.

In the afternoon the Noble Sarkar came out to his audience chamber and sent for a rider. He gave a box of grapes to Karam Singh Jahal, and ordered Dhonkal Singh commandant to accompany him (the Noble Sarkar) with one hundred Sikhs and Hindustani sepoys. The Noble Sarkar sent a word to Abdul Nabi Khan the representative of Colonel Sahib Bahadur, that he should remain their until his return in two or three days. It was stated that two thousand cannon balls sent by the Revenue Collector of the town of Gujrat had reached there. The Noble Sarkar ordered that it should be written to the aforesaid person to get ready about the same number more and to send the same over to him. When one quarter of the day was left he entered Harmandar, and offered one hundred and twenty-five rupees there. Two hundred Sikh sepoys accompanying Dhonkal Singh and Rasal Singh came in and presented themselves. The Noble Sarkar rode out, and, taking them along with his stirrups marched forward with the intention of taking a sacred bath at the temple of Tarn Taran. Sardar Jodh Singh of Ramgarh, Rani Sada Kaur, Kanwar Kharak Singh and the whole of his staff and servants remained in Amritsar. All went on well otherwise until nightfall.

1813 (3)

News of the Deorhi of Sirdar Ranjit Singh Bahadur. Thursday, dated 4th March, 1813 (30th Safar, 1228); the Royal Fort, Lahore.

Yesterday the Noble Sarkar kept on enjoying the dance of the dancing girls until the time when the night had passed one quarter, and later drank wine. He went into the zenana after the dance came to an end. When half of the night had passed he laid himself down to take rest. All went on well otherwise during the night.

To-day he got up when the day had advanced one quarter, and came out to the Saman Burj and the sirdars made obeisance to him. The messenger came and delivered a letter from Jiwan Singh Thanadar of Rawalpindi, in which it was written that according to the order of the Noble Sarkar he had sent rations of grain and other military stores and materials to the troops in the fort of Attock. Hakim Aziz-ud-Din Khan, and Sirdar Mat Singh and others, taking leave from the Noble Sarkar, had arrived near Khoshab and marched towards the fort of Attock without any break on the way. Samand Khan, Dost Muhammad Khan, Ahmad Khan, Duni Beg, and other sirdars had left Kashmir and reached near the "Ghat" of Khanpur on the way to Attock. Shahzada Ayub was reported to be carrying on some correspondence with the garrison master of Attock. The Noble Sarkar heard all this and made Munshi Karam Chand write out a reply to it. Later he went into the zenana, took his meals and laid himself down to take rest in the afternoon, while those who were present walked out. He got up again at about the third quarter of the day, and came out to the place set apart for the Royal throne and the sirdars usually present came in and made obeisance. It was stated that two cannons, mounted upon new planks and sent by the garrison master of Fatehgarh, had arrived. The Noble Sarkar came to inspect them, and, after observing two firings from each, caused them to be placed at the Deorhi. A messenger came and delivered a letter written by Abdul Rahim Khan, the garrison master of the fort of Attock, which had come from Nawab Ata Muhammad Khan, in which it was written that Shahzada Ayub had written to him to evacuate the fort of Attock and to establish the control and government of the king over it, and that he had not agreed to the surrender of that fort to him but would like to entrust it to the troops of the Noble Sarkar on their arrival. After considering its contents, the Noble Sarkar sent him a reply, that his troops were reaching him very shortly, and asked him to act according to his letter and to come himself to the presence of the Noble Sarkar and assured him that, on his arrival, all matters respecting his expenses would be properly settled. At nightfall the Noble Sarkar went into the zenana, listened to the music of the dancing girls, took his meals and laid himself down to rest when the night had passed one quarter.

Friday, 5th March, 1814 (1st Rabi-ul-Awwal)

The Noble Sarkar got up early in the morning, and came out to the Saman Burj, and the sirdars came in and made a courteous bow to him. A letter from Kanwar Kharak Singh, the eldest prince, came from Amritsar, and after considering its contents pertaining to his request to be allowed to come to the Noble Sarkar, he was ordered that at that time it was very essential for him to remain there. He was further told that he would be called from that place in two or four days and later would be made to depart towards Multan. A letter was issued to Raja Fateh Singh Ahluwalia, asking him to send his troops to Amritsar and to act according to the wish of Kanwar Kharak Singh. It was stated that it was rumoured that Sirdar Fateh Khan Wazir and Ata Muhammad Khan had gone to take hot bath, and that when Ata Muhammad Khan had entered the bathroom the "Wazir-i-Azam" had arranged the water to be made very hot and threateningly demanded the buried money from Ata Muhammad Khan. It was further added that as result of the altercation of the aforesaid Khan gave Sirdar Fateh Khan Wazir rupees forty lakhs and some of the jewels which were buried by him and he thus obtained his release. The Noble Sarkar heard this and went into the zenana while the sirdars and those who were present walked out. The Noble Sarkar took his meals and laid himself down to rest in the afternoon. He got up again at about the third quarter of the day, and came out. The sirdars usually present came in and made a courteous bow to him. The Noble Sarkar rode his special horse, and went to the Shalamar Gardens for recreation. Nur Khan, the Superintendent of that garden, presented him with one bunch of grapes and two "dails"[42] of fresh and green fruits and he was rewarded with rupees ten. Later the Noble Sarkar rode back from that place, entered the fort and went into the zenana. All went on well otherwise until nightfall.

1813 (4)

Deorhi of Sirdar Ranjit Singh Bahadur. Tuesday, dated 9ᵗʰ March, 1813 (5ᵗʰ Rabi-ul-Awwal, 1228, A.H.); the Royal Fort, Lahore.

Yesterday the messengers (Jauri) arrived and informed that Mahmud Shah Padshah had marched from the town of Peshawar and had entered his camp and intended to proceed towards Attock. Dewan Muhkam Chand was reported to have spoken to Hazrat Shah Shuja-ul-Mulk to make preparations for his journey alongwith him to Lahore. He was told in reply that as the Noble Sarkar had put in prison the ladies of his Harem, therefore, he did not see what he would do by going there, and that his aggressiveness he was afraid, might end his life. On hearing this the Noble Sarkar dictated a letter in privacy addressed to Diwan Muhkam Chand and got it despatched to him. To-day letters were despatched to summon Raja Fateh Singh Ahluwalia and Sardar Jodh Singh of Ramgarh from Kapurthala and Amritsar respectively. It became known that these persons had already been appointed to accompany Kanwar Kharak Singh to Multan. Namdar Khan, the Vakil of the Raja of Jasrota, be requested to be allowed to depart and was allowed to leave after being granted a shawl and a turban. A messenger arrived and delivered a letter from Nand Singh, the representative of the Noble Sarkar posted at the cantonment of Ludhiana, which stated that Rani Ram Kaur, the wife of the late Sirdar Baghel Singh, had presented herself to Colonel Nasir-ud-Daula Bahadur and had stated that Hari Singh, the son of Jodh Singh Kalsia, was interfering with the villages in her Taaluqa though she was under his patronage. Thereupon the Colonel Sahib Bahadur had assured her and written a letter to Hari Singh to stop interference with those villages or else he would be required to come over to Ludhiana to explain his conduct. The Noble Sarkar heard this and engaged himself in observing the dance of the dancing girls. All's well otherwise.

1813 (5)

Deorhi of Sirdar Ranjit Singh Bahadur. Thursday, dated 11ᵗʰ March, 1813 (7ᵗʰ Rabi-ul-Awwal, 1228 A.H.); the Royal Fort, Lahore.

Munshi Narain Dass, the brother of Munshi Devi Dass, reproduced in privacy the contents of the letter from Colonel Shah Muhammad Khan, which had been brought by the messengers (Jauri) to the Noble Sarkar. It appears that it stated that he wanted some help in meeting his expenses, urging also that if he could do any service for the court of the Noble Sarkar he should be asked to undertake the same without hesitation. The messengers (Jauri) were given rupees twenty by way of reward and entrusted with a letter. Another pair of messengers (Jauri) arrived and delivered letters from Munshi Devi Dass, Sirdar Mat Singh Bharania, Hakim Aziz-ud-Din Khan and others, in which they stated that they had left that place, and after reaching the bank of the river Attock, had encamped under the fort, and that Abdul Rahim Khan, the garrison master, who had been holding the fort on behalf of Nawab Ata Muhammad Khan had relinquished it had joined their army, entered their camp, and had helped in firmly establishing the garrison master of the Noble Sarkar over that place ...... (text mutilated) .... "If the Noble Sarkar may permit I may present myself to him, Dost Muhammad Khan, Duni Beg and Samand Khan, comrades of Sirdar Fateh Khan Wazir have come and set up their camp at a distance of twenty-four kos from Attock but are not advancing forward. Shahzadas Ayub and Abbas, sent by Hazrat Mahmud Shah have reached the other side of the river Attock. We have taken possession of the boats at Attock. The messengers (Jauri) would state other things verbally. Hazrat Mahmud Shah continues to be in his camp as before. Since the fort of Attock has been evacuated the aforesaid Hazrat is feeling very anxious in his mind." In reply it was written to them that they must keep their camp there and should inform the Noble Sarkar immediately when Dost Muhammad Khan might return to Sirdar Fateh Khan Wazir. A letter came from Sirdar Jodh Singh of Ramgarh in which it was written that he had marched from Amritsar and would present himself to the Noble Sarkar on the day after the following. Then some letters were issued to various places.

Friday, dated 12th March, 1813 (8th Rabi-ul-Awwal, 1228 A.H.)

A messenger brought a letter from Raja Fateh Singh Ahluwalia, in which it was written that according to the note of the Noble Sarkar he was preparing his march, had sent for his troops from various places and would reach the Noble Sarkar after the days of Holi.[43] It was written to him in reply that he should not delay but hastily reach the Noble Sarkar. The messengers (Jauri) brought in a letter from Diwan Muhkam Chand in which it was written that he had taken leave from Sirdar Fateh Khan Wazir, and marching from Kashmir, had set up his camp at a distance of four kos in the direction of Bhimbar and Rajauri, adding that Sultan Khan, Akbar Khan, Alam Khan, and other rajas of that district were assisting him. (This sentence is incomplete.)

Deorhi of Sirdar Ranjit Singh Bahadur. Saturday, dated 13th March, 1813 (9th Rabi-ul-Awwal, 1228 A.H.); the Royal Fort, Lahore.

Yesterday the Noble Sarkar remained busy in enjoying the dance of the dancing girls and in sprinkling lacdye on the occasion of Holi. Today Kishen Dass, the brother of Munshi Devi Dass, showed a letter addressed to him by his brother. It was written in there that from the day the"Thana" of the Noble Sarkar was established in the fort of Attock Hazrat Mahmud Shah was feeling sore in his heart, and had at that time written to Shahzada Ayub that though he was staying on the bank of the river for a long time he had not yet conquered the fort, and that what else could be expected of him. The messengers (Jauri) arrived and informed the Noble Sarkar that Diwan Muhkam Chand had marched further in this direction, adding that his luggage and effects, etc., were being brought to this side of the "ghats". All the sirdars offered congratulations and Nazars according to their rank on the occasion of the conquest of the fort of Attock.[44] The Noble Sarkar exempted every one from offering Nazar, saying that he would accept it only at that time when the fort of Multan would be conquered, as that would be the proper occasion of congratulations. Chet Singh commandant, who had been dismissed, was given rupees two hundred and entrusted with the battalion of Raushan Khan, and the latter's son was told that his father would be given some more important post.

Sunday, dated 14th March, 1813 (10th Rabi-ul-Awwal, 1228 A.H.)

A camel driver arrived and delivered a letter from Bhai Lal Singh, and the Noble Sarkar despatched a reply after considering it. The messengers (Jauri) brought a letter from Raja Sansar Chand of Kot Kangra, in which it was written that the Noble Sarkar must appoint some more troops in that direction so that the revenue be realized from the rajas of the mountainous regions. Mir Mazhar Ali, the Darogha of the horse driven cannons, was ordered to get ready another ten such pieces. A letter from the revenue collector of the town of Gujrat arrived together with rupees ten thousand of the collections from that place. The Noble Sarkar made over the amount to Rama Nand Sahu and discussed with his associates the matter of despatching troops to Multan. It was stated that Sirdar Jodh Singh of Ramgarh had come and entered the town. Agha Mahmud of the Rohilla tribe came from Kasur, paid his respects, presented his Nazar and requested for the improvement of his affairs. The

Noble Sarkar assured him. The messenger submitted a letter from Diwan Muhkam Chand, in which it was written that he had crossed over to this side of the "Ghat" and that the whole of his luggage and effects had reached the neighbourhood of Rajauri and Bhimbar. The messengers (Jauri) brought a letter from Munshi Devi Dass in which it was written that the government of the Noble Sarkar had been satisfactorily established over the fort of Attock, that most of the men of Abdul Rahim Khan had come out of the fort and had joined his camp while other who were left in a corner of the fort to protect the luggage, etc., would also leave the fort on that very day, and that the Noble Sarkar must rest assured about the control over that fort. He further added that Shahzada Ayub had written to him that the Noble Sarkar had great respect and friendly feelings for Hazrat Mahmud Shah who was always ready to do him some service but that by capturing the fort of Attock the Noble Sarkar had a little disappointed him, and added that he (Devi Dass) must write to the Noble Sarkar about this fort and urge upon him to remove this sadness from the Shah's heart. He further added that he had written to him in reply that after considering the matter he (Devi Dass) had written to the Noble Sarkar and the sorrow from his mind would be dispelled. Sirdar Jodh Singh of Ramgarh arrived, met the Noble Sarkar who stood up to show him respect and enquired after his health. All's well otherwise.

1813 (7)

News of the Court of Sirdar Ranjit Singh Bhadaur of Lahore. Tuesday, dated 12th April, 1813 (20th Rabi-us-Sani 1228 A.H.); the Village of Satura, eight kos on this side of Amritsar.

The Noble Sarkar got up early in the morning in the Shalamar Gardens and making his advance camp and the battalions of Mian Singh Hand, Chet Singh Depart ahead of him, took his meals with Kanwar Kharak Singh, the eldest prince. When the day had advanced one quarter he got into a horse driver carriage together Kanwar Kharak Singh, and, taking Nazars and other offerings from the zamindars of the neghbourhood and giving assurances to every one, reached the village of Satura after covering a distance of twelve kos, pitched his camp there, and entered into it at nightfall. The messengers (Jauri) came and submitted the news sent by Jai Karan Dass, the news agent. It came to be known that Sirdar Fateh Khan Wazir was staying near Dera Ghazi Khan, that some of his troops were encamped in the district of Khangarh and Muzaffargarh, that he was negotiating with Nawab Sarfraz Khan, the son of Nawab Muzaffar Khan of Multan regarding the revenue, that at that time the Nawab had paid as revenue and Nazrana seventy thousand rupees to Sirdar Fateh Khan, and that Sarfraz Khan was demanding Nazrana for King Mahmud Shah from other sirdars of that country. The Noble Sarkar heard all this and when the night had passed one quarter, took his meals, and retired to take rest.

Wednesday, dated 13th April, (21st Rabi-us-Sani 1228 A.H.); the Fort of Bhangian, Amritsar.

The Noble Sarkar got up early in the morning and came out. All the staff and the servants made their customary obeisance. Marching from the village of Satura on an elephant he went out on a ramble and reaching the village of Haidarpur took his meals there. Getting into the carriage again and covering a distance of eight kos he reached Amritsar and entered the fort of Bhangian. A salute of cannons was fired, and he rewarded the gunners with fifty rupees. He then laid himself down to rest but got up again after the third quarter of the day and came out once again. Hakim Imam-ud-Din presented him two rupees in cash and four mirrors framed in steel. The Noble Sarkar liked them and kept them for himself, offered one horse as Nazar and stated that his master also would present himself in a day or two. Narain Dass, the Vakil of Ramgarh, stated that Sirdar Jodh Singh was desirous of an interview and was told that he should come on the following day. The Noble Sarkar distributed one sweet pomegranate to every one of the special company and sent for one hundred rupees from the shop of Rama Nand Sahu. Riding a horse he went out on a ramble through the bazaars where he distributed one hundred rupees as charity among the poor. On his return he entered the fort of Bhangian. When the night had passed one quarter he went into the zenana, took his meals, and laid himself down to take rest.

1813 (7-B)
News of the Deorhi of Sirdar Ranjit Singh Bahadur of Lahore. Tuesday, dated 12th April, 1813 (20th Rabi-us-Sani 1228 A.H.); the Village of Satura, eight kos on this side of Amritsar.

The Noble Sarkar got up early in the morning in the Shalamar Gardens and ordered the march ahead of his own camp and the battalions of Mian Singh and Chet Singh. Taking his meals together with Kanwar Kharak Singh, gathering presents and Nazars from the Zamindars of the neighbourhood, and assuring every one, he reached the village of Satura after traversing a distance of twelve kos and halted in his camp. He entered into his tent at nightfall, when the messengers (Jauri) arrived and submitted the news regarding various events sent by Jai Karan Dass, the news agent. It was written that Sirdar Fateh Khan Wazir was staying near Dera Ghazi Khan, whereas some of his troops were encamped in the districts of Khangarh and Muzaffargarh that negotiations regarding revenue were going on with Nawab Sarfraz Khan, the son of Nawab Muzaffar Khan of Multan, that in those days the Nawab had paid to Sirdar Fateh Khan Wazir rupees seventy thousand as revenue and Nazrana, and that other sirdars of that district were preparing to pay their revenue and Nazrana to the king. The Noble Sarkar heard this, and, when the night had passed one quarter took meals, and later laid himself down to take rest.

Wednesday, 13th April, 1813 (21st Rabi-us-Sani); the Fort of Bhangian, Amritsar.

The Noble Sarkar got up early in the morning and came out and the staff and the servants made obeisance. He marched from Satura on the back of an elephant, and enjoying his trip, reached the village of Haidarpur, where he took his meals and then rode forward in a carriage towards the next stage of the journey. After covering a distance of eight kos he entered into the fort of Bhangian at Amritsar under a salute of cannons. The Noble Sarkar rewarded the gunners with rupees fifty and later laid himself down to take rest. He woke up again at about the third quarter of the day and came out. Hakim Imam-ud-Din presented him by way of Nazar rupees two in cash and four shield mirrors made fostel. The Noble Sarkar liked them and kept them for himself. The representative of Sultan Mehdi Ali Khan of Khanpur paid his respects, and offering a Nazar of a horse stated that his master would also come in a day or two to pay his respects personally to the Noble Sarkar. Narain Dass, the representative from Ramnagar stated that Sirdar Jodh Singh had come to see Noble Sarkar and wanted audience. The Noble Sarkar said that he should come on the following day. He gave one sweet pomegranate to each man of the company of special orderlies. Later he took rupees one thousand from the shop to Raman and Sahu and went riding his horse for recreation into the bazaar and after distributing rupees one hundred among the poor returned to the fort of Bhangian. Later he went into the zenana when the night had passed one quarter, and taking his meals, laid himself down to take rest.

Deorhi of Sirdar Ranjit Singh, Bahadur. Sunday, dated 18th April, 1813
(16th Rabi-us-Sani, 1228 A.H.); the Royal Fort, Lahore.

Yesterday the messengers (Jauri) brought in a letter from Pandit Ganga Ram who had been previously a Diwan to Louis Sahib. In it was written that according to the summons of the Noble Sarkar he had left Shahjahanabad and would soon present himself. After considering that letter the Noble Sarkar gave a reward of rupees four to the messengers (Jauri). To-day a messenger brought in a letter from Munshi Karam Chand in which was written that after leaving the presence of the Noble Sarkar he had reached the bank of the river Jehlum and intended to march on to the "Wazir-i-Azam" at Zafarabad. Munshi Narain Dass prepared a letter addressed to Sirdar Fateh Khan Wazir to the effect that in the past the Noble Sarkar and he had met together at Rohtasgarh[45] where mutual agreement had taken place, that if he would look carefully into what was agreed to in writing and decide to abide by it honestly he would not like to break his promises in the manner in which he had done, that if he had a mind to maintain firm relations he must first get the fort of Multan evacuated and surrender it to the Noble Sarkar and should also establish and recognize the Government of the Noble Sarkar over one-third of the country of Kashmir and also yield one-third of whatever treasure, property and other things had been seized by him from Kashmir in accordance with the terms of that agreement. It further stated that if he agreed to abide by these terms genuinely the Noble Sarkar would evacuate the fort of Attock and hand it over to him, that if he intended simply to talk against the Noble Sarkar he was at liberty to do so, that whatever help and service had been rendered to him already would be considered to have been wasted, that Munshi Karam Chand was being sent to him at that time, and that he was to consider everything contained in this letter as true and certain. This letter was sent to Munshi Karam Chand through a camel rider. Sirdars Jodh Singh of Kalsia and Dal Singh Bharania were ordered to march towards the fort of Attock.

Monday, dated 19th April, 1813 (17th Rabi-us-Sani, 1228 A.H.)

Gurdial, a representative of Sirdar Fateh Khan Wazir, came in, paid his respects to the Noble Sarkar through Diwan Bhawani Dass, presented one Ashrafi on his own behalf and a letter from his master regarding the fort of Attock together with a few fine woolen shoulder mantles, sheets of shawl kerchiefs, saffron, pods of musk and many other

63

gifts from the country of Kashmir, and submitted that it was proper for the Noble Sarkar to evacuate the fort of Attock and to hand it over to the king because only on that condition could continue the friendship of the two parties which otherwise would come to a break. The Noble Sarkar listened to these words and began to talk in a non-committal manner. Later the aforesaid person walked out and the Noble Sarkar sent rupees one hundred to his camp by way of entertainment. A letter from Nand Singh, the Thanadar of Rawalpindi, intimated that according to the orders of the Noble Sarkar he had sent five thousand maunds of grain, "Ghee" and various kinds of provisions to the fort of Attock, adding that the Noble Sarkar must rest assured with respect to the territory under his control. Nanak Chand Vakil submitted that Rustam Khan, sent by Diwan Muhkam Chand from the fort of Phillaur, had come to pay his respects to the Noble Sarkar who replied that he should be brought in at about the third quarter of the day. A letter from Kanwar Kharak Singh, the prince, arrived through a messenger, intimating that the troops of Hazrat Mahmud Shah had come from Peshawar and had reached the other side of the river Attock at a distance of eight kos from it. It also stated that the prince had considerably strengthened the fort of Attock and himself proposed to march towards Jehlum because the "Wazir-i-Azam" was reported to intend coming by that way, adding further that in a day or two he (the prince) would leave for that direction. The Noble Sarkar heard this and rewarded the messengers (Jauri) with four rupees. Manak Chand Vakil showed in Rustam Khan who presented one horse as Nazar, which was returned to him on the ground that he was granted exemption. He was employed on probation to deal with the papers concerning current matters. The messengers (Jauri) arrived and through the Munshi presented a letter from Raja Ranbir Singh of Bharatpur. Twenty rupees were awarded to this pair of messengers (Jauri). All's well otherwise.

It became known from the news that Kanwar Karam Singh of Patiala was staying on as before, and that after taking stock of all the stores, etc., with the help of Misar Budha Mal he had taken the same into his own possession. A letter from Chuni Lal and Bhir Chand intimated that the attacking party of the Noble Sarkar had reached the ditch, that the zamindars had attacked and killed ten out of them and had then retreated and established themselves in their own village, adding that the entrenchment was still intact and demands for the expenses, etc., had been met with. Thereupon a letter was issued to the representative of Rahmat Khan and others that they should enlist five hundred more men and lay waste the village of Malu.

Dated 18th Rabi-us-Sani.

Sirdar Gurdial Singh of Manimajra came and presented one garment and two horses with respect to his condolence about the late Raja Sahib Singh, and then left for the cantonment of Ludhiana on the following day. Rani Nurunissa of Malerkotla also left after offering her condolence. An estate of five villages was granted to the Afghans of Shamana.

Dated 19th.

A letter from Raja Bhag Singh intimated that he could not come on account of illness, adding that the Noble Sarkar should not feel it because he would come over to see him once at least as soon as possible. Sasasukh Kashmiri left the house of Chet Ram and went to Delhi. Rani Karam Kaur took over the management of the place. A letter for rupees three thousand regarding the balance of Mian Ghulam Rasul to be realized by him from the accountants, arrived. On the checking of the account of Nikahida, the jamadar of the stable, rupees six thousand were found to be due from him.

1813 (9)

News of the Deorhi of Sirdar Ranjit Singh Bahadur. Saturday, dated 8th May, 1813 (6th Jamadi-ul-Awwal, 1288 A.H.); the Royal Fort, Lahore.

Yesterday the Noble Sarkar remained sitting up to the time when the night had passed one quarter. It was stated that Ganga Ram Diwan, who was with Louis Sahib previously, had come from Amritsar and entered the town. The Noble Sarkar heard this and went into the zenana, took his meals, and laid himself down to take rest when the night had passed one and a half quarter. All went on well otherwise during the night. To-day he woke up early in the morning and came out to the garden where the sirdars usually present at the court presented themselves making obeisance. The Noble Sarkar showed his pulse to the physicians and according to their advice took some medicine. A messenger came and delivered a letter containing cordial sentiments from Bhai Lal Singh. The Noble Sarkar at once sent a reply to it after its consideration. After that ten thousand rupees were sent to meet the expenses of Topkhana. Narain Dass was instructed to convey the order of the Noble Sarkar to Mohsin Shah, a representative of Nawab Muzaffar Khan of Multan, that he must speedily pay up the revenue, and that it would be advisable for him to wait the arrival of Sirdar Fateh Khan Wazir otherwise he was at liberty to act according to his wish and could send for reinforcements immediately. The agent of Sirdar Jodh Singh of Kalsia stated that his master had written something. The Noble Sarkar replied that he already knew what it was, adding that it would soon become public. Sending for some rolls of Muradi cloth he caused them to be distributed among the poor in his own presence. Hukma Singh, the Thanadar of Lahore, was ordered to send two thousand maunds of wheat and other stores on camels to the army and repair the city walls and the ditch wherever these had crumbled down and had not been built. News of the events at Shahjahanabad arrived, and after hearing the same the Noble Sarkar rewarded the messenger with ten rupees and entrusted him with a reply. Ghulam Muhammad Khan, the gunner, who had previously been with Jahandad Khan, the garrison master of Attock, arrived, offered a Nazar and paid his respects and was assured that on the following day his name would be enlisted (Chirata Navisi). Karam Chand, the representative of Kharak Singh, the eldest prince, kept on talking something in whispers to the Noble Sarkar for two hours, and later walked out. The representative of Sirdar Jodh Singh of Ramgarh stated that Rani Sada Kaur had asked her soldiers to raid into the country of Ramgarh and cause disturbance there. The Noble Sarkar replied that she would be prohibited from doing so, adding that none would interfere in his country. The Noble Sarkar turned towards Hukma Singh and said to him that he wanted to inspect the troops of all the chieftains because all seemed to have small numbers of horsemen while they enjoyed very large estates granted to them for their maintenance.[47] He replied that it was for the Master carefully to look into every matter. A messenger arrived and stated that the brother of Sirdar Fateh Khan Wazir had appeared with four thousand horsemen on the road to the fort of Attock whereupon the communications of the Noble Sarkar with his men at that fort had been blocked, and whatever articles like grain, gunpowder, ammunitions, etc., were sent in that direction had returned. On hearing this the Noble Sarkar rewarded the aforesaid messengers (Jauri) with rupees twenty-five and appointed other messengers (Jauri) to go in that direction. A messenger came and delivered a letter from Munshi Devi Dass in which it was written that Karam Chand had gone to him from the army of "Wazir-i-Azam" and had stated that Sirdar Fateh Khan Wazir had called him to his presence for satisfying him about some of his demands and that for this purpose he intended to go to the Wazir's army. He further reported that there was a great dearth of grain, and that he would submit a report to the Noble Sarkar about whatever negotiations would take place on his arrival there. After hearing this the Noble Sarkar sent him a reply that the rations of grain would also reach him after the troops, and that he should go to the army of "Wazir-i-Azam" and act in whatever way would be best for the "Welfare of the Noble Sarkar and avoid all selfish considerations." A letter came from Imam-ud-Din Khan of Amritsar stating that one elephant, two horses, some suits of clothes left by the late Raja Sahib Singh and five thousand rupees in cash had come from Kanwar Karam Singh at Patiala and had been distributed in charity at the tank of Amritsar. In the afternoon the Noble Sarkar went into the zenana, took his meals, and laid himself down to take rest, while those who were present walked out one after the other. He got up again at about the third quarter of the day and came out to the place for the throne when four hours of the day were left and the sirdars made a courteous bow to him. Ganga Ram Diwan came in, paid his respects, and offered one Ashrafi and five rupees together with a small bottle containing perfumery. The Noble Sarkar turned his attention towards him, inquired after his health and gave him assurances, saying that he had heard that he was a very honest man and a good news agent and so had invited him from Shahjahanabad. He replied that he had no claim to be regarded as a good news agent but through the glory of his master he was enabled to perform his work satisfactorily. The Noble Sarkar inquired from him about the General Sahib,[48] Louis Sahib and other English Sahibs and was told that the English Sahibs had taken the country with the help of the sword. The Noble Sarkar said that some suitable work would shortly be proposed for him and asked him to remain assured in his heart. He walked out and the Noble Sarkar sent fifty rupees to his camp for his entertainment. Messenger came and delivered a letter from Munshi Devi Dass in which it was written that all the troops of the Noble Sarkar from various places were gathered together as before and were encamped near the fort of Attock, that after strengthening that fort he was leaving for the army of the "Wazir-i-Azam" along with Munshi Karam Chand and would submit a report of all the negotiations that would take place there on his arrival. On hearing this the Noble Sarkar became very angry and said that while troops of the Wazir had come to fight the troops of the Noble Sarkar, it was not good for the Munshi to go to the army of the "Wazir-i-Azam" without his permission which had not been given to him. He despatched a note to the Munshi expressing his displeasure and anger in the words that the Noble Sarkar had made Diwan Bhawani Dass of the low stature fully understand in privacy all the points and he must go to him. Letters were issued to all the chieftains of the army, asking them to be very watchful and alert. When the night had passed one quarter the dancing girls were called in and they presented themselves to the Noble Sarkar who kept on enjoying their dance up to the time when the night had passed one quarter and a half. All's well otherwise.

1813 (10)

News of the Deorhi of Sirdar Ranjit Singh Bahadur. Monday, dated 31ˢᵗ May, 1813 (22ⁿᵈ Jamadi-ul-Awwal, 1228 A.H.); the Royal Fort, Lahore.

The Noble Sarkar got up early in the morning and came out to the Saman Burj when the day had advanced four hours. The sirdars usually present came in and made a courteous bow. He showed his pulse to the physicians who made him drink a cold refreshing drink. The messengers (Jauri) came from the army of Sirdar Fateh Khan Wazir and said that his horsemen had captured some of the Sikhs and put them to death after shaving their beards, moustaches and the hair of their head. Another messenger (Jauri) took a letter from the Noble Sarkar to the "Wazir-i-Azam" to the effect that as soon as he should bring about the evacuation of the fort of Multan and hand the same over to the Noble Sarkar, the latter would immediately release the fort of Attock to him. The news reached Sirdar Fateh Khan Wazir that the troops of the Noble Sarkar were being appointed to march upon Kashmir, and, that through Jahandad Khan who appeared to have joined him (the Noble Sarkar), daily correspondence was going on with the latter's sirdars intended to win them over for the Noble Sarkar. On learning this the "Wazir-i-Azam" felt greatly agitated in his mind, consulted his associates and remarked that if the friendship between him and the Noble Sarkar would remain intact, well and good, otherwise the world would laugh at them, saying that friendly relations could not be maintained in spite of written agreements and promises. For that very reason he was reported to have sent a reliable person to Munshi Devi Dass whom he must have met by that time. On hearing this the Noble Sarkar felt greatly pleased and rewarded the messenger with twenty-five rupees. It was stated that Diwan Muhkam Chand had arrived and established his camp on the bank of the river Ravi with an army of ten thousand and horse and foot and several cannons, and that these troops were expected to cross over the river on the following day. The Noble Sarkar issued a letter to the Thanadar of Wazirabad asking him to provide sufficient grain. A messenger arrived and delivered a letter from the Thanadar of the town of Wazirabad, in which it was written that according to the order of the Noble Sarkar ten thousand horse and foot had gathered there. The Noble Sarkar considered the letter and wrote to him in reply to make these troops march forward. A letter was issued to Sirdar Desa Singh Majithia asking him to realize whatever revenue he could at that time from the rajas of the foot of the mountain and not to quarrel with them on any point and that the rajas would be properly dealt with after the end of the disturbances of Sirdar Fateh Khan Wazir. In the afternoon he went into the zenana, took his meals and laid himself down to take rest while those who were present walked out. He got up again at about the third quarter of the day and came out to the garden when four hours of the day were left. His associates and attendants presented themselves. The messengers (Jauri) arrived and delivered a letter from Munshi Devi Dass in which it was written that Sirdar Fateh Khan Wazir had sent him a message sueing for peace and friendship, and mentioning that he was at that time proceeding towards Peshawar under the stress of great necessity and was therefore sending his brother to the Noble Sarkar. He had further stated that as soon as he should bring about the evacuation of the fort of Multan and have it over to the Noble Sarkar he was perfectly sure that the Noble Sarkar would hand over the fort of Attock to him. He further added that some of the troops of the "Wazir-i-Azam" had crossed the river Attock, had met the troops of the Noble Sarkar which had already reached there and the former had dragged some of the horses into their camp and had captured some four or five of the latter's men whom they had killed outright. He further added that he had ordered his men to remain vigilant and watchful in their places, lest the troops of Sirdar Fateh Khan Wazir should make a raid upon the "Ghari". The Noble Sarkar heard this and felt greatly pleased and sent him a reply, that so long as the brother of Sirdar Fateh Khan Wazir did not reach the Noble Sarkar he should not go to Peshawar though he must cross the river Attock and remain very vigilant and watchful because no reliance could be placed in the Mussalman community, adding that he must not be neglectful in any manner. The Noble Sarkar told his associates that the arrival of Diwan Muhkam Chand was very desirable because Sirdar Fateh Khan Wazir had admitted whatever the Noble Sarkar had written to him. Those who were present talked in praise of the glory of the Noble Sarkar. After that he went into the zenana, took his meals and laid himself down to take rest when the night had passed one quarter. All's well otherwise.

1813 (11)

Deorhi of Sirdar Ranjit Singh Bahadur. Tuesday, dated, 8th June, 1813 (8th Jamadi-us-Sani, 1228 A.H.); the Royal Fort, Lahore.

Yesterday the Noble Sarkar kept showing the Koh-i-Noor,[49] which had been very kindly given to him by Hazrat Shah Shuja-ul-Mulk , to the jewellers from whom he asked its price. It was found in weight equal to three hundred and a few more "*surakhs*," and in value it was declared priceless as no other similar jewel existed anywhere else. To-day the messengers (Jauri) brought a letter from Munshi Devi Dass and the Noble Sarkar listened to its contents in privacy. It became known that the messengers for friendship and peace continued coming from the "Wazir-i-

Azam" as previously though nothing had yet been settled. The Noble Sarkar heard it and issued a letter addressed to that Munshi and other chieftains of the army and wrote them to link in all the boats in the river Attock except two which they must keep in their own control, that Diwan Muhkam Chand was being sent to them, and that they must act according to his advice and by mutual agreement in the matter of strengthening themselves in obtaining information from the other party with regard to peace and reconciliation. Ghafoor Khan Afghan came from Jhangsialan, paid his respects, presented one gold duecat as Nazar and stated that he had been in service at Jhang for a very long time, but that since the control of Hazrat Shah Shuja-ul-Mulk had become established there he had been dismissed from his post and did not know where to go from the door of the Noble Sarkar. The Noble Sarkar asked him the number of horsemen he possessed and was told that he had one hundred with him. The Noble Sarkar said that he would inspect their parade. Risaldar Ram Singh stated that salary to the amount of four thousand rupees had been ordered by the Noble Sarkar to be paid by Rama Sahu to him, but that he was not prepared to part with a single penny. On hearing this the Noble Sarkar despatched an urgent letter, ordering Rama Sahu to pay up that sum.

Letters were despatched to the rajas of the country of Kashmir, informing them of the remission of one year's revenue and asking them to proceed to Kashmir and establish their control on behalf of the Noble Sarkar. A camel rider arrived and delivered a letter from Diwan Muhkam Chand, in which it was written that after leaving the Noble Sarkar's presence, after an incessant march, he had reached Rawalpindi and proposed to march forward on the following day. It became known verbally through the camel driver that the troops of the said Diwan were going after him in that direction. All's well otherwise. It became known from a writing from Amritsar that the Noble Sarkar had exchanged turbans with Shuja-ul-Mulk. All's other otherwise.

1813 (12)

News of the Deorhi of Sirdar Ranjit Singh Bahadur. dated 9th of June 1813 (9th Jamadi-us-Sani, 1228 A.H.), Lahore.

Yesterday the Noble Sarkar kept on listening to the music of Attar Khan the singer on the flute up to the time when the night had passed four hours. After that Munshi Narain Dass came in and submitted a letter from Nand Singh, the representative of the Noble Sarkar posted at the cantonment of Ludhiana. It contained the news that Colonel Nasir-ud-Daula Bahadur had issued an order to Raja Jaswant Singh of Nabha that as Kanwar Karam Singh, the son of the late Raja Sahib Singh, had to be

70

installed on the throne of his father at the most auspicious hour just after the appearance of the first star on the 29th of Jamadi-us-Sani and the installation mark of kingship had to be applied to him at that time and as all the high and low sirdars of the environs of Patiala would be present there on that occasion, therefore he was at liberty to take leave only for a few days, for .. (text not decipherable). It further stated that the (Raja Jaswant Singh) replied to the Colonel that he would return within a week or ten days, and that thereupon the said Colonel approved his proceeding on leave and the said Raja did depart towards Nabha. After considering this letter the Noble Sarkar dictated a reply. When the night had passed one quarter he went into the zenana, took his meals and laid himself down to take rest. To-day he got up early in the morning, and came out. The staff and the servants made a courteous bow to him. After that he got into a palanquin, went to the bank of the river Ravi where he took a sacred bath, and distributed in charity to the Brahmans on the sacred occasion of the performance of his "sankalp"[51] and "Ekadashi,"[52] some fifty maunds of sweets, several huge trays full of slabs of sugar, fifty-one bottles containing syrup and eleven rupees in cash. Later when the day had advanced one quarter the Noble Sarkar rode from that place and returned into the garden where he distributed sweetened butter-cakes and other similar preparations of confectionary to about two hundred Brahmans, in addition to one rupee in cash to each of them. The Noble Sarkar also gave them in charity five cows, each covered by a shawl and being made to stand under a canopy with its horns decorated in gold and silver together with several other articles. At noon he went into the zenana, took his meals and laid himself down to take rest after eating "pulao."[53] Those who were present walked out one after the other. He got up again at about the third quarter of the day, and came out to the place set apart for the throne when four hours of the day were left. The sirdars usually present came in and made a courteous bow. The messengers (Jauri) arrived and made obeisance. He brought the news that five hundred horse and foot accompanying Ram Singh, the man incharge of the affairs of Kanwar Kharak Singh Bahadur, the prince, had established their camp in the "Sarai" of Hassan Abdal that on learning this Sirdar Fateh Khan Wazir had made some two thousand Durrani horsemen to march upon them, that the aforesaid horsemen fought with Ram Singh's troops that some fifty men were killed on both sides, that in the end the men of Ram Singh felt that they could not withstand the enemy, that they, therefore, took to flight, and that consequently horses and camels and other various things belonging to them were seized by the men of the "Wazir-i-Azam." On learning this the Noble Sarkar issued letters to the rajas of the mountainous regions to assemble together and march towards and join the victorious troops at Attock at the head of their armies. A letter was also issued to the chieftains of the army ordering them that they should not remain scattered in their stations, but must encamp at one place and fight the enemy. After that the Noble Sarkar went into the zenana, and, after eating something, laid himself down to take rest when the night had passed one quarter. All went on well during the night.

1813 (13)

Deorhi of Sirdar Ranjit Singh Bahadur. Tuesday, dated 15th June, 1813 (15th Jamadi-us-Sani, 1228 A.H.); the Place of Despatch as Before.

A messenger arrived and delivered a letter from Raja Sansar Chand. It was written to him in reply that he should assure all the rajas of his country and soon bring them along with himself and his troops to the Noble Sarkar who would be greatly pleased to receive them. The Noble Sarkar sent Ratan Singh to bring Bedi Sahib Singh, and called upon the Vakils of Multan to pay up the amount of revenue. The latter replied that the Noble Sarkar should send a reliable person with them to Multan and surely settlement of the revenue would be made on their reaching there. The Noble Sarkar held a private consultation with Himmat Singh Chillawala and ordered him to adopt some scheme by which all the Sikhs of that district might join him and come before the Noble Sarkar, so that the countries of Multan, Bahawalpur, etc., be conquered by all of them together and every one be given something according to his share, adding that he was prepared to give them a definite pledge and offered Raja Jaswant Singh as his guarantee. He replied that he would give a definite answer after thinking over the matter. Sirhandi Mal was ordered to have over all the papers of the Zamboorkhana[54] to Diwan Ganga Ram. A messenger came from the army and explained that the preparations (text mutilated) must be made. The Noble Sarkar replied that the forces of both sides had reached very close to each other and it looked probable that war would ensure shortly. A letter from Sirdar Dal Singh Bharania intimated that although according to the order of the Noble Sarkar he had made arrangements for sending grain to the fort of Attock separately for a force of thirty thousand horse and ten cannons, yet in accordance with the repeated letters of the Noble Sarkar which laid down that he should not plunge in war before the arrival of Diwan Muhkam Chand though he might continue sending grain to the fort of Attock, and that he must act according to the instructions of that Diwan he was at that time waiting for his arrival. The Noble Sarkar rewarded the messenger with rupees fifty and sent him a reply that the said Diwan was going to reach there very shortly and that he must act according to his advice. Diwan Ganga Ram was ordered quickly to study the papers relating to the Zamboorkhana and the like and to send one of his accountants to the battalions and the Zamboorkhana etc. Qazi Kalim-ud-Din delivered a letter from Raja Jaswant Singh of Nabha in which it was written that the Noble Sarkar should consider sure and certain whatever Himmat Singh Jhalla stated to him. Thereupon the Noble Sarkar held a private meeting with Himmat Singh and gave rupees one hundred to Qazi Kamal-ud-Din towards his (Qazi's) expenses, and said aloud that his Raja was certainly a well-wisher of the Noble Sarkar. One hundred rupees were given to the representative of Raja Bhag Singh toward his expenses. Hakim Aziz-ud-Din Khan stated that Shah Shuja-ul-Mulk had given away rupees fifteen hundred on the previous day in charity. The Noble Sarkar said that he had done well. Two thousand rupees were given to Jahandad Khan, and two thousand maunds of "Dal" of millet was sent to the army. Letters were sent to the rajas of the mountainous regions, asking them to present themselves before the Noble Sarkar with their troops with the assurance that the revenue of two years would be remitted to them. A messenger came from the army and stated that the troops of the Noble Sarkar had marched from Sarai Kala and had set up their camp near Hasan Abdal at a distance of five or six kos from the troops of Sirdar Fateh Khan Wazir, adding that his soldiers were standing ready day and night. The Noble Sarkar observed that now war would take place in that district on the arrival of Diwan Muhkam Chand there. All's well otherwise.

1813 (14)

Deorhi of Sirdar Ranjit Singh Bahadur. Wednesday, dated 23rd June, 1813 (23rd Jamadi-us-Sani, 1228 A.H.), the Place of Despatch as Before.

The Noble Sarkar said to the physicians that on account of his indisposition and also his anxiety about the war he could not sleep. Mangal Sain was ordered to keep ready another two thousand horsemen. Partab Singh Attarwala stated something to the Noble Sarkar in privacy regarding the affairs of the Badshah. Khushal Singh Jamadar was ordered to keep ready, because he was to be sent in some direction. He replied that he was quite ready and would depart when ordered. Pir Bakhsh, incharge of the police station, came in and stated that Mullah Hassan and Qazi Sher Muhammad Khan, the companions of Hazrat Shah Shuja-ul-Mulk, had written some letters on their own accord and under their own seals to Sirdar Fateh Khan Wazir, that as the messenger carrying those letters had been brought to him as a captive, therefore, he submitted those letters to the Noble Sarkar. It was written in them that the Noble Sarkar was all alone at that time in Lahore, that he had no troops with him, that if he (the Wazir) would send his troops it would not be difficult to capture Lahore and that when the Noble Sarkar would thus be surprised and captured, he, the Wazir, would be able to fight his armies with great chances of success, and that as there were no troops at Lahore he must send there whatever troops were available very soon. On learning this, the Noble Sarkar called upon Shahzada Haider, the son of Zaman Shah, Mullah Hassan, and Qazi Sher Muhammad Khan, and asked them as to what they had written, after conspiring among themselves, to Sirdar Fateh Khan Wazir. Those persons made no reply. The Noble Sarkar sent Mullah Hassan and Qazi Sher Muhammad Khan to Hazrat Shah Shuja-ul-Mulk with message that when there existed sincere friendship between him and the Noble Sarkar how could it be regarded proper for his associates to write such letters to the enemy, and that he might chastise them suitably or else the Noble Sarkar himself would punish them. He wrote in reply that these persons had written without his knowledge and that the Noble Sarkar was quite at liberty to treat them as desired. Thereupon the Noble Sarkar then put them in the custody of the battalion of Shadi Khan commandant, posting at the same time on hundred young Sikhs and the battalion under Sheikh Basawan to guard all the gates of the city walls and ordering them always to close the gates four hours before sunset and to open them after the day had advanced six hours. The messengers (Jauri) arrived and brought the news that Sirdar Fateh Khan Wazir, was encamped as before at a distance of seven kos from the troops of the Noble Sarkar, awaiting the arrival of further reinforcements from Peshawar. The Noble Sarkar heard this and then went into the zenana. All's well otherwise.

1813 (15)

News of the Deorhi of Sirdar Ranjit Singh Bahadur. Wednesday, dated 30th June, 1813 (1st Rajab, 1228 A.H.); the Royal Fort, Lahore.

Yesterday the Noble Sarkar remained sitting and enjoying the dance of the dancing girls until the night had passed four hours. After that he ordered for the preparation of sweet pudding in the name of Baba Nanak Shah to the value of rupees one hundred and twenty five. When the night had passed one quarter the dancing came to an end and the Noble Sarkar went into the zenana, took his meals and laid himself down to take rest. All went on well otherwise during the night. To-day he woke up early in the morning and came out to the Saman Burj. The sirdars made obeisance. The Noble Sarkar made an "Ardas"[55] upon the "Kharah" and distributed it to every one. Jassa Singh was ordered to march towards Kashmir at the head of his one thousand horsemen. Mohsin Shah, the Vakil of Multan, presented himself and delivered a letter from his master containing congratulations over his victory. Those who were present expressed their hope that Kashmir, too, would likewise be shortly conquered by the Noble Sarkar. The Noble Sarkar remarked that he wanted God's help in every undertaking. The Vakil of Hyderabad was called in and the Noble Sarkar talked to him in privacy for four hours. The Vakil said that it was impossible to establish any control over the country on the other side of the river Attock, without the co-operation of the Noble Sarkar, because, though the troops with Hazrat Mahmud Shah were inconsiderable, yet that country was extensive and difficult to manage. The Noble Sarkar said that after the establishment of control over the districts of Attock and Kashmir, arrangements would be made for the administration of those districts also. Two messengers (Jauri) were sent towards Peshawar for bringing news. The agent گماشته of Ramanand Sahu was ordered soon to get ready twenty-five pairs of gold bangles. The messengers (Jauri) came and brought the news that the people of Kashmir were being incited by the Subedar of that country to rise. The Noble Sarkar sent for Qazi Sher Muhammad Khan from his custody and asked him to pay fifty thousand rupees or to loose all hope of his life. He had become unconscious through the effects of his punishment and beating and could not utter anything from his mouth. After two hours when he recovered his sense he said that he did not possess even a cock-shell with him and was again sent back to his prison. When the day had advanced one quarter and a half the Noble Sarkar went into the zenana and laid himself down to take rest at noon after taking his meals. He got up again at about the third quarter of the day and came out to the place for the throne. The sirdars usually present came in and made a courteous bow. Sheikh Basawan, the commandant, was ordered to exercise great vigilance in guarding the gates of the city wall and in not allowing any letter written in Persian to leave without its inspection by the Noble Sarkar. Hazrat Shah Shuja-ul-Mulk was sent a word that he should keep Qazi Sher Muhammad Khan with himself as a hostage, that is, as a prisoner, and should pay rupees fifty thousand as his fine. The Shah sent a reply that he had nothing to do with the Qazi and that the Noble Sarkar might give him any punishment he liked. The Noble Sarkar turned his attention towards his associates and said that when the disturbance of the war with Durranis would be finished completely, he would make an offering of two thousand rupees in cash and one village to Harmandar Sahib adding that lakhs of rupees had been wasted in that campaign. He also remarked that if he had known that Sirdar Fateh Khan Wazir would behave towards him as he had done he would never have developed the least friendship with him. All stated that he should be very careful henceforth against the deceptions of other chiefs. The Noble Sarkar said that Diwan Muhkam Chand was a very brave man, for he plunged into war immediately on the arrival of the enemy and gained a victory over him. A letter from Kanwar Kharak Singh intimated that he had marched from the town of Ramnagar, had reached Sheikhupura, and would come to pay his respects to the Noble Sarkar on the following day or the day after. The representative of Mankera said that he had to say something in privacy, and the Noble Sarkar got aside and inquired from him about his message. He was told that his master had written to him that letters from Sirdar Fateh Khan Wazir, asking for help were repeatedly received by him, and that he had neither gone there personally nor he had sent his troops out of his regard for the friendship with the Noble Sarkar. The Noble Sarkar said that he would send an answer to it in a day or two. When the night had passed one quarter he went into the zenana, took his meals, and laid himself down to take rest. All's well otherwise.

Thurday, dated 1st July, 1813 (2nd Rajab, 1288 A.H.)

The Noble Sarkar got up early in the morning and came out to the Saman Burj when the day had advanced four hours. The sirdars usually present came in and made a courteous bow. Kanwar Kharak Singh, the eldest prince, came in, paid his respects and offered a Nazar of one tray of sweets. The Noble Sarkar enquired after his health. He said that he would set up his camp wherever he would be ordered. The Noble Sarkar said that he would propose the place. At the same time he sent one hundred newly recruited gunners to the victorious troops. It was stated that zamindars of the neighbourhood of Rawalpindi were committing robberies. On learning this the Noble Sarkar sent letter to the person incharge of Rawalpindi, pointing that the zamindars of that district had become very bold and asked him to punish one or two of them, so that the passage for communication might become clear and safe. The Noble Sarkar then went into the workshop and ordered the manufacture of cannons. He next rode to the place known as Kalkaji, enjoyed its sacred sight, offered an article made of gold worth five hundred rupees and fifty-one rupees in cash, and later receiving a ceremonial gift came back to his place. Later he went into the zenana, took his meals and laid himself down to take rest at noon, while those who were present walked out one after the other. He got up again at about the third quarter of the day and came out of the garden. The sirdars made their courteous bow. It was stated that four Mullahs were sitting in a village and one in Amritsar, endeavouring to cast an evil spell on the Noble Sarkar. The Noble Sarkar had them caught and handed them over to the battalion of Sheikh Basawan. A letter came from Sukh Dayal, the agent of Rama Nand Sahu, from Pind Dadan Khan, stating that early in the morning of the 11th of the month Diwan Muhkam Chand and other chiefs of the army gathered together and marched towards the fort of Attock with the intention of supplying rations of grain. From the other side Dost Muhammad Khan, the brother of Sirdar Fateh Khan Wazir, and other sirdars who had arrived near the "Bawli"[56] at about a distance of one and a half kos showed their readiness to plunge into war. It was also mentioned that the Durranies made a sudden attack and the artillery and the swivels were fired from this side, and that after a great deal of fighting and killing the enemy felt they could not withstand the shock and took to flight that most of the enemy were drowned in the river Attock, that Sirdar Fateh Khan, who stood in hiding just behind his troops lost heart and made his way to Kashmir, that only God knew where he would be able to escape afterwards, and that Diwan Muhkam Chand, Sirdar Dal Singh Bharania, and other sirdars had gone out in pursuit. The Noble Sarkar heard this and was gratified. Sultan Khan, the Raja of Bhimbar, arrived and the Noble Sarkar kept on talking with him until the night had passed one quarter. All's well otherwise.

1813 (16)

News of the Deorhi of Sirdar Ranjit Singh Bahadur. Thursday, dated 8th July, 1813 (9th Rajab, 1228 A.H.), Lahore.

Yesterday the Noble Sarkar remained sitting up to the time when the night had passed five hours and kept on enjoying the dance of the dancing girls. Afterwards he went into the zenana, took his meals there, and laid himself down to take rest when the night had passed one quarter. The dance came to an end. It went on well otherwise during the night. To-day he got up early in the morning and came out to the Saman Burj where the sirdars and attendants made their customary bow. Munshi Devi Dass came in, paid his respects, offered two "Ashrafis" as Nazar and then left.

Two cannons driven by horses, which had newly been constructed, were inspected by the Noble Sarkar who ordered for the construction of another five of the same pattern. Ram Singh, the man incharge of the affairs of Kanwar Kharak Singh, the eldest prince, arrived, and, offering a Nazar of one "Ashrafi" and five rupees, stated that they had plundered eighteen maunds of grain from the camp of the army of Sirdar Fateh Khan Wazir and had sent the same to the Fort of Attock, adding that, in addition to these, thousands of maunds of grain were pouring from the nieghbouring villages into the said fort. He continued describing details of the battle[57] for about one quarter and the rumours of how it had affected the enemy, that the "Wazir-i-Azam" had been wounded by a swivel shot and escaped towards Kashmir, that he was reported to have fled away from there and reached the bank of river Attock, and further that he was widely believed to have expired. The Noble Sarkar said that the last news was quite wrong, adding that it would be accepted as correct only when the exact information would come after due investigation, though there was no doubt that he had in fact been wounded, and that he (the Noble Sarkar) had despatched a messenger (Jauri) in that direction to ascertain the true facts. The aforesaid person having left, the Noble Sarkar went into the zenana when the day had advanced one quarter and a half, while others who were present walked out one after the other. The Noble Sarkar took his meals and laid himself down to take rest at noon. He got up again at about the third quarter of the day and came out to the place set apart for the throne تخت گاه. The sirdars came in and made their customary bow. Partap Singh Attariwala and Khushal Singh Jamadar were sent to the victorious troops to consult Diwan Muhkam Chand and other sirdars with regard to the conquest of the district of Kashmir. Hukma Singh Thanadar was sent to the fort of Attock to find out the state of the supplies there. The Noble Sarkar showed the treaty of Hazrat Shah Shuja-ul-Mulk to Ram Singh, the man in charge of his affairs. It was written therein that if the King of Kabul would fall into his hands he would be absolute master of the territory up to the other bank of the river Attock, while the Noble Sarkar would be absolute master up to this bank of the river Attock. The Noble Sarkar sat separately in privacy with Ram Singh and kept on talking with him until nearly a quarter of the day had passed. It appeared that the subject matter of their conversation was something concerning the case of Munshi Devi Dass and that some papers were examined. Afterwards he went into the zenana, took his meals, and laid himself down to take rest when the night had passed one quarter. All went on well otherwise during the night.

Friday, dated 9th July, 1813 (10th Rajab, 1228 A.H.)

The Noble Sarkar got up early in the morning and came out to the Saman Burj where the sirdars usually in attendance presented themselves with a customary bow. The Noble Sarkar showed his pulse to the physician who made him drink a cold refreshing drink. Ram Singh, the man in charge of his affairs, stated that the Noble Sarkar must ask Hazrat Shah Shuja-ul-Mulk to mention the names of Kashmir, Multan and Dera Ghazi Khan in the treaty,[58] whereupon the Noble Sarkar sent Bhai Gurbakhsh Singh to him (the Shah) along with the document of the treaty asking him to insert the names of those places in it. The Noble Sarkar asked the astrologers to tell him after due deliberation what would be the auspicious hours for his march towards Wazirabad. A message was sent to Hazrat Shah Shuja-ul-Mulk asking him to get ready to march towards Peshawar and the reply came that he was quite ready and the Noble Sarkar should appoint a large force with him, and that on his entry into Peshawar he would collect his own troops. The Noble Sarkar heard this and kept quite. He ordered Ganga Ram Diwan to audit the accounts regarding the seal of "Munshigari"[59] and understand all its details from Devi Dass, whereupon he submitted that three thousand rupees were due from the said Munshi. When the day had advanced one quarter and a half the Noble Sarkar went into the zenana, took his meals and laid himself down to take rest at noon. He got up again at about the third quarter of the day and came out to the garden when four hours of the day were left. The sirdars usually present came and made their customary bow. A messenger arrived and delivered a letter from Diwan Muhkam Chand, in which it was written that he had plundered and laid waste some of the villages belonging to "the bastards" and had sent over to the fort the grain and other stores that he had seized. The reply was written to him to the effect that he himself was a wise man and could do whatever he thought fit, that he should chastise the Yusufzai tribesmen whenever possible, and keep the Noble Sarkar informed of the facts whatever they might be about Fateh Khan Wazir. Ram Singh, the man in charge of his affairs, stated that all the sirdars were ever prompt in obeying Diwan Muhkam Chand except Ghaus Khan, the Darogha of the Topkhana, who did not pay so much heed to his orders. The Noble Sarkar said that he would be made to understand his position. At nightfall the Noble Sarkar rode out towards the bank of the river Ravi for recreation, and on return entered the fort and went over to the garden. It went on all well otherwise upto the time when the night had passed four hours.

1813 (17)

News of the Deorhi of Sirdar Ranjit Singh Bahadur. Tuesday, dated 13th July, 1813 (14th Rajab, 1228 A.H.); the Royal Fort, Lahore.

The Noble Sarkar got up early in the morning and came out to the Saman Burj when the day had advanced four hours. Bhai Gurbakhsh Singh, Kanwar Kharak Singh, Ram Singh Mukhtar, Diwan Ganga Ram and several other sirdars came in and made their customary bow. The Noble Sarkar talked to every one, telling his associates that on account of heavy rains and the floods in the river, etc., he had been very anxious that night, and that as soon as the floods should subside he would march to Wazirabad. The men of Mullah Jafar and Qazi Sher Khan were sent to the fort of Gobindgarh in Amritsar alongwith a guard of sepoys. A messenger came and delivered a letter from Bahadur Chand, a representative of the Noble Sarkar. It stated that he was about to enter Amritsar along with Hakim Imam-ud-Din Khan, the garrison master of the fort of Gobindgarh, asking him to keep the aforesaid men under his protection vigilantly. As Hakim Muhammad Ashraf Khan was also reported to be soon arriving there along with Bahadur Chand from Shahjahanabad the Noble Sarkar asked him further to receive the aforesaid Hakim, to provide with him suitable entertainment and meet his needs and to bring him along to the Noble Sarkar. In the meantime it began to rain and the Noble Sarkar went into the zenana. The sirdars and others who were present walked out, and he laid himself down to take rest at noon after taking his meals. The rain continued falling incessantly. He got up again at about the third quarter of the day and came out as usual to the Saman Burj when four hours of the day were left, and the rain had subsided. The sirdars came in and made their customary bow. The messengers (Jauri) arrived and stated that Sirdar Fateh Khan Wazir was encamped near Kundagarh, that although he had offered every encouragement to his companions yet his soldiers felt too starved to stay on and were proceeding towards Peshawar, and that, therefore, the Wazir himself was compelled to march thither. He added that Hazrat Mahmud Shah was without doubt encamped in the garden of Ali Mardan Khan as before, though he intended marching towards Jalalabad. The messengers (Jauri Cheeran   ?) arrived with the news for the king that he had delivered his letter to the Yusufzai sirdars, but the latter showed hesitation in coming. The King heard this and said that if they did not come they would be suitably punished, adding that the people of Peshawar were extremely frightened on account of the defeat of Sirdar Fateh Khan and most of the influential people were trying to keep aloof from him. On hearing all this the Noble Sarkar rewarded the messenger

80

with ten rupees and sent a letter to Diwan Muhkam Chand to establish effective control over all places on the other side of the river, but not to advance forward. The agent from Hyderabad came and stated that as soon as the troops of the Noble Sarkar should reach the district of Peshawar, his master would also come and join his troops. The Noble Sarkar said that that would be all right. It went on well otherwise up to the time when the night had passed four hours.

It was rumoured in Amritsar that about five thousand horsemen of Diwan Muhkam Chand had crossed to the other side of the river Attock with a view to plunder those parts but no definite and authentic news regarding the matter had arrived. Whatever details would be learnt would be despatched. All's well otherwise.

1813 (18)

News of the Deorhi of Sirdar Ranjit Singh Bahadur. Thursday, dated 21st July, 1813 (22nd Rajab, 1228 A.H.), Lahore.

Yesterday the Noble Sarkar remained in bed inside the zenana until noon and came out to the Saman Burj after getting up at about the third quarter of the day. Then only four hours of the day were left. The sirdars made their customary bow. Khushal Singh Jamadar and Partap Singh Attariwala, who had gone to the victorious troops, arrived, made a courteous bow, submitted a letter from Sirdar Fateh Khan Wazir addressed to Diwan Muhkam Chand at that place, and gave an account of that sirdar, of the Diwan and of other chieftains of the victorious army. They stated that Sirdar Fateh Khan Wazir had marched from Jahangir Noushehra towards Peshawar and contemplated going to Kabul, and that at the time of battle Donkal Singh commandant was not at fault, but it was Ghaus Khan of the Topkhana, who neither joined himself nor allowed his men to join (the victorious troops). The Noble Sarkar showed his displeasure. Hakim Muhammad Ashraf Khan entered along with Bahadur Chand, a Vakil of Noble Sarkar, and paid his respects. This respectable person presented a casket full of rubies. The Noble Sarkar showed kindness to him, made him sit on a stool made of straw, enquired after his health and remarked that or account of flood in the river he must have been put to great inconvenie ce. He replied that he had suffered no discomfort owing to his eagerness to see the Noble Sarkar. He then left and the Noble Sarkar sent after him five trays of fruit and two hundred and twenty-five rupees for his entertainment. The representative of Multan was told that he would never be allowed to leave. Thereupon a great discussion took place and

Diwan Bhawani Dass stood his surety and secured him permission to go to Multan with his brother. The messengers (Jauri) came and stated that Diwan Muhkam Chand had turned those men out of the fort of Attock who were there previously, and, after appointing other chieftains there instead had himself marched from that place and gone over to the district of Hassan Abdal where he had set up his camp, that he had begun punishing the zamindars who had risen in that district, and that representatives of every one had come to present themselves to him. The Noble Sarkar heard this and sent a letter to the aforesaid Diwan, stating that Lahna, the special ("Khidmatgar") of the Noble Sarkar, was going to him and he must act according to his message. The Noble Sarkar considered the letter of Maclif (probably Metcalfe) Sahib Bahadur, which Bahadur Chand had brought, on its presentation by the Munshi. It was written according to his wish that Hazrat Muhammad Ashraf Khan had been sent to him. When the night had passed one quarter the Noble Sarkar went into the zenana and laid himself down to take rest after his meals. The sirdars walked out and the heavy rain continued falling.

To-day the Noble Sarkar got up early in the morning and came out. The staff and the servants made their customary bow. Hazrat Muhammad Ashraf Khan came, met the Noble Sarkar, examined his urine and his pulse and said that after watching his urine and pulse for ten or fifteen days, he would be able to diagnose the disease and would then administer medicine to cure it. Then he walked out and the Noble Sarkar rode out to the bank of the river Ravi for recreation, and on his return entered the fort and later went into the zenana when the day had advanced one quarter, took his meals, and laid himself down to take rest at noon. He got up again at about the third quarter of the day and came out to the apartment set apart for the throne. The sirdars made their customary bow. The man incharge of the affairs of Kanwar Kharak Singh, namely Ram Singh, and the Kanwar, came in, and after conferring with the Noble Sarkar for two hours, left. The Noble Sarkar enquired about the Gurkha Raja and Amar Singh Thapa from Kishan Chand, the representative of the aforesaid Raja. He issued a letter to summon Ghaus Khan. Hira Singh Jhalla said that the Amil of Kangra had been made a captive by the people of ... (?) ... and had been brought to him. The Noble Sarkar said that he should be kept in confinement with a guard posted around his mansion. It began to rain heavily, but the Noble Sarkar continued his ramble, watching the playing of the fountains. He said to those who were present that his victory had been rendered possible merely through God's help and his good fortune, otherwise Ghaus Khan had left nothing undone to bring about his defeat, that he thought previously that Ram Singh was a capable man, but had now found out that he was absolutely stupid. Munshi Devi Dass was told that the Noble Sarkar had come to know that he had sold the ornaments and cloths of his house to pay up his amount to the Noble Sarkar, that the people had different opinions of him, and he gave him assurances. When the night had passed one quarter the Noble Sarkar went into the zenana, took his meals and laid himself down to take rest.

1813 (19)

News of the Deorhi of Sirdar Ranjit Singh Bahadur. Sunday, dated 24th July, 1813 (25th Rajab, 1228 A.H.); the Royal Fort, Lahore.

The Noble Sarkar got up early in the morning and came out to the Saman Burj when four hours of the day had advanced. The sirdars usually present came in and made their customary bow. In the meantime Hakim Muhammad Ashraf Khan came in and the Noble Sarkar made him sit upon a stool made of straw and showed him his pulse. The revenue collector of Kot Kangra was ordered to submit and explain his accounts to Diwan Bhawani Dass. He replied that he would do so. The representative of Sheikh Budha was entrusted with the duty of recording events in writing on behalf of the Noble Sarkar regarding the whole of the country and of appointing and maintaining messengers and news-writers at various places, who might transmit daily news. A messenger came and delivered a letter from Fateh Chand, the brother of the Raja of Ditarpur, in which it was written that he had reached Amritsar along with Naurang Rai, the companion of Raja Sansar Chand, together with four hundred musketeers, and that within a few days he will present himself to the Noble Sarkar. On hearing the contents of the letter the Noble Sarkar despatched a letter to Imam-ud-Din Khan, the garrison master of Gobindgarh, to send soon to the Noble Sarkar two horse-driven cannons. A letter came from Jiwan Singh, the Thanadar of Rawalpindi, containing a list of accounts of various kinds of grain and other stores which he had purchased and supplied to the troops in accordance with the Noble Sarkar's orders. After considering it, a reply was sent to him to the effect that the papers will be considered and the amount would be sent to him. In the afternoon the Noble Sarkar went into the zenana, took his meals and laid himself down to take rest. The sirdars and others who were present walked out. He got up again at about the third quarter of the day and came out to the garden when four hours of the day were left. The sirdars made their customary bow. A messenger came and delivered a letter from Alam Khan, the Raja of Akhnoor, stating that the ruler of Kashmir had written to all the rajas of that district to act in concert with him but that nobody paid any heed to his requests, that as collections of Kashmir had ceased he was feeling acutely the shortage of funds, and that if the Noble Sarkar would send troops, Kashmir could soon be conquered. Rama Nand Sahu, who according to the order of the Noble Sarkar had prepared twenty pairs of gold bangles, presented the same. These were handed over to Looni, the special bearer, who was instructed to direct the Sahu to get ready one pair of bangles beset with jewels. A letter came from Sirdar Dal Singh Bharania, stating that he had made his comrades enter the fort of Attock together with Kutub-ud-Din Khan, and that he himself intended to present himself to the Noble Sarkar to discuss certain matters. The Noble Sarkar went into the zenana and laid himself down to take rest when the night had passed one quarter. It went on well otherwise during the night.

Monday, dated 25th July, 1813 (26th Rajab)

The Noble Sarkar got up early in the morning and came out to the Saman Burj when the day had advanced four hours. The sirdars usually present came in and made their customary bow. The Noble Sarkar showed his pulse to Hazrat Muhammad Ashraf Khan. The Munshi of the Noble Sarkar produced a letter from Raja Jaswant Singh of Nabha and showed it to the Noble Sarkar in whispers. The representative of Sirdar Jodh Singh Ramgarh was ordered to write to his master to come riding all alone. Kanwar Kharak Singh was ordered to state how long his troops would remain there and when would they return. He replied that they would return very shortly. The Noble Sarkar said that Diwan Muhkam Chand was preordained to be successful for wherever he went obtained a victory. All rejoined that it was all due to the glory of the Noble Sarkar. A letter was sent to Mazhar Ali, the Darogha of the cannons driven by horses, calling upon him. Desa Singh Majithia came from the mountainous regions, paid his respects, offered a tray of sweets as Nazar and stated that Raja Mohindar Pal and Kangna Wazir of Noorpur, had come with him, and that nobody else had come. The Noble Sarkar said it was all right. The Noble Sarkar ordered the physician accompanying Shah Shuja-ul-Mulk to discuss his knowledge with Hazrat Muhammad Ashraf Khan. Thereupon the former put him a question and the later replied that whatever question he wanted to ask the same should be written down on a paper, and handed to him, so that he might write out the answer according to his undertaking, adding that no faith could be put in verbal statements, and that he had come there under orders of Mr. Metcalfe Sahib Bahadur out of regard for the Noble Sarkar and not for carrying on such discussions. Thereupon all kept quite. At noon he went into the zenana, took his meals there and laid himself down to take rest, while those who were present walked out one after the other. The Noble Sarkar got up again at about the third quarter of the day and came out to the Saman Burj when four hours of the day were left. The sirdars made their customary bow. The Munshi made the Noble Sarkar listen in whispers to a letter. It became known from it plainly that he had learnt from a letter of the Noble Sarkar to him that he had not kept his promises and was likely to reap the fruit of it in a few days. It mentioned further that at one time the Noble Sarkar had written to him that he should not be distracted but must present himself to the Noble Sarkar and remain firm with regard to his pledges, that that respectable person—the "Wazir-i-Azam"—had then answered that he had come to that district to collect troops and to give battle but that if the Noble Sarkar repeated his earlier advice, it would be quite fruitful, as he (the Wazir) was prepared now to act up to his promises by paying a large amount of the revenue of Kashmir by instalments and by bringing about the evacuation of the fort of Multan in favour of the Noble Sarkar. It was further emphasized that afterwards the Noble Sarkar must return to him (the Wazir) the fort of Attock in token of friendship or else there would be a serious battle in which both of them would suffer loss and no good would occur to either side. The Noble Sarkar heard this letter and smiled and said that its reply would be written out on the arrival of Diwan Muhkam Chand. He went into the zenana, took his meals, laid himself down to take rest when the night had passed one quarter. All's well otherwise.

1813 (20)

News of the Deorhi of Sirdar Ranjit Singh Bahadur. Monday, dated 2nd August, 1813 (4th Shaban, 1228 A.H.)

The Noble Sarkar got up early in the morning and came out to the Saman Burj when the day had advanced four hours. The sirdars usually present came in, and made their customary bow. A messenger came and delivered letters from Diwan Muhkam Chand and other chieftains of the victorious army. These mentioned that according to the order of the Noble Sarkar they had marched from their place, had reached and set up their camp at a distance of fifteen kos from Rawalpindi, and that they would present themselves very shortly after a continuous march. It was stated that Rajas of Nurpur and Jasrota had arrived with their troops in Amritsar, had set up their camps there and would be marching towards Lahore on the following day. The Noble Sarkar issued a letter to the Raja of Jammu, summoning him to his presence. The zamindars of the village of

Bahadurpur belonging to the territory of the Nakkas in the district of Gujrat came in and complained that the revenue collector of the place had robbed them completely of their household effects. The Noble Sarkar immediately caused a letter to be sent to the collector and also sent a staff bearer of his own with the zamindars, ordering him to restore to them all the property which he had tyrannically seized. It was stated that one canon driven by horses had been newly constructed and had been sent by Hakim Imam-ud-Din Khan, the garrison master of the fort of Gobindgarh. The Noble Sarkar came out, examined it carefully, and observed two or three firings of it and ordered its establishment at the Deorhi. When the day had advanced one quarter and a half, he went into the zenana, and those who were present walked out one after the other. The Noble Sarkar took his meals and laid himself down to take rest at noon. He got up again at about the third quarter of the day and came out to the garden when four hours of the day were left. The sirdars came in and made their customary bow. His associates and attendants stated that Sahib Singh Bedi was oppressing the people. The Noble Sarkar replied that on his arrival he would be made to understand everything, adding that being a person whom he must show reverence he could not speak to him harshly. Ramzan Khan, a reliable person of Hazrat Shah Shuja-ul-Mulk, came in and stated that Sirdar Fateh Khan Wazir had marched from Peshawar towards Kabul, but that the messenger of the Noble Sarkar had brought the news about his entry into Peshawar. Sher Muhammad Khan, the representative of Mir Sohrab Khan of Malpur, came in and stated that Sirdar Fateh Khan Wazir had firmly decided to march from Peshawar and go over to Kabul, but owing to the writing of Hazrat Mahmud Shah and Shahzada Kamran he had returned from the second stage of the journey and entered Peshawar again. On hearing this the Noble Sarkar sent two (Jauri) pairs of messengers in that direction to bring the news, and himself got busy in observing the dance of the dancing girls. When the night had passed one quarter he went into the zenana, took his meals and laid himself down to take rest, while those who were present walked out. It went on well otherwise during the night.

1813 (21)

Deorhi of Sirdar Ranjir Singh Bahadur. Wednesday, dated 4th August, 1813 (6th Shaban, 1228 A.H.), Lahore.

A messenger came and delivered a letter from Diwan Muhkam Chand and others, and stated that the sirdars had marched from their station and reached and camped at a distance of twenty-four kos on this side of Rawalpindi, and that they were coming by continuous march.

Another messenger came from Kashmir and brought the news that Muhammad Azim Khan was staying, brooding over his misfortunes, in Kashmir as before, and also stated that he (Azim) had written to the representatives of the rajas of the various Pargannas of Kashmir that their masters were procrastinating in coming and joining him, that it was not a good thing, that Sirdar Fateh Khan Wazir had found some of his sirdars having joined the Sikhs at the time of battle and had, therefore, gone to Peshawar, had put in prison some of those traitors, and was at that time contemplating returning again to the fort of Attock, that on his return he would first deal with their masters, and that the troops of the Noble Sarkar would never reach Kashmir, because it was very difficult, adding that whoever would come would be dealt with severely, that even if the Noble Sarkar came he would give him a pitched battle at least once, and that the future was in the hands of God. They replied that he had extended his hand of tyranny upon the people of that district so much that all had lost their senses, that it was for this reason that their masters were avoiding joining him. Thereupon he issued letters full of assurances to the rajas of that district urging that if they joined him they need to have no fear. The Noble Sarkar heard this and rewarded the messenger with ten rupees. The news came that the Rajas of Jasrota and Nurpur had arrived from Amritsar and camped outside the Mochi Gate. The Noble Sarkar said to his associates that he contemplated going to Amritsar and making offerings in accordance with the vow he had taken with regard to securing victory in the battle against the "Wazir-i-Azam." He had also to take a similar vow for the conquest of Kashmir for which the troops were coming to Lahore but would be sent there on the advice of Diwan Muhkam Chand. The messengers (Jauri) came from Peshawar and brought the news that Sirdar Fateh Khan Wazir was staying in Peshawar and trying to make collections from the people, and that the men of his army had reminded him of his promise made to them at Kundagarh, that whatever things they had lost in the loot following the battle, would be compensated for by the King but that nothing had yet been done.

[Text missing the last sentence being incomplete].

1813 (22)

News of the Deorhi of Sirdar Ranjit Singh Bahadur. Monday, dated 9th August, 1813 (11th Shaban, 1228 A.H.); the Royal Fort, Lahore.

The Noble Sarkar got up early in the morning and came out to the Saman Burj when the day had advanced four hours. The sirdars came in and made their customary bow. It was stated that the luggage of Raja Fateh Singh Ahluwalia had been despatched to Amritsar on that day because he was intending to depart towards his home. The representative of Himmat Singh Jhalla was ordered to go to Amritsar, where, on the arrival of the Noble Sarkar, some villages would be given to him to meet his payments. The Noble Sarkar also said that he would write to him ordering him to supply one "Kirpan"[60] by taking it from his master. He replied that whatever the Noble Sarkar should write, would be procured. He sat separately with Karam Singh Jahal and asked him to state how many villages were included in the estate of the late Sahib Singh. He replied that he had no knowledge whatsoever. The Noble Sarkar said that he had learnt it from certain people that these altogether were worth an estate of rupees fifty thousand, and that he proposed sending one of his accountants for the management of that property. It was reported that the revenue collector of Wazirabad had embezzled rupees thirty-five thousand of the revenues. On learning this the Noble Sarkar imposed a fine of rupees forty as a daily charge upon that collector.

Attar Singh of Faizullapur sought permission to leave for his home, and was ordered to stay there for a few days and told that he would be allowed to depart on the arrival of the Noble Sarkar at Amritsar. Raja Bir Singh of Nurpur was asked to state where he had left Raja Sansar Chand, and he replied that he (Sansar Chand) had sent some of his troops with him and would himself be coming to the Noble Sarkar after the rainy season. It was stated that Ganga Ram Jamadar had left for Sialkot at the head of two hundred sepoys, and that it appeared that he had some domestic dispute with the companions of Hukma Singh Chimny in which some two hundred men were killed and wounded on both sides. On learning this the Noble Sarkar was very angry and issued a letter summoning Hukma Singh. Raja Fateh Singh Ahluwalia asked for permission to depart, and was told by the Noble Sarkar that he himself would be leaving for Amritsar on the day after the next, but that in case he was delayed he would be allowed to depart. It was stated that a letter and a "Hundi" worth three lakhs of rupees from Sirdar Fateh Khan Wazir had reached one of his brothers, named Jabbar Khan, with instruction that he must pay the horsemen at the rate of thirty-five to forty rupees and the footmen at seven to ten rupees and should thus look after the troops and also that whatever he could realize from the Derajaat should also be spent on the maintenance of the army. It was further reported that the letters of the aforesaid person (the Wazir or Jabbar Khan) asking for troops had reached various places and that a careful augmentation of forces was in progress. It appeared, moreover, that the companions of Muin-ud-Daula Muhammad Khan of Mankera, and of Muzaffar Khan of Multan, etc., had presented themselves to that Khan, though it could not be discovered whether they had come under the orders of their masters or on their own initiative and with selfish motives. The Noble Sarkar heard all this and kept quite. He went into the zenana at noon, took his meals and laid himself down to take rest. Those who were present walked out one after the other. He got up again at about the third quarter of the day and came out to the place for the throne. The sirdars made their customary bow. Chaudhri Qadir Bakhsh and Naurang Singh said to the Noble Sarkar in privacy that Ghaus Khan, the Darogha of the Topkhana, had done many things during the war which did not justify his being true to his salt, that he could not be trusted in future, and that although his conduct might have led to the destruction of the whole army yet by the glory of the Noble Sarkar and the grace of God nothing amiss did happen. It was stated that Jahandad Khan had marched and gone to Wazirabad, and Baba Mehr Singh and Jamiat Bakhsh and other Sahibzadas had been quarrelling and fighting among themselves with arrows and gun for about a month over paltry matter of ... (?) ... in which fifty men were killed and wounded on both sides, and that in the end they had made peace between themselves. The Noble Sarkar said that it was well that they had settled their dispute among themselves and had not brought it to him. Fateh Singh Ahluwalia had private conference with the Noble Sarkar for about four hours, in which the latter remarked that he was very thankful to God that he had seen him hale and hearty with his own eyes. That respectable person replied that his life was given to him only for the purpose that he could avail of the sight of the Noble Sarkar, otherwise many chiefs of his army had committed many indescribable deeds of treachery. The Noble Sarkar said that everything was going on satisfactorily. He said to the representative of the Sirdar Gorkha that he must send for, in writing, one elephant of very fine gait for the Noble Sarkar from Sirdar Amar Singh Thapa, and offered its price. Hakim Aziz-ud-Din Khan and Manak Chand, the accountant, came in, and represented that Munshi Devi Dass had stated that whatever had been realized as revenue for the Noble Sarkar, had been paid into his treasury up to the last penny, that he accepted responsibility for all moneys, that Ram Dass was not with him, but that he (Ram Dass) had entrusted to him (Devi Dass) whatever monthly installments he had received. The Noble Sarkar asked them to go the camp of Ajudhia Dass and to ask Munshi Devi Dass to go there, too, and that the latter should explain the whole account to the former. A letter was sent to Raja Bhoop Singh, asking him to come together with other rajas and present himself, and that there would be no harm if (text not clear). A letter was sent to Raja Sansar Chand, asking him to come and present himself soon, because the affairs of the districts of the mountainous regions were to be considered on his arrival. The Noble Sarkar sent five thousand rupees to the fort of Attock, and rewarded the attendants upon horses, who had brought an Afghan sword from Jhang, with five hundred rupees. The Noble Sarkar ordered the reliable person of Raja Fateh Singh Ahluwalia to state how many troops their master possessed, and was told that he had some three thousand and five hundred horse and foot. The Noble Sarkar said that he would inspect their master's force on the Dussehra[61] day. Ram Nath Sahu stated that his property, which had been robbed by the dacoits near Wazirabad had not been discovered and restored to him. The Noble Sarkar replied that investigations would be made and his property recovered, and gave him assurances. When the night had passed one quarter the Noble Sarkar went into the zenana, took his meals and laid himself down to take rest. Those who were present walked out. It is reported that he would soon leave for Amritsar.

1813 (23)

NORTHERN INDIA NEWS EXTRACT;

(Second Leaf, the First Being Missing)

"It would be given to them but it should be given to us at this time." The "Wazir-i-Azam," replied that if they would be once again gain a victory over the enemy he would give them money incompensation for their property, and added that at that time they had no reason to make any demand for it. Thereupon the troops became displeased with the "Wazir-e-Azam." Rupees twenty were given to the aforesaid Jauri. After that the Noble Sarkar went into the zenana. All's well otherwise.

Dated 20th Shaban Wednesday, Corr.18th August. 1813

1813 (24)

Deorhi of Sirdar Ranjit Singh Bahadur. Saturday, dated 21st August, 1813 (23rd Shaban 1228 A.H.); the Fort of Bhangian, Amritsar.

A letter was despatched to Kanwar Kharak Singh, the prince, that he should bring Hazrat Shah Shuja-ul-Mulk, well guarded and in perfect safety. Another letter was sent to that Hazrat to the effect that the Noble

Sarkar had to consult him regarding certain matters, that therefore he should rest assured and come without delay with Kanwar Kharak Singh and Ram Singh, the man in charge of his affairs, and that certain matters could only be discussed on his arival. It was written to the garrison master of Attock that he must remain there and rest assured that he should take whatever stores he wanted from the "Thana" of Rawalpindi, that the troops of the Noble Sarkar would reach there very shortly and that necessary arrangements for establishing a cantonment there would then be completed. Two accountants, belonging to the Bania class from Shahjahanabad and sought employment. They were taken into service and deputed towards Kot Kangra as justices, after being made a grant of money to meet their expenses. The messengers (Jauri) came and delivered a letter from Sirdar Fateh Khan Wazir, urging upon the Noble Sarkar to release the fort of Attock and maintain friendly relations and stating that his demands also would be met, but that otherwise the Noble Sarkar must expect him there very soon. The Noble Sarkar considered the contents of the letter, smiled and said that in the month of Assuj,[62] the troops of the Noble Sarkar would go there to receive the "Wazir-i-Azam," and asked the Munshi to write a reply to the letter. The representative of Qazi Amar Singh Thapa presented a letter from his master, and the Noble Sarkar kept on talking with him in privacy for two hours. Dilsukh Rai, the representative of Raja Karam Singh of Patiala, presented five rupees on his own behalf and a letter from Nisar Budha Mal. He also presented another letter from his master together with one horse, one robe, four suits of clothes and several other gifts. The Noble Sarkar granted twenty thousand rupees in cash and two villages on the bank of the river Jhelum to Nihal Singh commandant, who had exhibited great valour in the battle against Sirdar Fateh Khan Wazir. The Noble Sarkar sent a message to Jawahar Singh, the represetative of Colonel Muhammad Shah Jahan, to write to his master to realise twenty five thousand rupees from the money-landers of Bikaner, and one hundred and twenty five thousand rupees from Multan by going there, adding that "Hundies" would be given in writing by the Noble Sarkar. In reply to a letter from the aforesaid Colonel it was written to him that all the matters had been very well explained to his representatives and would be communicated to him by his letter. All's well otherwise.

News of the Deorhi of Sirdar Ranjit Singh Bahadur. Thursday, dated 9th September, 1813 (13th Ramzan, 1228 A.H.); the Fort of Bhangian, Amritsar.

The Noble Sarkar got up in the morning and came out to his Diwan Khana when the day had advanced four hours. The sirdars usually present came in and made their customary bow. Rani Sada Kaur, the mother-in-law of the Noble Sarkar, and Kanwar Sher Singh and Tara Singh, the young princes, came in, met the Noble Sarkar and stated that if the Noble Sarkar undertook a campaign henceforth he must allow them also to take part in it. The Noble Sarkar said that he would, and asked the Rani whether her villages, which were in the possession of Sirdar Jodh Singh Ramgarhia had passed into her hands or not. She replied that she had established her control over them and that now she had no ill-will or enmity with him at all. When the day had advanced one quarter the Rani Sahiba and the princes walked out. The Noble Sarkar ordered Jai Karan Dass to engage in for service one hundred messengers together with "Mutsaddis"[63] the purpose of recording news, and sent them over to Peshawar, Kashmir, Kabul and Jalalabad, so that they might be sending daily news of those places. He replied that he would do so. The messengers (Jauri) came in and brought the news that Hazrat Mahmud Shah Badshah was at Kabul as before, and Sirdar Fateh Khan Wazir was also engaged there in collecting troops and that he had not presented himself before the King until that time, because the sirdars of the Durrani tribe had told the king that he had made worse the affairs of the king. The Noble Sarkar heard this and rewarded the "Jauri" with ten rupees. Desa Singh Majithia, who was present there, said, that when Sirdar Fateh Khan Wazir was busy in collecting troops the Noble Sarkar must also take care to organise his forces, and that it was not advisable for him to show negligence in that matter. When the day had advanced one quarter and a half he went into the zenana, took his meals, and laid himself down to take his rest at noon. At about the third quarter of the day he got up again and remained inside. It was stated that a person of the Jat tribe from among the brothers of the Raja of Nilamgarth (?) had come there with his family, and wanted to marry his daughter to the Noble Sarkar. The Noble Sarkar ordered Ram Singh his "Khidmatgar,"[64] to bring the girl and his mother inside the fort in a conveyance, because the Noble Sarkar would marry her after seeing her with his eyes. Thereupon the said bearer made them ride in a palanquin and brought both of them inside the fort. The Noble Sarkar cast a glance at the girl from head to foot, and kept talking with her mother for one hour and afterwards allowed them to depart. He came out to his Diwan Khana at nightfall and the sirdars presented themselves with a customary bow. Sujan Rae, the "Darogha-i-Adalat,"[65] was ordered to continue administering justice and keeping always before his eyes religious honesty and avoiding tyranny or cruelty to any of the poor. He replied that he would do so, adding that he had no power or courage to go against his wishes. When the night had passed one quarter he went into the zenana. Those who were present walked out one after the other. He took his meals and laid himself down to take rest. All went on well otherwise during the night.

Friday, dated 10th September, 1813 (14th Ramzan, 1228 A. H.)

The Noble Sarkar got up early in the morning and came out to his Diwan Khana when the day had advanced four hours. The sirdars came in and made their customary bow. The Noble Sarkar then went to a corner of the house all alone and sat down there and said to Nihal Singh, Mat Singh Bharania, and Bhai Gurbakhsh Singh, individually in privacy, that Shah Shuja-ul-Mulk had with him one saddle beset with jewels worth twenty eight lakhs of rupees and one big bedstead of turquoise fixed upon four legs, each of which was studded with one big diamond, and said that he proposed demanding these articles from him for himself. They said that the Noble Sarkar had full aurhority and he could do whatever he thought fit, but that already he had suffered a great deal of disrepute in his seizing the Koh-i-Noor gem from him, and these things could not be secured without inflicting further hardship, unpleasantness and humiliation. They further suggested that the Noble Sarkar might show kind attention, consideration, patronage and encouragement to him for the time being. The Noble Sarkar said that he was of the same opinion. He sent for Ram Singh, the man in charge of the affairs of Kharak Singh and order him to go to Shah Shuja-ul-Mulk on behalf of the Noble Sarkar, and tell him that he would shortly be sent towards Peshawar at the head of an adequate force. A letter was sent to Hukma Singh, the Thanadar of Lahore, that he should take due and proper care of the wives of the aforesaid Hazrat. When the day had advanced one quarter and a half he went into the zenana. Those who were present walked out. He took his meals and laid himself down to take rest at noon. He got up again at about the third quarter of the day, and came out to his audience chamber, where his sirdars and associates came and presented themselves. The messengers (Jauri) came and stated that Hazrat Mahmud Shah was still in Kabul, that Sirdar Fateh Khan Wazir had presented himself before the king, and that reproaches and retorts had been exchanged during the discussion between the "Wazir-i-Azam" and other sirdars of the Durrani tribes right in the presence of Hazrat Mahmud Shah over the defeat which they had suffered in the battle. He further reported that Sirdar Fateh Khan Wazir became displeased with those retorts and left the Darbar whereupon Hazrat Mahmud Shah summoned him and the Durrani sirdars on the following day, and brought about a peace between them. He further stated that after that every one of the sirdars sent for the troops of his own tribe, saying that the Shah would be able to march out within a month at the head of his warlike army, and that most of the men had come according to their call and the others were coming. The Noble Sarkar heard this and kept quiet, but later said to Manak Chand, the representative of Diwan Muhkam Chand, that as news about the approach of Sirdar Fateh Khan Wazir was afloat he must write to the Diwan that after completing his business he should get ready to come over the Noble Sarkar. When four hours of the night had passed, Ramzan Khan, a reliable follower of Hazrat Shah Shuja-ul-Mulk came in and said, that on account of the heat the temperature and disposition of the said Shah did not remain normal, whereupon the Noble Sarkar said that some other place would be proposed for him. When the night had passed one quarter those who were present walked out, and the Noble Sarkar went into the zenana, took his meals, and laid himself down to take rest. All's well otherwise.

1813 (26)

News of the Deorhi of Sirdar Ranjit Singh Bahadur. Saturday, dated 18th September, 1813 (22nd Ramzan, 1228 A. H.); the Fort of Bhangian, Amritsar.

The Noble Sarkar got up early in the morning and came out to the Diwan Khana when the day had advanced four hours. The sirdars usually present came in and made their customary bow. Sukh Dial, the agent of Rama Nand Sahu, was told that the work of the administration of justice, the charge of the seal of "Munshigiri," and other services connected with them, have been entrusted to him by the Noble Sarkar against rupees thirteen lakhs, but that he must administer justice with mercy and with religious honesty.[63] Folding his hands he replied that on the basis of contract justice according to religious honesty was a bit difficult to administer because one had to keep an eye on procuring money by means unlawful and illegitimate. The Noble Sarkar said that out of regard for him he postponed the granting of this contract for one year, and would now watch with what cleverness he would discharge his task. The Noble Sarkar granted him one turban gem, one plume, and one drum carried on a horse, whereupon he paid his respects, and took those things after presenting one Ashrafi and five rupees as Nazar. A messenger came and delivered a letter from Hukma Singh, the Thanadar of Lahore, which mentioned that the family of Hazrat Shah Shuja-ul-Mulk were being put to great inconvenience and trouble on account of heavy rain falling on their tents, and wanted to know the order of the Noble Sarkar. The Noble Sarkar heard this but did not make any reply. When the day had advanced one and a half quarter he went into the zenana and the sirdars who were present walked out. He took his meals and laid himself down to take rest. He got up again at about the third quarter of the day, and came out to his Diwan Khana where the sirdars usually present came and made their customary bow. Ram Singh, the man in charge of the affairs of Kharak Singh, the eldest prince, came and said that Hazrat Shah Shuja-ul-Mulk had sent for him on that day, and he wanted to know the orders of the Noble Sarkar in the matter. The Noble Sarkar said that he must go on the following day. Diwan Bhawani Dass of the low stature was told that on the day after the following Nand Singh the representative of the Noble Sarkar and the representative of Raja Bhag Singh, would both be allowed to depart. At nightfall a messenger came and said that on account of heavy rainfall about one hundred houses in Lahore had crumbled down to the ground and that about twenty-five men had been killed through their walls falling upon them, while many more were injured. The Noble Sarkar heard this and talked about it to the sirdars and his associates, saying that the downpour had been very serious that year in the district, and that such rainfall had never occurred before. Calling in the Munshi he ordered him to write out certain letters, then listened to the music of the flute by Attar Khan, and later went into the zenana, while those who were present walked out. He took his meals and laid himself down to take rest when the night had passed one quarter.

Sunday, dated 19th September, 1813 (23rd Ramzan 1228 A.H.)

The Noble Sarkar got up early in the morning and came out to his Diwan Khana when the day had advanced four hours. The sirdars usually present came and made their customary bow. A letter was issued to Hukma Singh, the Thanadar of Lahore, telling him that as it had been raining very heavily during that year he must be very careful in looking after the Ranjit Fort,[67] and that he should consider it his great responsibility. It was stated that Diwan Muhkam Chand had sent one Mustafa Khan Jamadar to the fort of Bhatinda at the head of two hundred footmen, in compliance with the request of Rani Lacheena. The Noble Sarkar said that the Diwan had done a very improper thing, because that country was in the possession of the English Sahibs, and at once issued a letter to him that he must not send any of his men to Bhatinda, and that in case he had sent some, he should call them back. When the day had advanced one and a half quarter the Noble Sarkar went into the zenana, and those who were present walked out. He took his meals and laid himself down to take rest. He got up again at about the third quarter of the day, and came out to his Diwan Khana where the sirdars made a customary bow. Rama Nand Sahu came in and showed a letter from a reliable person, who had come from Afghanistan, to the Noble Sarkar in privacy. It appears that it was written in it, that Sirdar Fateh Khan Wazir had marched from Kabul with sufficient troops, that it was rumoured that he had a mind to go towards Multan *via* the Derajaat, that Hazrat Mahmud Shah was also preparing to march in that direction, and that for certain he would start on the Eid after offering his prayers and listening to the sermon from the pulpit. It furter mentioned that he "Wazir-i-Azam" was hatching a conspiracy through correspondence with Nawab Muzaffar Khan of Multan. The Noble Sarkar heard this and said that it did not matter, adding that the situation would be dealt with satisfactorily. The Noble Sarkar explained all about the march of Sirdar Fateh Khan Wazir in privacy to Sirdar Mat Singh Bharania and Nihal Singh of Attari, and was assured by them that by the grace of God he (the Wazir) would again suffer defeat. They suggested that the Noble Sarkar must allow them to collect troops in any case. The Noble Sarkar kept quiet, and remained lost in his thoughts for about four hours, and latter called upon the Munshi and made him write letters to the sirdars who had gone on leave, and also to the rajas of the mountainous regions, summoning every one of them to his presence. Ram Singh, the man in charge of his affairs, stated that Hazrat Shah Shuja-ul-Mulk had asked him for some money to meet his expenses, and that he had given him one thousand rupees which he had taken from Duni Chand Saraf. It latter was issued to Hukma Singh, the Thanadar of Lahore, that he must make the wives of Hazrat Shah Shuja-ul-Mulk enter into the mansion of Shahzada Taimur in Lahore as previously. It was stated that Hakim Muhammad Ashraf Khan had left Lahore, and was expected to present himself before the Noble Sarkar on the following day or the day after. When the night had passed one and a half quarter, he went into the zenana, took his meals, and later on laid himself down to take rest when half of the night had passed. The heavy rain continued falling incessantly. All's well otherwise.

96

News of the Deorhi of Sirdar Ranjit Singh Bahadur. Monday, dated 20th September, 1813 (20th Ramzan, 1228 A.H.); the Fort of Bhangian, Amritsar.

The Noble Sarkar got up early in the morning and came out to his audience chamber when the day had advanced four hours. The sirdars usually present came in making a courteous bow. Nand Singh spoke in privacy to the Noble Sarkar for two hours, after which he was granted a robe of honour consisting of five garments and rupees one hundred in cash. He was then allowed to depart with the words that he must try to know everything hidden in the mind of Colonel Nasir-ud-Daula, and communicate the same daily to the Noble Sarkar. He replied that he would spare no pains in rendering service to the Noble Sarkar. He then walked out, and Kanwar Kharak Singh, the eldest prince, entered and talked about the control and administration of the country. He stated that the Noble Sarkar had done well and it was quite proper that the seal of "Munshigiri" had been entrusted to Sukha Nand *alias* Sukhdial, because in his mind he did not feel satisfied with Munshi Devi Dass. He stated that two or three men had petitioned to him for the grant of a contract of some estate and he wanted to know the intentions of the Noble Sarkar in the matter. The Noble Sarkar said that he must keep in mind the improvement and betterment of his affairs in every undertaking and should in that matter also act accordingly. The messengers (Jauri) arrived and delivered a letter from Pandit Nand Ram Kashmiri, who kept company with Sirdar Fateh Khan Wazir. The Noble Sarkar listened to its contents privacy, and caused a reply to be despatched. Then he went into the zenana and those who were present walked out. He took his meals. Rani Sada Kaur, his mother-in-law, came in along with Kanwars Sher Singh and Tara Singh and said that the Noble Sarkar had granted estates to Kanwar Kharak Singh but did not seem favourably disposed in showing kindness to Kanwars, Sher Singh and Tara Singh, adding that they, too, were his sons and he must be just to them, and that she was not asking the Noble Sarkar to do anything for her. The Noble Sarkar said that she must rest assured, for he would give something to them also. In the afternoon they walked out and the Noble Sarkar laid himself down to take rest. He got up again at the third quarter of the day and came out and the sirdars made a courteous bow to him. Duni Chand, a representative of Raja Bhag Singh, came in, and was allowed to depart with the grant of a robe of honour consisting of five garments and rupees one hundred in cash. The aforesaid person walked out and Manak Chand, a representative, submitted a letter from Diwan

Muhkam Chand, in which it was written that the zamindars of Hoshiarpur were trying to approach the Noble Sarkar with some recommendations regarding their case, and that the details of this case were as follows: "I had gone to the expedition of Kashmir and Attock under orders of the Noble Sarkar. In my absence the said zamindars did not pay a single penny to my son, Moti Ram, simply out of their bastardly character. Now I have asked from them for the revenue tax for the past and the present. They have made a complaint to the Noble Sarkar. There is no fault of mine in this case. I am still prepared to do whatever the Noble Sarkar may order me to do." In reply to this the Noble Sarkar wrote to him after due consideration of his note that he must take from those zamindars whatever was due and should not claim from them anything more. The messenger (Jauri) came from Peshawar and brought the news that Aggai Khan, the governor of Peshawar, had collected his troops and had despatched them towards Dera Ghazi Khan, and that it was rumoured there that Sirdar Fateh Khan Wazir had marched from Kabul towards Dera Ismail Khan, and that it was further reported that he had a mind to proceed towards Multan, though as a matter of fact he was still in his tent in Kabul and had not yet moved out of it on his forward march. He further added that Hazrat Mahmud Shah had asked for reinforcement from Mir Hyder Shah. The Noble Sarkar heard this and gave rupees twenty by way of reward to the aforesaid messengers (Jauri) and, after consulting the sirdars and his associates, went into the zenana. The sirdars and those who were present walked out. He took his meals and laid himself down to take rest when the night had passed one quarter. All's well otherwise.

1813 (28)

News of the Deorhi of Sirdar Ranjit Singh Bahadur. Sunday, dated 26th September, 1813 (30th Ramzan, 1228 A.H.), Amritsar.

The Noble Sarkar got up early in the morning and came out when the day had advanced four hours and his staff and servants made their customary bow. He inspected the drill of the battalion of the Hindustani Sepoys. When the day had advanced one quarter he came to the Diwan Khana, where the sirdars came and made their customary bow. He sent one thousand rupees to Hazrat Muhammad Ashraf Khan with the message that he must get ready from the bazaar whatever things belonging to him were stolen, and that his goods would be sent to him afterwards on their recovery. He was asked to rest assured about them. The messengers (Jauri) came from Kabul and brought the news that Hazrat Mahmud Shah was in

Kabul as before, that Sirdar Fateh Khan Wazir was outside that city as previously, that the latter had entered the red canopy of the Dera and had despatched his reliable person and runners with written messages to various places to summon the Durranies, Yusafzais and other tribes, that it was reported that the march of the "Wazir-i-Azam" towards the Deras secretly was quite probable, and that the people were flocking there from all directions. He further reported that the news had reached Hazrat Mahmud Shah, that a fight had taken place between the troops of Mir Haidar Shah, the ruler of Persia near Herat, in which the former had gained an upper hand; that it was the intention of Hazrat Mahmud Shah to march towards Peshawer as soon as the Durranies presented themselves to him; and that Sirdar Fateh Khan Wazir then would go to the Deras. The Noble Sarkar heard this and remarked that he wondered how the troops of Mir Haider Shah which, numbered only four or five thousand horsemen, overcame those of Fateh Khan. Those who were present replied that many people must have joined him and fought for him because for three hours the inhabitants of that place .... (text makes no sense). The Noble Sarkar rewarded the messengers (Jauri) with twenty rupees. He then went into the zenana at noon. The sirdars and those who were present walked out. He laid himself down to take rest after his meals. He got up again at about the third quarter of the day, and came out when four hours of the day were left. The staff and servants made their customary bow. Riding on a special horse, he enjoyed a pleasure trip through the bazaars of Amritsar distributed some two hundred rupees to the poor, and returned to the fort at about nightfall. He went into his council chamber as usual. The Noble Sarkar looked at the new moon, and ordered that a salute should be fired from the Topkhana from over the forts of Bhangian and Gobindgarh to mark its appearance. This was done accordingly. Sukh Dial, the agent of Rama Nand Sahu, stated that the representative Diwan of the Raja of Jammu requested for grant of the contract of some places for himself. The Noble Sarkar replied that he must bring from him an application on the following day, mentioning the places he wanted to take, and added that he would give him a contract. One Zulfiqar Ali — the wearer of weapons — came with twenty horsemen who appeared to belong to the forces of Nawab Mir Khan, paid his respects, and after presenting a horse and five rupees as Nazar, sought employment. The Noble Sarkar engaged him in service after assuring him generally. He then listened to the music of a flute and afterwards went into the zenana. The others walked out. He laid himself down to take rest after his meals when the night had passed one quarter. All's well otherwise.

*News of the Deorhi of Sirdar Ranjit Singh Bahadur. Sunday, dated 10th
October, 1813, (14th Shawwal, 1228 A.H.); the Tank of the Rani,
situated at seven kos from Jawalamukhi and eight kos from Kot Kangra.*

Yesterday the Noble Sarkar rode forward from Jawalamukhi at noon. On the way he took presents and Nazars from the zamindars of the villages, and, after covering seven kos arrived near the tank of the Rani a little before sunset. He set up his camp there, and entered into it. It was stated that some men had been causing great inconvenience on that day to the troops of the Noble Sarkar, who replied that they must all remain there. When two hours of the night had passed the messengers (Jauri) came and brought a letter from Kanwar Kharak Singh from a place at a distance of three kos from Amritsar. In it was written, that as there seemed to be sometime before the Noble Sarkar would return, he wished to be allowed to move forward, and that Sahib Singh Bedi had come to see him. After considering his letter the Noble Sarkar sent him a reply that he should not be hasty for in two days he would march back and his camp would soon be there. He made Munshi Karam Chand write a letter to the garrison master of the fort of Attock, and ordered it to be despatched to him through the messengers (Jauri). It was written in that letter, that as regards his statement about the inconvenience which was being felt by hires through shortage of funds, the Noble Sarkar had written to Rama Nand Sahu, who would shortly be supplying him with ten thousand rupees. The letter contained many words of assurance for the garrison master who was urged to maintain a firm control over that district. When the night had passed one quarter, he took his meals and laid himself down to take rest. All went on well during the night.

To-day he got up early in the morning and ordered march by the beat of drum. The messengers (Jauri) arrived and delivered a letter from Nawab Ata Muhammad Khan, which he had brought from the district of Rawalpindi. The Noble Sarkar handed it over to Munshi Karam Chand, and rode all along from the tank of the Rani. After covering a distance of eight kos he arrived near the fort of Kangra, where a tent was pitched into which he entered at noon. From over the said fort and the fort of Mangarh, salutes of cannons were fired in honour of his entry. He took his meals and laid himself down to take rest. He got up again when four hours of the day were left, and came out to the tent without poles. Bhim Singh of Hazara, the garrison master of that place, presented himself and offered two

Ashrafis and one horse as Nazar. The Noble Sarkar excused him the submission of the horse, and inquired from him all about that place. At nightfall Raja Sansar Chand came in and met the Noble Sarkar who kept on talking with him about Kashmir. The Raja said that it was advisable to send an expedition towards Kashmir at that time, for later it would begin to snow in that country. The Noble Sarkar said that on his return he would immediately despatch troops in that direction. The Thanadar of Kangra was ordered to make special arrangements for procuring grain and straw. He replied that he would do so. When the night had passed one quarter the Noble Sarkar took his meals and laid himself down to take rest, while those who were present walked out. It went on well otherwise during the night.

Monday, dated 11th October 1813 (15th Shawwal 1228 A.H.), Kangra.

The Noble Sarkar got up early in the morning, and took a sacred bath and changed his clothes. When the day had advanced four hours he rode out and went to the temple of Devi Nagarkot. On approaching the temple he alighted from his horse, entered it on foot when the day had advanced one quarter; enjoyed a sacred sight of the Devi, performed some rites peculiar to the place, and made an offering of his gold stuff, a gold threaded suit of clothes, one huge canopy, several necessary articles which he carried with himself, and twelve hundred rupees in cash. He remained standing for full four hours, and with his own hands distributed sweetmeats and five hundred rupees among the Brahmans. After this he received some sacred gifts from that place and returned to the village of Garhbara and went to the house of Holigur Gousayin, next, that august person made an offering of two hundred and fifty rupees to him, and mentioned to him the cherished problem of his mind. The Gousayin said that whatever objects the Noble Sarkar desired to achieve by the grace of God they would be realized by him and he must rest assured in his mind. When one quarter of the day was left the Noble Sarkar returned from that place and rode into Kangra where salute of cannons was fired. He walked through the fort, and the employees there presented him Nazars according to their ranks. At nightfall he rode from that place and came to his tent and ordered for the prepration of "hom"[68] that had to take place on the following day. After that he ate something and then listened to the "katha".[69] It went on well otherwise until the night had passed one quarter.

News of the Deohri of Sirdar Ranjit Singh Bahadur. Saturday, dated 16th October, 1813 (20th Shawwal, 1228 A.H.); the Village Jamalpur, Three kos Beyond Pathankot.

Yesterday the Noble Sarkar remained sitting until nightfall. He talked to Moti Rani, the son of Diwan Muhkam Chand in privacy, and made him depart with a grant of one pair of gold bangles and a robe of honour consisting of three garments, and with instructions to send his father immediately to Amritsar and to remain himself at the cantonment of Phillaur. He said to the representative of Raja Bhoop Singh of Haripur that he must send for his master hastily, because all chiefs were soon to be deputed to proceed towards Kashmir. He replied that, according to his order he would soon come and present himself within ten or twelve days, adding that the territory of his master being in the possession of the Noble Sarkar who actually collected its revenues he could not but be at his service. The Noble Sarkar said that his territory would soon be released to him, and that he should rest assured about it. Raja Omaid Singh of Jaswal stated that he wanted permission to leave for his home for ten days, so that he might make all proper arrangements before returning. The Noble Sarkar said that he would shortly let him go Kahdhara Singh was ordered to bring the Wazir of Chamba. The Noble Sarkar gave one rupee to each of the orderly horsemen. When the night had passed one quarter those who were present walked out, and the Noble Sarkar went into the tent, took his meals and laid himself down to take rest. It went on well otherwise during the night.

To-day he got up early in the morning and came out to the tent without poles where the sirdars made their customary bow. The messengers (Jauri) came and delivered a letter from Nawab Muzaffar Khan of Multan together with another from Muhammad Azam Khan, the Nazim of Kashmir. This second letter was in an envelope addressed to the Nawab of Multan by name. The first letter mentioned that he (the Nawab) was sincerely and with devotion ready to be obedient to him (the Noble Sarkar), and would have nothing to do with anybody else, that he was sending the letter of Nazim of Kashmir just as it was received by him in his name. The letter of the Nazim mentioned that the troops of the Noble Sarkar were leaving for that direction (Kashmir), that he (the Nawab) should collect all his forces from sundry places and send them into the territory of the Noble Sarkar to cause disturbance, and that he (the Nazim) would see him honoured and compensated by the King (Mahmud Shah) for his service. The Noble Sarkar heard this and remarked that it was all a rules for personal gain conceived in a very clever manner. A letter was sent to Kanwar Kharak Singh, the eldest prince, asking him to send all the troops that he could collect towards Gujrat, because the Noble Sarkar was firmly resolved himself to march towards Kashmir after his visit to Amritsar. When the day had advanced one and a half quarter, it was stated that all the troops of the Noble Sarkar had come from the Tank of the Rani and had joined the main army. The Noble Sarkar announced that his march would take place on the following day. At noon he went into the tent, took his meals, and laid himself down to take rest, while those who were present walked out. He got up again at about the third quarter of the day, and came out to the tent without poles when four hours of the day were left. His sirdars and attendant presented themselves. Urgent letters were despatched to Sirdar Jodh Singh of Kalsia and Diwan Muhkam Chand, asking them to present themselves speedily in Amritsar. The Noble Sarkar said to his associates that for some time past he had received no news about the country of Bokhara. They replied that whatever the messengers could learn about at that place from Kabul was always reported to him, adding that they had learnt that Mahmud Shah was at that time making preparations for his march from Kandhar towards Kabul, and that most probably he would have already started. Then talks went on about the passages to Kashmir, the associates saying that although the route *via* Sialkot was the shortest cut to Kashmir, yet it was quite impossible for the troops to traverse, and that men alone could negotiate that passage. The Noble Sarkar agreed with this view, adding that he would march only by an easier and straighter route. It was stated that some troops of Raja Bir Singh of Nurpur had arrived that day and had joined the Noble Sarkar's army, and that the Raja himself would come and present himself within two or three days. The Noble Sarkar made Munshi Karam Chand despatch letters to the rajas of the passes to Kashmir informing them that the Noble Sarkar after completing his visit to the sacred shrine of Jawalamukhi was coming back, and would this time by the grace of God himself conquer Kashmir, that they must keep ready personally in their places, and that they should definitely understand that the Noble Sarkar would soon be in Kashmir. It went on well until the night had passed four hours. It was being talked about that the Noble Sarkar was to go towards Amritsar on the following day, though it yet remained to be seen whether he would or not. All's well otherwise.

1813 (31)

News of the Deohri of Sirdar Ranjit Singh Bahadur. Friday, dated 22nd October, 1813 (26th Shawwal, 1228, A.H.); the Town of Gujrat.

Yesterday the Noble Sarkar continued sitting until the night had passed one quarter, and kept on talking with Jahandad Khan. The latter presented to the Noble Sarkar in privacy something in writing, probably some facts of Kashmir known to him urging that the Noble Sarkar must proceed in that direction promptly, and that it was not advisable for him to make any delay. The Noble Sarkar replied that that was his own intention but that he had to wait for the arrival of Diwan Muhkam Chand, adding that as soon he should arrive, the march in that direction would take place. The aforesaid person then said something with respect to the case of Nawab Ata Muhammad Khan, and the Noble Sarkar replied that he would invite that individual. When the night had passed one quarter and a half he walked out, and the Noble Sarkar went into the other tent, took his meals, and laid himself down to take rest when half of the night had passed. All went on well otherwise during the night.

To-day he got up early in the morning and came out to the tent set apart for audience when the day had advanced four hours. The sirdars and associates presented themselves. The zamindars of the village of Handoi, who had preferred a complaint to him on the previous day while he was out riding, came in and stated their own case. The Noble Sarkar asked the Thanadar of the town of Gujrat as to why he oppressed those zamindars. He replied that they had not paid a single penny of the revenue of the Noble Sarkar during the previous year on the pretext that it had been a dry season that they were delaying payment even with regard to the current year, that he had for that reason made a raid upon them and seized their cattle, and that they had consequently come with complaints to the Noble Sarkar. He further said that the Noble Sarkar was the master and the owner and might act upon whatever he thought proper and that he would strictly abide by his wishes. On hearing this the Noble Sarkar handed over those zamindars to the said Thanadar, and ordered that he must realize from them the revenue tax for the past and the current years as it was due, and should not exact anything more from them. The Vakil of Raja Chet Singh of Jammu came in, presented rupees five on behalf of his master and himself, and said that his master had collected all his troops, and would present himself before the Noble Sarkar whenever he would be ordered. The Noble Sarkar asked him to send for him. The representatives of the rajas of the hilly districts were warned that it was not right for their

104

masters that they had not come to present themselves according to their promise, and that they must soon be sent for. They replied that they would soon come and present themselves. When the day had advanced one quarter the Noble Sarkar took his meals, went to the other tent, and laid himself down to take rest at noon, while those who were present walked out. He got up again at about the third quarter of the day, and came out when four hours of the day were left. The sirdars came in and made a courteous bow to him. A messenger came and delivered a letter from Diwan Muhkam Chand, in which it was written that marching from Amritsar according to the order of the Noble Sarkar he was soon coming to present himself. The Noble Sarkar rode into the town of Gujrat, enjoyed a ramble through it, returned from there at nightfall, and re-entered the tent. The messengers (Jauri) arrived from Kashmir and said, that Muhammad Azim Khan was still encamped in Kashmir and had despatched his troops for the control and management of the "ghats" known as Kamangosha, Ayundhi, etc., and had distributed money among the men of his army to meet their expenses. The Noble Sarkar heard this, gave five rupees by way of reward to the aforesaid messengers (Jauri), and made them depart in that direction once again. A letter was despatched to Hukma Singh, the Thanadar of Lahore, asking him to send one newly constructed mortar promptly to the Noble Sarkar. Pandit Ram Chand, who was one of the associates of the Noble Sarkar, sought permission to leave. The Noble Sarkar said that his departure in those days could not be allowed. It went on all well until the time when the night had passed four hours.

1813 (32)

News of the Deorhi of Sirdar Ranjit Singh of Lahore. Wednesday, dated 27th October, 1813 (2nd Ziqaad, 1228, A.H.); the Village of Khera, situated on the Bank of River Jehlum.

When four hours of the night were left the Noble Sarkar got up, announced his march by a drum beat, and after making his entire luggage leave for the next stage of the journey before sunrise, came out into the tent, sat down on a carpet, and ordered the departure of the camp and other materials. Diwan Muhkam Chand, Munshi Mehtab Rai, Sirdar Dal Singh Bharania, and other sirdars came and made their customary bow. The Noble Sarkar, mounting an elephant and seating Diwan Muhkam Chand with himself in his special royal seat, turned his attention towards the next stage of his journey from the town of Gujrat. After covering a distance of seven kos he reached the village of Khera on the bank of the river Jehlum, and entered his camp when the day had advanced one quarter. Those who were present walked out, while the Noble Sarkar, after taking his meals, laid himself down to take rest at noon. He got up again at about the third quarter of the day and came out to the tent, which was used for audience, when four hours of the day were left. The sirdars made their customary bow. The messengers (Jauri) came from Kashmir and brought the news, that Muhammad Azim Khan was encamped in Kashmir as previously, and was in great fear in his heart that the Noble Sarkar might reach that country, and that a letter from Sirdar Fateh Khan Wazir had arrived there from Kabul, intimating plainly that Hazrat Mahmud Shah was returning from Kandhar. He also reported that the ruler of Kashmir had made satisfactory preparations for the defence of the "ghats." A messenger arrived and delivered a letter from Raja Fateh Singh Ahluwalia in which it was written, that owing to an urgent note from the Noble Sarkar he had marched from Amritsar, and after spending one night in Lahore, had crossed to the otherside of the river Ravi the next day and was expected to reach the presence of the Noble Sarkar within two days. A shawl and a turban were awarded to the brother of Pritam Singh Hazari, and he was allowed to leave for the Fort of Kot Kangra. Diwan Muhkam Chand presented himself and the Noble Sarkar kept on talking with him. All's well otherwise.

1813 (33)

A Sheet of the News of the Deorhi of Sirdar Ranjit Singh. Saturday, dated 30th October 1813 (5th Ziqaad, 1228, A.H.)

The Noble Sarkar got up early in the morning and came out to the tent set apart for audience when the day had advanced four hours. Diwan Muhkam Chand, Raja Sansar Chand and other high and low sirdars came and made their customary bow. The messengers (Jauri) came from Kabul and brought the news, that Hazrat Mahmud Shah Badshah had left Kabul and marched towards Peshawar on 10th Shawwal at the head of forty thousand horse and foot of the Yusafzai and other tribes that all the Mussalman sirdars had taken oaths on the Quran that once at least they would prove their sincerity and spirit of sacrifice, and that they had also told him (the King) that he on his part must also be prepared to grant them generous concessions. The messengers further reported, that Sirdar Fateh Khan Wazir was in Kabul, that a letter had reached the Governor of Peshawar for collecting materials that this governor was busy in collecting military stores, and that the king would come towards Attock from the upper side of Peshawar. After hearing this the Noble Sarkar rewarded the messengers (Jauri) with twenty rupees, and said to Diwan Muhkam Chand that the king was coming towards Peshawar, and that it would be good if a settlement was made with him. It was stated that Nihal Singh, Dhonkal

Singh, Ajit Singh, Mir Mazhar Ali and other commandants and the Darogha of the Topkhana driven by horses had arrived and set up their camps to the right of the victorious troops. When the day had advanced one and a half quarter the Noble Sarkar went into the zenana and those who were present walked out. He took his meals and laid himself down to rest at noon. He got up again at about the third quarter of the day, and came out to the tent set apart for audience when four hours of the day were left. The sirdars made their customary bow. Nawab Kutbub-ud-Din Khan of Kasur was ordered to present his soldiers for inspection by Diwan Muhkam Chand. He replied that he would do so. Diwan Ganga Ram was ordered to bring a list of all the military articles concerning the various Topkhanas and battalions after checking the same himself. Letters were despatched to the Thanadars of Lahore and Amritsar to send speedily carts full of gunpowder and balls to the Noble Sarkar. It went on well otherwise until the night had passed four hours.

1813 (34)

News of the Deorhi of Sirdar Ranjit Singh Bahadur. Saturday, dated the 13th November, 1813 (19th Ziqaad, 1228, A.H.), the (Village of Kheraon) the Bank of the River Jehlum.

Yesterday the Noble Sarkar remained sitting until the night had passed four hours, and continued talking with Diwan Muhkam Chand and Sukh Dial Sahu. It was stated that Kanwar Kharak Singh, the prince, had crossed the river Jehlum with his troops, and had set up his camp in the direction of Attock, and that Ram Singh, the man in charge of his affairs, had come over to this side of the river, but, after crossing it on the following day, would depart. A messenger came and delivered a letter from Hukma Singh, the Thanadar of Lahore, in which it was written that according to the Noble Sarkar's order he had asked Hazrat Shah Shuja-ul-Mulk serveral times to march but the latter had always put forward the excuse of his indisposition. The Noble Sarkar considered the letter and despatched a reply to the Thanadar, asking him once again that he must send that Hazrat to that direction. A letter was written out and despatched to that Hazrat also, pointing out to him that such time and opportunity would never recur to him again, and so he must come in that direction speedily. When the night had passed one quarter those who were present walked out, while the Noble Sarkar went into the other tent, took his meals there and laid himself down to rest. All went on well otherwise during the night. He got up early in the morning today, and came out to the tent set apart for audience when four hours of the day were left. The sirdars and attendants presented themselves. The Noble Sarkar talked to every one of them, and sent a verbal order to Raja Fateh Singh Ahluwalia, through his own staff bearer that he must cross the river Jehlum on that day and march towards Attock. Diwan Muhkam Chand and Raja Sansar Chand came in according to the summons of the Noble Sarkar who sat with them separately and held a private conference for about four hours. Munshi Karam Chand was made to write out letters to all the Thanadars on the other side of the river Jehlum up to the garrison master of Attock. It was plainly written in those that the army of the Noble Sarkar was marching in their direction that they must attend to it within their own boundaries and divisions for providing grain, etc., and should post immediately four horsemen and one extra horse at every fifth kos by way of a guard for the mails, because the Noble Sarkar would go to the fort of Attock riding on the horses of this mail service, while the troops would reach there after him. One letter was written out for Sirdar Fateh Khan Wazir, and was sent to him through the messengers (Jauri). It mentioned that the Noble Sarkar still adhered to the promises and agreements that he had made with him (Fateh Khan), and wanted him also to keep his pledges according to which he had agreed to pay to the Noble Sarkar eleven lakhs of rupees annually regarding Kashmir, to deliver him the fort of Multan to make one of his brothers and some troops to stay with him, adding that he had not yet fulfilled any one of those terms. It further asked that he might fulfil all the three conditions first, and then the Noble Sarkar would release the fort of Attock. It also contained a warning that in case these conditions remained unfulfilled the army of the Noble Sarkar would go to Kashmir and conquer it by a single attack. It finally concluded by saying that he would anxiously await a reply to this letter. At noon the sirdars and those who were present walked out, and the Noble Sarkar went into the other tent, took his meals and laid himself down to rest. He got up again at about the third quarter of the day, and came out when four hours of the day were left. The staff and the servants made their customary bow. He rode on his horse and went to the bank of the river Jehlum, sat down there, and watched the troops of Divan Muhkam Chand and Raja Fateh Singh Ahluwalia cross the river. At nightfall he returned from that place and entered his scarlet tent. Sheikh Salar Bakhsh came in, presented one gold duecat as Nazar and stated that he had been in the service of the Maharaja Bahadur Daulat Rao Schindia together with Colonel Johnson Sahib that on account of not being able to get his salary, he had left that service that he had come to present himself to the Noble Sarkar, that the Noble Sarkar's name like the sun and the moon was being mentioned all over the world, and that he was very well acquainted with all matters pertaining to the organisation and administration of a battalion. The Noble Sarkar heard this and replied that he should go and set up his camp in the Misl of Diwan Ganga Ram, adding that after making enquiries about him he would fix him up satisfactorily. He was given all assurances. This person then walked out. Roshan Khan, the well known Mistry, presented twenty-five newly constructed mortars, and was ordered to prepare more of the same kind. When the night had passed one quarter those who were present walked out. He went to the other tent, took his meals, and laid himself down to rest.

Sunday, dated 14th November, 1813 (20th Ziqaad, 1228, A.H.)

The Noble Sarkar got up early in the morning and came out to the tent set apart for audience when the day had advanced four hours. The sirdars came in and made their customary bow. The Noble Sarkar issued an order to all the rajas of the mountainous regions verbally through the staff bearer that they should immediately cross the river Jehlum together with their troops. A messenger came and delivered a letter from Bhai Lal Singh of Katihal, and the Noble Sarkar handed it over to the Munshi. The messengers (Jauri) came from Afghanistan and brought the news, that Sirdar Fateh Khan Wazir had marched from Kabul in this direction, had reached and encamped near Khaka-i (text not clear) which was one stage of journey from Kabul, that his brothers had gone in different directions towards their respective divisions to bring troops, that on their joining the "Wazir-i-Azam" he would march towards Peshawar, that Hazrat Mahmud Shah Padshah was staying on the other side of the Khyber Pass as previously that he was anxiously waiting for the arrival of the "Wazir-i-Azam", that the troops of the Qazilbashes and the Durranis had marched ahead from Rasulnagar towards Peshawar, and that the swivels had also very probably been sent secretly. On learning this the Noble Sarkar rewarded the messengers in the usual manner, and made them depart in that direction once again. It was stated that the troops of all the rajas of the mountainous regions had begun crossing the river Jehlum that the Topkhana of the Noble Sarkar, after crossing the "Ghat" of Muhamdipur, had gone over to the other side of the river, and established its camp. Ram Singh, the man in charge of the affairs of Kanwar Sahib, came in and stated that the Noble Sarkar had already promised, that whatever places would come into his possession at that time, would be granted to Kanwar Sahib, that as the division of Rawalpindi had newly been confiscated by the Noble Sarkar it should be granted by him to Kanwar Sahib. The Noble Sarkar heard this and told him to assure Kanwar

Sahib in every way and to tell him that presently his representations would be considered, and asked him to go back to Kanwar Sahib. When the day had advanced one quarter a half the Noble Sarkar went into the zenana, those who were present having walked out. He took his meals and laid himself down to rest at noon. He got up again at about the third quarter of the day and came out when four hours of the day were left. His sirdars and associates came in and made their customary bow. It was stated that Ram Singh, the man in charge of the affairs of Kanwar Sahib, had crossed the river Jehlum and gone over to the Kanwar. The Noble Sarkar rode out to the bank of the river Jehlum, sat down on a chair, and watched the crossing of the troops of the rajas of the mountainous regions. At nightfall he returned and entered his scarlet tent where his associates and attendants presented themselves. A messenger came and delivered a letter from the son of the late Jiwan Singh in which it was written that he had a great desire to kiss the feet of the Noble Sarkar, and was marching to present himself soon. It was written to him in reply that it would not be of any use for him to come over there because the Noble Sarkar himself was very soon coming in his direction, that soon places would be assigned to him to meet his expenses, etc., and that he should not entertain any fear. It was stated that Sirdar Fateh Singh Ahluwalia had crossed the river Jehlum and gone on further. The Noble Sarkar began to talk afterwards with Diwan Muhkam Chand and Sirdar Jodh Singh of Ramgarh. It went on well otherwise until the time when the night had passed four hours.

1813 (35)

Deorhi of Sirdar Ranjit Singh Bahadur. Dated 21st November, 1813 (17th Ziqaad, 1228, A.H.); near Rohtasgarh, five kos to the other side of the river Jehlum.

Yesterday, while the Noble Sarkar was sitting, a letter came from the Thanadar of Attock in which it was plainly written that the news had reached there that Hazrat Mahmud Shah was halting on the other side of the Khyber Pass, anxiously awaiting the arrival of the "Wazir-i-Azam" as previously, that four or five Yusafzai horsemen and others had got ready three or four thousand (text not clear) each, had despatched them towards Peshawar, and had emphatically ordered them to provide themselves with well-baked loaves of bread and to go towards the Noble Sarkar's country and begin plundering the same, and that the King had assured them that he would be following them soon with all his forces and warlike equipment. It further mentioned that it was being talked among the King's forces that some troops of the ruler of Bukhara had also departed in this direction, that these would soon reach the King, and that no reply had yet come from the king to the application sent to him by Nawab Muhammad Khan. The Noble Sarkar considered the contents of the letter, and sent a reply to the Thanadar of Attock, that his troops had left at that time in that direction, and that the Noble Sarkar himself would follow very soon. It became known verbally, through the messenger that Sultan Khan, the Raja of Bhimbar, had departed from the district of Attock with a view to meet the Noble Sarkar, and was expected to reach there in a day or two and that the mail service through horses had been set up according to the order of the Noble Sarkar right up to the fort of Attock. To-day the messengers (Jauri) came from Multan and stated that Nawab Muzaffar Khan had got the open lands about the town of Multan quite cleared, had caused all the wells in them to be completely closed up, had got ready four halting marks near the mausoleum of Hazrat Shams-i-Tabrezi, Takias of Darweshes, Chahar Bagh, etc., and had fixed two cannons on each of them had transferred all his goods and effects to the fort of Kot Shuja Khan himself had made very careful preparations for war, and that the Nawab had announced that both the fort of Multan and the town belonged to him. The Noble Sarkar heard this news, and rewarded them (Jauri) with four villages, and made them depart in that direction once again. He then held a private conference with Diwan Muhkam Chand and Sirdar Jodh Singh of Ramgarh with regard to this matter, and said that after gaining victory in the battle against Mahmud Shah he would certainly seize the fort of Multan in whatever way it would be possible. The representative of Sultan Khan, the Raja of Bhimbar, said that his master had come from the fort of Attock, and was only at a distance of twelve kos from the troops of the Noble Sarkar, and that he would present himself on the following day. The Noble Sarkar angrily asked why he had come away without any summons, adding that he had sent his troops in his direction, that he was to manage the "ghats" of the river Attock in conjunction with them; and that his coming away at that time was quite improper. He replied that his master had come to talk about certain matters. The representative of the Nazim of Multan presented a letter from his master, and said that he wanted to know what great fault had been committed by his master that the Noble Sarkar had decided to march against him. The Noble Sarkar replied that he must write to his master that if he agreed to become obedient and loyal to the Noble Sarkar, no harm would come to him, that if he would vacate the fort of Multan and surrender it to him he would be granted another fort instead, and that if in making preparations for war he had something else in his mind it was necessary to make him understand the position properly. Afterwards Diwan Muhkam Chand had a conversation regarding the departure of the troops tcwards Multan, submitting that they were steadfast and ready to depart in whatever direction the Noble Sarkar would order them, but requesting that the Noble Sarkar must wait and see the arrival of Sirdar Fateh Khan Wazir, and adding that after that he himself would be responsible for conquering the fort of Multan. All's well otherwise.

1813 (33)

News of the Deorhi of Sirdar Ranjit Singh Bahadur. Wednesday, dated 24th November, 1813 (30th Ziqaad 1228 A .H.)

The Noble Sarkar got up early in the morning, and came out to the tent set apart for audience and took his seat. Diwan Muhkam Chand, Bhai Gurbakhsh Singh, Bhawani Dass, Munshi Devi Dass, Hakim Aziz-ud-Din Khan and others came in and made the customary bow. The Noble Sarkar sent a verbal order to Raja Fateh Singh Ahluwalia through Bhai Gurbakhsh Singh to yield Jandiala out of his possession to the Noble Sarkar. One thousand rupees were granted to the representative of Bhai Lal Singh to meet his expenses. The Noble Sarkar held a private conference with Diwan Muhkam Chand, and told him that he intended to go to Lahore. He replied that he could do so, but said that the news about the arrival of Sirdar Fateh Khan Wazir was afloat. The Noble Sarkar said that it did not matter. The Noble Sarkar distributed fifty guns to as many men. He later despatched a letter to Nawab Muzaffar Khan of Multan asking him to send the representative of the Noble Sarkar back along with the sum of revenue. The messengers (Jauri) came and delivered letters from Mr. Metcalfe Sahib Bahadur and Kanwar Bahadur. After learning their contents the Noble Sarkar rewarded the messengers with fifty rupees, and entrusted them with the replies to those letters. Ramzan Khan, a reliable person of Shah Shuja-ul-Mulk, came and said that the king wanted to have a meeting with the Noble Sarkar, and was told that it would be arranged in a day or two. At noon the Noble Sarkar went into the other tent, took his meals, and laid himself down to take rest, while those who were present walked out. He got up again at about the third quarter of the day, and went into his scarlet tent. The sirdars came in and made their customary bow. A letter came from the garrison master through a messenger, in which was written that Hazrat Mahmud Shah, marching from Jalalabad, had reached near Jagta and was expected to enter Peshawar at night or in the morning, that Sirdar Fateh Khan Wazir continued to hold the station as previously, that he had gathered together ten or twelve thousand horse and foot although the troops from Kandhar

112

had not yet arrived that Shahzada Kamran, who was still in Kandhar, had written to the "Wazir-i-Azam" that for the present he or his troops could not come because of a disturbance which had arisen in that district, and that most of the men with the king had gone away disaffected. The Noble Sarkar learnt this and despatched a note to the above-mentioned garrison master, ordering him to continue supplying him with information regularly about Hazrat Mahmud Shah Badshah, Sirdar Fateh Khan Wazir, and Peshawar, etc. The Noble Sarkar enquired about the affairs of Attock from Diwan Muhkam Chand and about the state of the stores of grain, etc., in that place. The Diwan replied that the Noble Sarkar must rest assured, because the supplies in the fort of Attock were very ample. One white blanket was given to each of the several persons wearing the sacred thread, and twenty-five scarlet uniform waist-coats were given to the gunners of the battalion. The Noble Sarkar watched the dance of the dancing girls, and then went into the other tent when the night had passed one and a half hours, and took his meals. Those who were present walked out. All's well otherwise.

Dated 2nd December, 1813.

Colonel Ochterlony Sahib Bahadur went to the cantonment of Ludhiana after a tour through the mountainous regions, including Nooria, Jagadhari, Ambala, and Sirhind, etc., All the representatives and Munshis., who had accompanied his stirrup, went away. All's well otherwise.

1813 (36)
Deorhi of Sirdar Ranjit Singh Bahadur. Thursday, dated 25th November, 1813 (1st Zilhaj, 1228, A .H.), Rohtasgarh.

The Noble Sarkar was present in the tent set apart for audience when the messengers (Jauri) came from Peshawar and brought the news that Hazrat Mahmud Shah was encamped near Jagta as before, while Sirdar Fateh Khan Wazir had entered Jalalabad, had written a letter to Mahmud Shah that he would soon present himself, and that he need not worry, in the least, about his expenses because on his own arrival in Peshawar he would make all arrangement for the same. The letter further mentioned that he had written a letter to his brother Muhammad Azim Khan in Kashmir, assuring him that though at that time he was encamped in Jalalabad, yet he would soon march from there and conquer the fort of Attock. The Noble Sarkar heard this, and, rewarding the messengers (Jauri) with two rupees, sent them again in the same direction. The Noble

Sarkar said to his associates that Sirdar Fateh Khan Wazir and Hazrat Mahmud Shah were determined at that time to advance in this direction, and asked them what did they propose to do in the matter. They replied that for the time being they would continue their march forward, but in future would be guided by the advice from their next stage. The Noble Sarkar said that they were quite right, adding that the Rain battalion of the Sikhs must leave that place on the following day for Rohtas where it should fix its camp. A letter came from the sirdars of the army which had gone to Sikandah and Harthala, intimating that Makhad and Harsala authorities, after making warlike preparations, were ready to fight, and had sent their representative to the Noble Sarkar for negotiation, and asking for the Noble Sarkar's orders as to how they should act. It was written to them in reply that they should remain encamped wherever they were, and should not advance for the time being but await his further orders. A messenger came and delivered a letter from the garrison master of Attock in which it was written, that Hazrat Mahmud Shah was encamped as before, that preparations for his advance towards Peshawar were in progress and must have been completed by that time, that he was about to reach Peshawar very shortly, that the Governor of Peshawar had sent letters to the sirdars of the Yusafzai and Loralai tribes to get ready and present themselves to Hazrat Mahmud Shah when the latter would arrive in Peshawar, and that the various preparations were completed in Peshawar. The Noble Sarkar despatched a reply, and sent four messengers (Jauri) towards Peshawar to bring further news. It appeared that in the letter to the garrison master of Attock it was written, that he must manage the "Ghats" of Attock as best as he can and write to the Noble Sarkar for whatever stores, etc., he might need, so that the same might soon be sent to him. At nightfall, Sultan Khan, the Raja of Bhimbar, paid his respects and presented one horse as Nazar to the Noble Sarkar who kept on enquiring from him about the affairs of the fort of Attock in privacy for a long time, and then ordered him to march on the following day. All's well otherwise.

1813 (37)

Deorhi of Sirdar Ranjit Singh Bahadur. Thursday, dated 9th December, 1813 (13th to 15th Zilhaj, 1228 A.H.); Devariwal, near Rawalpindi.

A messenger arrived and delivered a letter from the garrison master of Attock in which it was written, that repeated letters from the garrison master of Makhad were reaching Hazrat Mahmud Shah in those days, informing him that the troops of the Noble Sarkar had reached and

114

encamped at a distance of twelve kos from that fort and were planning to bring about its evacuation, that though he and his men were ready to show their loyalty by sacrificing their lives yet it was essential that he (the Shah) should also help them with his troops, that hence he (the Shah) proposed despatching troops towards him and that some horsemen belonging to the Mughal and Durrani tribes had reached the other side of the river at the instance of the king but had gone back after reconnoitring the "ghat". After considering the contents, the Noble Sarkar despatched the reply, asking him (the garrison master of Attock) to guard the "ghats" with the greatest care, and to act generally in accordance with the instructions of Diwan Muhkam Chand. A letter came from the garrison master of Khanpur, demanding money to meet his expenses. The Noble Sarkar sent to him five hundred rupees and fifty horsemen immediately. The messengers (Jauri) came from Peshawar and brought the news that Hazrat Mahmud Shah Badshah was staying in a tent outside Peshawar as before, and that out of the Ruhila tribe whom he had engaged in service near the Khyber Pass, one thousand men had gone away because they could not get money and were starved, that the remaining ones also contemplated leaving, and that a letter had been received from Fateh Khan Wazir (by the King) in which it was clearly stated that he had gathered together all the troops from the district of Jalalabad and the Deras and would soon present himself. The Noble Sarkar heard this, and, rewarding the messengers (Jauri) in the usual manner, made him depart once again in that direction. A letter was despatched to Raja Fateh Singh Ahluwalia, asking him to reach the fort of Attock speedily. Letters were issued to Sirdars Jodh Singh of Ramgarh and Diwan Muhkam Chard, ordering them to bring about the evacuation of the fort of Makhad without any further hesitation or delay. All's well otherwise.

1813 (38)

News of the Deorhi of Sirdar Ranjit Bahadur. Saturday, datd 18th December 1813 (24th Zilhaj, 1228 A. H.); the Village of Taddeenwal, situated in the Country of the Fort of Attock Towards the North of it.

The Noble Sarkar got up early in the morning and came out to the tent set apart for audience when the day had advanced four hours. The sirdars usually present came in and made their customary bow. A messenger came and delivered a letter from Jodh Singh of Kalsia in which it was written that he had reached and encamped near Pind Dadan Khan and that he would soon present himself. On hearing the contents the Noble Sarkar sent him a reply that he must proceed towards Kundagarh, and establish an effective control over that district. Manak Chand Vakil submitted a letter from Diwan Muhkam Chand in which it was written, that he had marched forward from Makhad for about eight kos to the village of Pindi Gheb where he had encamped, that as the zamindars of that place contemplated running away on his approach he called them to his presence, and granted one turban to each of the four men from among them and with great assurances induced them to stay on. It was written to him in reply to do whatever he thought best. A letter came from Raja Fateh Singh Ahluwalia in which it was written, that he had reached Kundagarh and was about to establish control over that district. A messenger arrived and delivered a letter from Diwan Bhawan Dass of the low stature, mentioning that, after taking leave from the Noble Sarkar, he had reached the same day a distance of twenty kos from the victorious troops, that he would march from that place on the following day towards the town of Fateh Jang, and, by the grace of God and the glory of the Noble Sarkar, he would soon make collections from that district. The Noble Sarkar called upon four (Jauri) messengers, and awarding four rupees to each, sent them towards Peshawar to bring the news of the plans of march of Hazrat Mahmud Shah. When the day had advanced one quarter and a half the sirdars and others who were present walked out, and the Noble Sarkar went into the other tent, took his meals, and laid himself down to take rest at noon. He got up again at about the third quarter of the day and came out to his scarlet tent, when four hours of the day were left. His associates and attendants presented themselves. Raja Sansar Chand came and met the Noble Sarkar who stood up his full length out of respect and seated him on a chair. This Raja and Kanwar Kharak Singh, the eldest son, stated that their troops had marched towards Rawalpindi, while they had come all alone to present themselves. The Noble Sarkar replied that he, too, was very shortly to leave for that direction. The messengers (Jauri) came from Peshawar and brought the news, that Hazrat Mahmud Shah Badshah continued to stay in his camp outside Peshawar, that Sirdar Fateh Khan Wazir together with his forces had arrived at a place two kos distant from the troops of the king, that he had set up his camp there but did not seem to have courage enough to engage in warfare owing to the smallness of the number of his men and materials, and that it was difficult to forecast his plans though it was rumoured that he would present himself to the king. On hearing this the Noble Sarkar rewarded the messengers (Jauri) in the usual manner and made him go back once again. He said to his associates that staying in that district for a few days more would enable him to know the intentions of Sirdar Fateh Khan Wazir. A messenger came and delivered a letter from Sirdar Dal Singh Bharania which mentioned that Diwan Muhkam Chand, leaving him in the fort of Makhad, had marched away towards Mahdighat. When the night had passed one quarter those who were present walked out, and the Noble Sarkar went

116

into the other tent, took his meals, and laid himself down to rest. The guards, however, continued at their posts. All went on well otherwise the night.

Sunday, dated 19th December, 1813 (25th Zilhaj, 1228 A. H.)

The Noble Sarkar got up early in the morning and came out when the day had advanced four hours. The sirdars usually present came in and made their customary bow. He inspected the drill of the battalion of the Sikhs, and then went into the tent set apart for audience. A reply to the letter of Sirdar Dal Singh Bharania, which had arrived on the previous day, was despatched asking him to remain in that district with perfect assurance and to establish an effective control over the same. Diwan Ganga Ram presented a letter from Pandit Nand Ram, which mentioned that if the Noble Sarkar would send some reliable person to that place, all matters regarding the satisfactory settlement of salaries which were to be paid would be talked over. The Noble Sarkar wrote to him in reply that he had no such person with him, adding that he had nothing to do with him. A messenger came and delivered a letter from Dal Singh Bharania which mentioned that Nawazish Khan Khattak, the garrison master of Makhad, who had fled from that place and had hidden himself in the hills, had come out through a pass together with his family, and crossing the river Attock, had escaped towards Peshawar. A letter came from Raja Fateh Singh Ahluwalia which mentioned that after establishing an effective control over Kundagarh he was proceeding towards Chhachha Hazara to punish Sher Zaman Khan and other rebellious zamindars of the neighbourhood of Hakyak Matoor, and Bar, etc. When the day had advanced one quarter and a half the Noble Sarkar went into the other tent, took his meals, and laid himself down to take rest at noon while those who were present walked out. He got up again at about the third quarter of the day and came out to his scarlet camp and the sirdars usually present came in and made their customary bow. A messenger came and delivered a letter from Jodh Singh of Kalsia which mentioned that according to the order of the Noble Sarkar he had marched from Pind Dadan Khan towards Kundagarh, and was expected to join Raja Fateh Singh Ahluwalia very shortly. The messengers (Jauri) came in and stated that Hazrat Mahmud Shah Padsha continued to stay in his camp outside Peshawar, that Sirdar Fateh Khan Wazir had reached Peshawar, and had sent his reliable person with a letter to the king for negotiating peaceful relations and with a message that he would soon present himself personally, that it was rumoured there that the revenues of Kashmir and the reconciliation between the two parties would take place, and that the king's troops were feeling uncomfortable about their expenses. The Noble Sarkar heard this and made the messengers (Jauri) depart once again in that direction. The Noble Sarkar mentioned to his associates in the course of conversation that he himself had given a close thought to this matter and wished that somehow these disputes should be settled, so that the worries of both the parties might terminate. They replied that whatever he would order his representatives on his arrival, would be accepted because the enemy had not the power to indulge in war as there was great disunion among them. The Noble Sarkar said that whatever God would wish, would certainly take place. When the night had passed one quarter, those who were present walked out and the Noble Sarkar went into the other tent, took his meals and laid himself down to take rest. All's well otherwise.

1813 (39)

News of the Court of Sirdar Ranjit Singh Bahadur. Satruday, dated 25th December, 1813 (1st Muharram 1229 A. H.); the Royal Fort, Lahore.

The Noble Sarkar came out to the Saman Burj where Hukma Singh Thanadar, Mehr Singh, and other officials presented themselves and made their customary bow. All the money-lenders came in and presented Nazars according to their status and the Noble Sarkar inquired after the health of each. A messenger came and said that the Vakil from the town of Fateh Jang had arrived, and wanted permission to enter through the gate. The Noble Sarkar said that he might be allowed to enter. A camel rider came and delivered a letter from Diwan Muhkam Chand, which mentioned that he had marched from Mahdi Ghat towards Multan. A reply was immediately sent him that he should stay where he was for the time being, and act according to the order, which would follow. The reliable person from Nawab Umdut-ul-Nisa Begum, the wife of Hazrat Shah Shuja-ul-Mulk, came in, and after making a courteous bow and expressing the greetings on behalf of Begum Sahiba, gave something to be given away on charity after waying it round the head of the Noble Sarkar,[70] and inquired after his health. The Noble Sarkar replied that he was quite well and happy, and added that he should set the mind of Begum Sahiba at rest by telling her that he was coming shortly with the troops. The messengers (Jauri) came and delivered a letter from Diwan Muhkam Chand, which mentioned that just then a letter to his name had come from Sirdar Fateh Khan Wazir through Nand Ram Diwan, his messenger, and that had written as follows "still nothing is lost, give the fort of Attock to me so that the relations of friendship between the two parties may become strong," and that he had written to him in reply, "the fort of Attock would never be handed over to you, and that the country of Kashmir would soon he conquered by us." The Noble Sarkar heard this and kept quite. The representative of Khuda Dad Khan of Fateh Jang came in, paid his respects, presented one tray of sweetmeats on his own behalf and stated that his master was quite obedient to the Noble Sarkar and had intended to come personally but had sent him to submit that the troops of the Noble Sarkar, which had gone there, were laying waste the whole country, and that he was sent to pay the revenue to the Noble Sarkar. A letter was issued to Diwan Bhawani Dass of the low stature, Uttar Singh, and several others, ordering them not to interfere with the pastures and farms of that district on their arrival in the town of Fateh Jang, and not to cause any kind of destruction in that country.

Sunday, dated 26th December, 1813 (2nd Muharram, 1229 A. H.), the Place of Despatch as Before.

A letter was sent to Diwan Muhkam Chand asking him to stay in that district for a few days, and not to march in any other direction. It was stated that Raja Sansar Chand was coming together with other rajas of the mountainous regions by an incessant march. The messengers (Jauri) came and stated, that Hazrat Mahmud Shah Badshah and Sardar Fateh Khan Wazir continued to be in Peshawar, and that it could not be found whether they intended to come in this direction in view of there being no money with them, although they had gathered together troops from various places. The Noble Sarkar heard this and rewarded the messengers (Jauri) with ten rupees. It was stated that one person Nanak Potra was sitting at the Deorhi since several months. The Noble Sarkar called him in and sent him away with a grant of one fine woollen shoulder mantle, and a piece of agricultural land attached to a well-situated in the Taaluqa of Ramnagar. A messenger came and delivered a letter from the Raja of Rajauri, which mentioned that he intended to present himself as ordered, but that he was told that he should do so in Lahore as soon as the Noble Sarkar would regain his health. A letter was sent to Raja Fateh Singh Ahluwalia and Sirdar Jodh Singh of Kalsia that they should proceed to the district of Narthala and establish control over it. Munshi Ghulam Muhammad Hussain was called in and told something in privacy and made to go to Diwan Muhkam Chand. All else is well.

News of the Deorhi of Sirdar Ranjit Singh Bahadur. Saturday, dated 1ˢᵗ
January, 1814 (8ᵗʰ Muharram, 1229 A.H.); the Royal Fort, Lahore.

Last night the Noble Sarkar remained sitting until the night had
passed four hours, and the dancing girls remained present according to his
wish. Later, he felt slightly indisposed and went into the zenana. The
dancing girls went away. He took a little food and laid himself down to
take rest when night had passed one quarter. It went on well otherwise
during the night.

To-day he got up early in the morning and came out to the Saman
Burj when four hours of the day had advanced. Bhai Gurbakhsh Singh,
Desa Singh Majithia, Hukma Singh Thanadar and several other sirdars
came in, making their customary bow. It was stated that Hazrat Shah
Shuja-ul-Mulk had arrived in Lahore and entered his own mansion. Sardar
Desa Singh Majithia stated that the rajas of the mountainous regions
wanted permission to depart, because they had incurred debt through
lengthy travelling and felt embarrassed through shortage of straw, etc. The
Noble Sarkar replied that they might send their troops back to their homes
towards the mountainous regions, and themselves stay on until the arrival
of the Noble Sarkar in Amritsar, when they would also be allowed to
leave. The news came that Mir Izzat Ullah Khan, the news agent of the
glorious sahibs, coming from Peshawar had reached Shahdara, and needed
a permit to cross the river Ravi and enter the city walls. The Noble Sarkar
granted the permit. The sirdars and others who were present walked out
when the day had advanced one quarter, while the Noble Sarkar himself
went into the zenana, took his meals, and laid himself down to take rest at
noon. He got up again at about third quarter of the day and came out when
four hours of the day were left. The staff and the servants made their
customary bow. He went to the Saman Burj at nightfall after inspecting
the drill of the battalion of Mian Singh commandant. The sirdars came in
and made their customary bow again there. A messenger came and
delivered a letter from Diwan Bhawani Dass of the low stature,
mentioning that four cannons, eleven swivels, twenty (text not clear) and
much other material had been seized in the name of the Noble Sarkar from
the town of Fateh Jang, and that leaving his troops there, he would soon

present himself. After the consideration of the letter an order was passed for a reply to be sent to him. Hakim Muhammad Ashraf Khan came and presented a box of an electuary to the Noble Sarkar who explained to him the state of his health. It was reported that Mir Izzat Ullah Klan had arrived and entered the town. The Munshi presented the news of various sides. Later the Noble Sarkar went into the zenana, while those who were present walked out. He took his meals and laid himself down to take rest when the night had passed one quarter. It went on well otherwise during the night.

Sunday, dated 2nd January 1814 (9th Muharram. 1229 A.H.)

The Noble Sarkar got up early in the morning and came out to the place of audience when the day had advanced four hours. The sirdars who were usually present came and made their customary bow. Mir Izzat Ullah Khan, the news agent of the glorious Sahibs, who had come from the district of Peshawar met the Noble Sarkar and after mutual enquiries about each other's health they kept on talking about Afghanistan, Bokhara, etc. Pir Bakhsh, the police officer, was ordered to put the Mir up in the mansion of Jawala Singh and to look after his needs. The said Mir then walked out. Sarab Dayal Munshi was ordered to send one hundred rupees in cash, eleven trays of sweets and other articles of entertainment to his Dera, and he did accordingly. Manak Chand Vakil submitted a letter from the Diwan, mentioning that according to his order he had started from Rawalpindi towards Kalabagh. The Noble Sarkar despatched to him a reply after considering its contents, that for the present he must march towards the fort of Attock and not in any other direction. The Munshi should in privacy to the Noble Sarkar a letter that had come from Nand Singh, the Vakil of the Noble Sarkar at Ludhiana. The Noble Sarkar went into the zenana, and the sirdars and others who where present walked out. He took his meals and laid himself down to take rest at noon. He got up again at about the third quarter of the day and came out when four hours of day were left. The staff and the servants made their customary bow. He rode out on a horse to the bank of the river Ravi, and after recreation, inspected first the drill of the battalion of Sikhs and then the firing of the guns. On his return he entered the fort and went over to the Saman Burj where his associates and attendants presented themselves. The messengers (Jauri) came from Peshawar and brought the news, that Hazrat Mahmud Shah Badshah and Sirdar Fateh Khan Wazir continued to be in Peshawar, that the soldiers had presented themselves to the king and had submitted that he had promised to pay up their salaries on the arrival of Sirdar Fateh

Khan but that nothing had yet been paid, that at this the king had written to the "Wazir-i-Azam" to raise money from whatever place he could for such payments, and that accordingly the Wazir contemplated imposing some kind of tax or contribution upon the inhabitants of Peshawar, though it was not expected that he would be able to collect anything. The Noble Sarkar rewarded the messengers (Jauri), and sent them in that direction once again. Later, he went into the zenana, took his meals and laid himself down to take rest when the night had passed one quarter. All's well otherwise.

1814 (2)

Deorhi of Sirdar Ranjit Singh Bahadur. Wednesday, dated 6th January, 1814 (13th Muharram, 1229 A.H.); the Royal Fort, Lahore.

Manak Chand Vakil delivered a letter from Diwan Muhkam Chand, mentioning that he had despatched his horsemen to various places to collect money, and had instructed them not to molest those zamindars who would pay, but to punish others who persisted in their refusal. In reply it was written to him that he was a wise man and should do whatever he thought best for the country. The messengers (Jauri) came from Peshawar and brought the news, that Hazrat Mahmud Shah Badshah and Sirdar Fateh Khan were still in Peshawar and had inspected the parade of the troops . . . . (original mutilated) . . . horse and foot were taken down during the inspection of parade papers . . . . Khandala, Harbila, Shamshergarh, etc . . . . stated that Raja Fateh Singh Ahluwalia and Sirdar Jodh Singh . . . . had been turned out of their places and made over to the aforesaid persons . . . . they had about ten thousand men with them and in addition to that . . . . they themselves would collect all of their men if reinforcements came from the Noble Sarkar, so that . . . . battle be offered to them. Sirdar Fateh Khan had written to them in reply, that the troops of the Shahanshah would soon reach there to help them. The Noble Sarkar heard all this, and, rewarding the messengers (Jauri) with twenty rupees, sent them in that direction once again. A messenger from Rani Sada Kaur, the mother-in-law of the Noble Sarkar, came with a letter, mentioning that she had left for Amritsar according to the hint from the Noble Sarkar. He ordered a reply to be written to her that he proposed to be in Amritsar on the occasion of the "Sankarant." All's well otherwise.

News of the Deorhi of Sirdar Ranjit Singh Bahadur. Friday dated 14th January, 1814 (21st Muharram, 1229 A.H.); the Fort of Gobindgarh, Amritsar.

The Noble Sarkar got up early in the morning and came out to his Diwan Khana when the day had advanced four hours. The sirdars usually present came in and made their customary bow. He talked to every one of them, and ordered Sirdar Dessa Singh to go to Haripur with Raja Bhup Singh who would take his men from there and Mangarh for the proper management of his affairs. He also asked them to leave the brother of Munshi Sarab Dayal there and return themselves. They replied that they would do so. A messenger came and delivered a letter from Raja Fateh Singh Ahluwalia and Sirdar Jodh Singh of Kalsia mentioning that they had managed the affairs of that district very satisfactorily according to his order, and that after leaving their troops there had themselves started towards Lahore where they would soon present themselves. The Noble Sarkar sent a message to Raja Bhup Singh verbally through Shiam Singh, his own special bearer, that he must march together with the Sikh sirdars and establish control over Haripur and Mangarh. Rama Nand Sahu presented an instalment of forty thousand rupees as ordered, stating that he would pay up the remainder in a day or two, and that the details of whatever he had spent from his shop had been dictated in writing to Munshi Sarab Dayal. The Noble Sarkar approved of this. When the day had advanced one quarter the sirdars and others who were present walked out, and the Noble Sarkar went into the zenana, took his meals, and laid himself down to rest at noon. He got up again at about the third quarter of the day, and came out when four hours of the day were left. Those who were usually present made their customary bow. He rode out on his special horse and made a trip through the bazaar of Amritsar and the "Katra" of the Ahluwalias. Chet of Ram Saraf, standing in his shop, made a courteous bow to the Noble Sarkar while the latter was on his way towards the fort and also presented a tray full of sweatmeats as Nazar. On his return to the fort the Noble Sarkar went into his audience chamber where his associates and attendants presented themselves. Shiam Singh, the special bearer, came in and after conveying greetings from Raja Bhup Singh, stated that action would be taken according to the wish of Noble Sarkar. The Noble Sarkar asked about the case of the fort of Mala from Dal Sukh Rae, the Vakil of the Raja of Patiala, who replied that according to the order of the Noble Sarkar he had written about it to his master. Khuda Dad Khan of the town of Fateh Jang arrived and sought with folded hands his patronage and consideration. The Noble Sarkar assured him. He later went into the zenana, while the sirdars and those who were present walked out. He laid himself down to rest when the night had passed one quarter, after taking his meals. During the night all went on well.

Sunday, dated 15th January 1814 (22nd Muharram. 1229 A.H.)

The Noble Sarkar got up early in the morning and came out to the place of audience when the day had advanced four hours. The sirdars usually present came in and made their customary bow. It was stated that Sirdar Desa Singh Majithia had marched from that place along with Raja Bhup Singh of Haripur towards the mountainous regions. The Noble Sarkar called upon the Akalis and the men of Phula Singh Akalia, and listened to their dispute and claims about their shares of income. He ordered the men of Phula Singh that they should take only that portion as their share which was fixed as such since a long time, and should not claim anything more from the share of other Akalis, adding that if they claimed more than that in the future and the Akalis complained again, he and his men would be turned out of Amritsar altogether. In short this dispute went on until noon, and in the end they agreed to act according to the order of the Noble Sarkar and then went away. The Noble Sarkar went into the zenana, took his meals there and laid himself down to rest, while those who were present went away one after the other. He got up again at about the third quarter of the day, and came out when four hours of the day were left. Those who were usually in attendance made their customary bow. The Noble Sarkar, riding on his special horse, went to the tank of Harmandar, climbed up his own Bunga, enjoyed the sight around, and, ordering Hakim Imam-ud-Din Khan to see to its repairs, returned to the fort in the usual manner, and entered the audience chamber where his associates and attendants presented themselves. A shawl was granted out of kindness to Prem Singh an employee of Hakim Imam-ud-Din Khan. The Thanadar of Fatehgarh situated in the Taaluqa of the late Jaimal Singh Kanhya, who was there at that time on behalf of Kanwar Kharak Singh, the eldest prince, came in, paid his respects, offered two Ashrafis and one horse as Nazar and gave an account of that place. The Noble Sarkar mentioned that the Kanwar Sahib Bahadur was also coming there very shortly. The Munshi presented news of various sides, after which the Noble Sarkar began to listen to the music of the bards. It was stated that the rajas of the mountainous regions intended leaving for their homes. The Noble Sarkar replied that they would soon be allowed to depart when he himself would leave for Lahore. When the night had passed four hours the

124

sirdars and others who were present went away, and he went into the zenana, took his meals and laid himself down to rest when the night had passed one quarter. All's well otherwise.

1814 (4)

News of the Deorhi of Sirdar Ranjit Singh Bahadur. Thursday, dated 20th January, 1814 (27th Muharram, 1229 A.H.); the Twaifpul, at a distance of ten kos from Lahore.

Yesterday the Noble Sarkar remained inside the fort of Gobindgarh in Amritsar until the night had passed two hours. It was stated that the staff and servants for the conveyance were ready, and the Noble Sarkar ordered that he would ride out on the morning of the following day. He then took his meals and laid himself down to rest when the night had passed one quarter. All went on well during the night.

To-day he got up early in the morning and after taking his meal made the conveyance of the ladies proceed ahead, and himself came out when the day had advanced four hours. The sirdars made their customary bow. Rani Sada Kaur, the mother-in-law of the Noble Sarkar, came and met him and was told to go in the same direction together with Kanwars Sher Singh and Tara Singh. She replied that on that day it was "Choudas" [72] on the following day it would be "Amawas,"[73] and that on "Dooj" [74] she would leave for Lahore. The Noble Sarkar approved of it. Gobind Jas, son of Nand Singh, the Vakil of the Noble Sarkar, brought a letter from his father from the cantonment of Ludhiana, and stated that Colonel Nasir-ud-Daula had left the cantonment for Shahjahanabad, and that the mortars had been got ready by the Colonel and would soon be sent to the Noble Sarkar. When the day had advanced one quarter he got into a palanquin, moved from Amritsar towards Lahore, and all the sirdars and the rajas of the mountainous regions accompanied his stirrup. When he reached near the village of Attari, Shiam Singh and Hukma Singh Attariwalas offered a Nazar of two trays of sweetmeats. Hakim Imam-ud-Din Khan and other sirdars were now allowed to get back to Amritsar. The Noble Sarkar proceeded forward from that place, and, after covering a distance of fifteen kos reached the Tawaifpul sat down under the shade of trees, and later entered into a tent which was caused to be pitched up there. At nightfall a messenger came and delivered a letter from Hukma Singh, the Thanadar of Lahore, reporting that Damodar Mall, the Vakil of Sirdar Fateh Khan Wazir, had arrived and entered Lahore and would proceed to Amritsar on the following day to present himself. The Noble Sarkar sent a reply that as he himself was reaching there the following day therefore he should not send that person, and that he must be very careful about the watch and ward. Later, he went into his sleeping tent and laid himself down to take rest. All went on well otherwise during the night.

Friday, dated 21st January, 1814 (28th Muharram, 1229, A.H.); the Fort, Lahore.

The Noble Sarkar got up early in the morning and came out. The staff and the servants made their customary bow. He mounted an elephant, took his seat, made Bhai Gurbakhsh Singh sit by him in the special royal seat, and proceeded forward. On the way the zamindars of the neighbouring villages were asked to offer Nazars. When the day had advanced one quarter and a half the Noble Sarkar entered the Shalamar in a shower of rain, ordering others to proceed to Lahore and telling them that he himself would enter it at about the third quarter of the day. He took his meals and laid himself down to take rest at noon. He got up again at about the third quarter of the day, and came out to "Baradari" when four hours of the day were left. Hukma Singh, the Thanadar of Lahore, Mehr Singh, Gulab Singh, Mehtab Singh, Hukam Singh, Munshi Sarab Dial, and several other sirdars came in and made their customary bow. Nur Khan, the Superintendent of the garden, presented a "Dali" containing seasonable fruits, and was awarded ten rupees. A messenger came and informed him that Raja Fateh Singh Ahluwalia and Sirdar Jodh Singh of Kalsia had reached near Ramnagar on the bank of the river Chenab, had set up their camps there, and were riding on alone towards the Noble Sarkar. The Noble Sarkar rode out on a special horse towards Lahore. At nightfall, after covering a distance of ten kos, he reached the fort of Lahore and entered the Saman Burj. A salute of cannons was fired from over the fort in honour of his entry. The messengers (Jauri) came and stated that Muhammad Azam Khan continued to be encamped in Kashmir, was engaged in collecting troops, and looking after the new recruits and was also busy in strengthening the fortress sitauted in the mountains of Narain (i) and Sher Garh, etc. in Kashmir. He further reported that he (Muhammad Azam Khan) had sent funds to Ghulam Hussain, Umar Khan and his other sirdars to raise troops from all places, and had told them that their salaries would be paid by him and that correspondence by way of demanding troops continued. The Noble Sarkar heard this, rewarded the messengers (Jauri) with four rupees, and sent them back in the same direction again. When the night had passed two hours he went into the zenana, and those who were present went away. After taking his meals he

126

laid himself down to take rest when the night had passed one quarter. All went on well during the night.

Saturday, dated 22nd January, 1814 (29th Muharram, 1299, A.H.); the Royal Fort, Lahore.

The Noble Sarkar got up early in the morning and came out to the Saman Burj when the day had advanced four hours. The sirdars usually present came in and made their customary bow. Damodan Mal, the Vakil of Sirdar Fateh Khan Wazir, came in, paid his respects, and delivered a letter from his master with two Afghan horses of the Turkish breed, five closed baskets of grapes, four "Dalis" of pomegranates, pears and various other fruits from Afghanistan, and enquired after the health of the Noble Sarkar on behalf of the Wazir-i-Azam. The Noble Sarkar replied that by the grace of God he was getting on well.

It was plainly written in the letter, that he (the Wazir) had despatched his troops and would soon bring about the evacuation of the fort of Multan and deliver the same to the Noble Sarkar, and that he faithfully adhered to his agreements and promises so far and would continue doing so in the future, so that the friendship and sincerity between the parties might be strengthed still further. The Noble Sarkar asked Damodar Mal to state the size of the army with the "Wazir-i-Azam", and he replied that eight thousand men constituted his Durrani force (text not clear), and that it was most probable that the sirdars of the Yusafzais would also gather, and might have gathered in his absence. The Noble Sarkar remarked that among his master's troops there was a great disunion, and asked him to present himself again at about the third quarter of the day. He replied that he had something to say in privacy and the Noble Sarkar assured him that he would grant him a private interview. The said respectable person walked out and one hundred rupees were sent to him by the Noble Sarkar for his entertainment. The Noble Sarkar then made the Munshi write letters to the Rajas of Rajaur, Akhnur and such other places, mentioning that Diwan Muhkam Chand and some other sirdars would be arriving to hold a consultation and conference with them, so that troops might proceed in that direction in the month of Phagan, and urging that they should make preparations by themselves. A letter was issued to Sultan Khan the Raja of Bhimbar, to present himself soon to the Noble Sarkar who wished to talk to him. He went into the zenana, and the sirdars and other who were present went away. After taking his meals he laid himself down to rest at noon. He got up again at about the third quarter of the day, and came out to the Saman Burj when four hours of the day were left. His associates and attendants presented themselves. A messenger came and delivered a letter from Sirdar Fateh Khan Wazir, requesting that the Noble Sarkar would also send his troops towards Multan, that he was sending his troops there, and assuring him that he would first get that fort evacuated and delivered to him. After considering the letter the noble Sarkar said that if Fateh Khan Wazir would get the fort of Multan evacuated with the help of his own troops and deliver it to him and further give eleven thousand rupees annually as tribute for the revenues of Kashmir, he would certainly make over to him in return the fort of Attock. After that he said to his associates that he had no faith in the Durranis because although he (Fateh Khan) had written many statements supported with oaths in the name of God and the Prophet, etc., in his letter, yet there seemed to be some clever trick behind all those statements. A messenger came and delivered a letter from Sirdar Desa Singh Majithia, mentioning that he had reached, together with Raja Bhup Singh, at a distance of four kos from Haripur, and that by God's grace the control of the Noble Sarkar would soon be established over the forts of Haripur and Mangarh. When the night had passed two hours Raja Sansar Chand came and met the Noble Sarkar, who showed him great respect and made him sit on a chair. They went on talking together until the night had passed four hours. All's well otherwise.

1814 (5)

Deorhi of Sirdar Ranjit Singh Bahadur. Wednesday, dated 2nd February, 1814 (10th Safar, 1229, A.H.); the Royal Fort, Lahore.

Khushal Singh Jamadar stated that Munshi Devi Dass was present at the Deorhi, and the Noble Sarkar replied that he would be called in at the time of leisure. A robe of honour consisting of six garments was granted as a farewell gift to the Raja of Khanpur. A letter was sent to Jahandad Khan, the brother of Nawab Ata Muhammad Khan, calling him to the court. Fifty mortars were given to Jai Singh, a companion of Sirdar Dal Singh. The Noble Sarkar said to his associates that the skilled workmen of Lahore were not making good guns on the English style, and that they must think of a plan to get them from Shahjahajabad. They replied that they would do so (text torn) . . . . said that he would pay to the Noble Sarkar the amount proposed by Rama Nand Sahu, and requested that the division of Wazirabad (text torn) be entrusted to his charge. The Noble Sarkar said that he should pay up the amount and then the aforesaid division would be given to him. Very urgent summons were sent to Diwan Muhkam Chand. A robe of honour consisting of seven garments was granted to Raja Bir Singh of Nurpur and another of three garments to his companion Sheo Dayal, according to his request, as farewell gifts and they were told that if the troops of the Noble Sarkar went to the mountainous regions to collect revenue, they must join them at the head of their troops. The Vakil of the Nazim of Multan presented a letter from master, stating that he was obedient to the Noble Sarkar in every respect and had nothing to do with anybody else. The Noble Sarkar said that he would reply after thinking over it. A letter came from Munshi Amir Beg, the garrison master of the fort of Attock, through messengers (Jauri), mentioning that the troops appointed there had to get salaries for about four months and were worrying him with repeated demands. After considering its contents, the Noble Sarkar sent a letter to Amar Singh, the Thanadar of the place to pay ten thousand rupees for the salaries of the troops in the fort there, and that he would be allowed reduction in his account. All's well otherwise.

1814 (6)

News of the Deorhi of Sirdar Ranjit Singh Bahadur. Monday, dated 14th February, 1814 (22nd Safar 1229 A.H.); the Royal Fort, Lahore.

The Noble Sarkar got up early in the morning and came out to the Saman Burj when the day had advanced four hours. The sirdars usually present came in and made their customary bow. Raja Fateh Singh Ahluwalia came alongwith his companions to see the Noble Sarkar who made him sit in a chair, and talks of friendship and unity went on between the two. The Raja said that at that time he was going to his place on necessary business but would return soon to his presence. The Noble Sarkar approved of his intention and granted a robe of honour consisting of seven garments, five pieces of jewellery and one horse to him, and a robe of honour consisting of five garments to Chaudhri Qadir Bakhsh, Mehr Chand and the other three persons, respectively, as farewell gifts. Those respectable persons then walked out. It was reported that Raja Sansar Chand had met Diwan Muhkam Chand and had marched away to his native country. Manak Chand and Narain Dass, the Vakils, stated that if the Noble Sarkar permitted Diwan Muhkam Chand and Sirdar Jodh Singh of Ramgarh who had arrived, they might present themselves. The Noble Sarkar ordered that they should be called in. It was stated that the battalions of the Noble Sarkar having marched from Shahdara, were coming after crossing the river Ravi. Diwan Muhkam Chand and Sirdar

Jodh Singh Ramgarhia came in with their companions, and the said Diwan presented five gold ducats and two horses, Munshi Mehtab Rae, his companion, presented five rupees, Sirdar Jodh Singh Ramgarhia offered two trays of slabs of sugar; and their ten or twelve companions submitted Nazars according to their ranks. The Noble Sarkar enquired after their health, asked about the state of that district of Attock and of the fort of Makhad, etc., and enquired where the troops accompanying them were at that time. They replied that they had come according to the summons of the Noble Sarkar after satisfactorily establishing their control over that district, and had allowed their troops to proceed to their respective places. The Noble Sarkar allowed them to go away, with the words that they would be called in again at leisure when many other things would be talked. When the day had advanced one and a half quarter the Noble Sarkar went into the zenana and laid himself down to rest at noon. He got up again at about the third quarter of the day and came out, whereupon the staff and the servants made their customary bow. Manak Chand, the Vakil of Diwan Muhkam Chand, came in and reported the arrival of Fateh Khan of Sahiwal in search of employment, and was told that the Diwan could bring him to the presence of the Noble Sarkar on the following day. It was stated that Raja Fateh Singh Ahluwalia had left for Kapurthala. The Noble Sarkar rode out to the bank of the river Ravi for recreation. When he reached near the battalions, a salute from the cannons was promptly fired, and the messengers, the commandants and others presented themselves and offered Nazars according to their ranks. At nightfall he returned, entered the fort and went through the "Baradari" into the newly laid out garden where his associates and attendants presented themselves. The messengers (Jauri) came from Kashmir and brought the news, that Muhammad Azim Khan continued to encamp in Kashmir, and that since the troops of the Noble Sarkar had returned from the district of Attock to this side, he was engaged in augmenting his own forces and had stationed the whole of them outside Kashmir, and that it was rumoured there on the strength of a statement made by the representative of the Nazim of Multan, that Hazrat Mahmud Shah and Sirdar Fateh Khan Wazir had marched from their stations in that direction. The Noble Sarkar heard this and awarded the messengers (Jauri) four rupees. A messenger came and delivered an envelope containing the news of Shahjahanabad, and was awarded five rupees. After learning the contents of the news, the Noble Sarkar went into the zenana, took his meals, and, when the night had passed one quarter, laid himself down to take rest in his sleeping chamber. All's well otherwise.

News of the Deorhi of Sirdar Ranjit Singh Bahadur. Tuesday, dated 22nd February, 1814 (1st Rabi-ul-Awwal); the Royal Fort, Lahore.

Yesterday the Noble Sarkar sat inside until the night had passed four hours, and continued enjoying the dance of the dancing girls. He sprinkled lacdye over those girls and his associates while watching their pleasant dance. When the night had passed one quarter he went into the zenana, all others having walked out. He took his meals and laid himself down to rest. To-day he got up early in the morning and came out when the day had advanced four hours and took his seat in the Saman Burj where the sirdars made their customary bow. He kept on talking with every one of them asking them questions and receiving answers. Sirdar Jodh Singh of Kalsia came in, met the Noble Sarkar and sought permission to leave. The Noble Sarkar granted his request, and gave him a robe of honour consisting of five garments, one horse and one mortar, and said that he could go at that time to the district of Doaba, but should return when summoned, and that he must not cross the river Satluj to enter into his territory. He replied that he would abide by his order. A messenger came and delivered a letter from Hakim Imam-ud-Din Khan, the garrison master of Gobindgarh, mentioning that Sirdar Jodh Singh of Ramgarh had reached there and sent his troops to his territory, and that he was forwarding this news for formation. A letter came from Raja Sansar Chand, mentioning that he had sent his troops to Sirdar Desa Singh Majithia is requisitioned by him, and had himself reached Sujanpur safely. In the meantime another messenger came and delivered a letter from Sirdar Desa Singh Majithia, stating that the sons of Fateh Singh Kanhya still continued to quarrel among themselves, and that he contemplated attacking the fort of Jhirka and reducing it. A reply was immediately despatched, that there was no necessity for such attack, that the fort would be reduced merely by continuing his blockading it for a day or two, and that a direct attack would involve loss of many lives. When the day had advanced one quarter and a half the Noble Sarkar went into the zenana, those who were present having walked out. He took his meals and laid himself down to rest at noon. He got up again at about the third quarter of the day and came out when four hours of the day were left. He inspected the drill of the battalion of Sheikh Basawan, the commandant, and granted one gold necklace to two persons respectively. At nightfall he went to the Saman Burj as usual, and his associates and attendants came in and presented themselves. Two sons of Sirdar Jodh Singh of Kalsia came in and expressed their desire to be granted permission to leave. The Noble Sarkar said that they must remain there, whereupon they kept quite. The Noble Sarkar granted a robe of honour consisting of four garments and on a horse to each of them out of his kindness. The dancing girls then presented themselves. He wanted their dance until the night had passed one quarter, and later went into the zenana, took his meals and laid himself down to rest when the night had passed one quarter and a half.

Dated 23rd February, 1814 (2nd Rabi-ul-Awwal)

The Noble Sarkar got up early in the morning and came out when the day had advanced four hours. The sirdars usually present came in and made their customary bow. The messengers (Jauri) came from the district of Peshawar and said, that Hazrat Mahmud Shah Badshah had marched from Peshawar towards Dera Ismail Khan. It was rumoured that he would go to Kandhar. He further stated that the contractors had come from Kandhar to the King, had reported that Ata Muhammad Khan continued to stay in Kandhar together with Shah Ayoob, that both were collecting the Durrani and Ucchakzai troops with the intention of marching towards Kabul, that at the same time it was rumoured that the Durranis had prevented them from proceeding towards Kabul on the plea that a hasty action like that was not right, but that it would be more expedient for them to attempt reducing Kabul and Peshawar into their possession gradually. The messengers further stated, that Ata Muhammad Khan had decided to despatch some troops towards Kabul, and had personally sent letters on his own behalf to the sirdars of Kabul and Peshawar, in which he appeared to have urged them to rise and cause disturbance in their territories, that he had promised them rewards for such service, and finally, that Hazrat Mahmud Shah Badshah (in consequence of this move of Ata Muhammad Khan) was in great perplexity and had sent for Sirdar Fateh Khan Wazir. On hearing this the Noble Sarkar rewarded the messengers (Jauri) with twenty rupees, and sent them back in that direction once again. A messenger came and delivered a letter from Nawab Muzaffar Khan of Multan, mentioning that he had despatched his representative with the instalment of money to the Noble Sarkar, which would reach him very soon. The Noble Sarkar sat separately, and made Pir Bakhsh Kotwal to understand something in privacy. It became known later, that the Noble Sarkar was posting him in the house of the Begum of Hazrat Shah Shuja-ul-Mulk, with instructions that he should gain influence with her and should steal out of her possession whatever cash, articles and jewellery be with her and bring the same to the Noble Sarkar who would suitably reward him for this service. The Kotwal replied that gradually he would try to achieve the object for which he was being appointed. When the day had advanced one quarter and a half the sirdars and others who were present went away, and the Noble Sarkar went into the zenana, took his meals and laid himself down to rest at noon. He got up again at about the third quarter of the day, and came out to the Saman Burj when four hours of the day were left. His associates and attendants presented themselves. A messenger came and delivered a letter from Diwan Muhkam Chand, mentioning that he had reached Kapurthala. It was stated that the troops of the Noble Sarkar had reached the division of the Raja of Bhimbar, and had set up their camp there, and that the troops of Kanwar Kharak Singh the eldest prince, had reached Shahdara. A letter was sent to the garrison master of Attock, asking him to exercise all due vigilance and care in keeping that place under control. The Noble Sarkar then went into the zenana, and the sirdars and others who were present went away. After taking his meals, he laid himself down to rest when the night had passed one quarter. All's well otherwise.

1814 (8)

News of the Deorhi of Sirdar Ranjit Singh Bahadur. Thursday, dated 3rd March 1814 (10th Rabi-ul-Awwal, 1229 A.H.); the Royal Fort, Lahore.

The Noble Sarkar got up early in the morning and came out to the garden and sat down there. Bhai Gurbakhsh Singh, Hakim Aziz-ud-Din Khan, Hakim Rae, Har Bhaj Rae, Diwan Bhawan Dass of the low stature, Karam Chand, Sukh Dial, Munshi Diwan Ganga Ram, Rasal Singh, Mian Singh, Dhonkal Singh, etc., the commandants; and Nihal Singh, Partap Singh, Jai Singh of Attari, Dal Singh Bharania, Jodh Singh Soorianwala, Shiam Singh Nakka, Hari Singh Nalwa, Himmat Singh Chillawala, Dhanna Singh Malwai, and several others came in and made their customary bow. The Noble Sarkar inspected the drill of the company of the special Sikhs but excused the battalions from drill on account of the Holidays. Gulab Rae Jamadar was given two hundred rupees in the course of his account to meet his expenses. A letter came from Raja Bhag Singh, stating that the Thanadar of Kot Kapura was involved in a dispute with the zamindars of his division, and requested that he must be stopped from such interference, and should be made to desist from such proper acts. The Noble Sarkar heard this and rewarded the messenger, saying that a reply

133

would be sent in a day or two. In the meantime Kanwar Kharak Singh, the eldest prince had come. He said that according to the order of the Noble Sarkar he had sent Ram Singh to Hazrat Shah Shuja-ul-Mulk. A letter came from the garrison master of Attock, stating that he had sent his troops with Dewa Singh of Ropar with a view to punishing the zamindars of Kundagarh, that by the blessing and glory of the Noble Sarkar those who were under his displeasure would be punished, that control would again be restored over that region, and that more troops ought to be deputed in that direction. It was written to him in reply that Gulab Singh Kakar and Charat Singh of Shahdara had already been sent in that direction with their horsemen, and that if he wanted anything at any time to meet his requirements he must realize it from that very place. A letter came from Diwan Muhkam Chand, intimating his arrival in the cantonment of Phillour and sending a detailed account of that district. The Noble Sarkar enquired about Sirdar Fateh Khan Wazir from Divan Bhawani Dass. He replied that he continued to be in Dera Ismail Khan and was busily engaged in looking after his troops and issuing letters to the Nawabs of Multan and Bahawalpur for military help. He further stated that there were two or four thousand horsemen in Peshawar, that contributions were being levied upon that town, that the travellers were being robbed on the highway, that Muhammad Azim Khan, the brother of the afore said sirdar, was still in Kashmir where he was engaged in maintaining two or four thousand horse and foot with him, that inspite of all these preparations great fear existed among the inhabitants of that town on their hearing reports about the approach of the army of the Noble Sarkar, and that especially the money-lenders were terror struck. In the afternoon the Noble Sarkar went with the eldest prince into the zenana, took his meals and laid himself down to rest. Those who were present went away. He got up again at about the third quarter of the day and came out. His staff and servants made their customary bow. Riding a horse, he went to the mausoleum of Jahangir for recreation, returned from there at nightfall, and entered the fort and watched the dance of the dancing girls until one quarter of the night had passed. Later, he went into the zenana, took his meals and laid himself down to rest. All went on well otherwise during the night.

Friday, dated 4th March, 1814 (11th Rabi-ul-Awwal)

The Noble Sarkar got up early in the morning and came out to the Diwan Khana when the day had advanced four hours. Bhai Gurbakhsh

Singh, Hakim Aziz-ud-Din Khan, Himmat Singh Jhalla and several other sirdars came in and made their customary bow. A letter was sent to Diwan Muhkam Chand, asking him to keep on sending regularly full accounts of that district. The Darogha of the swivels was granted five thousand rupees through Rama Nand Sahu to meet his requirements, and was ordered to go at the head of all swivels to Jhirki in the division of Nadhan Singh, the son of Fateh Singh Kanhya, and to reduce it into his possession after forcing the evacuation of the inhabitants. He replied that he would do so. Ram Singh, the man in charge of the affairs of Kanwar Kharak Singh, the eldest prince, came in and said, that he had gone to Hazrat Shah Shuja-ul-Mulk, and had told him according to the order of the Noble Sarkar that he should himself surrender whatever articles of jewellery, turquoise and emeralds, etc., were with his Begams, that otherwise they would be seized in some other way, and that the Shah had replied that at that time he had nothing with him, that whatever he had possessed, had already been seized by them, and that he was left only with his life which also they could destory if they liked. He further reported that he had himself felt helpless in the end, and had therefore returned to the Noble Sarkar. The Noble Sarkar heard this, whispered something into his ears, and asked him to take some maid-servants alongwith him at about the third quarter of the day to send them inside the Haram, and to tell them to snatch and bring out whatever articles of jewellery, pearls, and such other boxes they might find there. The above-mentioned agreed to do likewise. Sarbuland Khan and his other companions were awarded one shawl each as a farewell gift, and allowed to depart. A letter and a horse came from Nawab Kutub-ud-Din Khan of Kasur, and in reply the Noble Sarkar wrote him to purchase and send two more horses. A letter came from Sukha Nand and Bahadur Singh, the representatives of the Noble Sarkar, stating that they had met Nawab Muzaffar Khan and were now proposing to proceed towards Bahawalpur. The Noble Sarkar sent for lacdye and sprinkled it over his associates and attendants on account of the Holi, and watched the dance of the dancing girls. When the day had advanced two quarters and three hours the sirdars and others who were present went away, and the Noble Sarkar entered into the zenana, took his meals and laid himself down to rest. He got up again at about the third quarter of the day, and came out of the Saman Burj when four hours of the day were left. His associates and attendants presented themselves. Partap Singh of Attari, having been granted a robe of honour consisting of three garments, was made to depart for chastising the zamindars. The village of Shishmahal, situated near Lahore, was granted to Himmat Singh Jhalla as jagir. Ram Singh, the man in charge of the affairs of the Noble Sarkar, came in and stated that he had one to the Dera of Shah Shuja-ul-Mulk, had demanded the jewellery, had then sent five maid-servants into the ladies inside the place that they had brought every thing that they could find in the interior such as jewellery, turquoise, pearls, small boxes, carpets and the like, and that Hazrat Shah Shuja-ul-Mulk had wept and cried aloud that he could not resist the will of God saying that they could take away whatever they liked. The Noble Sarkar told him to present all the various articles on the following day, for he wanted to see them. He replied that he would do so. At nightfall the Noble Sarkar rode out into the town, and enjoying a trip through it, returned to the fort when four hours of the night had passed. He went into the zenana, took his meals and laid himself down to take rest. All went on well otherwise during the night.

Saturday, dated 5th March, 1814 (12th Rabi-ul-Awwal, 1229, A.H.), the Days of the Holi.

The Noble Sarkar got up early in the morning and went into his sleeping chamber. As the rain was falling heavily and it was the day of Holi he ordered that nobody should be allowed to come in. He drank wine, listened to the music of the dancing girls, later took his meals, and laid himself down to rest at noon. He got up again at about the third quarter of the day, and came out to the garden when four hours of the day were left, and those who were accustomed to be present made their customary bow. The commandants of the battalions were ordered to go into their cantonments and engage themselves in enjoying Holi but must not allow any of the soldiers to enter the town. It was stated that Hazrat Shah Shuja-ul-Mulk had not taken his food since two days on account of his grief for the property and materials that had been   seized from him. The Noble Sarkar, after hearing this, engaged himself in enjoying Holi with his associates. Shahzada Haider was summoned and told to surrender big pieces of jewellery which he might have, and was assured that in that case his property would be delivered back to him by Ram Singh. That respectable person replied that his life was there and that the Noble Sarkar could kill him. Such conversation went on with this Shahzada for some time. Later the Noble Sarkar went into the zenana and those who were present went away. He sprinkled coloured water upon his body, and taking his meals laid himself down to rest. All's well otherwise.

News of the Deorhi of Sirdar Ranjit Singh Bahadur. Tuesday, dated 5th
April, 1814 (13th Rabi-us-Sani, 1229, A.H.), Lahore.

The Noble Sarkar got up early in the morning and came out to the
garden where Bhai Gurbakhsh Singh, Sirdar Mat Singh Bharania, Himmat
Singh Chillawala, Sukh Dial, Diwan Ganga Ram and others presented
themselves, making their customary bow. A letter from Aziz Khan and
Sheikh Budha, the commandants, intimated, that according to his order
they had marched with their battalions from the district of Chirki, and,
passing through Manjah, had gone over to Ghaus Khan, the Darogha of
the Topkhana, and that they had sent Nadha Singh, the son of Fateh Singh
Kanhya, to the Noble Sarkar, guarded by two sentinels. A reply was sent
to them that they must always remain obedient to the said Khan and write
regularly to the Noble Sarkar about all events, and that their monthly
allowances would soon be sent. An order was sent to Nihal Singh
commandant that he must get ready because in a day or two he was to go
towards Kot Kamalia. Chet Ram Sarraf presented twenty-five gold
necklaces. The Noble Sarkar ordered Daulat Ram Modi, the supplier of
military provisions, that he must keep supplying grain on camels to meet
the requirements of the battalions and to send one hundred camels laden
with gunpowder and shells *via* the river Ravi by means of boats towards
Kot Kamalia. It was stated that Nadhan Singh Kanhya had come guarded
by two sentinels from the battalion of Aziz Khan. The Noble Sarkar
ordered him to be made over to Shadi Khan Jamadar and said that he
would be set free on the payment of twelve hundred rupees. A letter was
sent to the Darogha of the swivels that he should go to that place with all
his swivels. Chet Singh commandant requested that he should be granted
two cannons for his battalion. The Noble Sarkar replied that those would
be given to him. Gulab Singh, the then Jamadar of the attendants upon
horses, was ordered that he, with all such attendants, should present
himself. In the afternoon the Noble Sarkar went into the zenana, took his
meals and laid himself down to rest. He got up again at about the third
quarter of the day, and came out to the garden and held a court there. The
Darogha of the workshop said that more balls had been prepared and was
ordered to make them over to the "Kotha." Hukma Singh Thanadar was
ordered to sell off wheat. Sobha Singh, the revenue collector of Gujrat,
was allowed to depart after being granted three garments. The Noble
Sarkar distributed fifty rupees in charity. After enjoying a dance of the

dancing girls, he went into the zenana, took his meals, and laid himself down to rest when the night had passed one quarter. All's well otherwise.

1814 (10)

Deorhi of Sirdar Ranjit Singh Bahadur. Monday, dated 11th April, 1814 (19th Rabi-us-Sani, 1229, A.H.); the Shalamar Gardens, Lahore.

The Special Royal horses اسپان خاصه were sent to Amritsar. Six gunners from among the companions of Mir Mazhar Ali, the Darogha of the Topkhana driven by horses, who were in prison with the Noble Sarkar, were pardoned for their faults and released after being granted one "Ilaqa" each. A robe of honour consisting of three garments was given to Hakim Nur-ud-Din Khan who was allowed to depart towards Wazirabad and Sialkot. Then villages in the division of Taragarh were given to Garwa Singh. Sukh Dial stated that he had sent five hundred rupees to the camp of Shah Shuja-ul-Mulk who had returned them. Diwan Bhawani Dass stated that Ram Singh, the manager of the affairs of Kanwar Kharak Singh had already seized the boxes belonging to Shah Shuja-ul-Mulk while he was on his way to Rawalpindi, and that it appeared that Hari Singh, the representative of the Noble Sarkar, had stolen some articles of jewellery out of them. The Noble Sarkar sent for that person. He sent a message to the camp of Shuja-ul-Mulk, asking him to send his reliable person to accompany his stirrup up to Amritsar. The ironsmiths of Kotli presented ten guns. When six hours of the day were left the Noble Sarkar rode with his associates and other attendants and entered the Shalamar Gardens. Kanwar Kharak Singh came together with Ram Singh and stated that he had left all the troops with him at Sheikhupura, and had come all alone to take a sacred bath at Amritsar. The Noble Sarkar said it was all right. All's well otherwise.

1814 (11)

News of the Deorhi of Sirdar Ranjit Singh Buhadur. Monday, dated 18th April, 1814 (26th Rabi-us-Sani, 1229 A.H.), Amritsar.

The Noble Sarkar got up early in the morning and came out to the Diwan Khana where he took his seat. Bhai Gurbakhsh Singh, Hakim Aziz-ud-Din Khan, Mat Singh Bharania, Diwan Muhkam Chand and others came in and made their customary bow. The gunners گوله اندازان of the fort of Gobindgarh were awarded one hundred rupees. The Vakil of Bhai Lal Singh was granted a robe of honour consisting of five garments and one hundred rupees in cash, and allowed to depart after being told that there was one horse with Bhai Lal Singh which was liked by the Noble Sarkar, and which he should bring to Amritsar for him. Five gunners were engaged in service and ten gold necklaces were granted to the men of the Sikh company. It was stated that Yusaf Ali, the "Darogha-i-Adalat" was outriding when a Sikh, in a state of inebriation, struck him with a sword and wounded him. On learning this an order was given that the Sikh be traced, and for this purpose letters were despatched to the commandants to make a search with the aid of their battalions. The Vakil of Raja Sansar Chand stated that the Noble Sarkar was expected to release the villages belonging to the division of the fort of Janki which had been confiscated by him. The Noble Sarkar replied that they would be released. A letter came from Sahib Singh, the Jamadar of the messengers, stating that Sardar Fateh Khan Wazir had entered the district of Dera Ghazi Khan, and that some of his troops had crossed the river Sind near Khangarh and Muzaffargarh. The representative of Nawab Sadiq Ali Khan of Bahawalpur was, further, reported to have gone to the presence of the "Wazir-i-Azam," to have expressed on behalf of his master that he was his house born friend, and an old loyal follower, that until that time he had been maintaining diplomatic relations with the Noble Sarkar out of sheer expediency, but that in the future he would abide by his (the Wazir's) orders, that the "Wazir-i-Azam" after taking pledges had sent this representative back towards the Nawab with a robe of honour consisting of seventeen garments for him and with the request that he must send his troops under some reliable leader and submit Nazrana henceforth to him instead of the Noble Sarkar. The Noble Sarkar despatched messengers (Jauri) to ascertain the truth about this news. At noon he went into the zenana and laid himself down to rest, those who were present having gone away. He got up again at about the third quarter of the day, and came out to the audience chamber. He held a private conference, with Diwan Muhkam Chand, and after that rode out for recreation and later went into the Royal fort, took his meals, and laid himself down to rest. All's well otherwise.

1814 (12)

News of the Deorhi of Sirdar Ranjit Singh Bahadur. Friday, dated 29th April; 1814 (8th Jamadi-ul-Awwal, 1229 A.H.). Dinanagar as Previously.

The Noble Sarkar got up early in the morning and came out to the tent set apart for holding the court. Bhai Gurbakhsh Singh, Himmat Singh Chillawala and others came in and made their customary bow. The news came that Kanwar Kharak Singh had reached near the Kot of Sukhrae, and was expected to join the victorious troops in the evening or the next morning. Sada Sukh, the guard, requested for a jagir and was told that he would be given one. It was stated that the control over the fort of Makhadgarh had not been satisfactorily established owing to the rebelliousness of the zamindars of the neighbourhood, and the Noble Sarkar said that five thousand horsemen would soon be sent to that district to achieve that object. Ten well-known Sikhs were engaged in service. The Noble Sarkar asked about the state of the troops of Wazir Fateh Khan Sirdar from his Vakil Damodar Mal. A letter was sent to Hukma Singh, the Thanadar of Lahore, asking him to get the city wall and the ditch constructed and repaired properly. Lachhman Singh, the garrison master of Pathankot, was emphatically ordered to store up the floor of wheat and grain and other such cereals and was then allowed to leave. A letter from Nawab Sarfraz Khan of Multan arrived, mentioning that Fateh Khan Wazir was camped near Dera Ghazi Khan, and engaged in collecting troops and dry provisions, and that he (the Nawab) had sent the thousand rupees as Nazar to him, though in reality he was loyal and faithful to the Noble Sarkar. The Noble Sarkar enquired about the improvement of the drill of the battalion of the Sikhs from Lachhman Singh commandant through Desa Singh Majithia, who replied that the Sikhs were doing well in drill. The Noble Sarkar said that more Sikhs should be recruited in that battalion and that mortars would be supplied to them. The son of Diwan Ganga Ram, presenting a Nazar of five rupees, paid his respects. At noon the sirdars and others who were present went away, and the Noble Sarkar laid himself down to rest after taking his meals. He got up again at about the third quarter of the day and came out to the tent set apart for the court, where those usually present made their customary bow. Money was realised from Sukh Dial and given to Ahmad Khan of Jhang to meet his requirements. The Noble Sarkar purchased four gold threaded saddles through Desa Singh, and ordered Karam Chand accountant to prepare a detailed statement of the salaries of men in charge of the swivels and present the same to him. He said that he would do so within four days. At night he took his meals after going into his palace, and then laid himself down to rest. All's well otherwise.

1814 (13)

News of the Deorhi of Sirdar Ranjit Singh Bahadur. Saturday, dated 21st May, 1814(30th Jamadi-ul-Awwal, 1229 A.H.); the Town of Wazirabad, on the Bank of the River Chenab.

The Noble Sarkar got up early in the morning and came out. The staff and the servants made their customary bow. Riding a horse he went to the bank of the river Chenab into his tent where Bhai Gurbakhsh Singh, Sukh Dial, Himmat Singh Chillawala and several other sirdars came and made their customary bow. A letter from Mustakim Khan of Muzaffarabad urged that the Noble Sarkar should send a sufficient force in that direction, and that he would bring about the surrender of Kashmir. The Noble Sarkar ordered Mazhar Ali, the Darogha of the cannons driven by horses, to take from the Noble Sarkar as much gunpowder as he required and keep ready. Later, He sat in privacy with Diwan Muhkam Chand and Hakim Aziz-ud-Din Khan and said, that the zamindars of the neighbourhood of Kashmir were asking for military help on promise that they would bring about the surrender of Kashmir for the Noble Sarkar, and that at that time his armies were all collected, while more troops were expected to join them in a few days. He asked them their advice about sending troops towards Kashmir. The Diwan said that at that time the troops of the Noble Sarkar were feeling extremely uneasy and distracted by the severity of the summer and that the rainy season was fast approaching, and hence the expedition to Kashmir must be postponed and only the revenue tax be demanded from the Nazim of that country. The Noble Sarkar said that as rumours regarding the intended expedition towards Kashmir had spread far and wide, it did not appear advisable or expedient at that time to return without achieving the object, and added that after the arrival of Kharak Singh, the eldest prince, he would send him at the head of an army towards Kashmir. He emphatically asked Kangna Wazir of the Raja of Nurpur to pay up the revenue tax, and the latter replied that he would shortly do so. It was stated that Muhammad Azim Khan, the Nazim of Kashmir, had died. The Noble Sarkar said that this news was not to be believed, and at once called upon one pair of messengers (Jauri) and made them depart towards Kashmir to find out the truth. He took twelve thaousand rupees from Sukh Dial, and kept the sum to himself. The news about the events of Shahjahanabad came, and the Noble Sarkar remarked that the facts about the glorious sahibs appeared to be fuller and better. Diwan Ganga Ram said that if the Noble Sarkar would order him, he would gather through his own agency some detailed account about the English Sahibs. He replied that the Diwan might do so. The Noble Sarkar got up from that place at noon, went into his own tent, took his meals and laid himself down to rest, while those who were present went away. Getting up again when four hours of the day were left, he went to the tent set apart for audience, where the sirdars came in and made their customary bow. Sirdar Himmat Singh Chillawala stated that in those days reliable persons had been appointed by the English Sarkar to make investigations about the contracts of all the ferries of the river Jamna, which belong to the Sikhs, and added that shortly the administration of justice would be established in that country. The Noble Sarkar said that it should be written to Lala Chandi (?) Dass to send a full account of the council of the English Sahibs to him. Later, enjoying a pleasure trip through the garden he went into the zenana, while the sirdars and others who were present went away.

1814 (14)

Deorhi of Sirdar Ranjit Singh Bahadur. Tuesday, dated 24th May, 1814 (3rd Jamadi-us-Sani, 1229 A.H.), on the Bank of the River Chenab.

Early in the morning the Noble Sarkar rode out and engaged himself in shooting birds and fowls and other game in the open land at a distance of nine kos from the victorious army, and later sat down on a carpet under the shade of trees. He said to those who were present that his forces had reached and encamped near Rajauri and were awaiting news about Kashmir, after receiving which they would advance further. The Noble Sarkar next rode out, and later returned to his tent when four hours of the night had passed. A letter from the garrison master of Attock informed that Sirdar Fateh Khan Wazir had marched towards Kabul mentioning also that the writer would write later after ascertaining further facts.

Wednesday, dated 25th, May 1814 (14th Jamadi-us-Sani, 1229, A .H.)

Rama Nand Sahu reported on the basis of letters received from Peshawar that Sirdar Fateh Khan Wazir had hurriedly escaped to Kabul owing to the severity of summer, leaving four thousand horse and foot in Peshawar, and that the troops of Muhammad Azim Khan, thre ruler of Kashmir, were engaged in controlling the "Ghats". In the meantime Kanwar Kharak Singh, the prince, arrived and met the Noble Sarkar who made a "sarwarna"[70] of one thousand rupees over his head, and distributed it to the poor. He sought permission immediately to proceed towards Kashmir, assuring that by the grace of God he would conquer it in a single attack. The Noble Sarkar said that that was the only thing which he cherished most in his heart. It was reported that the battalion of Dhonkal Singh had arrived and joined the victorious army. Imam Bakhsh, the Kotwal of Lahore, arrived with two thousand maunds of gunpowder and paid his respects. Agge Khan, the Vakil of Raja Sansar Chand paying his respects, stated that he had come with one thousand horse and foot of his master. The Noble Sarkar said to those who were present that on account of the severity of summer the expedition to Kashmir was called off and postponed. Ram Singh, the manager of the affairs of Kanwar Kharak

Singh, said that it was not advisable for the Noble Sarkar to return towards Lahore without establishing his control over that country and thus realising the object of his mind adding that if the heat that summer was so excessive the Noble Sarkar could for the present remain where he was and move further with the expedition to Kashmir after the rainy season. The Noble Sarkar ordered the commandants of all the battalions and other chiefs of the army to cross the river Chenab and fix their camp at Gujrat. He immediately distributed fifty maunds of gunpowder among the battalions, and ordered Hakim Aziz-ud-Din Khan to see that the axe men and the stone breakers level up the pits and heights of the passage to Kashmir. Later he went into the zenana. All's well otherwise.

1814 (15)

News of the Deorhi of Sirdar Ranjit Singh Bahadur. Tuesday, dated 24th May, 1814 (3rd Jamadi-us-Sani, 1229 A.H.); the Town of Wazirabad, on the Bank of the River Chenab.

The Noble Sarkar got up early in the morning and came out before sunrise. His sirdars and associates came in and made their customary bow. Along with them the Noble Sarkar rode out towards the open land for a hunt. Alighting from their horses at a distance of nine kos from the victorious troops, they engaged themselves, in shooting birds and fowls. At noon they sat down under the shade of trees. The Noble Sarkar took his meals along with his associates who had gone with him and later laid himself down to take rest. He got up again when four hours of the day were left and sat down upon his carpet. His associates began to talk about the expedition to Kashmir. The Noble Sarkar said that his troops had reached near Rajauri and fixed their camp and were waiting anxiously for news from Kashmir, after which they would move a little forward. He rode back and entered his tent when the night had passed four hours. Those who were present made their customary bow. A letter came from the garrison master of the fort of Attock mentioning that Sirdar Fateh Khan had marched towards Kabul, and that he would write again on gaining further rows. After considering the contents of that letter the Noble Sarkar went into the zenana, took his meals and laid himself down to rest during the night.

Wednesday, dated 29th May, 1814 (8th Jamadi-us-Sani 1229 A.H.).
Singh.

The Noble Sarkar got up early in the morning and came out to the tent set apart for the court, and Bhai Gurbakhsh Singh, Hakim Aziz-ud-Din, Sukh Dial, Diwan Muhkam Chand and several others came in and made their customary bow. Rama Nand Sahu brought letters which had come from Peshawar and reproduced their contents, stating that Sirdar Fateh Khan Wazir had gone towards Kabul on account of the severity of the summer, leaving four thousand horse and foot in Peshawar, and that troops of Muhammad Azim Khan were engaged in the management of the "ghats". In the meantime Kharak Singh, the eldest prince, came in, paid his respects to the Noble Sarkar who made a "sarwarna" of one thousand rupees over his head and gave it away to the poor. The Kanwar said that he wanted to be allowed to proceed to Kashmir at that time, and that he hoped by the grace of God to conquer it in only a single attack. The Noble Sarkar said that that was what he most cherished in his heart. In the meantime it was stated that the battalion of Dhonkal Singh commandant had arrived and joined the victorious army. The Noble Sarkar said that his battalion must encamp on the bank of the river Chenab. Imam Bakhsh, in charge of the police station of Lahore, arrived with two thousand maunds of gunpowder and paid his respect. The Noble Sarkar had a talk with Sirdar Fateh Singh Ahluwalia in privacy. Zaqi Khan, the Vakil of Raja Sansar Chand, arrived, paid his respects, and stated that he had brought with him one thousand horse and foot of his master. The Noble Sarkar said that he had done well, and addressed those who were present that on account of the severity of summer the expedition to Kashmir had been called off. Ram Singh, the man in charge of the affairs of Kanwar Kharak Singh, represented that returning to Lahore without establishing control over that country and without achieving that object was not desirable, and that so long as it was expected to be very hot the Noble Sarkar could stay there, and could go on the expedition to Kashmir after the end of the rainy season. After that all the commandants of the battalions and all the chiefs of the army were ordered to cross the river Chenab and fix their camps in Gujrat. At noon those who were present went away, and the Noble Sarkar went into the other tent, took his meals, and laid himself down to rest. He got up again at about the third quarter of the day and remained for some time inside the tent. Later he came out to the garden of Sukh Dial when two hours of the day were left. The sirdars came and made their customary bow. Fifty maunds of gunpowder were distributed among the battalions. Hakim Aziz-ud-Din Khan was ordered to tell emphatically all the axe men

144

and stone breakers to level all the pits and heights on the way. At nightfall the Noble Sarkar sent forty rupees for entertainment to the representative of Sirdar Nahinga Singh of Thanesar. He then went into the zenana, took his meals and laid himself down to rest during the night. All's well otherwise.

<h1 style="text-align:center">1814 (16)</h1>

News of the Deorhi of Sirdar Ranjit Singh Bahadur. Friday, dated 27th May,1814 (6th Jamadi-us-Sani, 1229 A.H.); the Town of Wazirabad, on the Bank of the River Chenab.

The Noble Sarkar got up early in the morning and came out. The staff and servants made their customary bow. He rode out on his horse to his tent which was pitched on the bank of the river Chenab and took his seat. Bhai Gurbakhsh Singh, Hakim Aziz-ud-Din Khan, Sukh Dial, Bhawani Dass, Sirdar Mat Singh Bharania, Himmat Singh Chillawala, and several other sirdars came in and made their obeisance. Sirdar Jodh Singh of Kalsia entered, offered one horse as Nazar, and paid his respects. The Noble Sarkar enquired after his health and ordered him to cross the river Chenab, and proceed forward towards Rajauri. The Noble Sarkar talked to Raja Fateh Singh Ahluwalia in privacy and asked him also to cross the river Chenab with his troops. This person then walked out. In the meantime a letter had arrived from Nand Singh, the Vakil at Ludhiana, informing that he had sent thirty gunners and thirty workmen according to the Noble Sarkar's order. He later wrote him a reply, after considering the letter, and rewarding the messenger with two rupees. The Noble Sarkar enquired about the state of the passages to Kashmir from Jahandad Khan and Ghulam Muhammad Khan, the brothers of Ata Muhammad Khan, and authorised them to take whatever they wanted to meet their requirements from the treasurer of the Noble Sarkar. They were also told to accompany the troops of the Noble Sarkar to Kashmir, and were promised the divisions of Soudhra and Sambharial as Jagirs on their return from Kashmir. They replied that they would do so, adding that the Noble Sarkar would come to know what sacrifices they were capable of making for him. A letter from Shadi Khan commandant from Lahore intimated that he was carefully guarding the town of Lahore and the Deorhi of Hazrat Shah Shuja-ul-Mulk Fateh Kha. of Sahiwal was ordered to engage one hundred well trained horsemen to accompany him, and was told that their salaries would be paid by the Noble Sarkar. At noon he went into the other tent, took his meals and laid himself down to rest, while those who were present walked out. He got up again at about the third quarter of the day and came out to the tent as usual, where his associates and attendants presented themselves. He inspected one hundred infantry men and ten horsemen and engaged them in service. Then he held a parade of the horsemen of Jodh Singh of Suhriyan. News about the events of Shahjahanabad arrived, and the Noble Sarkar rewarded the messenger with six rupees on hearing it. A letter came from Sheikh Ahmad, the Amil of Jullundur, that he had got ready two thousand balls for the swivels according to order and would make them reach wherever the Noble Sarkar would wish. A letter was sent in reply, asking him to send those shell for the swivels to the Noble Sarkar. The zamindars of Kot arrived, presented one rupee as Nazar, and paid their respects. The Noble Sarkar assured them in every way two hundred rupees were given to Sultan Mahdi Ali Khan of Khanpur to meet his requirements. A letter, containing cordial sentiments, came from Raja Jaswant Singh of Nabha. It was stated that Sirdar Jodh Singh of Kalsia and Raja Fateh Singh Ahluwalia had marched away together with their troops according to his order towards the "ghat" of Ramnagar. The Noble Sarkar, after watching dance of the dancing girls, took his meals when one quarter of the night had passed, and later laid himself down to rest. All's well otherwise.

1814 (17)

Deorhi of Sirdar Ranjit Singh Bahadur. Wednesday, dated 1ˢᵗ June, 1814 (11ᵗʰ Jamadi-us-Sani, 1229 A.H.), the Fort of Gujrat.

Sukh Dial Sahu was ordered to send fifty thousand maunds of cereals like wheat, millets, pulses, etc., to Rajauri. Karam Chand was ordered to distribute cartridges among the battalions. Action was taken according to the orders. Diwan Muhkam Chand was told that although he was unwell, yet the Noble Sarkar regarded him as a father to himself and, felt convinced that the expedition to Kashmir would not succeed without his going there, and that he had no such confidence in any of his sirdars or chiefs. He replied, that so long as he was alive he would not allow the Maharaja Bahadur personally to go on any expedition, that he could do whatever he liked after his death, and that if that was the wish of the Noble Sarkar he must order all the chiefs and sirdars of the army to be loyal and obedient to him and not to show the least hesitation or avoidance at the time of battle. The Noble Sarkar said that nobody could dare to be disobedient to him, adding that if anybody would disobey him he would not benefit by it. He also said that if it be the Diwan's advice he would like to go over to Rajauri and stay there, lest Sirdar Fateh Khan Wazir might cross the river Attock and reach the district of Bhimbar. The Diwan replied that the Wazir had no such courage, and gave the Noble Sarkar full assurances on that account. The revenue collector of the town of Gujrat was ordered to send five hundred maunds of baked millets to Rajauri. The representative of Kanwar Kharak Singh was ordered to distribute gunpowder and ammunitions to his troops. One messenger (Jauri) belonging to the Muslim communtiy was sent to Kashmir for bringing news. An estate worth five thousand rupees was granted to Mehr Singh Rukanwala in the country of the late Jamal Singh. All's well otherwise.

1814 (18)

Deorhi of Sirdar Ranjit Singh Bahadur. Thursday, dated 2nd June, 1814 (12th Jamadi-us-Sani1229, A.H.)

Dhonkal Singh, Sheikh Basawan and other commandants of the battalions were ordered to march forward and fix their camps near the "sarai" of Daulatnagar. They marched away. Raja Fateh Singh Ahluwalia came, accompanied by Chaudhri Qadir Bakhsh. The Noble Sarkar said to him in private that he had no confidence in anybody except him and Diwan Muhkam Chand. The Raja replied that the Noble Sarkar should have no fear in the least, that he was always ready to sacrifice his life and to do all he could for his good according to his wishes. The Noble Sarkar told Naurang Singh, a reliable person of Raja Sansar Chand to leave with his own troops on the following day for Lahore and most emphatically warn the chiefs of the army to be most vigilant in protecting and guarding Lahore. The officers of the army were urged to sacrifice their lives in the expedition to Kashmir, and promised that by the grace of God they would be given twice as many Jagirs as they already possessed, after its conquest. A letter was sent to the Thanadar of Lahore to load fifty thousand rupees upon camels and send them soon to the Noble Sarkar. Two thousand rupees granted as salaries for the special royal horse attendants.

Friday; dated 3rd June, 1814 (13th Jamadi-us-Sani, 1229 A. H.)

The messengers (Jauri) arrived from Kashmir and stated that Muhammad Azim Khan, the Nizam of Kashmir, had appointed five thousand horse and foot at each of the places of "Garhi" up to the "Ghat", and himself had established his camp on the "Ghat" of Pirpanjal with twenty thousand horses and foot. He had destroyed the bridges over those streams which the people had to cross on their way to and from Kashmir and the fighting continued as before. On hearing this the Noble Sarkar rewarded them, and made them depart in that direction once again. He issued an order to the commandants of the battalions of the mules to get ready for loading. Emphatic summons were sent to Sheikh Basawan, Sheikh Budha and Ghaus Khan. A letter from garrison master of Attock informed, that Sirdar Fateh Khan Wazir's forces had come and fixed their camp near the "Ghat" of Muzaffarabad, and that therefore the zamindars of that district had revolted. The Noble Sarkar wrote in reply that his troops would soon be reaching there for their chastisement, adding that he must exercise great care and vigilance. Kanwar Kharak Singh was told that although he had already distributed money among his troops, yet he must stay on for a few days and should march forward after regaining complete health. Dial Singh and other chieftains were ordered to march forward from that place on the following day and to fix their camps near Daulatabad. All's well otherwise.

1814 (19)

News of the Deorhi of Sirdar Ranjit Singh Bahadur. Thursday, dated 9th June, 1814 (19th Jamadi-us-Sani, 1229 A. H.), the Sarai of Nowshera.

The Noble Sarkar got up early in the morning and came out and sat down in a mosque in the Sarai of Nowshera, where Bhai Gurbakhsh Singh, Sukh Dial Singh, Himmat Singh Chillawala, Diwan Bhawani Dass, Hakim Aziz-ud-Din Khan, Sirdar Mat Singh Bharania and other sirdars arrived and made their customary bow. Letters were sent to Akbar Khan of Rajauri and Ruhullah Khan of Punchh, calling upon them to present themselves to the Noble Sarkar immediately, and informing them that in case they made delay they would be made to suffer, for then the Noble Sarkar would first turn them out and proceed to conquer Kashmir afterwards. The messengers (Jauri) came from Kashmir and stated, that Muhammad Azim Khan, the Nazim of Kashmir, had well secured the "Ghats" of Pirpanjal, Bahramgalla, and Sistan, etc., and himself was camped on this side of Kashmir, that he was in terror of the approach of the Noble Sarkar's forces, and that it was most probable that he would evacuate Kashmir and flee on learning about the approach of his troops. The Noble Sarkar heard this and rewarded the messengers with twenty-five rupees. He then sent an order to the commandants of the battalions immediately to advance forward with their battalions and establish their camps near the "sarai" of Akbarpur (one word in the text not clear). Raja Fateh Singh Ahluwalia and Sirdar Jodh Singh of Kalsia came in, and the Noble Sarkar held a lengthy private conference with them regarding Kashmir. Jai Karan Dass, the news writer, stated that only eighteen thousand horse and foot were with the Nazim of Kashmir, whereupon the Noble Sarkar replied that its reduction would be effected within a few days. When the day had advanced one quarter those who were present walked out, and the Noble Sarkar went into the zenana, took his meals and laid himself down to rest at noon. He got up again at about the third quarter of the day, and came out to the other tent when four hours of the day were left. His associates and attendants presented themselves. Balak Ram Risaldar was ordered to station himself there with two thousand horsemen and not to allow any person to go near the army. All the chieftains of the army and the employees were ordered to distribute among their companions flour, grain and other kinds of food stuff for eight days. A letter came from Akbar Khan of Rajauri stating that he was over loyal and obedient to the Noble Sarkar that the Noble Sarkar should send Pandit Raja Ram to him, and that he would present himself after receiving pledges on oath from him. Action was taken according to his letter and Pandit Raja Ram was sent to him. A letter was sent to the garrison master of Manglan, asking him to send grain. The staff charge of the flourings was ordered to take the tent of the Noble Sarkar to the "sarai" of Akbarpur (one word in the text not clear). The action was taken according to the order. When four hours of the night had passed the officials went away. The Noble Sarkar took his meals, and later laid himself down to rest when the night had passed one quarter. All's well otherwise.

1814 (20)

News of the Deorhi of Sirdar Ranjit Singh Bahadur of Lahore. Thursday, dated 16th June , 1814 (26th Jamadi-us-Sani, 1229, A. H.); the Village of Panth Sarai Badshahi, six kos Beyond the Town of Rajauri.

The Noble Sarkar got up early in the morning and came out to the tent where the staff and the servants made their customary bow. All the rajas of the mountainous regions were called to his presence, and he inspected their horsemen and infantry, and ordered them to leave their horses behind and advance ahead all alone. They said that they would do so at about the third quarter of the day. A letter together with ten thousand rupees arrived from the revenue collector of the town of Gujrat. The Noble Sarkar sent him a reply, acknowledging the receipt of the money and requiring that rations of grain must also be sent over to him, laden on oxen. Two hundred rupees were given to Sultan Mahdi Ali Khan to meet his own requirements. Letters were sent to the garrison master of the fort of Attock and other chieftains there, stating that it appeared that Sirdar Fateh Khan Wazir intended to cross over to Kashmir, and hence they must act together to check him at the "ghat" of Muzaffarabad which they must not allow him to cross. At noon the Noble Sarkar went into the other tent, took his meals, and laid himself down to rest. Those who were present went away. He got up again at about the third quarter of the day, and came out to the other tent when the day had advanced four hours. All his associates presented themselves. Ordering all the chieftains of the army to march forward to Behramgalla, he enquired from his associates if they had received any news from Kashmir just recently. They stated that all the passages to Kashmir were closed up and it was most difficult to use the tracks. The Kotwal of the army said that the flour was available for the army at the rate of four seers for a rupee. The Noble Sarkar said that the rate had gone so high, because the rations of grain had not yet reached, and ordered Sukh Dial Sahu immediately to send two thousand maunds of flour to the district of Behramgalla. One, Bakhtawar Khan commandant, came in search of employment. He paid his respects and was well assured that he would be given a letter of authority to take charge of a battalion. At nightfall those who were present went away, and the Noble Sarkar went into the other tent, took his meals, and laid himself down to rest.

Friday, dated 17th June, 1814. (27th Jamadi-us-Sani, 1229 A .H.)

The Noble Sarkar got up early in the morning and came out to the tent set apart for the court. Bhai Gurbakhsh Singh, Hakim Aziz-ud-Din Khan and several others came in and made their customary bow. The Noble Sarkar ordered Raja Fateh Singh Ahluwalia, Sirdar Jodh Singh of Kalsia and Ramdial to march immediately towards Behramgalla. They obeyed the order. A letter was sent towards the town of Gujrat to Rama Nand Sahu to send promptly twenty thousand rupees in cash. Five thousand rupees were distributed in the presence of the Noble Sarkar to the special royal attendants upon horses. Sirdar Mat Singh Bharania, who according to the order of the Noble Sarkar had gone out for the construction of a bridge over the Bal Nala stream, which was situated at a distance of two kos on this side of Behramgalla, against the two or three thousand infantry of Ruhullah Khan of Punchh who were already on the top of the mountain, returned and said that the troops accompanying Ruhullah Khan had established themselves there and had begun fighting against the troops of the Noble Sarkar, and that whoever tried to approach the stream were fired upon by them and killed by their bullets. He also stated that from his side not a single shot was fired without the Noble Sarkar's order. The Noble Sarkar replied that all the chieftains of the army could fire without any hesitation. In the afternoon the Noble Sarkar went into the other tent, took his meals, and laid himself down to take rest.

When two hours of the day were left he got up again, and came out to the tent set apart for audience at nightfall. The sirdars made their customary bow. The Noble Sarkar called upon Ghaus Khan and Mazhar Ali, the Superintendents of the Topkhana, and ordered them to despatch the whole of the Topkhana towards Behramgalla, to post cannons on great heights and destroy the entrenchments of Ruhullah Khan. The Noble Sarkar sent the messengers (Jauri) belonging to the Muslim community, towards Behramgalla, and after taking his meals, laid himself down to rest. It became known that on the top of the hill fighting continued with the troops of Ruhullah Khan of Punchh for two hours, in which, about five hundred men were killed and wounded on both sides, and that, in the end, the brave men took possession of the hill and the "Ghat." On the following day a detailed account would be sent. All's well otherwise.

1814 (21)

Deorhi of Sirdar Ranjit Singh Bahadur. Saturday, dated 2nd July 1814 (13th Rajab, 1229 A.H.), Punchh.

It was stated that five soldiers of the battalion of Sheikh Budha, the commandant, had been killed and about the same number wounded by robbers on the way, and that the rest were dying through starvation. On hearing this the Noble Sarkar distributed half a seer of flour to every one. A letter from Diwan Muhkam Chand advised that the Noble Sarkar must stay himself in Rajauri, and despatch his forces towards Kashmir, that he should state how much money he wanted to meet the expenses so that it should be sent, and that he should have no confidence in Akbar Khan and other rajas of the mountainous regions, but on the contrary should be very much alert with regard to them. It was written to him in reply that his advice would be followed, and that he should send fifty thousand rupees soon. Raja Fateh Singh Ahluwalia and Sirdar Jodh Singh of Kalsia stated that their troops were dying of starvation. The Noble Sarkar granted five hundred rupees in payment of an account to meet the expenses of Ghaus Khan, the Darogha of the Topkhana. The news came that the zamindars of the neighbourhood of Mandi had plundered the bazars of the village of Thatha. Sukh Dial was ordered to distribute rations of grain for four days among the battalion of the Sikhs and one seer of the "Pakka"[76] measure among each of the other battalions. This was done according to orders. The Noble Sarkar asked Akbar Khan of Rajauri the state of the road to Kashmir *via* Tosha Maidan, and was told that on that route very little grain etc., was available, that water was likewise scarce, and that the route *via* Baramula appeared to be quite good. A letter was sent to the zamindars of

Bakha Pestarwala, telling them that if they would come to the Noble Sarkar with their hearts full of assurance, patronage and consideration would be shown to them. Later, the Noble Sarkar rode out, and inspecting the "Garhi" of Punchh, went back to his tent. All's well otherwise.

1814 (22)

Deorhi of Sirdar Ranjit Singh Bahadur. Tuesday, dated 5th July, 1814 (16th Rajab, 1229 A.H.), Punchh.

Letters were sent through Sujan Rae, the Administrator of justice, to the Raja of Kotli and several others and to the various zamindars of the various districts, calling upon them to come to the presence of the Noble Sarkar. Akbar Khan said that that country was a Jagir worth three lakhs of rupees, and that the march should be made forward only after its settlement. The Noble Sarkar replied that he thought likewise. It was stated that Zabardast Khan; the zamindar of Rajpura, had come with a gaunt horse and jointed the troops of the Noble Sarkar. The news came that from among the troops which had been deputed with Sujan Rae, the administrator of justice, four thousand Sikhs had deserted with their guns owing to the scarcity of grain. Zabardast Khan zamindar came with the horse granted to him by the Noble Sarkar, and stated that he had heard on the way that the "Thana" of the Noble Sarkar had become established in Pir Panjal. The Noble Sarkar replied that it was quite wrong and, granting him a robe of honour consisting of three garments, ordered him to supply grain to the army. He replied that he would as far as it lay in his power. It was stated that out of the company of the Sikhs, which had gone over to the mountains for bringing about the evacuation of the "Garhi," only two men had returned and nothing was known about the whereabouts of the rest. Cartridges were distributed among the battalion of Dhonkal Singh commandant, and one Benares "Dupatta" was granted to Hira Singh commandant.

Wednesday, dated 6th July. 1814 (17th Rajab, 1229 A.H.)

On enquiring by the Noble Sarkar, Akbar Khan of Rajauri stated that one route to Kashmir was fifty kos in length, the other was forty kos, the third twenty-six kos, and there was yet another by the foot of the mountain, adding that the routes *via* Baramula and Pir Panjal were quite straight and in good condition. The Noble Sarkar said that if the roads had been clear he would have entered Kashmir within three days, but that at that time he was feeling helpless. It was written to the zamindars of the neighbourhood of Kashmir that they should present themselves before the Noble Sarkar in perfect confidence. The Noble Sarkar rode out to inspect the "ghats" and the stations but returned without making any observation; because the night had come on. The messengers (Jauri) brought the news that Muhammad Azim Khan, the Nazim of Kashmir, had strengthened the "ghats" and was well established in the fort and the town, adding that the rate of grain was very high even there. Fifty rupees were given as reward to those messengers (Jauri). It was stated that Diwan Muhkam Chand had newly recruited in Lahore something like ten thousand footmen and was arranging for their maintenance. All's well otherwise.

1814 (23)

Deorhi of Sirdar Ranjit Singh Bahadur. Friday, dated 8th July, 1814 (19th. Rajab, 1229 A. H.), the Town of Punchh.

The Noble Sarkar inspected the drill of his special orderly Sikhs and granted one "Ilaicha" to every two of them. Sirdar Mat Singh Bharania and several other chiefs of the army were ordered to march towards Rouri, situated at a distance of four kos from that place in the direction of Kashmir. They marched away accordingly. Sujan Rae Adalti and Sheikh Yusaf were appointed to look after the safety of people going to and coming from Amarpur Chumak, and also were ordered to distribute two thousand rupees as an instalment in the course of an account in the battalion of Sheikh Basawan. Raja Fateh Singh Ahluwalia sought permission to take alongwith him all the wounded to the town of Gujrat. The Noble Sarkar, allowing this, told him to march ahead together with Sirdar Jodh Singh of Kalsia. He replied that he would march at about the third quarter of the day. A letter from Sarbuland Khan of Rouri intimated that the troops of Mohammad Azim Khan, the ruler of Kashmir, were stationed there, and for that reason he could not present himself to the Noble Sarkar. Five hundred rupees were given to Sondhi, the son of Mian Khairata, to meet his expenses, after being ordered to march forward. The rajas also were made to march. It was written to the garrison master of Attock that no news about that district had reached the Noble Sarkar for a few days, and that he should continue writing regularly. On enquiring by the Noble Sarkar, the man incharge of the police for the bazaar stated that, at that time, flour was selling in the market at the rate of seven "kacha"[77] seers per rupee, and that even at that rate it could be procured with great difficulty. It was stated that Isa Khan, the Wazir of the Raja of Kotli, had joined the army. The Noble Sarkar heard it and sent one thousand rupees

153

for his entertainment. The news reached some Sikhs, while on the way to the village of Thatha, were by the Mulkias. All's well otherwise.

Dated 29th of July, 1814.

It became known in the cantonment of Ludhiana that in the town of Phillaur a salute of eleven guns had been fired both at the third quarter of the day and at nightfall. It became known that the "ghat" of Kashmir had fallen into the possession of the Noble Sarkar, and it was rumoured at the same time that Kashmir itself had been conquered. Again the news came that in Phillaur drums had been beaten to express joy on the rumour that Kashmir had been conquered.

Dated 30th July of the aforesaid year.

The messengers (Jauri) who had left for the cantonment of Ludhiana for Nand Singh, the Vakil of the Noble Sarkar, arrived and reported that Sahma Raja Kaka had joined the troops of the Noble Sarkar on the way to the "ghat" that at that time the troops of the Noble Sarkar had crossed and entered Kashmir, and that the said Raja supplied rations consisting of all kinds of grain to the troops of the Noble Sarkar, with the result that in the army the grain could be had at the rate of twenty seers a rupee. He further informed that Muhammad Azim Khan, the Nazim of Kashmir, had run away, that Kashmir had come into the possession of the Noble Sarkar, that though no direct news or letter had come from Kashmir it was rumoured everywhere that Kashmir had in reality been conquered, and that he would write later on further investigation. All's well otherwise.

1814 (24)

News of the Deorhi of Sirdar Ranjit Singh Bahadur. Friday, dated 5th August, 1814 (18th Shaban, 1229 A. H.), the Village of Sandha.

Marching from the place where a bridge crosses the rivulet, the Noble Sarkar entered safely the village of Sandha at about noon after exercising great care about his stores and effects. It was stated that Ram Singh, the manager of the affairs of Kanwar Kharak Singh, together with Akbar Khan of Rajauri, leaving Behramgalla for the place where Sirdar Dal Singh Bharania and others were, had reached the village of Thatha, and had put Akbar Khan in custody, and that Sirdar Mat Singh Bharania, who had been seriously wounded, had expired. The Noble Sarkar sent

154

Bhai Gurbakhsh Singh to his son for condolence. It was stated that Sirdar Dal Singh Bharania, Rant Dial and several other sirdars had hastily marched away from Sistan all through the night had entered the village of Thatha, that on the previous day many men had been killed and wounded on the way, that a great deal of property of the army had been plundered, and that some two thousand guns, about the same number of swords and many other implements of war belonging to the Sikhs, had been taken away by the zamindars of those regions. Pehlwan Khan, the brother of the Raja of Kotli, paid his respects and stated that henceforth no loss would occur to the Noble Sarkar, and that his stores and effects would be made to reach Lahore in perfect safety. The Noble Sarkar felt greatly relieved and gave him a robe of honour consisting of three garments with a pair of gold bangles.

Saturday, dated 6th August, 1814 (19th Shaban, 1229 A. H.), the Bridge over a stream situated at five kos on this side of Sandha.

The flow of water of the village Sandha was stopped, and the pool was made stationery on the top of a hillock, and thus the stores and effects etc., were made to cross. It reached a distance of five kos from Sandha where the Noble Sarkar had encamped. It was stated that while on the way fighting had broken out between the battalion of Sheikh Budha and the Malkiya tribesmen, and that several were killed and wounded on both sides. The Noble Sarkar praised the men of the battalion concerned and said that on his arrival in Lahore he would engage two or three battalions of the "Najibs" in his service.

Sunday, dated 7th August, 1814 (20th Shaban, 1229. A. H.), the Village of Kotli.

Marching onward they reached the village of Kotli and entered the tent. The Noble Sarkar said that the road *vide* Amarpur Chumak was difficult to pass, and that, therefore, he noted to march *via* Bhimbar. Raja Fateh Singh Ahluwalia ordered not to proceed forward without an order from the Noble Sarkar, because the cannons and other materials had not yet joined the army, and that the following day would be of halt. All's well otherwise.

1814 (25)

News of the Deorhi of Sirdar Ranjit Singh Bahadur. Thursday, dated 25th August, 1814 (9th Ramzan, 1229 A. H.); the Royal Fort, Lahore.

The Noble Sarkar got up early in the morning and came to the place for holding the court. Bhai Gurbakhsh Singh, Diwan Muhkam Chand, Sirdar Dal Singh Bharania, Sukh Dial, Hakim Aziz-ud-Din Khan and other sirdars came in and made their customary bow. A letter came from the men at Fatehgarh and Behramgalla, intimating that the troops of Ruhullah Khan of Punchh had arrived and besieged the "Garhi", and that they wanted to know the order of the Noble Sarkar in the matter. After considering it he despatched a reply that they should stay there for a little time when more troops with rations of grain would reach them. A letter was sent to Akbar Khan of Rajauri that he should keep the new men in service and send them to the "Garhi" of Behramgalla, after assuring them that their salaries would be paid by the Noble Sarkar. Two hundred rupees were given to Sherbaz Khan to meet his requirements. A reply full of cordial sentiments was sent to the letter of Raja Sansar Chand. The Noble Sarkar held a private conference with Diwan Muhkam Chand and Rani Sada Kaur, his mother-in-law, and said that the province of Kashmir had remained out of his hands simply on account of (the conduct of) the troops of Bhayya Ram Singh, the traitor, that in this expedition lakhs of rupees had been sent and a great deal of disgrace and insult had been incurred by him from the view-point of his rivals and that at time he had no other sympathetic friend beside them. They replied that they were prepared to make all sacrifices for him, even including their lives and property, although it was very unfortunate that the Noble Sarkar did not accept their earlier suggestion, *viz.* that it was advisable for him to stay on in the town of Gujrat or in Rajauri and to send only his troops forward, because in that case all things might have turned out quite satisfactorily through his prestige. They also said that, even then, by the grace of God and by his own glory, they would, in the month of Chet, make themselves responsible for the conquest of Kashmir, provided the Noble Sarkar would keep himself assured, call Bhayya Ram Singh to his own presence, and scold him suitably. The Noble Sarkar said that he would do so. Fixing an allowance of ten rupees a day he sent two horsemen to bring Bhayya Ram Singh to his presence. After that all went out and the Noble Sarkar went into the zenana, took his meals, and at noon laid himself down to rest. When four hours of the day were left he awoke again and came out to the garden where he instructed Sabit Khan Afghan to recruit horsemen. The Noble Sarkar rode out and inspected the city walls, and later on went into

156

the fort after enjoying a pleasure trip. He kept on talking to his associates until the night had passed four hours, and took his meals and laid himself down to rest when it had passed one quarter. All's well otherwise.

1814 (26)

Deorhi of Sirdar Ranjit Singh Bahadur. Sunday, dated 4th September, 1814 (18th Ramzan, 1229 A.H.), Lahore.

A letter was sent to Kanwar Kharak Singh, the eldest son, asking him to present himself soon together with Sultan Khan, the Raja of Bhimbar, after distributing salaries to his troops. Salaries were distributed among the battalion of Sheikh Basawan, the commandant, while the price of the various articles belonging to the Noble Sarkar, which had been lost in the battle, was deducted from them. At the request and responsibility of Sujan Rae Adalti, Sheikh Yusaf was set free with the order that he must go to the district of Manjha, should capture the Sikhs who had run away from the battlefield and bring them to the presence of the Noble Sarkar. The aforesaid person departed. Sukh Dial was ordered to get ready short uniform tunics of "Banat" and bags for storing foods.[78]

(به سکهدیال بنا بر تیار کوئی بانات و لوشه دان حکم دادند)

A letter came from the revenue collector of Sujanpur with a Hundi of five thousand rupees. It was written to him in reply that he should speedily present himself with the papers of annual contributions. Umaid Singh Jaswal was granted a robe of honour on his departure towards his home. Shadi Khan commandant was warned that no theft be allowed to take place in the town. All's well otherwise.

1814 (27)

News of the Deorhi of Sirdar Ranjit Singh Bahadur. dated 15th September, 1814 (29th Ramzan, 1229 A.H.), Lahore.

The Noble Sarkar got up early in the morning and came out to the place fixed for the court. Bhai Gurbakhsh Singh, Diwan Bhawani Dass, Sukh Dial, Hakim Aziz-ud-Din Khan, and other sirdars came in and made their customary obeisance. The Noble Sarkar said to Hakim Aziz-ud-Din Khan in privacy that a very large sum of money had been spent in the expedition to Kashmir, and that it was necessary for all of them — the three brothers — who were great well-wishers of the Noble Sarkar, to give

157

him one hundred and fifty thousand rupees each. The Hakim, folding his hands, replied that his life and property were entirely at the disposal of the Noble Sarkar, that he had only sixty thousand rupees with him. The Noble Sarkar heard this and kept quiet. Sukh Dial was ordered that out of the fifteen rupees which formed the daily allowance of Sabat Khan Afghan, ten rupees should be given as such to Sherbaz Khan and five rupees to Sultan Khan, the brother of Bakhshi Ruhullah Khan of Punchh, and that a Jagir would also be granted to Sabat Khan. Hukma Singh Thanadar was emphatically ordered to keep watch over the town of Lahore and specially to exercise great vigilance with regard to Hazrat Shah Shuja-ul-Mulk. The Kotwal came and stated, that two Afghans took one grocer away from the city, seized a gold bracelet from his person, and then killed and buried him, that the relatives of the grocer, on learning this, went after those Afghans in great fury and murdered them, and that although the latter had only done this by way of revengefulness yet they had no authority from the Noble Sarkar to have done so. A letter came from the garrison master of Attock, stating the troops which had been sent forward had not yet reached there, while the zamindars of that district had raised to their heads in revolt, adding that the brother of Sirdar Fateh Khan Wazir was collecting a force in Peshawar, though it was impossible for him to succeed in raising money. In the afternoon the Noble Sarkar took his meals and laid himself down to take rest. He got up again at about the third quarter of the day and came out. The staff and the officials made their customary bow . . . . (the text mutilated) . . . . The Noble Sarkar went in, enjoyed the dance of the dancing girls, and later on took his meals when half the night had passed and laid himself down to rest. All's well otherwise.

1814 (28)

Deorhi of Sirdar Ranjit Singh Bahadur. dated 15th September, 1814 (29th Ramzan, 1229 A.H.), Lahore.

Hakim Aziz-ud-Din Khan was told in privacy that as a huge amount of money was expected to have been spent on the expeditions to Kashmir, it was necessary that they all the three brothers—should give to him one hundred thousand rupees. He folded his hands and said that, though he had the whole of his property and life ready for sacrifice for the Noble Sarkar, yet at that time he only had sixty thousand rupees with him and that the Noble Sarkar could take at once. The Noble Sarkar heard this and kept quiet. Sukh Dial was ordered that out of the daily allowance of fifteen rupees which were being paid to Sabat Khan Pathan on behalf of the Noble Sarkar, ten rupees should be paid daily to Sherbaz Khan and five rupees to Sultan Khan, the brother of Bakhshi Ruhullah Khan of Punchh, and that a Jagir would soon be granted to Sabat Khan. A letter came from the garrison master of Attock mentioning that the troops which the Noble Sarkar had despatched in that direction had not reached there by that time, and that the zamindars of that district had risen in revolt. He further added that the brother of Sirdar Fateh Khan Wazir was collecting troops in Peshawar but it would not be possible for him to raise money. After considering these contents the Noble Sarkar rode out and went to the Shalamar Gardens where enjoyed the dance of the dancing girls for some time. All's otherwise.

1814 (29)

Deorhi of Sirdar Ranjit Singh Bahadur. Friday, dated 16th September, 1814 (1st Shawwal), the Village of Patteki.

The Noble Sarkar marched from the Shalamar Garden early in the morning and, on his arrival in the village of Patteki entered his camp.

Saturday, dated 17th September, 1814 (2nd Shawwal 1229 A.H.), Amritsar.

The Noble Sarkar ordered his departure in the morning and entered Amritsar when the day had advanced one quarter. He remained after that in the fort of Gobindgarh. He ordered Kanwar Kharak Singh, the eldest prince, to look after the equipment of his troops very carefully, to show consideration and patronage to every one, and never to remain ignore of his affairs. Kanwars Sher Singh and Tara Singh, the princes, were told that they would soon be granted Jagirs. Nand Singh, the representative of the Noble Sarkar, after paying his respects presented a letter from Colonel Nasir-ud-Daula Bahadur and stated that he had brought Munshi Abdullah Khan, a reliable person of the Colonel Sahib Bahadur, with him and had set up his camp in the mansion of Sukha Nand. The Noble Sarkar relied that he had done well. The Noble Sarkar enquired after the health of Colonel Sahib Bahadur and of other sahibs from him. The dance of the dancing girls began and the Noble Sarkar kept on watching. All's well otherwise.

News of the Deorhi of Sardar Ranjit Singh Bahadur. Wednesday, dated 28th September, 1814 (13th Shawwal, 1229 A. H.), Lahore.

The Noble Sarkar got up early in the morning and came out to the Saman Burj. The sirdars usually present came in and make their customary bow. Hamir Singh, the Vakil of the Raja of Patiala, came in and made his obeisance and was ordered to state if he had received any news about Raja Bhag Singh. He replied that he knew only one thing and that was that the said Raja having left the town of Jind along with Kanwar Partap Singh, had gone over to Hansi, had met Mr. William Frazer Sahib,[77] the elder, and Colonel Arnold Sahib Bahadur, and had set up his tent outside Hansi, adding that no further definite and final news had yet been received. He further stated that the English Sahibs had also sent for Kanwar Fateh Singh, the eldest son of the aforesaid Raja and it remained to be seen what would be decided. Hukma Singh Thanadar was told that he was given the post of keeping all kinds of provision for feasts and entertainments in his custody. He declined it, but the Noble Sarkar, granting him a robe of honour consisting of three garments, issued to him a letter of authority prepared in his office for the same work regarding Lahore, Pathankot, Sialkot, etc. The Noble Sarkar asked Diwan Singh of Fatehgarh why he had run away from the "Garhi" at Behramgalla. He replied that the troops of Ruhullah Khan of Punchh and Akbar Khan of Rajauri had established such entrenchments around the "Garhi" that no water or grain could reach him from without, that he had nothing else but grain left with him, that therefore he grew helpless and felt hard-pressed, and that he was thus forced to surrender it to them. A letter was sent to Raja Fateh Singh Ahluwalia, ordering him that he must get ready his troops, for he would be sent towards Attock in the month of Katak. Hakim Aziz-ud-Din stated that the Raja was a little annoyed at heart with the Noble Sarkar who replied that whatever the people talked was quite wrong, because they had been friends for a very long time, adding that if by chance any annoyance existed in his mind against the Noble Sarkar, his grievances would be removed within one hour of their meeting together. The representative of Raja Akbar Khan of Rajauri came in, offered five rupees as Nazar, and paid his respects. The Noble Sarkar, after enquiring after the health of his master, asked him to state how many men from among those who had accompanied Muhammad Azim Khan had been killed in the battle. He replied that five sirdars and about a thousand men of his tribe had been slain, adding that at that time that Khan was setting right the "Garhis". In the afternoon the Noble Sarkar went into the zenana, took his meals, and laid himself down to rest, while those who were present went away. When four hours of the day were left, he got up again and came out to the garden where the sirdars and his associates presented themselves. He asked Qazi Kamal-ud-Din as to how it was that the representative of Bhai Lal Singh had not come with the horse, and was told that he would be coming that day or on the day following. Jalal, the carpet layer, was granted one Benares Dupatta. At nightfall the Noble Sarkar rode out to the bank of the river Ravi for recreation, and, on return, went into the zenana. He took his meals and laid himself down to rest when the night had passed one quarter. All's well otherwise.

1814 (31)

News of the Deorhi of Sirdar Ranjit Singh Bahadur. Friday, dated 30th September, 1814 (15th Shawwal, 1229 A.H.); the Royal Fort, Lahore.

The Noble Sarkar got up early in the morning and came out to the Saman Burj where, as usual, the sirdars came in and made their customary obeisance. The Noble Sarkar ordered Mat Singh Bharania to show his troops on parade which was to be held on the Dusehra Day, when he must present them properly equipped. Moolraj, the accountant of the special royal horse attendants, was made to realize the salary of these attendants for six months from the late Jaimal Singh's son, who was at that time in prison but whose release was now ordered. Johri Mal was granted a robe of honour consisting of three garments and was allowed to leave for his home. Chet Singh commandant stated that the sepoys of his battalion had seized the house and goods of the late Gur Singh, according to the order of the Noble Sarkar. The Noble Sarkar told him to deliver all the confiscated articles into his treasury. Hukma Singh, the Thanadar of Lahore, was asked to keep all the necessary documents concerning the various Pargannas. Sujan Rae, the dismissed "Adalti", was called in and set at liberty, after having been made pay something by way of Nazrana. The Noble Sarkar ordered Sukh Dial to pay the price of two hundred guns which had arrived from Kotli, and asked that another two hundred similar guns should be constructed. A reliable person came from Hazrat Shah Shuja-ul-Mulk, asking permission on behalf of the said Shah to leave that place. The Noble Sarkar replied that he would be allowed to depart. In the afternoon those who were present walked out, and the Noble Sarkar went into the zenana, took his meals, and laid himself down to rest. He got up again at about the third quarter of the day and came out to the place for the court when four hours of the day were left. His associates presented themselves. The messengers (Jauri) came and stated that Muhammad

Azim Khan, the ruler of Kashmir, was busily engaged in arranging his troops and in strengthening the forts, the "Garhis", the "Nakkas" (passages), etc., that Ruhullah Khan of Punchh had become his resourceful adviser, and that the ruler of Kashmir still continued to stay in the neighbourhood of Baramula. Rewarding the messengers (Jauri) with ten rupees, he rode out to the bank of the river Ravi for recreation, and, on return at nightfall, went over to the garden. It was stated that Qaji Amar Singh Thapa, the Paymaster of the Gurkha troops, was posting the newly recruited sepoys on the "ghats" and "nakkas", and was visiting the various places in his division with a view to strengthen them. After hearing this he went into the zenana, took his meals and laid himself down to rest when the night had passed one quarter. All went on well during the night.

Saturday, dated 1st October, 1814 (16th Shawwal, 1229 A.H.)

The Noble Sarkar got up early in the morning and came out to the place fixed for the court where, as usual, the sirdars came in and made their customary obeisance. One Kandhara Singh by name, was given charge of fifty new horsemen and also granted a Jagir worth seventeen thousand rupees. He accepted his charge. A messenger came and delivered a letter from the garrison master of Makhad, mentioning that the zamindars of that district were in revolt, were girding up their lions, and were busy in plundering the country-side and waylaying the travellers. It expressed a hope that the Noble Sarkar would soon despatch adequate forces in direction to punish them. After considering the contents it was written to him in reply that he should remain alert and vigilant, and that after the Dusehra festival troops would be sent to that place for punishment of zamindars. A letter was sent to the garrison master of Gobindgarh, ordering him to get ready caps and other articles of the uniforms for the battalions speedily and to send them over the Noble Sarkar.[78] The Noble Sarkar distributed two rupees to each of the Brahmans by name. A letter was sent to Sirdar Desa Singh Majithia, asking to march soon together with his troops to the fort of Attock. Fazaldad Khan, the zamindar of the district of Gorak, paid his respects, presented one horse and Nazar and was ordered to pay up promptly the revenue-tax for his division. At noon those who were present went away and the Noble Sarkar went into the zenana, took his meals, and laid himself down to rest. He got up again at about the third quarter of the day and came out to the garden when four hours of the day were left. His associates and attendants presented themselves. He inspected the accounts of Sukh Dail, and despatched a letter full of cordial sentiments to Akbar Khan of Rajauri.

162

The revenue collector of Shahdara was ordered to undertake the repair of the mausoleum and the garden of Jahangir Badshah in the best possible manner. Raja Garba Singh was allowed to leave for his home with a grant of a robe of honour consisting of seven garments. The Noble Sarkar sent fifteen rupees to Chhajju Bhagat.[79] He fixed fifty thousand rupees to be realized from the daughter of the late Mian Khairata and made over Qazi Amir-ud-Din and other employees to the late Khairata to her. He held a private conference with Munshi Abdullah Khan, a reliable person of Nawab Nasir-ud-Daula Bahadur. At nightfall those who were present went away and the Noble Sarkar went into the zenana, took his meals and laid himself down to sleep for the night. All's well otherwise.

1814 (32)

Deorhi of Sirdar Ranjit Singh Bahadur. Wednesday, dated 5th October, 1814 (20th Shawwal, 1229 A.H.), Lahore.

A letter from Diwan Muhkam Chand intimated that he would present himself to the Noble Sarkar after a week, after distributing salaries to his troops. Sujan Rae "Adalti" who had been dismissed from his post was appointed "Darogha" on his presentation of five thousand rupees as Nazrana. Fourty-two prisoners were released. It was written in reply to a letter from Dewa Singh, who was appointed in the fort of Attock, that he should stay there for a few days more, that he should give two thousand rupees to the representatives of Sarbuland Khan and others appointed in the fort of Attock, and should give them through their Vakils. The daughter of the late Mian Khairata, the Darogha of the Topkhana, delivered to the Noble Sarkar ten thousand rupees out of the fifty thousand. He ordered the ironsmiths to prepare five hundred cannon balls each weighing ten seers. A letter from the garrison master of Attock intimated that Ghafoor Khan had marched away from Peshawar towards Attock up to a distance of ten kos under the direction of Sirdar Fateh Khan Wazir, that the people owing to the fear of his approach had been fleeing in various directions, and requested that the Noble Sarkar should speedily send reinforcements. All's well otherwise.

1814 (33)

Deorhi of Sirdar Ranjit Singh Bahadur. Thursday, dated 13th October, 1814 (28th Shawwal, 1229 A. H.), Lahore.

The Vakil of Raja Fateh Singh Ahluwalia stated that his master was ill, and requested the Noble Sarkar to send Hakim Khair Shah Khan to treat him. The Noble Sarkar replied that he would do so. Dhana Singh Malwai said that, according to the order of the Noble Sarkar, he had the troops of Rani Sada Kaur and those of Ramgarh enter the fort of Attock. The Noble Sarkar said that he had done well. A letter from the accountant, in charge of the affairs of the garrison master of the fort of Kangra, intimated that one Prem Singh and a Qadir Bakhsh Machhi, who were appointed in that fort and entered into a conspiracy with Raja Bhoop Singh of Haripur, that they had promised to deliver that fort to that Raja, that the latter had come to the fort with two hundred men, but that by the glory of the Noble Sarkar he (the writer) becoming aware of the fact had put in prison both of those persons and turned the followers out of the fort, and that Prem Singh had managed to escape while Qadir Bakhsh was still in person. After considering the contents the Noble Sarkar sent him words of praise and appreciation in reply, and asked him to send Qadir Bakhsh to his presence with great caution and care. It was written to the garrison master of Attock to write to the Noble Sarkar an account of Sirdar Fateh Khan Wazir, after finding out the details. Mehtab Rae, the accountant of Diwan Muhkam Chand, was admitted into a private conference which went on for a long time. Munshi Abdudllah Khan, who had come under summons of the Noble Sarkar stated with reference to negotiations which were going on between him and Himmat Singh and Bhir Singh Bahadur, that whatever decision the Noble Sarkar wanted to give, he must send in writing in a letter to Colonel Sahib Bahadur. Talks about various topics and the English Sahib continued after that for a while. All's well otherwise.

1814 (34)

News of the Deorhi of Sirdar Ranjit Singh Bahadur. Wednesday, dated 25th October, 1814 (11th Ziqaad, 1229 A.H.), Lahore.

The Noble Sarkar got up early in the morning and came out to the garden. Bhai Gurbakhsh Singh, Himmat Singh Chillawala, Sirdar Karam Singh, Jodha Singh Pinpi, Ram Singh, Hakim Aziz-ud-Din Khan, and several other sirdars came in and made their customary obeisance. The Noble Sarkar inspected the drill of the orderly youths and later watched the firing of the guns. Karrori Mal came in to pay his respects through Ramanand Sahu, and the Noble Sarkar enquired after his health. He ordered Sujan Rae, the dismissed "Adalti," that he should daily keep him informed about the battalions. Sheikh Budha stated that he wanted some cloth for making bags to contain gunpowder, and was ordered to purchase it from the bazaar, and was told that its price would be paid by the Noble

164

Sarkar. Khushal Singh, Jamadar, stated that he had already sent two hundred horsemen to Mandi and maintained them there, and that they expected to be given something to meet their expenses. The Noble Sarkar ordered him to take five hundred rupees from Ramanand Sahu and give it to them. Action was taken according to the order. Ramanand presented ten rolls of muslin which were liked and taken by the Noble Sarkar who ordered him to purchase fifty pairs of shawls for his use. It was stated that Sheikh Ahmad, the Amil of Jullundur, had embezzled five thousand rupees from the revenues of the Noble Sarkar who said that investigations would be made and the money would be realised from him. Sukh Dial was ordered to get ready, under his own personal attention, one "howdah" for the use of the Noble Sarkar. Ram Kishen, the writer of the news of Shahjahanabad, sent the news of that place, and the Noble Sarkar, on learning it, gave six rupees by way of reward to the messenger. A letter was sent to Raja Bir Singh of Nurpur to send soon to the Noble Sarkar one pair of trained falcons. It was stated that the troops of the English Sahibs had gathered together in the cantonment of Ludhiana, and were about to march towards the country of the Gurkhas, The Noble Sarkar heard this and kept quiet. He told Dhonkal Singh commandant that salary for two months would be distributed among his battalion on the following day. In the afternoon those who were present went away, and the Noble Sarkar went into the zenana, took his meals and laid himself down to take rest. He got up again, at about the third quarter of the day, and came out to his audience chamber when four hours of the day were left. The sirdars usually present came in and made their customary obeisance. Sukh Dial Sahu was ordered to explain his accounts to Munshi Devi Dass, whereupon he replied that he would not like to explain it to that person. The Noble Sarkar inspected the orderly youths, and gave one gold necklace to each of the row of them. He ordered Duni Chand, Chet Ram, and other "sarrafs" to get ready very soon a gold necklace worth five hundred rupees. Chet Ram, something in privacy, and was told that he would be called from Ramgarh, presented a letter containing cordial sentiments from his master. The Noble Sarkar awarded two rupees to the messenger, and a Jagir worth two thousand rupees in the division of Pathankot to one, Raju Singh. Karam Chand was ordered to distribute salary of two months among the battalion of Dhonkal Singh, and was told to take some money and purchase two horses from the merchants. A letter from the garrison master of Makhad intimated that the zamindars of that place had revolted. The Noble Sarkar rewarded the messenger with five rupees. He held a parade of the camels of the battallion of Chet Singh commandant, and gave them two hundred rupees to meet their expenses, ordering them also to keep ready with all equipments. It was stated that the disposition of Sherbaz Khan, the nephew of Ruhullah Khan of Punchh, who was in Lahore at that time, was abnormal owing to high temperature, and the Noble Sarkar sent Munshi Devi Dass to enquire after his health. Fazaldad Khan of Daska paid two thousand rupees regarding revenue into the treasury of the Noble Sarkar. Shadi Khan commandant stated that ten thieves were in prison with him for a long time, and was ordered to release them with a warning. When the night had passed one quarter those who were present went away, and the Noble Sarkar went into the zenana, took his meals and laid himself down to take rest.

Thursday, dated 27th October, 1814 (12th Ziqaad, 1229 A. H.)

The Noble Sarkar got up early in the morning and came out to the Saman Burj when the day had advanced four hours. The sirdars usually present came in and made their customary obeisance. He inspected the papers of Sukh Dial Sahu for four hours, and after that rode out to the bank of the river Ravi, went into a boat, enjoyed a trip on the river, sent for two cannons from Ghaus Khan's Topkhana, and watched their firing. He came out of the boat and a Brahman approached him with some complaint. He ordered for his arrest and gave him into the custody of Khushal Singh Jamadar. When the day had advanced one quarter the Noble Sarkar returned from that place, entered the fort and sent four bows for Raja Sansar Chand. He ordered Raja Ram Pandit that he should always perform "Hom" in honour of Deviji on behalf of the Noble Sarkar. A robe of honour consisting of seven garments, a turban gem, a bejewelled under-turban, and one horse were granted to Raja Sultan Khan of Bhimbar as tokens of his kindness. At the time of noon he went into the zenana, took his meals and laid himself down to take rest. He got up again at about the third quarter of the day and came out to the garden. The sirdars came in and made their customary obeisance. The Noble Sarkar inspected the drill of the special orderly youths and watched the firing of the guns. The representative of the Raja of Suket-Mandi came in, presented two rupees on his own behalf, and one gaunt horse and a letter from his master, and the Noble Sarkar enquired after his health. Chhajju Misar, the Amil of Kot Kangra, came in, presented a Nazar of one tray of sweetmeats and paid his respects to the Noble Sarkar who enquired about the affairs of that district and the rajas of the mountainous regions. Khushal Singh Jamadar stated that Sher Singh of Jodhpur was present at the "Deorhi," and was told that he would be called in on the following day. Mazhar Ali, the Darohga of the cannons driven by horses, was given one cannon. Misri Khan Ruhila was ordered to go to Wazirabad to protect the people from thieves and robbers there. It was stated that Hazrat Shah Shuja-ul-Mulk was suffering great inconvenience on account of the shortage of funds, and the Noble Sarkar ordered that he should be paid two thousand rupees to meet his expenses. The Noble Sarkar inspected some young men and engage ten of them in his service. It was stated that one hundred maunds of gunpowder, sent by the Amil of Kot Kamalia, had arrived, and the Noble Sarkar ordered that it should be deposited in the "kotha". Action was taken according to the order. After that Kandhara Singh was awarded one mortar, and was ordered to maintain fifty more horsemen. A letter came from Nihal Singh Attariwala, stating that he would soon come to present himself to the Noble Sarkar. The representative of the Raja of Jasrota stated that he wanted to know the orders with respect to himself. The Noble Sarkar replied that his master had taken ten thousand rupees from him at Punchh, and he must return that sum. Munshi Devi Dass was ordered to distribute one hundred rupees among the poor every day. Shadi Khan commandant was ordered to realise five hundred rupees from Jawala Singh, the son of Mat Singh Bharania, regarding the balance of his revenue. Rae Sukh, the Darogha of the Topkhana of Khairata, stated that some iron was needed for cannons, and was told that he would be given the same. A letter came from the son of Nawab Muzaffar Khan of Multan stating that he had sent his revenue with his representative, and hoping that it would reach him (the Noble Sarkar) very soon, adding at the same time that he should not send his troops in that direction. It was reported that Hazrat Mahmud Shah, Sirdar Fateh Khan Wazir, and Shahzada Kamran had combined together in Qandhar and were proposing to march towards Dera Ghazi Khan, that Ata Muhammad Khan, the Nazim of Kashmir, had been captured by them and that they were busy in gathering troops. After hearing this the Noble Sarkar went into the zenana, and, after taking his meals, when the night had passed one quarter, laid himself down to take rest. All's well otherwise.

1814 (35)

Deorhi of Sirdar Ranjit Singh Bahadur. Wednesday, dated 26th October, 1814 (11th Ziqaad, 1229, A.H.), Lahore.

The Noble Sarkar inspected the drill of the orderly youths and the firing of the guns. Sujan Rae, who had been dismissed from the post of "Darogha-i-Adalat," was ordered to explain daily to the Noble Sarkar the affairs of the various battalions. Khushal Singh Jamadar was given five hundred rupees at his own request to meet the expenses of two hundred horsemen which he had engaged in service at Mandi. Ten rolls of muslin were taken from Ramanand Sahu who was told to purchase fifty pairs of fine shawls for the Noble Sarkar. Sukh Dial was ordered to get ready one silver "howdah" for the use of the Noble Sarkar. It was stated that Sheikh Ahmad had embezzeld five hundred rupees from the revenues of Jullundur. The Noble Sarkar said that investigations would be made and the sum would be realised from him. He carefully considered the news of the events of Shahjahanabad and rewarded the carrier of the news. A letter was sent to Raja Bir Singh of Nurpur asking him to send a couple of falcons, trained to be kept on the hand. It was stated that the English troops had assembled in the cantonment of Ludhiana with a view to conquer the country of the Gurkhas. The Noble Sarkar gave one gold necklace to each of the two orderly youths and ordered Duni Chand and other brokers and dealers in gold to get ready several gold laces. A letter came from Sirdar Jodh Singh of Ramgarh and the Noble Sarkar rewarded the messenger after considering the letter. One, Raju Singh by name, was granted a Jagir worth two thousand rupees in the divisions of Pathankot. Dhonkal Singh commandant was ordered to distribute salaries for two months to the men of his battalion. Two horses were purchased from a merchant. A letter from the garrison master of Makhad intimated that the zamindars of that district had revolted. The Noble Sarkar inspected the parade of the battalion of Chet Singh commandant, gave two hundred rupees towards their expenses, and ordered that they should get ready, well equipped and accounted. Munshi Devi Dass was sent to bring news about Sherbaz Khan, the brother of Raja Ruhullah Khan of Punchh, who was sick at that time.

Thursday, dated 27th October (12th Ziqaad.)

The Noble Sarkar sent four bows to Raja Sansar Chand, and in token of his kindness gave a robe of honour consisting of seven garments, a turban gem, a bejewelled under-turban and one horse to Raja Sultan Khan of Bhimbar. The representative of the Raja of Suket-Mandi presented two rupees on his own behalf and one gaunt horse and a letter from his master Chhajju Misar, the revenue collector of Kot Kangra, presented cannon to be driven by horses was granted to Mazhar Ali Darogha. Misri Khan Ruhila was ordered to go to Wazirabad to establish guard against robbers and dacoits, and also to send two thousand rupees to Hazrat Shah Shuja-ul-Mulk to meet his expenses. one hundred maunds of gunpowder, sent by the revenue collector of Kot Kamalia, reached the Noble Sarkar and was stored into the "kotha". Quandhara Singh was granted one mortar, and was also told to recruit and maintain fifty more horsemen. Munshi Devi Dass was ordered to distribute one hundred rupees daily to the poor on behalf of the Noble Sarkar. A letter came from the Nawab of Multan, intimating that he had sent the revenue tax through his representative and requesting that troops should not be despatched against him. It was stated that Hazrat Mahmud Shah, Sirdar Fateh Khan Wazir, and Shahzada Kamran had combined together in Qandhar and were planning to march towards Dera Ghazi Khan, that Ata Muhammad Khan, the Nazim of Kashmir, had been thrown into prison, and that troops were being collected together. The Noble Sarkar heard this and went inside. All's well othersiwe.

1814 (36)

News of the Deorhi of Sirdar Ranjit Singh Bahadur. Thursday, dated 3rd of November, 1814 (19th Ziqaad, 1229 A. H.), Lahore.

The Noble Sarkar got up early in the morning and came out to the garden when the day had advanced four hours. Bhai Gurbakhsh Singh, Jawala Singh, Jal Singh, Sukh Dial, Hukma Singh, Himmat Singh Chillawala, Diwan Ganga Ram, Hakim Aziz-ud-Din and other sirdars came in and made their customary obeisance. The Noble Sarkar inspected the drill of the orderly youths and observed the firing of the guns. A letter came from Hari Singh and Shiam Singh, reporting their own arrival. A letter from Diwan Muhkam Chand relating to the affairs of Phillaur was brought in and the messenger was awarded five rupees. Bhai Gurbakhsh Singh stated that Kanwar Partab Singh, the son of Raja Bhag Singh, sought suitable employment under the Noble Sarkar who replied that he should be told to wait for a few days, and should be assured that he would be invited within ten or fifteen days to an interview. A letter from Raja Fateh Singh Ahluwalia intimated that he had mustered his troops and would present himself on the occasion of Diwali. After considering the contents the Noble Sarkar rewarded the messenger with two rupees. Qazi Kamal-ud-Din, the representative of Raja Jaswant Singh of Nabha, was asked to state whether the Raja had reached Nabha or not. He replied that he had not yet reached there. The Noble Sarkar after inquiring about the health of Bhai Lal Singh from his reliable person Sheikh Ramzani and talking to him for two hours, told him to go and tell his master that he would be invited on the arrival of Governor Sahib Bahadur in the district of Shahjahanabad. Ramanand Sahu came in and requested that the Noble Sarkar should give some place on contract to Karori Mal. The Noble Sarkar told him to take security from him for the lease and promised to grant him a place. Diwan Ganga Ram requested for money to meet his expenses and was told that it would be given to him. A letter from Nand Singh, the Vakil of the Noble Sarkar, intimated that he had reached the cantonment of Ludhiana, and had an interview with Colonel Nasir-ud-Daula Bahadur, adding, that the Colonel Sahib had marched away towards the mountainous regions. The messenger was awarded two rupees. Khushalmal Adalti was emphatically ordered to pay up to the treasury of Noble Sarkar whatever income he had realised from the administration of justice. A reliable person was sent to bring Sirdar Jodh Ramgarhia. It was stated that the Sikh forces, beyond the river Satluj, had gone away with Colonel Nasir-ud-Daula Bahadur. The Noble Sarkar heard this and went into the zenana at noon, took his meals, and laid himself down to rest. He got up again when four hours of the day were left and came out to the garden. His associates and officials came in and made their customary obeisance. An order was sent to the Darogha of the swivels to leave for Amritsar. Four hundred rupees were given to Bhawani Dass of the low stature to meet his expenses. The Vakil of the Raja of Chamba requested some money to meet his expenses and also sought permission to leave. The Noble Sarkar told him to stay on for a few days. The Vakil of the Raja of Baklidamtorwala was sent for and asked to give some information about that district. He replied that the brother of Sirdar Fateh Khan Wazir was tyrannising over that district, and that if the troops of the Noble Sarkar should go there he could be punished. After that the Noble Sarkar rode out to the river Ravi for recreation, and, inspected the drill of the battalion of Mazhar Ali, and the firing of his Topkhana. When the night had passed two hours, he went round through the bazaar and then entered the fort and later on the zenana. When the night had passed one quarter, he took his meals and laid himself down to take rest. All's well otherwise.

1814 (37)

News of the Deorhi of Sirdar Ranjit Singh Bahadur. Friday dated 4th November, 1814 (20th Ziqaad, 1229 A.H.), Lahore.

The Noble Sarkar got up early in the morning and came out to his audience chamber when the day had advanced four hours. The sirdars usually present came in and made their customary bow. The Noble Sarkar inspected the drill of the special orderly youths, جوانان ازوئی خاص observed the firing of the guns, and granted mortar to ten Sikh soldiers. The representative of Ahmad Khan of Jhang was called in and allowed to depart with a message for his master that he should collect his troops and present himself. This person was also granted a robe of honour, consisting of three garments, at the time of his departure. Ten camels were purchased from the merchants through Sukh Dial Sahu, Sahib Singh, the messenger, requested the Noble Sarkar to grant him his salary, and was told that he would be paid. The Darogha of the garden of Shalimar came in and presented a "Dali" of flowers, which the Noble Sarkar distributed among his associates. Later, he sent for the elephants and inspected them. A letter came from the representative of the Noble Sarkar, who had gone over to Multan, mentioning that he had reached there, that he had a talk with Nawab Muzaffar Khan of Multan regarding the revenue tax, that the Nawab had told him in reply that the representative of Sirdar Fateh Khan Wazir was demanding it on one side and the Noble Sarkar was asking for it, on the other, and that he had no such means as to be able to pay it to pay both. On learning this the Noble Sarkar asked Dal Singh Bharania what steps were to be taken at that time. He replied that the revenue tax could not be realised from Multan without the despatch of troops in that direction. The Noble Sarkar said that he would do so on his arrival in Amritsar, and then continued discussing this matter for two hours. Ten rolls of "Mahmudi" and "Gulbadan" respectively, were purchased by the Noble Sarkar through Sukh Dial Sahu. At noon those who were present walked out and he went into the zenana, took his meals, and laid himself down to rest. He got up again at about the third quarter of the day and came out to the garden, when the day had advanced four hours. His associates and attendants came in and made their customary obeisance. The Noble Sarkar inspected two young men and recruited them in the battalion of Chet Singh and ordered Sukh Dial Sahu to send the necessary amount of rations of grain to the battalion of the Sikhs. Two hundred rupees were given to Rae Singh, the Darogha of the Topkhana, to meet his expenses. The revenue collector of Amirpur Chumak was ordered to explain the account of his division to Karam Chand, the accountant. A letter came from Raja Hari Singh of Nurpur, mentioning that he had despatched his representative who would soon present himself and would make a verbal statement, which the Noble Sarkar should consider as true and genuine. A letter containing cordial sentiments was addressed to Raja Gurkha and entrusted to his representative to be sent by him. Jawala Singh was ordered to send for five pairs of oxen from his division for carrying the cannons. He replied that he would do so. The Noble Sarkar distributed two hundred rupees to the poor, and then rode out to the open fields for recreation and returned at nightfall. He entered the fort, went into the zenana, and took his meals there. When the night had passed one quarter he again took some food and laid himself down to rest. All's well otherwise.

1814 (38)

Deorhi of Sirdar Ranjit Singh Bahadur. Friday, dated 4th November, 1814 (20th Ziqaad, 1229, A. H.), Lahore.

The Sikh sepoys were granted one mortar each. The representative of Ahmad Khan of Jhang was ordered to go to his master and to tell him to come to the Noble Sarkar alongwith his troops. He was also granted a robe of honour consisting of three garments, as a farewell gift. Ten camels were purchased. A letter of a reliable person of the Noble Sarkar came from Multan, which mentioned that Nawab Sarfraz Khan had been asked to pay the revenue tax to the Noble Sarkar, that he had replied that the representative of Sirdar Fateh Khan Wazir was also demanding it, and that he could not afford to pay the tax to both of them. After considering that letter Sirdar Dal Singh Bharania was asked what was to be done in the matter. He replied that no revenue tax would be realised from that place without the troops of the Noble Sarkar going there. The Noble Sarkar said that he would make some arrangement about the matter on his reaching Amritsar. Two sepoys were recruited and were made to join the battalion of Chet Singh. Two hundred rupees were given to Narain Singh, the Darogha of the Topkhana, to meet his expenses. A letter came from Raja Hari Singh of Nurpur, stating that his representative had left for the court of the Noble Sarkar, who should accept as true whatever statement he would make verbally. A letter containing cordial sentiment was addressed to the Gorkha Raja and entrusted to his representative for despatch. Jawala Singh was ordered (The remaining text is missing.)

1814 (39)

Deorhi of Sirdar Ranjit Singh Bahadur. Sunday, dated 6th November, 1814 (22nd Ziqaad, 1229 A .H.); the Fort of Gobindgarh, Amritsar.

Early in the morning the Noble Sarkar rode out, reached the village of Kallowal, and took his meals there. Dal Sukh Rae, the representative from Patiala, was asked to state the news about the march of Colonel Nasir-ud-Daula Bahadur and the district of Patiala. He requested that the Noble Sarkar might allow Humair Singh to depart. The Noble Sarkar said that he would do so on reaching Amritsar. Ajit Ram, the representative of Bhai Lal Singh, presented a letter containing cordial sentiments from his master, and the Noble Sarkar delivered him a reply in writing. After that

Sabat Khan Afghan stated that if the Noble Sarkar intended to engage him in service it would be good, otherwise he should be allowed to depart. The Noble Sarkar replied that he should rest assured that he intended to show him consideration and patronage. He then rode out and reached Amritsar after traversing a distance of seventeen kos. Kanwar Kharak Singh, the prince, came forward to receive him together with Bhayia Ram Singh, his authorized agent and manager. Imam-ud-Din Khan, the garrison master of Gobindgarh, and several others of his employees, came, made their customary obeisance, and offered Nazars according to their ranks. The Noble Sarkar entered the fort of Gobindgarh in Amritsar and a salute was fired from the cannons. Kanwar Kharak Singh said that it had become known to him that Diwan Muhkam Chand had died in the town of Phillaur. The Noble Sarkar said that that was so and expressed a great deal of sorrow remarking that such a wise and intelligent person of the age at that time was not at all available. A letter was sent to Moti Ram, the son of the deceased Diwan, by way of condolence. All's well otherwise.

1814 (40)

News of the Deorhi of Sirdar Ranjit Singh Bahadur. dated 15th November, 1814(2nd Zilhaj, 1229 A. H.), Amritsar.

The Noble Sarkar got up early in the morning and came out to the tent set apart for audience. The sirdars usually present came in and made their customary obeisance. The Noble Sarkar ordered the staff in charge of the floorings to pitch a "Kanat" near the "Bunga" of the Noble Sarkar besides the tank of Amritsar because he intended watching the sight of the fair from there. Kahan Singh, the son of Bhai Harbhaj Rae, presented two boxes of rubies. A letter from Nand Singh Vakil intimated that Colonel Nasir-ud-Daula Bahadur had conquered the "Garhi" of Nalagarh and established his "Thana" there. The Noble Sarkar began to praise the bravery and courage of the glorious Sahibs immediately on hearing this news, and continued talking about them for two hours. Ram Singh Gadwai was ordered to hold a parade of his horsemen. The representative of the Raja of Mandi sought permission to leave, and was told that the revenue tax of the Noble Sarkar had not yet been paid into his treasury. He replied that he had written to his master and would submit to the Noble Sarkar whatever reply would come. A messenger came and delivered a letter from Nawab Abdul Samad Khan of Dera. After considering it the Noble Sarkar sent him a reply asking him to send two riding horses. This messenger was awarded five rupees. Kanwar Kharak Singh and Bhayia

Ram Singh came in and presented themselves. Ram Singh was questioned about the district of Jammu. He replied that disturbance and unrest still prevailed there, and that he had sent a battalion for the punishment of the zamindars of that place. The Noble Sarkar told him to send more troops, so that they might be punished effectively. The Noble Sarkar distributed two hundred rupees among the poor, and granted one shawl; in token of his kindness, to Chet Singh commandant. In the afternoon he went into the other tent, took his meals, and laid himself down to rest while those who were present walked out one after the other. He got up again at about the third quarter of the day and came out. He rode out to his "Kanat" tent where sirdars made their customary obeisance. He continued enjoying the sight of the fair. Dal Sukh Rae, the Vakil of the Raja of Patiala, was sent for and asked to give some account of the Gurkhas, the Noble Sarkar remarking that he had learnt that the Colonel Sahib Bahadur had conquered the "Garhi" of Nalagarh. He replied that the glory of the glorious Sahibs was very great and their good fortune was making progress every day. For two hours the same talk went on after which that person sought permission to leave. He was told that his departure would be conveniently arranged after a little time. Kanwar Kharak Singh and Bhayia Ram Singh came in and the Noble Sarkar showed the Koh-i-Nur gem to his associates. He told Munshi Devi Dass that if he wanted to take a contract of the seal of the Noble Sarkar, he must agree to pay one hundred and seventy thousand rupees. That person agreed to it. Imam Khan Kotwal was ordered to send five maunds of linseed oil. He replied that he would do so. When the night had passed two hours the Noble Sarkar rode from that place and went to his own tent. Rama Nand Sahu came and requested that the Noble Sarkar should visit his shop according to the old established custom, just as he did in the past after the "Diwa". The Noble Sarkar got up at that very time and went to his shop on foot. The Sahu presented by way of Nazar five trays containing fruits and sweetmeats, five "Ashrafis" and one horse. The Noble Sarkar rode from that place and went to his own tent, took his meals there, and laid himself down to rest for the night. All went on well during the night.

Wednesday, dated 16th November (1814 3rd Zilhaj, 1229, A.H.)

The Noble Sarkar got up early in the morning and rode out to the shop of Rama Nand Sahu. All his associates and sirdars went there to present themselves. The Noble Sarkar ordered Sukh Dial Sahu to pay up the balance of the revenue tax of the division of Pind Dadan Khan, Khushab, etc. He replied that he would do so, and further submitted that the Noble Sarkar could take back all the places and every thing else from him, but must allow his seal to remain with him as previously. The Noble Sarkar heard this and kept quiet. He inspected red "banat" and some other articles from Danu Mal Sarraf, and purchased the same. He asked Rura Mal and Harkishen Dass Sahu of Amritsar to take the seal of the Noble Sarkar on contract jointly. They replied that they would act according to his wishes. When the day had advanced one and a half quarter, he got up from that place, went to the tent, passed into the interior, took his meals, and laid himself down to rest. He got up again at about the third quarter of the day and came out to the tent set apart for audience, where his associates and attendants presented themselves. Baba Naurang Singh stated that Raja Fateh Singh Ahluwalia was leaving Kapurthala on that day or the day following, and would soon be coming. The Noble Sarkar heard this and kept quiet. News of Shahjahanabad, sent by Jamiat Singh, the news agent, was delivered and listened to Rani Sada Kaur, the mother-in-law of the Noble Sarkar, was ordered to present herself on the following day, because, something had to be talked to her. Sirdar Nihal Singh Attariwala was ordered to despatch his troops expeditiously to the fort of Attock. He replied that he would do so. A letter came from Qaji Amar Singh Thapa, mentioning that the English Sahibs contemplated conquering the country of Multan in those days, that though they were at war with him, yet they were on terms of well-established friendship with the King (probably Mahmud Shah), and that at that time it was very necessary for the Noble Sarkar to send him military assistance. The Noble Sarkar heard this and kept quiet. Rama Nand Sahu stated "that the seal must be given to Sukh Dial, but the Noble Sarkar did not make any reply. Sherbaz Khan said that he wanted to know his orders regarding himself. The Noble Sarkar replied that he must accept a Jagir worth four thousand rupees in the division of Amirpur Chumak. He replied that that would not be sufficient for his maintenance. The Noble Sarkar heard this and kept quiet. The messengers (Jauri) were sent towards Hardwar and the Dera of Ram Rae for bringing speedily certain information about those places. Sirdar Dal Singh Bharania stated that Dhana Singh Malwai had shown great . . . . ., spirit of sacrifice in the expedition of Kashmir and expected . . . . . (text mutilated). The Noble Sarkar went to the camp of Bhai Asa Singh and remained there talking for two hours and . . . . . (text mutilated). He himself laid down to rest during the night. All's well otherwise.

News of the Deorhi of Sirdar Ranjit Singh Bahadur. Friday, stated 18th, November, 1814 (5th Zilhaj, 1229, A.H.), Amritsar.

The Noble Sarkar got up early in the morning and inspected the drill of the orderly youths. (خانه بروئ خا) observed the firing of the guns, and then went to the tent where he held his court. The sirdars came in and made their customary obeisance. Moti Ram, the Darogha of the mint, presented one tray of slabs of sugar and paid his respects. A letter from the revenue collector of Sarae Kala conveyed information about that place. The Noble Sarkar considered it and kept it to himself. Some workmen of Kotli had brought two hundred mortars which they presented to the Noble Sarkar, who liked and accepted them. Akbar Khan, the brother of Sherbaz Khan, came in, presented a tray of slabs of sugar, and paid his respects to the Noble Sarkar who enquired from him about the affairs of the mountainous regions, and Punchh etc. He stated that the ruler of Kashmir had granted Ruhullah Khan a robe of honour, a bejewelled under-turban and fifty thousand rupees in cash in recognition of his services. For two hours such talks went on. After that it was written in reply to the letter of the Gurkhas that there existed a relation of friendship and unity between the glorious Sahibs and the Noble Sarkar, therefore, no help of any kind could be given to them by the Noble Sarkar. Sher Singh and Tara Singh were ordered to send for their troops. Five thousand Afghan apples were purchased and sent to Lahore, and Kalian Singh, the Thanadar of that place, was ordered to make them into jam which he should keep in his custody. Fifty special royal horsemen were awarded one mortar each. After taking his meals, he laid himself down to rest at noon, but got up again at about the third quarter of the day and held a court, where all his associates and attendants presented themselves. A messenger arrived and delivered a letter containing cordial sentiments from Ahmad Khan of Jhang and was awarded four rupees. A letter, summoning Rajab Ali of Maharajakot, was sent. The Noble Sarkar listened to the details of the accounts of men appointed in the fort of Gobindgarh from his accountant. Dal Sukh Rae, the representative of the Raja of Patiala, was told that he would be allowed to depart very shortly. A letter from Nand Singh, the representative of the Noble Sarkar, containing an account of the Colonel Sahib Bahadur, arrived. Nadhan Singh presented one tray of slabs of sugar and paid his respect Sukh Dial stated that he had paid up fifty thousand rupees consitituting the balance of the revenue tax, and the Noble Sarkar replied that he had done well. The Noble Sarkar inspected the drill of the battalion of Dhonkal Singh. It was stated that Colonel Nasir-ud-Daula

176

Bahadur had conquered the fort of Balagarh and laid a siege around the fort of Ramnagar in the division of the Gurkhas. The Noble Sarkar remarked that the fortune of the English Sahibs was in the ascendant. He announced that he would soon march towards Tarn Taran. When the night had passed one quarter, he went into the other tent, took his meals, and laid himself down to rest. It went on well otherwise during the night.

1814 (42)

Deorhi of Sirdar Ranjit Singh Bahadur. Wednesday, dated 15th December 1814 (21st Zilhaj, 1229 A.H.); the village of Tadinwal, in the Taaluqa of the Fort of Attock, Towards the North of it.

It was stated that the sepoys of the Noble Sarkar had taken leave from him and gone over to the fort of Gandha Ghar where they had established their camp, and that they had mounted cannons on every tower of it towards the river Attock, though at the same time they were feeling a shortage of gunpowder and balls. The Noble Sarkar heard this and ordered his bearer, Moti, to despatch ten carts laden with balls and five carts with gunpowder in that direction. A messenger came and stated that Muhammad Azim Khan continued to tyrannise over Kashmir, that he had told his councillors that the "chat" of Attock, belonging to the Noble Sarkar, had been taken by his troops who at that time were supposed to have reached the "Ghat" of Makhad etc., for establishing control over those regions, that thus the way for the troops of Afghanistan was supposed to have been opened up, though in reality that way was under the control of the Noble Sarkar, that he was holding out hopes to them of the coming of the troops from Afghanistan and exhorting them to maintain their respective forces ready for war. The Noble Sarkar heard all this, and, rewarding the messenger with four rupees, spoke to his associates and attendants that, by the grace of God, he would achieve the conquest of Kashmir in the month of Phagan. The representative of the Nazim of Multan arrived and stated that whatever revenue tax was due from his master would be paid in instalments, and asked how it was that the Noble Sarkar was planning to despatch troops in that direction. The Noble Sarkar replied that at that time he stood in great need of money and hence if the balance of the amount demanded from him be paid immediately, no troops need be sent in that direction. He replied that the Noble Sarkar must wait for ten days adding that he was writing to his master and might present the whole amount very shortly. The Noble Sarkar said that he would do so. The messengers (Jauri) came from Peshawar and brought the news, that Hazrat Mahmud Shah continued to be in Peshawar, that the Governor of

177

Peshawar had taken a loan of two lakhs of rupees from the money lenders and submitted the same to Mahmud Shah, who had ordered that amount to be distributed among his troops. A letter came from Fateh Khan Wazir from Kuldaig, which is situated at twenty-five kos from Peshawar, stating that he would soon come and present himself. The Noble Sarkar heard this, and, rewarding the messengers (Jauri), made them depart once again in that direction. All's well otherwise.

1814 (43)

Deorhi of Sirdar Ranjit Singh Bahadur. Monday, dated 20th December, 1814 (26th Zilhaj, 1229 A.H.); the Village of Tadinwal, in the Taaluqa of the Fort, Towards the North of it.

A messenger came and delivered a letter from Sirdar Jodh Singh of Kalsia, mentioning that he had met Raja Fateh Singh Ahluwalia who had appointed him to punish the rebellious zamindars of that district, that he would soon march for that purpose, and that the representative of Sher Zaman Khan from Chhacha Hazara had reached there but had not yet held any meeting with him. It was written to him in reply that he should act according to the wish of the said Raja. A messenger came and delivered a letter from Amir Beg, the garrison master of Attock, mentioning that the representative of Sirdar Fateh Khan Wazir had come from Peshawar on the other side of the river Indus with a view to present himself to the Noble Sarkar, that he was accompanied by a troop of one hundred horsemen, that he had asked for a boat to bring him across the river to this side that for this reason he wanted to know the order of the Noble Sarkar in the matter, so that he might act accordingly. It was written to him in reply that he should be allowed to cross the river, but that the "Ghats" must, all the same, be effectively guarded. Dal Sukh Rae, representative of Raja Karam Singh Bahadur, came in and delivered a letter from his own master and another from Misar Budhamal, the latter's reliable manager, plainly dealing with the case of the fort of Malan. The Noble Sarkar asked him where was the Raja Sahib at that time, and was told that he was in Sherpur but intended proceeding to Patiala, where he might have already reached. He expressed his feelings of discomfort about his expenses, whereupon the Noble Sarkar gave him two hundred rupees. Raja Sansar Chand came and met the Noble Sarkar who very respectively made him sit down and continued talking to him about hunting, and telling him that he (the Noble Sarkar) had never hunted a leopard. A letter came from Diwan Bhawani Dass of the low stature, mentioning that he had reached the neighbourhood of the town of Fateh Jang, had laid siege to two or three villages, had forced the zamindars of the place to approach him, and that talks about the revenue tax from the ruler of Fateh Jang were in progress. He further added that he would send a detailed account later. The Noble Sarkar heard this and ordered for a despatch of a reply to him. All's well otherwise.

News of the Sirdar Ranjit Singh Bahadur. Wednesday, dated 1st
February 1815 A.D. (20th Safar, 1230 A. H.), the Fort of Lahore.

On account of the rainfall, the Noble Sarkar kept on drinking wine and listening to the music of the flute in the company of Khushal Singh Jamadar. At about the third quarter of the day he ordered Sultan Mahmud, the son of the late Ghaus Khan, Aziz Khan, Sheikh Badha and other commandants of the battalions to keep ready at their various places, for they would have to proceed towards Multan very shortly. Two men of Mohsin Shah, a representative from Multan, stated that his camp being fixed near that of the representative of Sirdar Fateh Khan Wazir, he was being seriously inconvenienced by a great deal of nuisance, and requested his camp to be removed to a distance. The Noble Sarkar replied on the following day or the day after it would be shifted to some other mansion. Five camels were sent to the battalion of Sewa Singh for purposes of carrying load.

Thursday, dated 2nd February (21st Safar, 1230 A. H.)

The Noble Sarkar ordered Kanwar Kharak Singh, the eldest prince, to present himself soon alongwith Bhayia Ram Singh. Fifteen sepoys were newly recruited. One man was sent to bring Rani Sada Kaur and her grand-childern. One hundred rupees were sent to Mohsin Shah, the Vakil of Multan, for his entertainment. Sirdar Dal Singh Bharania was told that he would be given some other Jagir. A letter from Karam Singh Jahil stated that he had spoken by way of advice to Nihal Singh Attariwala according to the order of the Noble Sarkar, that he had advised him to give up fraternising with Phula Singh Akalia, to turn him out of that place, and to join the troops of Muhkam Chand, but that he did not agree to his suggestions. He (Karam Singh) requested that the Noble Sarkar should send him further instructions as to how he should act in the future. It was stated that Misar Chhajju had fled away, and, thereupon, the Noble Sarkar ordered Sukh Dial to punish him. Muhammad Ali Khan, a Vakil of Sardar Fateh Khan Wazir, presented himself to the Noble Sarkar according to his summons and was ordered to say something about his master. He replied that he did not know where he was encamped in those days. The Noble

Sarkar told him that he would be allowed to depart after a short time from Amritsar, where the Noble Sarkar was shortly going with his camp. Sujan Rae was ordered to give daily an account of his battalion to Hakim Aziz-ud-Din Khan. The Noble Sarkar enquired after his health from Jahandad Khan, the brother of Ata Muhammad Khan, who had come to pay his respects, and told him to take twenty rupees daily from Hakim Aziz-ud-Din Khan. A letter was sent to Hukma Singh Chimni to present himself. A letter of authority was given to Sukh Dial with regard to wax, which was demanded by the workers in the workshop for the construction of a mortar. Dal Singh Bharania and others were told that after a few days' stay at Amritsar, an expedition would be sent from that place for conquering Multan and collecting revenue tax from Bahawalpur and other places, and that afterwards the Noble Sarkar would go and set up his camp in the districts of Jhang and Sialkot. Mehr Chand, a representative of Raja Fateh Singh Ahluwalia, having been granted a robe of honour consisting of five garments, was ordered to go and bring his master at the head of his forces to Amritsar. All's well otherwise.

1815 (2)

Deorhi of Sirdar Ranjit Singh Bahadur. Thursday, dated 9th February, 1815 (28th Safar, 1230 A.H.), Lahore.

The Noble Sarkar ordered Aziz Khan and other commandants to get together the camels which are intended for carrying the load of the battalions. Orders for their presentation to the Noble Sarkar were sent accordingly to Sada Singh Nakai and Nihal Singh Malla. A horse was granted to Fateh Chand, the brother of Raja Sansar Chand of Kangra. Chet Singh commandant was pardoned for his offence, was set free from the person, granted a robe of honour and sent back to his battalion. The Noble Sarkar granted one horse to Raja Sherbaz Khan of Punchh. Later, he asked the astrologer to find the auspicious hour for his departure for Amritsar. They said that Basant Panchami day was the most auspicious day. A letter, expressing cordial sentiments, came from Nawab Muhammad Khan of Bhakhar, and a similar reply was sent to him. The messengers (Jauri) were sent to bring news about Sirdar Fateh Khan Wazir. Dal Singh Bharania was ordered to get ready, for he, at the head of his forces, was to be appointed to proceed towards Multan and Bahawalpur that very day or the day following. Letters of invitation were sent to the zamindars of Maharajakot. Ten newly-manufactured lances were sent to the camp of Sultan Mahmud. A letter, summoning Kanwar Kharak Singh, who had been caught, were sent over to the camp of Ghaus Khan. The news came that Nawab Governor Sahib Bahadur had gone to Meerut, and the Noble Sarkar remarked that it was to be seen where Bhawani Dass would hold an interview with him. The garrison-master of Kangra was sent an order to furnish a detailed list of accounts of dues of the men of rank and position, so that the amount covering their salaries be despatched accordingly. In the country of the Punjab heavy rain continued falling incessantly from the 2nd to the 10th February, and the skies are still overcast with the clouds. The grain is selling at a very cheap rate. All's well otherwise.

1815 (3)

News of the Deorhi of Sirdar Ranjit Singh Bahadur. Thursday, dated 2nd March (19th Rabi-ul-Awwal, 1230 A. H.); the Royal Fort, Lahore.

The Noble Sarkar got up early in the morning and came over to the Saman Burj where the sirdars came and made their customary obeisance. The Noble Sarkar ordered Hira Singh commandant to arrange the drill of his men both times. One horse, sent by Fazal Dad Khan of Daska, was presented to the Noble Sarkar. A letter, summoning Budha Singh Nakka, was sent. Nihal Singh Attariwala requested the Noble Sarkar to grant some Jagir to Phula Singh Akali. The Noble Sarkar said that it would be granted. A letter came from the Raja of Mandi, expressing cordial sentiments. The Noble Sarkar granted a robe of honour, consisting of three garments to Bisakha Singh for his services in connection with the administration of justice out of (one word in the text not clear) Khushal Mai. The Noble Sarkar granted fifty rupees to two bearer-coolies to meet their expenses, and made them depart for bringing water from the Ganges. Hakim Muhammad Ali Khan came and administered a mild aperient to the Noble Sarkar who was afterwards allowed to remain by himself. By the time the day had advanced two quarters and three hours, the medicine had produced the desired effect. Later, he took his meals and laid himself down to take rest. He got up again when only two hours of the day were left and went again into his sleeping chamber where his associates and attendants presented themselves. The Noble Sarkar told the physicians that the taking of an aperient was certainly a means of recovering health. They said that the Noble Sarkar was quite right. The Noble Sarkar ordered Basant Rae, the astrologer, to assist Bisakha Singh in the administration of justice. Each of the zamindars of Dhannigheb was awarded a piece of long cloth piece for a pair of trousers and allowed to leave. The Noble Sarkar ordered Sukh Dial to arrange the despatch of five hundred maunds of gunpowder to the fort of Attock. He replied that he would do so. It was stated that the zamindars of Hasan Abdal had come to see him. The Noble

Sarkar directed that they should come on the following day. He inspected the drill of the special orderly youths, observed the firing of guns, and ordered Dhanni Sahae Khidmatgar to bring the income of the administration of justice from Khushal Mal. The Noble Sarkar enjoyed the music of a flute by Attar Khan, and later, went inside and laid himself down to take rest when the night had passed one quarter.

Friday, dated 3rd March, 1815 (20th Rabi-ul-Awwal)

The Noble Sarkar got up early in the morning and came out to the garden where the officials and sirdars came in and made their customary bow. Hakim Nur-ud-Din Khan said that if the Noble Sarkar liked he would go to Wazirabad for collecting the revenue tax. The Noble Sarkar replied that he could go. A letter came from Raja Fateh Singh Ahluwalia mentioning that he had marched from Kapurthala according to the order of the Noble Sarkar and was crossing the river Beas at that time, and that he would reach his presence soon after collecting his forces. The Noble Sarkar said to his associates that he could see none among the employees of that Raja who might be able to manage the affairs of the whole of his territory. They replied that Chaudhri Qadir Bakhsh held an absolute control over all his affairs, and, whatever he proposed, always did take place. The Noble Sarkar said that Misar Prabhdial would be the best man, but the said Chaudhri would kill him. He said to Nihal Singh Attariwala that, for the time being, he had granted only forty rupees a day to Phula Singh Akalia, but that some Jagir would also be proposed for him later. The representative of Raja Sansar Chand came and stated that his master wanted a loan of two thousand rupees. The Noble Sarkar immediately gave him one thousand rupees, and said that the other thousand would also be shortly given to him. He told Narain Dass, the brother of Diwan Bhawani Dass, that he would soon be sent to Sirdar Fateh Wazir. He submitted that he could not go, and requested that somebody else might be sent there. The Noble Sarkar remarked that all his accountants seemed to tremble at the fear of the said Khan. The Royal horsemen requested for some money to meet their expenses, and the Noble Sarkar replied that they would be given the same. A letter was sent to Fida Khan, summoning him. One thousand rupees were sent as salary of the gunners through Dhonkal Singh. Ghulam Muhammad Khan, the brother of Jahandad Khan, presenting himself, stated that in spite of the fact that the Noble Sarkar had promised him consideration and patronage, nothing at all had been done for him. The Noble Sarkar gave him an assurance that he would be granted a Jagir and some cash to meet his expenses. He ordered Karam Chand to disburse payment for two months to the men of Mazhar Ali. The ironsmiths submitted that they had prepared five thousand iron-balls, and the Noble Sarkar ordered Hakim Imam-ud- Din Khan to make them reach the fort of Gobindgarh at Amritsar, on camels. The zamindars of Chumka came in and complained as follows, "Bhayia Ram Singh has leased out our country to Sultan Khan, the famous man. He is treating us very cruelly. If the Noble Sarkar wants to rob us he may do so with his own hand." The Noble Sarkar consoled and assured them that Bhayia Ram Singh would be spoken to regarding their case, and that henceforth no cruelty would be visited on them. It was stated that Ram Dial, the son of Diwan Moti Ram, had come and entered the town of Lahore. Talks about the fort of Ramgarh continued with those who were present, who stated that only one hundred maunds of maize were its produce. The Noble Sarkar observed that the Gurkhas were foolish to have started fighting against the English Sahibs because they would never be successful, adding that had they been wise, they would have maintained friendship and amicable relations with them. The son of Hakim Rae presented one tray of slabs of sugar as Nazar, and paid his respects to the Noble Sarkar who enquired after his health. In the afternoon he went into the zenana and laid himself down to take rest after his meals. He got up again at about the third quarter of the day, and came out to the garden where his associates and attendants presented themselves. Hakim Aziz-ud-Din Khan stated that he had gone to Hazrat Shah Shuja-ul-Mulk according to the order of the Noble Sarkar, and had asked him to give the "Hundi" about the large sum of money, that the Shah had replied that the "Hundi" was not with him but was with the ladies of his Haram, and that if the Noble Sarkar wanted to take his life he could, otherwise he should let him alone and take all the property that belonged to him (the Shah). The Noble Sarkar heard this and kept quiet. Sukh Dial stated that fifty guns with butts had come from Jandiala, and the Noble Sarkar replied that he would have looked at them on the following day. It was reported that Sukha Singh — a horseman — had come from Raja Jaswant Singh. The Noble Sarkar called upon Daya Singh, a companion of Khushal Singh, and ordered him to proceed with his battalion to Daudpur and to bring Manohar Singh, a zamindar of that place after effecting his capture, and to use military force in case the zamindars showed any opposition. The tailors of the Noble Sarkar came in with two suits of clothes made of brocade, and presented them to the Noble Sarkar who granted them twenty-five rupees as a reward. Dian Singh commandant presented a tray of slabs of sugar in celebration of his own marriage, and the Noble Sarkar distributed the same to those who were present. The experts in charge of the horsemen of the Noble Sarkar stated that dealers in horses had brought some for sale from Dera Ismail Khan. He replied that they would be called in on the following day, and after that he went into the zenana to take his meals and thereafter laid himself down to take rest when the night had passed one quarter. All's well otherwise.

1815 (4)

News of the Deorhi of Sirdar Ranjit Singh Bahadur. Thursday, dated 18th May, 1815 (8th Jamadi-us-Sani), Dinanagar.

The Noble Sarkar got up early in the morning and came to the tent set apart for the court. The officials and sirdars came in and made their customary bow. Pirthi Bilas, the Vakil of the Gurkhas, and Sheo Dat Rae, a reliable person of Raja Maha Chand of Bilaspore, and others, presented themselves and requested that the Noble Sarkar should speak to the Shahs (money-lenders or bankers) of Amritsar to lend them five lakhs of rupees on their promise of a quick repayment. They further requested him to take a written agreement from the Gurkhas and to help them cross the rivers Jamna and Ganges together with a conveyance (Baghi) carrying their effects. The Noble Sarkar said that he would do so, but would first write all about their request to the English Sahibs. Naurang Singh, a reliable person of Raja Sansar Chand of Kot Kangra, was called in and ordered that he should help Desa Singh Majithia and Diwan Bhawani Dass, who were being sent with their forces, presented with them towards the mountainous regions for collecting revenue tax from Kulu and other places. He replied that he would do so. The Noble Sarkar then made Naurang Singh, Diwan Bhawani Dass and Desa Singh Majithia to depart with the grant of a robe of honour consisting of five garments to each. He further ordered all the rajas to march away together with the said Diwan, and they all walked out. A letter from the garrison master of Manglan intimated that Raja Akbar Khan of Rajauri had in those days, together with the other rajas of that region, set up a siege around that fort, and that, if some troops would speedily be deputed to reinforce him, it would be all right. In reply he was thoroughly assured. In the afternoon the Noble Sarkar went to the other tent, and laid himself down to rest after taking his meals. All those who were present walked out. The Noble Sarkar got up again at about the third quarter of the day, and came out to the tent set part for audience in the usual manner. The sirdars came in and made their customary bow. The Noble Sarkar called in Ram Dial, the news-writer of the English Sahibs, and told him that he had just received a letter from Nand Singh, the representative of the Noble Sarkar himself, stating that the fort of Malawan had been conquered, that Kanwar Amar Singh Thapa had come and held an interview and that the son of Qaji Amar Singh Thapa, who was firmly entrenched in the fort of Jitak in the direction of Nahan, had vacated it and gone away. For about four hours this conversation continued, after which the said respectable person went away, and the Noble Sarkar himself held a private conference with Bhai Gurbakhsh Singh, Dhanna Singh Malwai and some other associates. The Noble Sarkar said,[80] "Though apparently sincere friendship is supposed to exist between myself and the English Sahibs, yet in reality our relations are merely formal and conventional. Therefore, I had thought out to myself that if ever the English Sahibs would act differently in their dealings with me, I would call upon the Gurkhas and make friends with them, and in case they showed any hesitation I intended to make over the fort of Kangra to them to win their comradeship. Now they have gone away from the mountains, and it can't be said when they would next cherish a desire for the above-mentioned region. I never expected such thing to happen, as would make the mountainous regions become empty of them so suddenly"[*]. They replied that the Noble Sarkar was certainly a very wise man, and so he need not be afraid of anything at all, adding that every thing would turn out quite satisfactory.

The Noble Sarkar went into the other tent and laid himself down to rest during the night after taking his meals. Captain Bridge Sahib Bahadur is still in the cantonment of Ludhiana. It was stated that Ram Dass, the son of Qaji Amar Singh Thapa, was coming, and Captain Bridge Sahib Bahadur had gone to a distance of half a kos to receive him, and, after meeting him, had brought him to put up in his own bungalow. He was further reported to have greatly assured that person and had shown him great hospitality and kindness. Munshi Abdul Naib Khan and Nand Singh, the Vakils of Lahore, had entered Ludhiana. Two staff-bearers and two spear-holders of the Noble Sarkar were accompanying Qaji Ram Dass. Evidently something had reached for the expenses of the said Qaji. The

---

[*] The original reads as follows:—

"ارشاد نمودند ظاهره چنان دریافت شد که هر چند قیمابین سرکار و صاحبان انگریز بهادر دوستئی دلی
است لیکن ازطرفین صرف ظاهرداری بکار می برد. لهذا بجانی خود همین تجویز می داشتم که
اگر ماوصاحبان انگریز بهادر سوال وجواب نوع دیگر بعمل خود آمد گورکها را طلبیده رفیق خود خواهم
کرد. اگر نام برده چیزے عذر درسرکار کند قلعه کانگره باوشان داده اوشان را رفیق خود کرده خواهند
شد. حالا مشارالیه ازان کوه خارج شدند. ثانی الحال داعیه این ملک کے خواهد کرد. مارا این قدر توقع نه
بود که یک بیک این طور ملک کوهستانی خالی خواهد شد."

186

news came that Qaji Ranchur Singh had come out of the fort of Jitak, but had gone back once again into it and established himself there. Later, the news came that General Ochterlony Sahib Bahadur had, on Tuesday, reached Panjore *(i)*, that the garrison master of that place had come forward to receive him that he had taken him along with himself into the fort and presented him the necessary provisions for entertainment and two thousand rupees in cash. Yesterday, on the morning of Wednesday, he had marched away towards Mani Majra. It is reported that he would put up at Ratan Garh, while the camp of the army would be in the town of Sisan.

1815 (5)

News of the Deorhi of Sirdar Ranjit Singh Bahadur. Friday, dated 26th May, 1815 (16th Jamadi- us-Sani 1230 A.H.), Dinanagar.

The Noble Sarkar got up early in the morning and came out to the tent set apart for the court. The sirdars came in and made their customary bow. Nasir Khan, a Vakil of Raja Sansar Chand, reported that the English Sahibs had conquered the fort of Malawan, and that Qaji Amar Singh Thapa had been shown into the presence of the General Sahib Bahadur, and was kept there as a man in custody. The Noble Sarkar observed, "The Gurkhas did not show any want of earnestness in the battle, but were rendered helpless through their supplies running short. Raja Sansar Chand, with his brother, considered himself a great man of valour, but had suffered defeat on several occasions in his fight against Qaji Amar Singh, and could never score a victory over him. It was only through the reinforcements from the Noble Sarkar which went to assist Raja Sansar Chand that the Gurkhas were driven out of the country of Kangra. The English Sahibs are men of great forbearance, while the Gurkhas were practising great tyranny in the mountainous regions. Now the latter have been driven out of that country."[*] After that Sherbaz Khan stated that the brother of Sultan Khan of Bhimbar had written to request for his brother's release. The Noble Sarkar replied that he himself intended to set that Khan free, though he could not confidently say whether he, Raja Akbar Khan of

---

[*] The original reads as follows:—

"خود بدولت فرمودند که گورکھاها در جنگ قصورنه همه بهم نارسیدن غله لا چار شدند. و
صند وقچه راجه سنسار چند برادرمشار الیه که خود رابجوانمردی نامزد می داردفعه کا جی امرسنگھ
جنگ خورده لیکن یک دفعه فتحیاب نه شد. دریں جانب بکمک راجه سنسار چند رسیده گورکھا هارا
ازملک کانگڑه خارج. و صاحبان انگریز بهادر صاحب داعیه هستند و گورکھا هادر ملک کوهستان
بسیار زیادتی می کردند. حالا خارج شدند."

187

Rajauri, would also raise trouble or not. He further added that he would be released on the arrival of Ram Singh, but he must give assurance that he would not create any mischief like Akbar Khan and Dewan Singh. In the afternoon the Noble Sarkar went inside, and laid himself down to rest after taking his meals, while those who were present walked out.

He got up again at about the third quarter of the day, and came out to the tent set apart for audience when four hours of the day were left. His associates and attendants presented themselves. Letters from Ram Dial and Sirdar Dal Singh came from Kot Kamalia, intimating that Nawab Sadiq Muhammad Khan had not yet shown any inclination to pay up the revenue tax, stating simply that he had very old friendship with the Noble Sarkar, and that many times in the past he had been excused from the payment of the revenue tax and the Nazrana. They further requested that they might know the order of the Noble Sarkar, so that they might act accordingly. The reply was sent to them, that they should somehow or other realize Nazrana from the Nawab of Bahawalpur, and should not mind if they could secure a little less than the full sum. After that the Noble Sarkar continued talking to his associates for a while, and later rode out for recreation to the open land. On his return, he went in as usual and enjoyed the dance of the dancing girls, and later, laid himself down to take rest after taking his meals when the night had passed one quarter. All's well otherwise.

1815 (6)

News of the Deorhi of Sirdar Ranjit Singh Bahadur. Monday, dated 19th June, 1815 A.D., (10th Rajab, 1230 A.H.); Wazirabad, on the Bank of the River Chenab.

A messenger came and presented a letter from the garrison master of Mangalan, which stated, "Just the other day the Malkiya tribe rose and fought with the troops of the Noble Sarkar. In the end they found that they could not withstand opposition, and took to flight. Some fifty persons were killed and wounded on both sides." After inspecting the reports of that district and its neighbourhood, the Noble Sarkar talked about them to his associates. A messenger came and presented a letter from the garrison master of Nowshera, which mentioned, "It is rumoured here that Sirdar Fateh Khan Wazir is continuing to stay in Peshawar, that he had collected about twenty-five thousand men of the Yusafzai tribe and had despatched them to the fort of Attock, and that he had sent some of his troops to Kashmir *via* Tibet on the request of Muhammad Azim Khan, the Nazim of Kashmir." A representative of Bhai Lal Singh presented a letter from his master, and, after talking something in privacy to the Noble Sarkar, walked out. After that the Noble Sarkar rode out, and, making a ramble around the troops, went into the zenana. All's well otherwise.

1815 (7)

News of the Deorhi of Sirdar Ranjit Singh Bahadur. Friday, dated 30th June, 1815 (21st Rajab 1230 A.H.); the Town of Wazirabad, on the Bank of River Chenab.

The Noble Sarkar got up early in the morning and came out to the tent set apart for audience. The officials and the sirdars came in and made their customary bow. It was reported that Chaudhri Qadir Bakhsh had not yet left for Rajauri. The Noble Sarkar felt very angry on learning this, and, summoning that person, asked him as to why he had not departed. He replied that he was just leaving. The Noble Sarkar ordered him to leave all his effects behind and to proceed immediately to bring Akbar Khan, the Raja of Rajauri, and remarked that if he (Akbar Khan) would accompany him back, it would be all right, otherwise some other plan would be adopted for the purpose. That person obeyed the order and took his way in that direction. A messenger came and submitted a letter from Sujan Rae, stating that he had disbursed salaries for two months to the battalion of Dhonkal Singh according to the order of the Noble Sarkar, and that he now proposed to distribute salaries among the other battalions. After considering this letter the Noble Sarkar sent him a reply, asking him to send regularly accounts of those regions to him. A light shower of rain fell, and the Noble Sarkar went into the other tent and laid himself down to take rest at noon after his meals. He got up again at about the third quarter of the day and came out to the tent without poles when four hours of the day were left. He then went to the bank of the river Chenab and sat down there, his associates and attendants presenting themselves. A letter was sent to Desa Singh Majithia to present himself soon after the realization of revenue tax from the Raja of Kulu, in case its assessment had been settled. In the meantime the messenger (Jauri) came and brought the news that Shahid Khan, the brother of Sultan Khan—the Raja of Bhimbar, had set up the camp of his misfortune near the village of Kagri, high up on the mountain at a distance of four kos from the fort of

189

Mangalan, and that troops of the Noble Sarkar had also left to fight him, and were expected to reach the "Sarai" shortly. A letter from Gobind Singh Ahluwalia came from the fort of Attock. It mentioned that he would soon present himself according to the order. It further stated that one day the horsemen of Hari Singh Nalwa had gone towards Kundagarh long with a "Ghari" (i), Sherbaz Khan of Kundagarh had come out to fight them, and that they had continued fighting for two hours. Many men from either side had laid their lives in the field of battle, and in the end, the said Khan felt that he could no longer fight. He suffered a defeat and fled away, and the horsemen of the Noble Sarkar brought the, 'Ghari' (i) along with them in perfect safety. In reply, it was written to him that he must invite Sherbaz Khan to himself, and personally bring him to the Noble Sarkar after giving him great assurances. At about nightfall it began to rain very heavily and the Noble Sarkar went into the other tent. After taking his meals he laid himself down to take rest during the night, and, those who were present, walked out. The rain continued falling.

Saturday, dated 1st July, 1815 (22nd Rajab, 1230 A.H.)

The Noble Sarkar got up early in the morning, and went into the tent and indulged in drinking wine and in merry-making, etc. It continued to rain from morning till the evening with great force. None of those, given to make their customary bow, appeared at all. Letters from Kanwar Kharak Singh and Bhayia Ram Singh arrived. After due consideration, it was written to them in reply to present themselves soon. A letter was sent summoning the zamindars of Jini Gheb. A letter expressing cordial sentiments came from Raja Sansar Chand of Kot Kangra. Munshi Devi Dass stated that Mirza Rahim Beg, the representative of Colonel Muhammad Shah Khan, wanted a reply to the letter of his master. The Noble Sarkar said that he would be soon given a suitable answer. The zamindars of Jalalabad came, paid their respects, and offered one rupee each as Nazar. The Noble Sarkar kept on enquiring after their health for a while, and ordered them to procure ten pairs of oxen from their division. The Noble Sarkar made a pleasure trip through the fair of Sarwar Sultan. He gave one rupee to each of a group of Sikhs. Later, the dancing girls came in, and he kept on enjoying their dance until the night had passed one quarter, and continued drinking wine all the time. The rain continued falling in torrents. All's well otherwise.

Deorhi of Sirdar Ranjit Singh Bahadur. Thursday, dated 13th July, 1815 (5th Shaban, 1230, A.H.); the Town of Wazirabad, on the Bank of the River Chenab.

Early in the morning the Noble Sarkar got up and went to the tent set apart for audience. The officials and sirdars came in and made their customary bow. Abdul Nabi Khan, a Vakil of Bhai Lal Singh of Kathal, submitted a letter from his master together with a horse having a silver harness and many other gifts and five rupees on his own behalf. The Noble Sarkar enquired after the health of the Bhai Sahib, and continued talking with the Vakil for about an hour. The latter then walked out. Pindi Dass, a representative of Nawab Muhammad Khan of Mankera, was called in. He was granted a robe of honour consisting of five garments, and allowed to depart. The representative of Sirdar Jodh Singh of Ramgarh stated that Rani Sada Kaur was molesting his master. He requested the Noble Sarkar to bring about a settlement between them, otherwise a fight would occur and many lives would be lost uselessly. The Noble Sarkar said that such settlement would be brought about on the arrival of his master. The representative of Nawab Sadiq Muhammad Khan came in and presented a letter from his master, clearly mentioning that though he had paid up the tribute allotted to him in full, yet the troops of the Noble Sarkar were interfering with his country. The Noble Sarkar replied that his tribute had been fixed at ninety thousand rupees for a long time, while he had paid up only forty thousand, adding that he must pay the remaining sum at Amritsar, and that then the troops would be called back. A letter came from Nawab Abdul Samad Khan, the ruler of Dera Ghazi Khan, which stated, "here is my representative coming into your presence. Whatever he states verbally may be regarded by your Noble Sarkar as true and certain." In the afternoon the sirdars and others who were present walked out and the Noble Sarkar went in, and, taking his meals went to sleep. He got up again at about the third quarter of the day, and when four hours of the day were left, he came out and entered the tent set apart for holding the court. The officials and sirdars came in and made their customary bow. The nephew of the Raja of Jasrota came in and offered one horse Nazar. For a while the Noble Sarkar kept on enquiring after his health. Rama Nand Sahu said that contract to supply all the requisite things, needed for the administration of justice, be granted to him. The Noble Sarkar asked him to submit a fixed sum of seventeen lakhs of rupees. Rama Nand kept quiet on hearing this demand. The representative of the country belonging to Damtorwala, presented a complimentary letter from his master to the

Noble Sarkar. The latter asked him to send for his master, for he intended to hold consultation with him and to depute him to Kashmir to assist in its conquest. He replied that he would do so. It began to rain, and the Noble Sarkar enjoyed the music of the bards. Later, he went in, took his meals, and went to sleep during the night.

Friday, dated 15th July, 1815 (6th Shaban, 1230 A. H.)

The Noble Sarkar got up early in the morning and came out and inspected the drill of the Gurkhas. He entered the tent set apart for audience, and the sirdars came in and made their customary bow. A note was sent to the garrison master of Rohtasgarh, informing him that some goods consisting of articles, like Pashmina cloth, belonging to certain merchants, were sent by Sirdar Yar Muhammad Khan from the other side of the river Indus and were on way to Kashmir and Amritsar, that the zamindars of Kundagarh and the dacoits of the neighbourhood of Rohtasgarh had plundered that property and taken it away, that he must investigate the whole situation, recover the property and send it and the dacoits promptly to the Noble Sarkar, and that otherwise he was likely to suffer. The messengers (Jauri) came from Attock and stated that just in those days, some peculiar epidemic had swept over the fort of Attock and most of the soldiers and the Sikhs had fallen ill and died. He further stated that the Afghans were showering balls of cannons over that fort, from which the swivels were being fired at them. Santokha Bakhshi came from the Raja of Jasrota, presented a gaunt hourse on behalf of his master and expressed a wish for being vowed to depart. The Noble Sarkar granted him a robe of honour consisting of six garments and one hundred rupees in cash as a farewell gift. In the afternoon he took his meals and went to sleep. He got up again at about the third quarter of the day, and came out in the usual manner. His associates and attendants presented themselves. The representative of Ahmad Khan of Jhang presented two horses and one camel sent by his master and then walked out. Budh Singh, the son of Ganda Singh Safi, was granted a robe of honour consisting of four garments, and was allowed to depart. The news arrived that a quarrel had broken out between Sarbuland Khan Bharich of Rohri and Ruhullah Khan of Punchh, that some men had been killed and wounded on both sides, and that Ruhullah Khan had despatched his troops for the punishment of Sarbuland Khan. It began to rain in torrents, and the Noble Sarkar, calling in the dancing girls, engaged himself in drinking wine and enjoying their dance. When one quarter of the night had passed he took his meals and went to take rest. Dawinde Khan of Kamona is still at Amritsar, and Raja

Ram Dial of Jarbarah, who had gone from Amritsar to the mountainous regions, had returned and again entered Amritsar. All's well otherwise.

1815 (9)

News of the Deorhi of Sirdar Ranjit Singh Bahadur. Sunday dated 16th July, 1815(8th Shaban, 1230 A. H.), the town of Wazirabad.

The Noble Sarkar got up early in the morning and came out to the tent set apart for audience. The sirdars came in and made their customary bow. Karam Chand Vakil came in and presented letters from Kanwar Kharak Singh and Ram Dial, the son of Diwan Moti Ram, which stated, "We wanted to present ourselves to the Noble Sarkar during these days, but have postponed our intention on hearing about the approach of Sirdar Fateh Khan Wazir. We have removed our camp from this place to the neighbourhood of Kot Kamalia, which is at a distance of sixty or seventy kos from the river Attock. Whatever be the case, the Noble Sarkar must rest assured regarding the affairs of this country." After due consideration, a reply was despatched to the Kanwar, wishing him to come all alone to Noble Sarkar who had something to speak to him, and leaving Diwan Ram Dial with his troops at that place. A messenger came and submitted a letter from Chaudhri Qadir Bakhsh, a companion of Raja Fateh Singh Ahluwalia, which mentioned that he had spoken to Akbar Khan of Rajauri to present himself to the Noble Sarkar, that he showed hesitation and avoidance, that Shah Shuja-ul-Mulk had left Chamba and marched away towards the mountainous regions, that the troops of Kashmir, which were with him (the Shah) had refused to accompany him at the time of his departure from Rajauri towards Chamba, but had turned their march towards the "Sarai Shahi" near Daulat Nagar where they had set up their camp, and that it was reported that they intended to proceed to reinforce Ruhullah Khan of Punchh. After due consideration, the reply was sent that if Akbar Khan seemed to avoid coming over to the Noble Sarkar it did not matter, and he (the Chaudhri) was to leave him and come over to his (Sarkar's) presence. A letter from Mohsin Shah, a representative from Multan, arrived, mentioning that he had left Multan and reached Diwan Moti Ram, and that after taking leave from him shortly he would present himself. In the afternoon, the sirdar and others who were present, walked out, and the Noble Sarkar went into the other tent and laid himself down to rest after taking his meals. He got up again at about the third quarter of the day, and came out to the tent set apart for audience when four hours of the day were left. Associates and attendants came and presented themselves. A letter from Hukma Singh, the Thanadar of Lahore, brought the news that it had heavily rained and most of the houses and walls had fallen, and that he had submitted the report simply for the sake of information. After consideration, he was sent a reply to repair all breaches in the usual manner. A letter was issued to the garrison master of Gobindgarh which lies in Amritsar, asking him to give or send to Hukma Singh, the Thanadar of Lahore, whatever he might require from him. The Noble Sarkar enjoyed the music of the bards and then went over to the other tent. After taking his meals he went to rest when the night had passed one quarter. All's well otherwise.

The account of the cantonment of Ludhiana is this Colonel Nelson Sahib Bahadur is the ruling authority over the army, and Captain Ross Sahib Bahadur is the master of the whole administrative and financial machinery. General Ochterlony Sahib Bahadur marched from the village of Hari on the 11th Shaban, halted in the village of Shahi, and reached Hariana on the 12th.

The Gurkha troops continue to encamp in the cantonment of Ajmergarh, and Colonel Nicholson Sahib Bahadur is the commanding officer there. Captain Bridge Sahib Bahadur, who had gone from Ludhiana to Nahan for its settlement, had set up a new camp there. The Gurkha troops are encamped near Nahan as servants of the English Company Bahadur.

1815 (10)

Deorhi of Sirdar Ranjit Singh Bahadur; the Town of Wazirabad, on the Bank of the River Chenab, where the Noble Sarkar remained up to the 18th July, 1815.

A letter from Jai Karan Dass, the news-writer, arrived and mentioned that the men besieged in the fort of Kangra had fled, that Raja Fateh Singh Ahluwalia had entered the fort, and that the son of Shahid Khan, with two other chieftains, had been captured. The Noble Sarkar felt very happy to hear this and ordered for a salute from the Topkhana, which took place accordingly. A note was sent to Raja Fateh Singh Ahluwalia and others to punish those who were besieged wherever they might found. A letter from Hukma Singh Chimny from the fort of Attock intimated that

Sirdar Fateh Khan Wazir had entered Kabul after satisfactorily arranging his troops posted at Khairabad. All's well otherwise.

1815 (11)

(First leaf of the text is missing)

Some say that the messengers (Jauri) had been taken to Ludhiana to General Ochterlony, and some say that the said Shah is still in Kishtwar. Nothing is known for certain. Three hundred labourers, carpenters and masons have gone over to the other side of the fort of Attock for the construction of the Nadir Shah Tower, which is situated within the range of the said fort. All's well otherwies.

Shahzadas Kamran and Usman, the sons of Zaman Shah, who had left Herat and gone over to Haji Feroz-ud-Din were later had departed from there on the pretext that they were proceeding on a pilgrimage to the House of Allah at Mecca, entered Multan after travelling through the countries of Nasir Khan, Mir Sohrab Khan of Malpur, and Nawab Sadiq Muhammad Khan. At their departure Mir Sohrab Khan presented them fifteen hundred rupees, and Sadiq Muhammad Khan made them a gift of three thousand rupees. Nawab Sahib Shahnawaz Khan sent brother to receive Shahzada Kamran, and presented twenty-five "Ashrafis" to Shahzada Nasir and seven "Ashrafis" to Shahzada Usman. Delicious food and daily expenses were also supplied to Shahzada Kamran by the said Nawab. The Shahzadas intended to go to Shah Shuja-ul-Mulk next. All's well otherwise.

News from Amritsar, dated 22nd July 1815 A.D.

It became known that Sirdar Ranjit Singh was still staying Wazirabad. The Noble Sarkar enquired about the conditions of the district of Kandhar and other places from Jahandad Khan, and gave him two thousand rupees to meet his expenses. Dal Singh Bharania entered Lahore together with his troops and the sum of forty thousand rupees which had realised from Multan, and later, about to proceed towards Wazirabad. Events of Attock were also being reported as desired. Sirdar Sahib Bahadur (the Noble Sarkar) was planning to collect his entire forces and to proceed upon an expedition to Kashmir. The news came that the cantonments and barracks of all the troops would be fixed in the district of Rajaur and the "sarai" of Nowshera. All's well otherwise.

Deorhi of Sirdar Ranjit Singh Bahadur. Thursday, dated 27th July, 1815 (19th Shaban 1230 A.H.)

Kanwar Kharak Singh and Bhayia Ram Singh came from the district of Kot Kamalia according to the summons of the Noble Sarkar, and presented trays, full of slabs of sugar on the occasion of making their customary bow. Gulab Rai, who was posted at the Basti Gate of the city wall was called in and ordered to explain how his guarding that gate could be considered satisfactory when Hazrat Shah Shuja-ul-Mulk had fled away during his charge. After showing his great displeasure the Noble Sarkar threw him into prison. Letters were sent to Mian Singh, Dhonkal Singh and other commandants to present themselves together with their battalions promptly. Harnath Singh of Patiala presented himself to the Noble Sarkar, and offering one horse as Nazar, talked of his own affairs.

Friday, dated 28th July, 1815 (20th Shaban)

Hukma Singh Thanadar reported the capture of fifteen thieves. The Noble Sarkar ordered their ears and noses to be cut off and they be banished from the town.[83] He ordered Sheikh Budha, Aziz Khan another commandants to take money and distribute salaries for two months among their battalions. The revenue collector of Hariana was sent for Bhayia Ram Singh was ordered to state how he had realized the revenue tax of Multan. He replied that he had himself become a surety and made himself responsible for the payment of the revenue tax. Izzat Rai, the merchant, stated that the Noble Sarkar could take five thousand rupees as fine from him and pardon his fault. The son of Jodh Singh of Suriyan made a request in the course of his interview, that he be allowed to go home on leave. The Noble Sarkar replied that he would be allowed to leave on the following day.

Saturday dated 29th July, 1815 21st Shaban 1230 A.H.)

Sirdar Dewa Singh of Ropar, and Nihal Singh of Attari presented trays of sweetmeat as Nazars, and stated, on the occasion of their presentation, that Diwan Bhawani Dass was also shortly coming after them. The money realised as revenue tax from the mountainous regions was entrusted to Desa Singh Majithia. Albel Singh, the son of Himmat Singh Jhallwalla, stated that he had brought his troops with him. The Noble Sarkar said that he had done well, and remarked casually that

Sultan Khan, the Raja of Bhimbar, would soon be released. Sirdar Jodh Singh of Ramgarh came in to pay his respects, and the Noble Sarkar seated him in a chair and held a friendly conversation with him. Khushal Singh Jamadar stated that he had come after leaving Fateh Singh Man in the fort of Kangri. Rama Nand Sahu was sent for. Diwan Moti Ram was ordered to send his troops towards Phillaur. The Noble Sarkar rode out to the open land for recreation and hunt, and, after enjoying the dance of the dancing girls on his return, went into the zenana. It began to rain. All's well otherwise.

1815 (13)

News of the Deorhi of Sirdar Ranjit Singh Bahadur. Tuesday dated 1st August 1815 (24th Shaban, 1230 A.H.); the Royal Fort, Lahore.

The Noble Sarkar got up early in the morning and entered the Saman Burj. The sirdars came in and made their customary bow. Nihal Singh Nakai requested for the grant of the division of Nakka to him, promising to pay a large sum of money for it, and to be ready to render service in the future. The Noble Sarkar heard it and kept quiet. Chaudhri Qadir Bakhsh whispered something into the ears of the Noble Sarkar. Munshi Devi Dass was ordered to state if any news regarding Sirdar Fateh Khan Wazir had reached him. He replied that he was reported to be still staying in Peshawar. The representative of the Raja of Bhador was granted a robe of honour and was allowed to depart. An estate worth five thousand rupees was granted to the son of Munshi Jodh Singh. A letter was sent to Nawab Sarfraz Khan of Multan, stating that Mohsin Shah, his representative, had not yet reached the presence of the Noble Sarkar, and he was ordered to send him promptly, as something had to be talked to him verbally. When the day had advanced one quarter, the Noble Sarkar got up from the court and went into the zenana. The sirdars and those who were present walked out. He laid himself down to take rest after his meals. He got up again at about the third quarter of the day and came over to the garden. His associates and attendants came in and presented themself. Pandit Kaka Ram came in, paid his respects, and offered one tray of sweetmeats as Nazar. The Noble Sarkar kept on enquiring after his health for a while. It was stated that Kutub-ud-Din Khan of Kasur was present at the gate. The Noble Sarkar replied that he should come on the following day. A note was sent to the garrison master of Sialkot to send over the two horses of the Noble Sarkar, which were with him. The dancing girls were called in and the Noble Sarkar engaged himself in enjoying their dance. When four hours of the night had passed, the Noble Sarkar went into the zenana and laid himself down to rest during the night, after taking his meals.

Wednesday, dated 2nd August, 1815 (25th Shaban 1230 A. H.)

The Noble Sarkar got up early in the morning and came out. The staff and the servants made their customary bow. He rode out towards the open land. After making a pleasure trip he returned to the fort and entered the Saman Burj. The sirdars came in and made obeisance. The Noble Sarkar inspected the drill of the newly-recruited Gorkhas and watched the firing of guns. Kutub-ud-Din Khan of Kasur presented one tray full of slabs of sugar and complained that Nihal Singh Attariwala was molesting him with regard to certain villages, and wished that the Noble Sarkar would stop him from doing so. The Noble Sarkar replied that he would. Narain Dass, a representative from Ramgarh, stated that his master expected that he would be granted leave to depart. The Noble Sarkar said it would be granted to him. He showed his pulse to the physicians and said that he felt very fit and cheerful. Sirdar Dewa Singh of Ropar requested for the remission of seven hundred rupees of the revenue tax, which had been imposed on him regarding Mini. The Noble Sarkar replied that such revenue tax could never be remitted. Harnath Singh Nihala, presenting a tray of sweets as Nazar, paid his respects to the Noble Sarkar who enquired after his health. A note was sent to Mian Singh Har, inviting him to present himself. A representative of Raja of Dilaipur offering a Nazar of two rupees presented himself. The Noble Sarkar enquired after his health. He stated that he had brought two thousand rupees, the balance of his revenue tax due to the Noble Sarkar. The Noble Sarkar told him to deliver that money to his agent, Rama Nand. In the afternoon the Noble Sarkar went into the zenana and laid himself down to rest, after taking his meals. He got up again at about the third quarter of the day and came out. The staff and the servant made their customary bow. He rode out into the open field, and, after galloping the horse for a while, returned to his own place, and sent a word to Kishen Dass, a representative of Bahawalpur, to present himself on the following day. After that he enjoyed the music of the bards, and later entered the zenana and went to rest during the night after taking his meals. Raja Fateh Singh Ahluwalia spent one night at Amritsar and left for Kapurthala on the following day. Rani Sada Kaur is ill for a long time and Sher Singh and Tara Singh are with her. Shah Shuja-ul-Mulk is still in Kishtwar. All's well otherwise.

The Noble Sarkar got up early in the morning and came over to the Saman Burj. Bhai Gurbakhsh Singh, Jodh Singh Surnanwala, Karam Singh of Rangar Nangal, Himmat Singh Chillawala, Budh Singh, the son of Amar Singh - the Raja of Sansi, Jai Singh, Shiam Singh, Karam Chand, Diwan Bhawani Dass, Diwan Ganga Ram Pandit, Nanak Chand, Narain Dass, a representative from Ramgarh, and other sirdars entered into the presence of the Noble Sarkar and made their obeisance. Diwan Ganga Ram Pandit said, "All the battalions had arrived near Shahdara yesterday and camped there. To-day all of them had to cross the river Ravi, but owing to the river being in floods, they have to stay still. To-morrow they would enter Lahore." Sabit Khan Afghan requested for money to meet his expenses. The Noble Sarkar told him to take one hundred rupees from Munshi Devi Dass. Bhawani Dass Akal presented a tray of slabs of sugar as a Nazar and paid his respects. The Noble Sarkar enquired after his health and assured him that consideration and patronage would be shown to him. Karam Chand accountant was ordered to prepare a correct list of men in the battalion of Bakhtawar Singh, so that the salaries be disbursed accordingly. A letter was sent to the revenue collector of Kangra to collect the revenue tax of that place and deliver it to the local garrison master. Another was sent to the garrison master of Gobindgarh, asking him to send Sheikh Yousaf Khan and Shadi Khan to the Noble Sarkar together with two thousand soldiers. Ash Karan, a representative of Raja Dhonkal Singh of Jodhpore, sought permission to depart. The Noble Sarkar replied that he was going to Amritsar on the occasion of "Sankarant" of Bhadon, and would allow him to leave from that place. In the afternoon the sirdars and those who were present walked out, and the Noble Sarkar went into the zenana and laid himself down to rest after taking his meals. He got up at about the third quarter of the day and came out to the garden. The officials and sirdars came in and made their obeisance. Kanwar Kharak Singh, the eldest prince, came and presented eleven big trays containing large slabs of sugar in celebration of his marriage. Dal Singh Bharania was ordered to get ready one hundred maunds of gunpowder from his division and told that its price would be deducted from the account of the Noble Sarkar. Jawind Singh was ordered to retain the division of Khairabad with him. He begged to be excused, saying that the horsemen with him were very many and the estate with him was very small. The Noble Sarkar said that further consideration and patronage would be shown to him. Two carts laden with gunpowder sent by the revenue collector of Shahpur, reached the court of the Noble Sarkar who sent a further order for the manufacture of another similar amount and for its despatch to him. Hira Singh commandant was told that the battalion of Nihal Singh would be put under his charge. He replied that he was willing to accept its responsibility. Sukha Nand, a representative of the Noble Sarkar, stated that after a great search he had procured a pod of musk, and if the Noble Sarkar would wish, he would present it. The Noble Sarkar asked him to bring it on the following day. A letter was sent to Sukh Dial, asking him to present himself soon in case he had realised the revenue tax from Pind Dadan Khan. After that a son of Dhanna Singh Malwai presented a tray of sweets and made his obeisance. The Noble Sarkar kept on enquiring after his health for a while, and for two hours continued talking about various subjects in his presence. Later, he rode out to the bank of the river Ravi and returned to his place after recreation. Afterwards, he went into the zenana and laid himself down to rest during the night, after taking his meals.

1815 (15)

News of the Deorhi of Sirdar Ranjit Singh Bahadur. Friday dated 17th August 1215 A.D. (12th Ramzan 1230 A.H.), Lahore.

The Noble Sarkar got up early in the morning and entered the Saman Burj. Bhai Gurbakhsh Singh, Himmat Singh Jhalla, Sirdar Jodh Singh of Kalsia, Karam Singh, Hardass Singh, Jawala Singh; Sada Singh, Hari Singh, Arjan Singh, Diwan Bhawani Dass, Karam Chand, Munshi Devi Dass, Hakim Aziz-ud-Din Khan and other sirdars entered the presence of the Noble Sarkar and made their customary obeisance. A letter from Diwan Moti Ram intimated that he had reached Phillaur and that the General Sahib Bahadur had entered the cantonment of Ludhiana. Two rupees were awarded to the messenger. Namdar Khan Gujar reported that Muhammad Azim Khan, the Nazim of Kashmir, was actively engaged in reorganising his troops and in fortfying the "ghats" and passages of the mountainous regions. The Noble Sarkar kept quiet on hearing this. He, addressing his associates, said that twenty thousand footmen must be selected and sent on the expedition to Kashmir. Kutub-ud-Din Khan of Kasur was told that he would be allowed to depart on the following day. Hari Singh Nalwa requested the Noble Sarkar to pay very careful and favourable consideration to the brother of Shiam Singh Nakka. A letter from Sukh Dial intimated that he would leave for the presence of the Noble Sarkar, just after the realization of the revenue tax from Pind Dadan

Khan. The Noble Sarkar gave five thousand rupees to the Dogra horsemen to meet their expenses. Dhonkal Singh commandant reported that flint was required for the guns. The Noble Sarkar said that it would be supplied. A letter from Mathra Dass intimated that Ahmad Khan of Jhang Sial offered him only fifty thousand rupees as revenue tax for the whole year, and asked the Noble Sarkar his orders in the matter, so that he might act accordingly. He was sent a reply to take whatever was offered and press hard for the remainder. The Noble Sarkar asked Munshi Devi Dass if he would accept a contract for supplying provisions for the whole of his country. He replied that he would accept it. Sheikh Basawan stated that if the Noble Sarkar approved this suggestion.[84] Dhonkal Singh commandant was ordered to set right his battalion, and present the same on the following morning to the Noble Sarkar for purposes of showing their drill. Gulab Singh, the jamadar of the special royal horsemen, reported that Rup Chand Sarraf had been ordered by the Noble Sarkar to pay him five thousand rupees but had refused to make any payment. The Noble Sarkar replied that he would get the money. Moti Ram, the Darogha of the mint, presented a tray containing slabs of sugar as Nazar and paid his respects. The Noble Sarkar showed his pulse to the physicians and complained that he felt an unpleasent taste. They replied that they would soon give him a tonic the use of which would restore him to perfect health. Diwan Singh, the brother of Hukma Singh, was ordered to arrange for an inspection and parade of his horsemen. Sada Singh asked permission to leave and was told to stay on for a few days more. Ten new Gurkhas were recruited. Abid Khan was asked to go over to the other side of the river Satluj, and to tempt the Gurkhas to come with him to the court of the Noble Sarkar. He replied that he could not do so. In the afternoon the sirdars and others who were present, walked out together, and the Noble Sarkar went in, took his meals and laid himself down to take rest. He got up again at about the third quarter of the day and came over to the garden. The associates and attendants came in to present themselves. Mazhar Ali, the Darogha of the cannons driven by horses, submitted that wooden planks were required for mounting the cannons. The Noble Sarkar said that he must go to the "Mistri Khana" (workshop) and get them prepared as he liked. Twenty five Sikh horsemen were recruited. One Benares Dupatta was given to the son of Nizam-ud-Din Khan of Kasur who was then allowed to depart. Two Gurkhas were granted one golden necklace each. Sawan Singh of Patti was ordered to arrange for an inspection and parade of his troops. He replied that he would do so on the following day. A note was sent to the garrison master of Gobindgarh, ordering him to get prepared for despatch one silver houdah. Bakhtawar Singh commandant was ordered to grant leave for two months to his men. He replied that he would do so. The workmen of Lahore presented ten guns and the Noble Sarkar liked and accepted them. At nightfall the Noble Sarkar rode out for recreation through the open land. On his return he entered the fort, went into the zenana, took his meals and retired to rest during the night. All's well otherwise.

1815 (16)

News of the Deorhi of Sirdar Ranjit Singh Bahadur. Saturday dated 18th August 1815 (13th Ramzan 1230 A.H.); the Royal Fort, Lahore.

The Noble Sarkar got up early in the morning and came out to the garden after enjoying the sacred sight of the Granth Sahib. Those who were accustomed to be present, made obeisance. He inspected the drill of the special orderly youths and the firing of a volly of guns and conversed with those who were present. A messenger came and delivered a letter from Sher Dil Khan of Kundagarh, which mentioned that if the Noble Sarkar sincerely agreed to favour him and granted him a Jagir, he would always be ready to render him service. After due consideration he was sent a reply that if he should come immediately with his men on receiving this letter, honour and patronage would be shown to him. The battalion of Dhonkal Singh commandant arrived in accordance with the order of the Noble Sarkar who inspected their drill and observed the firing of the guns. Six soliders of that battalion were wounded through the exploding of some guns. The Darogha of the workshop was called in and the Noble Sarkar very angrily warned him that he must get the guns constructed very well and that otherwise he would be severely punished. A letter from the garrison master of Makharbar intimated that some zamindars had gone to present themselves to the Noble Sarkar and requested that he should assure them that they would be shown honour and patronage. The news came that a woman wearing a sacred thread, was sitting at the gate and complaining that the nephew of Rama Nand had committed rape on her daughter. She wanted him to be punished. The Noble Sarkar said that punishment would be meted out to him. A certain person gave information that Diwan Bhawani Dass of the low stature had embezzled a portion of the revenue tax of the mountainous regions, realised by him for the Noble Sarkar. The latter replied that it would be claimed from him at the time of auditing his accounts. A representative of Kanwar Kharak Singh was ordered to state where Bhayia Ram Singh and Kanwar Sahib were at that time. He replied that at time were in the mansion of Sobha Singh. Munshi Devi Dass was ordered to gain information regarding the events of

Peshawar, Kabul etc, and to report them. The representative of Raja Bhup Singh of Haripore was allowed to depart with a grant of a robe of honour consisting of three garments. He was ordered to present himself again after two months, and was promised honour and patronage on his return. A Sikh made a statement regarding the affairs of his Jagir, and the Noble Sarkar purchased two bows and handed them over to the "Tosha Khan." A letter from the Raja of Suket intimated that he had despatched his representative to the Noble Sarkar and requested that the latter should consider whatever he would express as true and correct. A letter from the revenue collector of Kot Kamalia intimated that he would soon present himself according to order. The Noble Sarkar distributed one hundred rupees to the poor and the needy. Diwan Bhawani Dass submitted that Kishan Dass Vakil had left Multan and was expected to reach Lahore that day or on the day following. Salaries for six months were granted to labourers in advance. A letter was sent to the garrison master of Attock, stating that Sher Dil Khan of Kundagarh had sent a message to the Noble Sarkar, and asked him to give him assurances and to send him over to him. The Noble Sarkar inquired about the state of the ramparts of the city from Hukma Singh Thanadar. In the afternoon the sirdars and those who were present walked out, and the Noble Sarkar went into the zenana and laid himself down to rest after taking his meals. He got up again at about the third quarter of the day and came out to the garden. The sirdars made the customary bow. Diwans Bhawani Dass and Ganga Ram stated that they had disbursed the salaries for two months among the battalions of the Sikhs and others, adding that some of them still remained to be paid. The Noble Sarkar said that they would be paid their expenses out of the "Tosha Khana." Mian Singh requested the grant of a Jagir. The Noble Sarkar replied that it would be given. Shiv Dial Singh requested the grant of the contract of the division of Hajipur after its assessment. The Noble Sarkar said that he must pay eighty thousand rupees annually to the Noble Sarkar as its revenue tax. He replied that the said Jagir did not admit of such a yield. The Noble Sarkar ordered Ganga Ram to distribute salaries for two months among the battalion of Dhonkal Singh. He replied that he would do so. Those who were present represented that Sirdar Jodh Singh of Kalsia had shown great earnestness and enthusiasm in the service of the Noble Sarkar, who replied that he would be granted another Jagir. He said to Himmat Singh Jhalla that the battalions of the glorious sahibs were very efficient, because they never showed the least hesitation to plunge into war. For about two hours such conversation went on. He rode out for recreation through the forest, and on his return to the fort, entered the zenana, and laid himself down to rest during the night after taking his meals. All's well otherwise.

1815 (17)

News of the Deorhi of Sirdar Ranjit Singh Bahadur. Thursday, dated 24th August, 1815 (19th Ramzan, 1230, A.H.)

The Noble Sarkar got up early in the morning and came out to the Saman Burj. The sirdars came in and made their customary bow. The Noble Sarkar inspected the drill of the special orderly youths. It was stated that Nihal Singh, a Vakil of the late Sirdar Jodh Singh Ramgarhia, had left for Amritsar. Sirdar Sahib Bahadur said that, though all the sirdars must have felt sad on the death of Jodh Singh Ramgarhia, yet Rani Sada Kaur must have felt very happy over it. The associates rejoined that the Noble Sarkar was quite right. A letter from Sarbuland Khan of Kundagarh intimated that there was no doubt he had been an ally of Muhammad Azim Khan at the time when the Noble Sarkar arrived in those regions, but as he had quarrelled with him and they were not on good terms, he pledged himself that if the Noble Sarkar would plan an attack upon Kashmir he would render loyal service. The Noble Sarkar wrote to him in reply to send his representative. Dhanna Singh Malwai stated that according to the order of the Noble Sarkar, Raja Jaswant Singh of Nabha had made over the village of Moran to him. The Noble Sarkar replied that he had done well. A letter from Sirdar Desa Singh Majithia intimated that he had reached the neighbourhood of the fort of Kangra, adding that whatever facts he could ascertain, he would communicate the same faithfully. In reply, it was written to him to survey the country, to hold a parade of the inmates of the fort, and to note down these results and return to the Noble Sarkar, after establishing a proper control over that fort and distributing salaries to the garrison. In the afternoon the sirdars and other who were present walked out and the Noble Sarkar laid himself down to rest after his meals. He got up again at about the third quarter of the day and came out to the garden. His associates and attendants presented themselves. He ordered the despatch of a letter to Raja Fateh Singh Ahluwalia, asking him to send his representative. Out of his kindness he granted a Benares Dupatta to Sunder Singh. Ram Singh Kalla said that he had brought a horse for the Noble Sarkar. Jauri Singh of Rukian was granted some villages in the division of Kot Kamalia and allowed to depart. It was reported that Jodh Singh was present. The Noble Sarkar heard it and kept quiet. It was further reported that Mehtab Singh and Nihal Singh of Ramgarh were in Amritsar, and had sent the ashes of the late Jodh Singh of Ramgarh to the Ganges at Hardwar. Later he went into zenana and laid himself down to rest during the night, after taking his meals.

1815 (18)

News of the Deorhi of Sirdar Ranjit Singh Bahadur. Sarurday, dated 26th August, 1815 (20th Ramzan, 1230, A.H.); the Royal Fort, Lahore.

The Noble Sarkar got up early in the morning and came out to the Saman Burj, where the sirdars came in and made their customary obeisance. He inspected the drill of the special orderly youths and witnessed the firing of the guns. He asked Narain Dass, a representative of Ramgarh, to name some reliable person, through whom a robe of honour might be sent to his master by way of condolence. He replied that the Noble Sarkar could do whatever he wanted. Somebody said that Rani Sada Kaur had managed to bring the late Jodh Singh under the influence of an evil spell which caused his death. The Noble Sarkar remarked that it was quite wrong. He said to one, Captain Bakhshi Singh, that the newly re-cruited battalion would be put under his charge. One hunderd young men came from Maajah in search of employment, and the Noble Sarkar selected twenty five "Najib" youths from among them. He announced that two new battalions would be formed. Karam Chand stated that he had received several letters from various sides, and if the Noble Sarkar ordered him he would explain their contents. The Noble Sarkar replied that he would listen to them later on. Kutub-ud-Din Khan of Kasur was allowed to depart towards his home, with a grant of one Benares Dupatta. Sarab Dial, the agent of Munshi Devi Dass, was granted a pair of gold bangles as a mark of favour. Qazi Kamal-ud-Din, a representative of Raja Jaswant Singh of Nabha, came in, paid his respects, offered two rupees as Nazar and said, that according to the order of the Noble Sarkar the village of Moran had been made over to Dhanna Singh Malwai. The Noble Sarkar said that he had done well. The messengers (Jauri) came from Rajauri and reported, that at the instigation of Raja Akbar Khan a disturbance was afloat again in the district of Kangra. The Noble Sarkar replied that the mischief-makers would be suitably punished. He told the Qazi that another Jagir would soon be granted to Gulab Singh, the son of the late Sahib Singh of Gujrat. A note was sent to Hukma Singh to send to the Noble Sarkar all the various people who were staying in the fort of Attock.

Bhayia Ram Singh, on being questioned, stated that the condition of the district of Jammu was the same as before. Two thousand rupees were granted to Sahib Singh, the Jamadar of the messengers. The representative of Raja Dhonkal Singh of Jodhpore asked for leave to depart. The Noble Sarkar replied that he would be allowed to depart after a little time. Dhonkal Singh commandant stated that one hundred men of his battalion had been lost in Kangri. The Noble Sarkar replied he could recruit more men in their place. Sheikh Basawan stated that one hundred young men of his battalion were left at that place for purposes of watch and ward, and requested for money to meet their expenses. The Noble Sarkar ordered Sukh Dial to send to Raja Mahar Chand of Bailaspur, asking him to send news regularly about himself. A letter from Nand Singh, the representative of the Noble Sarkar, arrived and brought news about General Sahib Bahadur. He awarded two rupees to the bearer of the letter. In the afternoon, the Noble Sarkar went into the zenana and laid himself down to rest after taking his meals. He got up again at about the third quarter of the day and came out to the garden, where his associates and attendants presented themselves. He asked Shiv Dat Rai "Bad-farosh" to explain, if he had any news about the Gurkhas. He replied that he would submit it as soon as he heard any. Kanwar Kharak Singh came in and requested to be granted the division of Gujranwala. The Noble Sarkar replied that it was in the charge of Hari Singh Nalwa who remained present day and night rendering service to the Noble Sarkar, adding that some other Jagir would be granted to him. He asked Dhanna Singh Malwai if he was satisfied with the grant of the village of Moran. He replied that Raja Jaswant Singh would never have given it to him, and that he had secured it simply through the blessings and the glory of the Noble Sarkar. A note was sent to the revenue collector of Jullundur to send ten thousand rupees in cash promptly. Himmat Singh Jhalla asked for order regarding Narinjan Lal Vakil. The Noble Sarkar heard it and kept quiet. A note was sent to Attar Singh, asking to present himself soon. A bearer was sent to bring Nadhan Singh Ayu. A note was sent to Rama Nand Sahu to get ready and send gold-threaded trappings. Another was sent to Diwan Moti Ram to send the zamindars of Faridkot. Two horses, sent by the revenue collector of Dhanigheb, reached the court of the Noble Sarkar, who awarded eleven rupees to their grooms. Hukma Singh, the Thanadar of Lahore, stated that four thousand rupees had been paid to the Noble Sarkar for the purchase of grain. A letter came from Ajit Singh, the son of Gurdit Singh Ladhowala. The Noble Sarkar took his meals at nightfall and laid himself down to rest.

Sunday, dated the 27ᵗʰ August, 1815, A.D. (21ˢᵗ Ramzan, 1230, A.H.)

The Noble Sarkar got up early in the morning and came out to the Saman Burj, where the sirdars made their customary obeisance. He inspected the drill of the special orderly youths. Hakim Aziz-ud-Din Khan stated that Attar Singh of Faizullahpur had come to the "Deorhi," complaining about his salary. A note was sent to him that his salary would be paid very soon, and he was warned, that if he would be disobedient he would suffer. The representative of Raja Dhonkal Singh of Jodhpore came in, and was allowed to depart with one Benares Dupatta, a turban, a roll of white long cloth, another of muslin and two bows for the Raja. Diwan Chand stated that two pairs from among the oxen of the Topkhana, which had been sent to Manjah for grazing, had not returned. The Noble Sarkar replied that they would be brought back after a search. He sent for a cannon driven by horses from the camp of Mazhar Ali, had it fired five or six times, and then granted a gold bangle to each of the two gunners. A letter from the revenue collector of Hajipur intimated that dacoits, belonging to the division of Rani Sada Kaur, were making plundering raids in the villages of the Noble Sarkar. He sent him a reply, assuring him that they would be punished suitably. The brother of Hukma Singh Chimny applied for grant of the division of Sialkot, and the Noble Sarkar gave him some assurance. He took his meals at noon and laid himself down to rest. He got up again at about the third quarter of the day, and came out to the garden where his associates and attendants presented themselves. It was stated that the son of Fazal Dad Khan of Daska sought permission to leave, and the Noble Sarkar replied that he must wait for a few days. He granted two silver and gold *(i)* to the two special staff-bearers. The news came that some of the zamindars of the neighbourhood of Makhad had again raised disturbance. The Noble Sarkar replied that they would be suitably punished. It was stated that Ratan Singh Gajraki did not pay salaries to his men. The Noble Sarkar said to his associates that it would be very good thing if the fort of Rattu, belonging to the Raja of Chamba, came into the possession of the Noble Sarkar. They replied that through the blessing of his glory it was not difficult to acquire, and that as soon as the Noble Sarkar would decide to capture it, it would come into his· possession. Bhayia Ram Singh stated that, should the Noble Sarkar order, he would take his troops to Sheikhupura and post them there. The latter approved of the idea. He took his meals and laid himself down to rest during the night. All's well otherwise.

Deorhi of Sirdar Ranjit Singh Bahadur. Monday, dated 4th September, 1815 (29th Ramzan, 1230, A.H.), Lahore.

Rama Nand Sahu personally presented a tray full of slabs of sugar as Nazar. Shiv Dat Raj, a Vakil of the Raja of Bilaspur, informed what he had learnt verbally from men who had reached Ludhiana, that Hazrat Shah Shuja-ul-Mulk was reported to have gone to Manimajra through the mountains and was most probably reaching Ludhiana that evening or the following morning. The Noble Sarkar replied that if the news had been true, Nand Singh, his representative, who was present there, must have written about it. Kanwar Kharak Singh was ordered to get ready to accompany the Noble Sarkar who was proceeding towards Amritsar in the near future. The representative of the Kanwar stated that Turab Ali merchant was ready to stand surety for Rama Nand Sahu to the extent of five thousand rupees. The Noble Sarkar ordered that the sum assured be taken from him and the Sahu be set at liberty. The news arrived that Sirdar Budh Singh of Faizullahpur had died according to the will of God. The Noble Sarkar replied that there was no escape from his will. A letter was sent to Raja Akbar Khan of Rajauri, asking him to send his reliable person. A letter from the garrison master of Rohtasgarh intimated that the zamindars of that district had again raised disturbance in those days, and were committing robberies. The Noble Sarkar wrote to him in reply that he should chastise them. Rama Nand Sahu stated that Raja Ram Pandit, the son of Ram Chand Pandit, had arrived in obedience to his summons, and that the son of Nand Ram Pandit was quarrelling with him unjustifiably. The Noble Sarkar said that he would be fined and that their differences would be settled. Two horses were given to Mazhar Ali, the Darogha of the cannons driven by horses, for the purposes of dragging them out of the stable. Dhonkal Singh commandant was ordered to get ready some cartridges. Jahandad Khan was sent an order to present himself soon to the Noble Sarkar.

Tuesday, dated 5th September (30th Ramzan 1230 A.H.)

The Noble Sarkar mentioned to Hakim Aziz-ud-Din Khan casually that when Hazrat Shah Shuja-ul-Mulk would reach Ludhiana, a letter would be sent to General Sahib Bahadur demanding his return. The Hakim replied that English Sahibs were very powerful and would never send him back. The Noble Sarkar inspected the drill of a battalion, and granted one piece of trousers to each of four men. A verbal order was conveyed to Malik Muhammad Khan of Siestan through the messengers (Jauri) to send his representative at once to the Noble Sarkar. A letter was sent to Hakim Nur-du-Din, asking him to send the balance of the money realised from Wazirabad and Zafarwal, etc. Fifty youngmen were newly recruited. Himmat Singh Jhallawala was told that the Noble Sarkar would call back Nand Singh, his Vakil, who was stationed with the General Sahib Bahadur. A letter was sent to the Raja of Nurpur, asking him to present himself. The Noble Sarkar distributed two hundred rupees among the beggars and then went into the zenana. All's well otherwise.

1815 (20)

Deorhi of Sirdar Ranjit Singh Bahadur. Friday, dated 15th September 1815 (10th Shawwal, 1230 A.H.), Lahore.

The Noble Sarkar said to Pindi Dass that he had granted a robe of honour and an elephant for his master, the ruler of Mankera, and that these would soon be given to him. A letter from Raja Fateh Singh Ahluwalia expressed a wish for the fort of Zahure, stating that whatever money accrued to the Noble Sarkar from that place in the past, would be paid to him in the future also. In reply he was asked to send his representative, Mehr Chand, for through him alone the proper answer regarding the matter would be conveyed to him. Mehr Singh Jagirdar was emphatically ordered not to discontinue the charities to Hindus and Muslims which had become customary, assuring him that he would be allowed a deduction from the account of the Noble Sarkar. A general talk, regarding the march towards Amritsar, took place. The Noble Sarkar ordered Bhayia Ram Singh, to get ready for his departing towards Jammu. Hari Singh Nalwa was ordered to go home, make payments to his troops and to return along with them to present himself on the occasion of Dusehra. A letter came from Nand Singh, the representative of the Noble Sarkar from the army of General Ochterlony, stating that Partap Singh, the son of Raja Bhag Singh, had died at Shahjahanabad. The Noble Sarkar remarked that his brother Fateh Singh must have felt very happy over it. Khushal Singh was ordered to look after and maintain the horsemen, with the assurance that he would be granted their salaries. The news arrived that Shah Shuja-ul-Mulk was still encamped in Kishtwar, and had one thousand horse and foot in his service. On hearing it, the Noble Sarkar sent the messengers (Jauri) with one other person to bring further news about them. Nihal Singh Attariwala was summoned. The Noble Sarkar purchased one elephant from a merchant. The Vakil of Raja Sansar Chand, on enquiring, stated that his master was at that time staying at Alimpur. The Noble Sarkar granted a robe of honour consisting of three garments to Pirthi Dass, a representative of Raja Gurkha.

Saturday, dated 16th September (11th Shawwal, 1230 A .H.)

A letter from the garrison master of Attock intimated that Sardar Fateh Khan Wazir had marched away towards Kabul, and that Purdil Khan, Purdhan Khan and others were staying in Peshawar. In reply he was asked to continue writing about the events of that place. The representative of Mankera stated that, after collecting his troops, Sirdar Fateh Khan Wazir would return very shortly, and suggested that it would not be good to be indifferent about his return. The Noble Sarkar said that the matter would be thought over. The son of the Ghaus Khan, the Darogha of the Topkhana, was ordered to get ready four large cannons for despatch towards the fort of Phillaur. Dewa Singh of Ropar was sent a letter, asking him to keep all his troops together, for the Noble Sarkar wanted to review them on his arrival there. Sheo Dat Rai, a representative of the Raja of Bilaspur, was told that the Noble Sarkar was soon leaving for Amritsar and would allow him to depart from there. Dhayia Ram Singh was ordered to distribute pay to the soldiers of Kanwar Kharak Singh monthly, and warned that otherwise, he would be made to suffer. Qazi Amir-ud-Din, a representative of the Noble Sarkar, who had gone over to the army of Sirdar Fateh Khan Wazir, was sent a letter, stating that rumours about the arrival of the said wazir were afloat, and that, being in that district, he must regularly write about the conditions over there. Kanwar Kharak Singh was asked whether he was aware that the troops of Bhayia Ram Singh were living upon the rations belonging to him. He replied that the said Bhayia alone was responsible for them, and that he had nothing to do with them. The Noble Sarkar said that such carelessness was quite improper and advised him to be alert about his own affairs. Later he went inside. All's well otherwse.

Deorhi of Sirdar Ranjit Singh Bahadur. Monday, dated 18th September, 1815 (13th Shawwal, 1230, A.H.), Lahore.

The Noble Sarkar got up early in the morning and came out to his place in the Saman Burj. Bhai Gurbakhsh Singh, Badha Singh, Phula Singh, Himmat Singh, Hakim Rai, Hakim Aziz-ud-Din, and other sirdars, big and small, came in, making obeisance. Khushal Singh, the representative of Raja Karam Singh of Patiala, was granted a robe of honour consisting of three garments and allowed to depart with a message for that Raja and Misar Budh Mal, that they must pay, at least once, a visit to the Noble Sarkar. He replied that he would do so, and then went away. Sabit Khan Afghan asked for some money to meet his expenses. The Noble Sarkar made Munshi Devi Dass give him one thousand rupees. A letter from Bhai Lal Singh of Kaithal explained, among other things, the circumstances under which Kanwar Partab Singh, the son of Raja Bhag Singh, and others had died. The Noble Sarkar awarded five rupees to the messenger. He warned Sheikh Budha and Aziz Khan, the commandants of the battalions, to get ready, for they had to be ordered to proceed in some direction. They replied that they would do so. Himmat Singh Jhalla stated that a representative of Raja Akbar Khan of Rajauri had arrived. The Noble Sarkar, ordering him to bring him along to the court on the following day, remarked "Rajauriwala is a very treacherous man. He has friendship with the Nazim of Kashmir and is acting as a hypocrite in his relations with us. It does not, however, matter much, for the lesson would be brought home to him." Sisoo Rao, the representative of Raja Raghu Ji Bhonsla of Nagpur, came in and asked for permission to depart, for he had greatly run into debt. The Noble Sarkar told him that he would be allowed to depart on his (Noble Sarkar's) arrival in Amritsar. Mian Singh and Hira Singh, the commandant, took leave for ten days and went to their homes. The Noble Sarkar showed his pulse to the physicians and said that he felt unwell and bilious. They suggested that he must take an aperient. The Noble Sarkar approved of it and said that he would do so. Sirdar Dal Singh Bharania came and presented a tray full of slabs of sugar as Nazar. The Noble Sarkar enquired after his health. Bhai Gurbakhsh Rai stated that Mushtaq Rai Chotra had come to seek permission to present himself personally. The Noble Sarkar said that he would be invited at some other time. It was stated that Kanwar Kharak Singh, the eldest prince, was still putting up in the Shalamar Gardens. A note was sent to Dewa Singh of Ropar, reminding him of the loan of two thousand rupees which had been temporarily taken by him, and requiring him to repay the same. Another was sent to Kanwar Kharak Singh, ordering him to write regularly above the district of Jammu and above Diwan Singh Dadu. A letter from Raja Isari Sain of Mandi explained the conditions pervailing in the mountainous regions. The messenger, being awarded six rupees, was entrusted with a reply, couched in cordial terms, to the Raja, who was asked to write regularly about the events of that place. Munshi Devi Dass was asked to state whether his brother Kishen Dass had come from Multan or not. He replied that he would come soon. In the afternoon, the Noble Sarkar entered the zenana, took his meals, and went to sleep. He got up again about the third quarter of the day, and came out to the garden when four hours of the day were left. His associates and attendants presented themselves. Hardas Singh Donia came, and presenting two rupees, stated that he had gone to Raja Fateh Singh Ahluwalia according to orders, and had asked him to come over to the presence of the Noble Sarkar. He further added that Fateh Singh Ahluwalia was unwell at that time and had, therefore, sent his representatives who would soon arrive. One, Shiv Dial accountant of Wazirabad, was called in, and ordered to investigate the truth about the report that certatin accountants were embezzling money of the Noble Sarkar. He replied that he would do so. The Noble Sarkar inspected the drill of the gunners of Ghaus Khan and the firing of the cannons. An order was sent to the gate-keepers of Lahore, not to allow any armed person to enter the town. A letter from Ram Dial, the son of Diwan Moti Ram, informed of his own condition. The messenger was awarded two rupees, and a reply was sent to him to equip and get ready his troops. The revenue collector of Shahdara was sent an emphatic order to pay up the revenue tax. A letter was sent to the Raja of Nurpur, asking him to send Prem Singh, the son of Kangana Wazir, to the Noble Sarkar. A note was sent to Nand Singh, the garrison master of Attock, to collect the zamindars of Hassan Abdal, Sarai Kala and other places, and to send them over to the Noble Sarkar. The Noble Sarkar distributed cartridges to the battalion of Bakhtawar Singh, and ordered that they must get ready, for the camp of the Noble Sarkar was about to leave for Amritsar. A letter, from Prem Singh of Sadipur, explained the conditions prevailing there. The bearer of this letter was awarded two rupees. The Noble Sarkar told Hakim Aziz-ud-Din Khan that Hakim Imam-ud-Din Khan had embezzled part of the revenue of the division of Pattoki. He replied that some one had misrepresented the matter to the Noble Sarkar, and represented that all collections, made by him, could be accounted for, adding that, if anything turned out to be due from his brother, he himself would be prepared to pay double the amount. The Noble Sarkar rode out for recreation to the garden of Khushal Singh. The gardener presented him with a basket of seasonable fruits. After two hours he returned from that place, went into the zenana, took his meals and went to sleep for the night.

1815 (22)

News of the Deohri of Sirdar Ranjit Singh Bahadur. Monday, dated 30th October, 1815 (26th Ziquad, 1230 A.H.), Sialkot.

The Noble Sarkar got up early in the morning and came out to the tent set apart for audience. The sirdars came in and made obeisance. He ordered Shiam Singh Nikka to summon his five hundred horsemen and arrange their parade. He replied that he would do so, adding that his horsemen were quite ready. Bhayia Ram Singh stated that five hundred rupees in cash must be sent towards Jammu through Dawender Khan of Kamona to meet the expenses of his troops and for the settlement of that district. The Noble Sarkar agreed. He told Namdar Khan Gujjar to rest assured, for very soon a military expedition would be sent to the mountainous regions. He said that that was the proper time for bringing about the subjugation of Kashmir. The Noble Sarkar replied that he himself had that very thought in his mind. Qazi Kamal-ud-Din, a representative of Raja Jaswant Singh of Nabha, presented himself to the Noble Sarkar, making the customary bow. He delivered a letter from his master, containing cordial sentiments and stating that Ratan Singh Garjaki had taken some of the villages belonging to his (the Raja's) sister into his own possession, and requesting that these should be released. The Noble Sarkar said that he must rest assured, adding that he was shortly leaving for the town of Gujrat where he would very attentively listen to their grievances. Diwan Bhawani Dass of the low stature reported that Sirdar Fateh Khan Wazir had reached Jalalabad after an incessant march from Kabul, and was reported to be marching from that place towards Peshawar. He further added that probably he had already entered the latter place and had despatched some of his troops towards Kashmir *via* Tibet, and that since the mother of Hazrat Muhammad Shah Padshah had died, that Resort of the World had not left Kabul for any direction. In the afternoon, the sirdars and others who were present walked out, and the Noble Sarkar went into the other tent, took his meals and laid himself down to rest. He got up again at about the third quarter of the day, and came out to the tent set apart from audience as usual. His associates and attendants presented themselves. One carriage, which a year ago had been sent by General Ochterlony Sahib Bahadur, was at this time granted to Khushal Singh Jamadar as a mark of favour. A note was sent to Hukma Singh, the Thanadar of Lahore, enjoying upon him always to keep on

213

sending news about Lahore, and to remain very vigilant and alert in guarding the town. The Noble Sarkar called in Rae Singh, the father of Dundu, and, after giving him full assurances and granting him a robe of honour consisting of five garments, deputed him to go and fetch the Raja Dunu who had turned hostile. The Noble Sarkar sent one horse out of kindness to the camp of the Raja of Jammu for his use. Riding out towards the forest for recreation and hunting, he entered his tent, on his return, at about nightfall. He went in, took his meals and laid himself down to rest when a quarter of the night had passed. All's well otherwise.

1815 (23)

Deohri of Sirdar Ranjit Singh Bahadur. Tuesday, dated 31ˢᵗ October, 1815 (27ᵗʰ Ziqaad, 1230 A.H.), Sialkot.

The Noble Sarkar inspected the drill of the Gurkhas, and also of the troops of Kanwar Kharak Sigh, and said to Bhayia Ram Singh that his force was very small. He replied that some of his troops had gone to Jammu, Mangalan and other places. The Noble Sarkar ordered Dhonkal Singh commandant to get ready, for his departure in some direction was soon to be ordered. He further ordered the two hundred horsemen and several other companions of Bhayia Ram Singh to leave for the fort of Ranjitgarh, which was under Sahib Singh Bedhi, and was situated only at a distance of two kos from that place, and to bring it under their control, saying that its garrison master had, on the previous day, directed his troops to fire from the cannons on his (the Noble Sarkar's) troops. The Noble Sarkar further directed them to march away afterwards, towards the district of Jammu. They left immidiately. The Shahs presented trays containing sweetmeats in celebration of the Diwali Day. It was reported that Shahzada Haidar, the son of Zaman Shah, who had been blinded and was putting up with Hazrat Shah Shuja-ul-Mulk, having exchanged pledges with Muhammad Azim Khan, the ruler of Kashmir, had gone to the other side of Kishtwar. The representative of the Raja of Jasrota and Namdar Khan Gujar were sent to bring Dudu Diwan. Bhayia Ram Singh was ordered to send one thousand gunners with two cannons to accompany Dwinde Khan of Kamona. He said that he would do so. A letter was sent to Raja Fateh Singh Ahluwalia that he should promptly send the son of Sultan Khan of Bhimbar, who was in custody with him, to the Noble Sarkar. A letter from Nawab Ahmad Khan of Jhang Sial arrived together with ten camels. Ten rupees were awarded to the person who brought them. In reply he was sent a letter, asking him to send his troops. At nightfall the Noble Sarkar rode out, watched the illuminations in the army and the town of Sialkot and on his return, witnessed a dance of the dancing girls. All's well otherwise.

News of the Deorhi of Sirdar Ranjit Singh Bahadur. Wednesday, dated 15th November, 1815 (12th Zilhaj, 1230 A.H.); the Stage of Journey, the Village of Kotla at the Foot of the Mountain.

The Noble Sarkar got up early in the morning and came out. The staff and the servant made a bow, and the drum was beaten to announce the march. The baggage was sent ahead, and the staff in charge of the flooring was called upon to carry the royal tent and fix it near the village of Kotla, which is twelve kos from Bhimbar, the Noble Sarkar saying that he himself would reach there quickly. They departed according to his orders, while the Noble Sarkar himself went into the other tent. Diwan Ram Dial stated that, should the Noble Sarkar permit his father Diwan Moti Ram, he would come in to pay his respects. The Noble Sarkar replied that he would be called in on his (Noble Sarkar's) arrival at the next stage of the journey. Taking his meals, he started from the place of his halt in a palanquin towards the next stage of the journey. He went along, enjoying a hunt on the way, to his camp which was fixed near the village of Kotla, after covering a distance of ten kos. A salute was fired from the cannons to mark his arrival. The Noble Sarkar went into the other tent and laid himself down to take rest. He got up again at about sunset, and came to his tent made of the Turkish canopy of scarlet colour. His associates and attendants presented themselves. Moti Ram, the son of Muhkam Chand, came forward and paid his respects. He offered one Ashrafi, eleven rupees and one horse as Nazar. The Noble Sarkar, out of kindness, excused him from presenting the horse and enquired after his health. For two hours he continued enquiring about the affairs of the district of Phillaur, and held a private consultation with him. It seemed quite evident that he was going to be deputed to join the expedition to Kashmir. When four hours of the night passed the Diwan walked out. The representative of the Raja of Jasrota arrived to inform that his master had reached the army together with Desa Singh Majithia. The Noble Sarkar ordered that he would be called in on the following day. Abdul Rahman Khan reported that he had recruited fifty horsemen according to the order of the Noble Sarkar whom he requested to inspect them, so that others might then be recruited. The Noble Sarkar replied that he would do so in a day or two. The garrison master of Kotla came in, paid his respects, offered five rupees as Nazar, and stated that most of the villages of that district had been rendered waste by the Raja of Rajauri. The Noble Sarkar said that they must be populated and made prosperous again, adding that some troops would be permanently stationed there. Sadhu Singh, the brother of Hukma Singh Chimny, stated that, though he was effectively managing his Jagir in the division of Shergarh, yet the zamindars of some two or four villages were still very powerful and had not yet submitted. The Noble Sarkar replied that he must maintain more men and punish those short-sighted fools. When one quarter of the night had passed, the sirdars and others who were present went away and the Noble Sarkar went into the other tent after warning the troops to remain vilgilant and alert. He took his meals later and laid himself down to take test. All's well otherwise.

1815 (25)

News of the Deorhi of Sirdar Ranjit Singh Bahadur. Sunday, dated 19th November, 1815, A.D.) 15th Zilhaj, 1230 A.H.), the village of Kotla.

Mir Mazhar Ali Darogha was ordered to take two or three cannons dragged by horses to Diwan Ram Dial, and to act according to his wish. A fine woollen shawl was granted to the former, who was then made to depart towards Rajauri. One, Moman Shah by name, was ordered to go to Punchh and to keep writing about the condition of that place. The Noble Sarkar, out of his kindness, granted one spear and one gold-threaded saddle to each of the fifty-five swivels and the same threaded saddle to each of the fifty horsemen of his own "Risala" and appointed twenty-five swivels and the same number of axe men to accompany Ram Dial. The Noble Sarkar held a parade of the "Risala" of Dula Singh Malwai and others, and made them depart also with Ram Dial. One, Kotha Wazir, offered a Nazar of five rupees on behalf of the Raja of Nurpur, and stated that his master would come and present himself shortly. Mehr Chand, a representative of Raja Fateh Singh Ahluwalia, was ordered to write to his master to post two hundred horsemen at Shahdara near the Tawaifpul which was close to Lahore, for guarding the road and keeping a watch against thieves and highwaymen. The zamindars of the district of Bhimbar presented Nazars according to their possessions and stated that the fort of Guman, situated near the northern village on the top of the mountain, was so located that if it came into the possession of the Noble Sarkar, his control over that district would be firmly established. On hearing this the Noble Sarkar sent a horseman to Diwan Ram Dial to instruct him verbally to conquer that fort. A representative of Rahimullah Khan, the brother of Akbar Khan of Rajauri, presented himself and, offering a Nazar, stated that the disagreement between him and Akbar Khan still continued, adding

216

that if the Noble Sarkar patronized him, he would seize Akbar Khan from wherever it would be possible and deliver him up to the troops of the Noble Sarkar on their arrival on the scene. The Noble Sarkar said that he would think over the matter on the following day and ordered him to present himself again. Later, he went into his tent. All's well otherwise.

Deorhi of Sirdar Ranjit Singh Bahadur. Thursday, dated 14th December, 1815, A.D. (12th Zilhaj, 1230 A.H.), Amarpur Chumak.

A Vakil of the Rani of Kotli stated that the Rani had come together with her victorious army according to the wish of the Noble Sarkar, and reached a distance of ten kos from that place; adding that on the following day she would join the triumphant troops. The Noble Sarkar replied that he must write to the Rani to vacate Kotli and to assure her that some other Jagir would be granted to her. One, Fateh Din Khan, left under the order of the Noble Sarkar to bring Zabardast Khan, the son of Ruhullah Khan of Punchh, according to his own request. The Noble Sarkar also asked this representative to write to him that he should come over to the Noble Sarkar in a spirit of obedience and loyalty, assuring him that high honour and patronage would be granted to him, but warning him at the same time that in case of disobedience, his fate would be the same as that of Akbar Khan of Rajauri. The messengers (Jauri) came in and stated that Hazrat Mahmud Shah Padshah had entered Peshawar and was determined to proceed to the mausoleum of Pir Ghulam Pir which was situated in the direction of Kashmir adding that Sirdar Fateh Khan Wazir was proposing to present himself to the Noble Sarkar with a view to take the fort with his consent. He further added that two donkeys by the said Wazir alongwith him from Peshawar, had reached his army and were at the time with Gujar Mal Vakil. On hearing it, the Noble Sarkar awarded ten rupees to the bearers and made them go back in the same direction. A letter from Hukma Singh Chimny, the garrison master of Attock, intimated that Hazrat Mahmud Shah had entered Peshawar and deputed the son of Ahmad Khan Torazai towards Kashmir *via* Tibet and that he (the Hazrat) himself intended to march towards Attock, and requested for the despatch of reinforcements. In reply, it was written on him that he should rest assured that he would be sent as many men as he needed. A letter was sent to Sultan Mahmud, the Darogha of the Tophkana, to march from the river Jehlum, and settling up his camp near the town of Fateh Jang, wait the orders which would be sent to him later and act according to them. Sirdar

Desa Singh Majithia and Phula Singh Akalia were sent an order in writing to proceed towards Rohtas and Hassan Abdal.

Friday, dated 10th December, 1815 (13th Muharram 1230 A.H.)

Gujar Mal Vakil presented a small bag containing a letter from Sirdar Fateh Khan Wazir, in which was written, "Evacuate the fort of Attock and make it over to us. Hazrat Mahmud Shah's authority will be restored over it. Come over to this district and we will hold an interview. I will make over to your Noble Sarkar the fort of Multan after getting it evacuated by mutual help. As to the revenue tax of Kashmir it would be paid as it would be assessed." The Noble Sarkar said that this could never be, adding that the fort of Attock could be handed over to him only after the said Wazir handed over the fort of Multan by getting it evacuated and after his agreeing to pay a fixed amount of revenue for Kashmir. The Vakil requested the Noble Sarkar to send some reliable person alongwith him, adding that he would personally take him to the Wazir and bring about the settlement of the affair. The Noble Sarkar approved of this proposal. A letter from Nihal Singh Attariwala intimated, "At the time of my entering into and establishing my Thana over the fort of Karachi, I granted one fourth of the villages of the town connected with the fort to the people who were besieged in it. 1 am stating this simply for your information." The Noble Sarkar held a conference and consultation about his own departure with Raja Sansar Chand. Later, he went into the other tent . All's well otherwise.

1816 (1)

Deorhi of Sirdar Ranjit Singh Bahadur. Saturday, dated 13th January 1816 (12th Safar, 1231 A.H.), Amritsar.

The Noble Sarkar went to the tank of Harmandar Sahib early in the morning because it was the "Sankrant" day, and, taking his bath and offering charities and Nazars before the Granth Sahib and the other shrines of Guru Sahib, came over the place where he always held his court. He got himself weighed seven times with "Ghee", "Shakartari" rice, "Mash", linseed vessels of copper, bronze, gold and silver, all of which he distributed together with five cows and some pictures of gold and silver worth two thousand rupees, by way of charity, among those who wore the sacred thread. He afterwards returned to his place after distributing one rupee to each of them and serving them with "Halwa" and "Puris". The Raja of Nurpur was asked by means of a letter to come to Lahore. A letter from Karam Chand intimated that he, together with Hari Singh Nalwa and others, was engaged in realizing the revenue tax of Chandal Bar, and that, after making collection, he would march ahead. Sardar Dewa Singh of Ropar presented a tray full of slabs of sugar and stated, that leaving his troops in the district of Nowshera, he had come all alone to pay his respects to the Noble Sarkar. The latter replied that he had done well. A letter was sent to Attar Singh of Faizullahpur, asking him to take himself along with his troops to Hari Singh Nalwa. Shiv Dial stated that Khushwaqt Rae,[85] the news agent of Muntazim-ud-Dawala Bahadur, expected some favour and also wanted permission to go to Patiala to attend the marriage of the daughter of Dal Sukh Rae, his brother. The Noble Sarkar replied that he would be called in at the time of leisure. He enquired about the condition of the wine cellars in Amritsar, Lahore etc., from Diwan Ganga Ram. The Vakil of Rani Sada Kaur stated that Kanwars Sher Singh and Tara Singh had come, and were desirous of paying respects to the Noble Sarkar. The latter replied that they must come on the following day. Later, he rode out for recreation and to see the life of the bazaar. All's well otherwise.

1816 (2)

Deorhi of Sirdar Ranjit Singh Bahadur. Friday dated 19th January, 1816 (18th Safar, 1231 A.H.), Amritsar.

Rama Nand Sahu, presenting a tray of sweetmeats and paying his respects, requested that the lease of the salt mines might be allowed to remain with Sukh Dial and Roop Chand as before, adding that if the Noble Sarkar wanted any increase in the stipulated sum he was ready to pay it even from his own pocket. The Noble Sarkar replied that it would be increased by one hundred thousand rupees. Thirty thousand rupees were received from the revenue collector of Jullundur. A robe of honour of five garments was given to Ajudhia Dass, who was ordered to explainfully to the accountants the finances of the country. It was reported that Sirdar Fateh Khan Wazir, marching from Peshawar, had set up his camp near Kundagarh and intended to cross over to this side of the river Sind. The Noble Sarkar heard this and despatched the messengers (Jauri) to bring further news. Thirty-one thousand rupees were decided to be the amount of fine which was to be paid by Raja Bir Singh of Nurpur for his absence. A robe of honour consisting of five garments was awarded to Nasir Khan, the zamindar of Makhad, as a farewell gift. He was further ordered to make search for the property of the money-lenders which had been robbed in that district. Fifty footmen were newly recruited. Sujan Rae Darogha stated that the Sikhs of the battalions were demanding salaries for six months. The Noble Sarkar said that they would be paid in a day or two. At the request of the Vakil of the Raja of Bhadarwala, it was written to the revenue collector of Dinanagar that "Pashmina" worthful thousand rupees which was the property of that Raja had been stolen in his district, and that he must recover it promptly and restore it to its owner, or else he was likely to suffer. It was written to the garrison master of Kangra that he must take thirty thousand rupees from Narain Dass, the revenue collector of that place, and send it over to the Noble Sarkar. One fine woolen shawl was granted to Baqae Khan, a reliable person of Rani Sada Kaur. Besakha Singh Adaltiă stated that Khatries of Sultanpur had requested him that the Noble Sarkar might accept thirty thousand rupees from them, and get them back their property from Raja Fateh Singh Ahluwalia. The Noble Sarkar replied that they must be assured and told that their case should be settled. He asked Rani Sada Kaur, his mother-in-law, as to how much money Sirdar Bir Singh possessed. She replied that if the Noble Sarkar exercised extortion, lakhs would come into his possession. Later, he rode out for recreation through the bazaars, etc. All's well otherwise.

Deorhi of Sirdar Ranjit Singh Bahadur. Sunday, dated 4th February, 1816 (4th Rabi-ul-Awwal, 1231, A.H.), Amritsar.

The Noble Sarkar inspected the drill of the company, and awarded one fine woolen shawl to its Subedar. News about the events of Shahjahanabad arrived, and six rupees were awarded to the bearer. Diwan Bhawani Dass came over from Lahore after completing the marriage ceremonies of his son and made his customary bow. A letter from Kanwar Kharak Singh, the eldest prince, intimated that he was busily engaged in constructing a formidable fort, and that he would present himself to the Noble Sarkar, after completing his arrangements for the proper control and settlement of the country and the fort. The Noble Sarkar asked Mehr Chand, the Vakil of Raja Fateh Singh Ahluwalia, whether his master had written anything about the Nazrana of the Noble Sarkar and the confiscation of the property of Preet Khatri, a resident of Sultanpur. He replied that he was loyal to the Noble Sarkar in every way, and would never go against his order. The Noble Sarkar emphatically ordered Narain Dass, the revenue collector of Kangra, to pay into the treasury the revenue tax for the autumn crop. Desa Singh Majithia stated that Nathu, the Wazir of Chamba, was terror struck by the imprisonment of Raja Umed Singh Jaswal, and was reported to be contemplating running away. The Noble Sarkar ordered Khushal Singh Jamadar to make himself secretly aware of his intentions. Diwan Ram Dial and Sirdar Dal Singh Bharania were sent an order to march from Rohtasgarh, go over to the other side of Rawalpindi, and to keep ready for an engagement in case Sirdar Fateh Khan Wazir and the zamindars of Attock approached them. The special horsemen (سواران خاصگی) were despatched for bringing about the evacuation of the houses of that Raja, and the Taaluqa of Rajpura Duti out of that Raja's territory was made over to Raja Sansar Chand.

Monday, dated 5th February 1816 (5th Rabi-ul-Awwal, 1231 A.H.)

The Noble Sarkar gave a letter of authority to Diwan Bhawani Dass for distributing salaries for two months among the battalion of Dhonkal Singh commandant. Taj Ram reported that Jahandad Khan, the brother of Ata Muhammad Khan, had come according to the order of the Noble Sarkar and desired to pay his respects. The Noble Sarkar replied that he must come on the following day. The revenue collector of Jullunder, presenting a tray of sweetmeats, paid his respects. The Noble Sarkar told Mehr Chand Vakil to write to Raja Fateh Singh Ahluwalia to despatch some of his troops, for bringing about the evacuation of the country of Raja Jaswal. He granted one suit of clothes, yellow in colour, to Sujan Rae, the Darogha of the battalions, as a mark of his favour. Hakim Ruhullah Khan stated that Munshi Devi Dass took bribes from everybody. The Munshi, who was present, replied that he had acquired everything through the blessings and glory of his master and repudiated the accusation. At this the Noble Sarkar smiled. Granting one fine woolen shawl to Kanwars Sher Singh and Tara Singh, his own princes, he told them to send some of their troops for bringing about the evacuation of the country of Raja Jaswal. They replied that they would do so. It was reported that the troops of Raja Karam Singh had conquered Phaura and then gone back to Patiala. It was stated that Suba Singh, the son of Sirdar Jodh Singh of Kalsia, had arrived there with a force of three hundred horsemen. Diwan Bhawani Dass requested the Noble Sarkar to forbid Hakim Ruhullah Khan from picking quarrels with everybody. The Noble Sarkar said that he would be asked to desist. At nightfall, he rode out for recreation to the bazaar in the town. All's well otherwise.

1816 (4)

Deorhi of Sirdar Ranjit Singh Bahadur. Tuesday, dated 6th February, 1815 (6th Rabi-ul-Awwal, 1231 A.H.), Amritsar.

The Noble Sarkar sent his audience tent towards the sacred town of Tarn Taran. Suba Singh, the son of Sirdar Jodh Singh of Kalsia, presented himself and offered a tray of sweetmeats as Nazar to the Noble Sarkar, who enquired after his health and asked him why his father had not yet come, he replied that he had to stay behind owing to a disturbance created by his (Suba Singh's) brother, named Harao Singh, and that he would present himself within a month. Gulab Singh, the grandson of Duni Chand, the Vakil of Raja Bhag Singh of Jind, was allowed to depart with a robe of honour of five garments for Duni Chand, and another of seven garments and an elephant for Kanwar Fateh Singh. The Noble Sarkar purchased five bejewelled under-turbans and one pair necklace from Koto Mal Sahu, and gave one of the under-turbans to Ram Lal, the brother of Khushal Singh Jamadar. He granted a robe of honour of five garments to Nathu, the Wazir of the Raja of Chamba; assuring him, at the same time, that he would be made to depart in a manner befitting his rank. Hakim Imam-ud-Din Khan was sent an order that he should establish the government of the Noble Sarkar in all the places belonging to Raja Umade Jaswal, and to send him over the Noble Sarkar after giving him a Jagir worth something like twelve thousand rupees. The Noble Sarkar asked

Raja Sansar Chand whether he had sent any reliable person to bring about the evacuation of the Taaluqas of Rajpura and Nathi. He replied that he would be· sending there his brother, Fateh Chand, and Naurang Singh Kotwal. The Noble Sarkar said that he would go to the sacred places of Tarn Taran on the following day, and asked him (Raja Sansar Chand) also to get ready. He replied that he would do so. The Noble Sarkar gave marching orders to the battalions and others, and himself rode out and went to Harmandar Sahib, he returned to enter his palace after making an offering of large sums of money to the Granth Sahib. All's well otherwise.

1816 (5)

(Heading Torn). (Probably) 7ᵗʰ February, 1816

The Noble Sarkar got up at about the third quarter of the day, and came out to the tent set apart for the audience. He held a court, where his associates and employees presented themselves. Letter from Jawala Singh, Karam Singh Jahil, and others intimated that the "Thanas" of the Noble Sarkar had been established in all the places belonging to the Raja of Nurpur, and that they were awaiting further orders. After considering them it was written in reply, that they should present themselves promptly to the Noble Sarkar. A letter was sent to Sirdar Garba Singh Bharatgarhia, asking him immediately to come over to the Noble Sarkar together with his troops. Sohba Singh, the son of Sirdar Jodh Singh of Kalsia, arrived according to the summons of the Noble Sarkar, who remarked that, as he had come to render service after such a long time, he should pay something as fine. He replied that he was his obedient servant and would do whatever he would be ordered. Dewa Singh of Ropar stated, that if the Noble Sarkar would allow, he would leave for his own home. The Noble Sarkar replied that he would be given a letter of authority to leave on the following day. Hukma Singh, the Thanadar of Lahore, stated that he wanted to know whatever were the orders for himself. The Noble Sarkar replied that he must come on the following day, when he would be given instructions about certain matters and then allowed to depart. The Akalis · and the other "Babas" of Tarn Taran requested alms, and the Noble Sarkar gave them one hundred rupees. He himself rode out towards the tank at Tarn Taran, and, making an offering of five hundred rupees in cash and to horses equipped with gold-threaded saddles to the Granth Sahib and staying there for a few hours, returned and entered his camp. The zamindars of that place came in, paying their respects and each offering one rupee as Nazar. The Noble Sarkar enquired after their health and greatly assured them. When four hours of the night had passed he took his meals and laid himself down to rest. All went on well otherwise during the night.

Thursday, dated 8th February, 1816 (8th Rabi-ul-Awwal, 1231 A.H.)

The Noble Sarkar got up early in the morning, and came out to the tent set apart for audience. Himmat Singh Chillawala, Nihal Singh, Partap Singh, Jai Singh Attariwala, Diwans Moti Ram and Ganga Ram, Hakim Aziz-ud-Din Khan, and other high and low sirdars came in and made their customary bow. A letter was despatched to Raja Fateh Singh Ahluwalia to present himself promptly. Hakim Aziz-ud-Din Khan was ordered to administer suitable punishment. to all the robbers and dacoits of the "Manjah". He replied that he would do so. The messengers (Jauri) came and brought a letter from the garrison master of Attock that as to the news about Sirdar Fateh Khan Wazir …. (nearly half of the leaf is torn.)

Tej Ram stated that the revenue collector of Hajipur was awaiting permission to pay his respects to the Noble Sarkar, who replied that he must be brought in tomorrow. He ordered the staff in charge of the floorings, at the same time, to take his camp to the district of Nowshera. Action was taken according to the order. One, Captain Baje Singh, who had become tired of the enmity of Khushal Singh Jamadar came in and presented his resignation. The Noble Sarkar replied that he was at liberty to do whatever he liked, that if he wanted to stay on he could, and that it was a matter of his own sweet will to stay or go. Thereupon that person obtained a permit to leave, and asked for another to cross the "ghat" on the way to Ludhiana. The Noble Sarkar gave him the letter of authority. Diwan Ganga Ram stated that salaries had been distributed in all the battalions, and that the battalion of Sikhs had been paid for six months but were expecting further payment. The Noble Sarkar replied that they would soon be given whatever was required. It was stated that the dacoits and robbers of the district of Manjha had left their villages and were on flight, out of the fear of the Noble Sarkar. Two hundred horsemen were appointed to bring the zamindars of Kallowal. The zamindars of the village of Chanab came in, paying their respects and offering one horse as Nazar. The Noble Sarkar enquired after their health and ordered them to pay five hundred rupees into the treasury in connection with straw and grass, or else they were likely to suffer. They replied that they were obedient servants of the Noble Sarkar and would act according to his order. Dhonkal Singh, Harna Singh and other commandants of the battalions came in and were ordered to distribute military equipments among their battalions, and to remain very careful about their duties. They replied that they would act according to the order of the Noble Sarkar. In the afternoon, he went into zenana, took his meals and laid himself down to rest. He got up again, at about the third quarter of the day and came to the tent set apart for audience. His associates and attendants presented themselves. Misar Ganesh Datt of Karunjawal Phulkiwala requested for the payment of his salary and was assured that he would be paid. Hukma Singh Thanadar was ordered to go to Lahore, to remain very alert and watchful in his guard during the day and at night, never to be negligent in that matter, and to continue writing regularly to the Noble Sarkar. The Noble Sarkar rode out to the bank of the tank at Tarn Taran and stayed there for two hours. Later, he rode out for recreation to the open land, from where he returned and entered his tent at nightfall. All persons having walked out, the Noble Sarkar went to the zenana, took his meals and laid himself down to rest when the night had passed one quarter. All's well otherwise.

1816 (6)

News of the Deorhi of Sirdar Ranjit Singh Bahadur. Saturday, dated 10th February, 1816 (10th Rabi-ul-Awwal, 1231, A.H.), the Town of Patti.

The Noble Sarkar got up early in the morning and came out to the tent set apart for audience. Diwans Moti Ram and Ganga Ram, Shiv Dial, Nihal Singh, Partap Singh Attariwala, Himmat Singh Chillawala, Hakim Ruhullah Khan and several other officers and sirdars came in and made their customary bow. The staff in charge of the floorings was ordered to send the camp of the Noble Sarkar towards Patti. Action was taken according to the order. An urgent call was sent to Munshi Devi Dass. Orders were given to the zamindars of Nowshera to arrange for the payment of five thousand rupees as Nazrana. They replied that they had no means to meet that demand. After a great deal of discussion which was characterized by excuses and refusals, two thousand rupees were imposed upon them and they were ordered to pay the same to Khushal Singh Jamadar. An Englishman[88] who had come from Hansi for the last three or four months, came in and stated that the Noble Sarkar had promised, during his stay in the towns of Bhimbar and Amarpur to show him honour and patronage and that no action had been taken to fulfil that promise until then, with the result that he had not even been paid the allowance of three rupees a day which the Noble Sarkar had fixed for him. Thereupon the latter gave him two hundred and twenty-five rupees, and told him that he could go back to his house for the time being but might come again at any time he liked, taking his (the Noble Sarkar's) house to be his own. That person left reluctantly in the company of a messenger whom the Noble Sarkar deputed to see him off. Diwan Singh, the son of Hukma Singh Thanadar, was made to depart towards the fort of Attock, after being awarded one turban and one fine woolen shawl. Narain Dass, the representative from Ramgarh, was ordered to send for Sirdar Bir Singh to the court of the Noble Sarkar. He replied that he would do so. A letter from Kanwar Kharak Singh came with information about the district of Jammu and the messenger was awarded two rupees. A note was sent to him in reply, asking him to leave behind Thakur Davende Khan of Kamona with adequate forces at that place, and to present himself to the Noble Sarkar promptly. Two hundred horsemen were sent to arrest and bring the zamindars of the village of Nandpur. In the meantime, Jawala Singh, Karam Singh Jahal and several others had come in and stated that they had effected the evacuation of all the places in the division of the Raja of Nurpur, and had established the government of the Noble Sarkar over them, and that about one hundred thousand maunds of grain, fifty thousand maunds of gunpowder and ammunition, two hundred swivels, ten cannons, two elephants, two hundred horses and many other things had been seized by them for the Noble Sarkar from that place. The Noble Sarkar heard this and kept quiet. A letter came from Hakim Imam-ud-Din Khan, stating that he had reached the country of Raja Umed Singh Jaswal, and hoped that by the grace of God he would soon force him to evacuate all the places belonging to him and would present himself soon, after establishing the Thanas of the Noble Sarkar in those places. The Noble Sarkar heard its contents and wrote to him in reply that he should give a Jagir worth twelve thousand rupees to that Raja after the establishment of his own government, and should then return and present himself. Each of the zamindars of the village of Nowshera was granted one turban and one lion-cloth of muslin. When the day had advanced one quarter, the Noble Sarkar took his meals and, marching from that place, rode out and entered his tent in the town of Patti after covering seven kos, when one quarter of the day was left. The garrison master of the place came in, paid his respects and offered one horse as Nazar. The Noble Sarkar enquired after his health. He sent two hundred men of the battalion of the Sikhs to bring the zamindars of the village of Dhariwal and Sarhali. Diwan Moti Ram stated that he wanted to say something in privacy and was told that he would be heard at the time of leisure. After that the dancing girls of the town of Patti were called in, and the Noble Sarkar watched their dance which came to an end when the night had passed four hours. Later, he went into the other tent and laid himself down to rest after his meals when the night had passed one quarter. All went on well during the night.

Sunday, dated 11ᵗʰ February, 1816 (11ᵗʰ Rabi-ul-Awwal 1231 A.H.)

The Noble Sarkar got up early in the morning, and came out to the tent set apart for audience. The officials and sirdars came in and made their customary bow. The Noble Sarkar ordered the revenue collector of Patti to pay into his treasury ten thousand rupees. He said to Diwan Moti Ram, that if he liked to suggest that some troops be appointed to go to the other side of the river Satluj to bring about the evacuation of the fort of Ferozepur, the Noble Sarkar would do it. He replied that the Noble Sarkar was a wise man and might do whatever he thought fit. Two hundred horsemen were despatched to capture and bring the tribe of Kul. Baba Naurang Singh, a reliable person of Raja Fateh Singh Ahluwalia, came in and was ordered to say where the Raja was. He replied that he would soon present himself. A letter from Diwan Ram Dial and Sirdar Dal Singh Bharania intimated that they had marched towards Rawalpindi from Rohtasgarh according to the order of the Noble Sarkar. The Noble Sarkar, awarding two rupees to the bearer of the news, wrote to them in reply to remain very alert and careful in matters of watch and ward during the day and at night, and to send regularly the news of the place. A letter was issued to Bakhshi Sultan Singh of Punchh to send the collections in hand soon to the Noble Sarkar. Khushal Singh Jamadar said that the sepoys of the Noble Sarkar who had gone to arrest and bring the zamindars of the village of Dhariwal, did not find them there, and that they, therefore, had plundered the said village and returned. The Noble Sarkar replied that they had done well. A letter from the garrison master of Phillaur intimated about the conditions which prevailed in that district, and the news bearer was awarded one rupee. The revenue collector of Hajipur, presenting one tray of sweetmeats, paid his respects, and was ordered emphatically to pay up the balance of the revenue tax. Himmat Singh Jhalla stated that a letter had come from Raja Bhag Singh of Jind, and the Noble Sarkar replied that he would listen to it at the time of leisure. At noon, the Noble Sarkar went into the other tent and laid himself down to rest after taking his meals. Those who were already present and others walked out. He got up again at about the third quarter of the day, and came out to the tent set apart for audience as usual His associates and attendants presented themselves. A letter from Phula Singh Akalia came to intimate "Just in these days Shahid Khan, the brother of Sultan Khan, the Raja of Bhimbar, had raised a disturbance in union with some zamindars. I proceeded with an adequate force to oppose them and gave them battle. Not being able to resist they took to flight." The Noble Sarkar felt very happy on hearing this, awarded two rupees to the news-bearer, and wrote to him in reply never to be indifferent about the mischief of those short-sighted people, and to continue sending information of that place. Haaker Mal requested some money to meet his expenses and was given two hundred rupees. The representative of Raja Bhup Singh of Haripur stated that his master would come shortly and present himself according to the summons of the Noble Sarkar. The Noble Sarkar rode out to see the fort of Patti and after a trip through it, proceeded towards the open land and returned at nightfall. He then entered his tent, took his meals and laid himself down to take rest. All's well otherwise.

1816 (7)

News of the Deorhi of Sirdar Ranjit Singh Bahadur. Saturday, dated 11th February, 1816 (10th Rabi-ul-Awwal, 1231, A.H.), the Town of Patti.

The Noble Sarkar moved his camp from the previous place to the town of Patti, and imposed two thousand rupees as Nazrana on the zamindars of Nowshera, the work of collections being entrusted to Khushal Singh Jamadar. The Noble Sarkar gave two hundred and twenty-five rupees to an English Sahib who had been here since four months, and who had been promised an allowance of three rupees a day but had not been paid anything until that time. He told the Sahib to go to his house at that time, saying that he could come again whenever he liked, without being in the least formal about his visits. At his request the Noble Sarkar gave him a messenger to see him off. Diwan Singh, the son of Hukma Singh Thanadar, having been granted a turban and a shawl, was allowed to depart towards the fort of Attock. A letter came from Kanwar Kharak Singh, containing an account of the district of Jammu. It was written to him in reply that he should have Thakar Devende Khan of Kamona there with an adequate force, and himself come back promptly to the Noble Sarkar. The Noble Sarkar sent two hundred horsemen to arrest the zamindars of the village of Nandpur. Jawala Singh, Karam Singh and several others came in and stated that they had established the control of the Noble Sarkar over all the places belonging to the Raja of Nurpur, and had seized about one hundred thousand maunds of grain, fifty thousand maunds of gunpowder, two hundred swivels, three cannons, two elephants, two hundred horses and several other articles belonging to that

Raja. A letter from Hakim Imam-ud-Din Khan intimated that, on reaching the country of Raja Umed Singh of Jaswal, he would by the grace of God, establish the authority of the Noble Sarkar over all places belonging to him, and would present himself to the Noble Sarkar afterwards. It was written to him in reply that, after establishing such control he would give a Jagir worth twelve thousand rupees to the Raja and then return. The Noble Sarkar marched forward for seven kos, and entered his tent at the place mentioned above. The garrison master of the town of Patti presented one horse as Nazar. He sent two hundred men of the battalion of the Sikhs for capturing the zamindars of the villages of Dhariwal and Sarhali.

Sunday, dated 11th February, 1816 (11th Rabi-ul-Awwal, 1231 A.H.)

The Noble Sarkar asked for ten thousand rupees from the revenue collector of Patti, and said to Diwan Moti Ram that if he advised him, he would send some of his troops to the other side of the river Satluj to bring about the evacuation of the fort of Ferozepur. He replied that the Noble Sarkar was a wise man and could do whatever he thought fit. After that the Noble Sarkar sent two hundred horsemen to capture the Kul tribe. A letter from Diwan Ram Dial, Sirdar Mat Singh Bharania and others intimated that they had left Rohtasgarh and had marched towards Rawalpindi according to the order of the Noble Sarkar. In reply it was written to them that they must be very alert and careful in matters of watch and ward during the day and at night, and must keep sending accounts every day. Summons of call were sent to Bakhshi Sultan Singh of Punchh. Khushal Singh Jamadar said that, on account of the flight of the zamindars, the sepoys of the Noble Sarkar who had been appointed to bring them, had plundered the village of Dhariwal. The Noble Sarkar said that they had done well. A letter from the garrison master of the fort of Phillaur intimated some news of that place. A letter came from Phula Singh Akalia stating that just in those days Shahid Khan, the son of Sultan Khan, the Raja of Bhimbar, had created disturbance there by joining some of the zamindars, whereupon he had gone to oppose them, and, feeling that they could not stand, they had taken flight. It was written to him in reply that he should never be indifferent about the mischief of those short-sighted people, and should always be writing about them to the Noble Sarkar. After that the Noble Sarkar rode out with a view to inspect the fort of Patti. All's well otherwise.

News of the Deorhi of Sirdar Ranjit Singh Bahadur. Wednesday, dated 14th February, 1816 (14th Rabi-ul-Awwal, 1231 A.H.), the Town of Khemkaran in the District of Manjah.

The Noble Sarkar got up early in the morning at the place known as the village of Mukani, and came out to the tent. His associates, attendants and others presented themselves. He ordered the staff in charge of the floorings to take his camp and fix the same near the town of Khemkaran at a distance of twelve kos from that place. They acted according to the order. Diwan Moti Ram requested to be allowed to go to Phillaur as some affairs were getting worse. The Noble Sarkar replied that he must stay on for another few days. A messenger came and presented a letter from Hukma Singh Chimny, the garrison master of Attock. It was written therein that Sirdar Fateh Khan Wazir was still encamped as previously in the neighbourhood of Ghat Akora. The Noble Sarkar awarded two rupees to the messenger. Six villages in the division of Manjah were granted to Jawahar Singh and Ram Singh to form part of their Jagir. Narain Dass, a representative from Ramgarh, stated that Sirdar Bir Singh had also come from Amritsar according to the order. The Noble Sarkar ordered him to bring him in his presence at about the third quarter of the day. The zamindars of the villages of Mukani were ordered to pay five hundred rupees as Nazrana. Dal Singh Kallat (which is a sub-caste of the Jats) was ordered to hunt out all the dacoits and robbers in the Manjah. When the day had advanced one quarter, he took his breakfast and rode out from the village of Mukani and marched on to the next stage of the journey. Hunting and enjoying himself on the way, he entered his camp in the town of Khemkaran after traversing twelve kos, when four hours only of the day were left. A salute was fired from the cannons. The zamindars of the place came in and offered one rupee each as Nazar. The Noble Sarkar ordered them to pay up one thousand rupees by collecting the same. A letter was sent to Ahmad Khan of Jhang to reach the court at that very place along with his troops present with him at the time. Rajab Ali Khan Afghan of Maharajkot came in, paid his respects and offered one horse as Nazar to the Noble Sarkar, who very cordially enquired after his health. Sirdar Bir Singh of Ramgarh came and had a meeting with the Noble Sarkar who showed him great courtesy, and made him sit on a chair. Both enquired after each other's health. The Noble Sarkar asked him also about the state of his brother, Diwan Singh. Tej Ram said that Gaba Singh of Bharagarh had come to the Deorhi of the Noble Sarkar, wanting to pay his respects. The Noble Sarkar replied that he should come on the following day. News about the events of Shahjahanabad arrived, and the Noble Sarkar awarded six rupees to the bearer. Letters, expressing cordial sentiments, were sent to Raja Jaswant Singh of Nabha and Bhai Lal Singh of Kaithal. When the night had passed four hours the Noble Sarkar went into the other tent, took his meal, and laid himself down to rest when the night had passed one quarter.

1816 (9)

News of the Deorhi of Sirdar Ranjit Singh Bahadur. Wednesday, dated 6th March, 1816 (6th Rabi-ul-Sani, 1231, A.H.), the Bank of the River Beas.

The Noble Sarkar got up early in the morning and came out to the tent set apart for audience. The sirdars came in making their customary obeisance. He ordered the staff in charge of the floorings to send his camp on towards Jalmer. News about the events of Shahjahanabad arrived, and, after considering it, the Noble Sarkar gave reward as usual. One, Faqirullah, the Jamadar of the Rohillas, was asked to cross the river and set up his camp. He said that he would do so. Dhonkal Singh and other commandants were called in, and ordered that as the vanguard of the army and the attention of the troops were directed in another direction, therefore, they must now show any negligence by exercise the utmost vigilence in matters of guard and watch. Harsukh Dass, the agent of Rama Nand Sahu, was told that fifty thousand rupees for distribution as salary among the battalions were needed. He replied that, at that time, he did not have sum with him but expected it to arrive, on that very day from Amritsar, saying that, on its receipt, it would be made over to the treasury of the Noble Sarkar. A note was sent to the revenue collector of Pakpattan to send Sheikh Kamal, the eunuch. Bhai Gurbakhsh Singh stated that somebody had left fifty thousand rupees as a trust with that eunuch, and that as the trustor had passed away, the Noble Sarkar should take that money from him. The Noble Sarkar replied that his means and resources would be investigated. The zamindars of this side of the river Satluj, of the neighbourhood of the division of Bahawalpur, presented one horse each and paid their respects. The Noble Sarkar assuring them and granting them one turban and one loin-sheet to each, allowed them to depart. In the afternoon, he got up from the court, went into the other camp, took his meals and laid himself down to rest.

He got up again at about the third quarter of the day, and came out in the usual manner to the other tent. His associates and attendants presented themselves. Bhai Sahj Singh and Kishen Das, the Vakils, coming from across the river, stated that they had negotiated with the reliable persons of Bahawalpur regarding the revenue tax according to his orders, and that they had been told that the ruler of Bahawalpur could not pay one hundred thousand rupees but would be willing to pay a lesser amount. Kishen Dass added, that being a loyal and sincere friend of the Noble Sarkar, he had brought eighty thousand rupees with one fine horse from them after making assessment. The Noble Sarkar replied that he accepted his decision, but asked further for a written acceptance for eighty thousand rupees for himself and five thousand rupees for his associates and a time limit for their payment. He (Kishen Dass) replied that they would make the payments conveniently. Thereupon the Noble Sarkar granted robe of honour, consisting of seven garments to each of the reliable persons of Bahawalpur and made them depart together with Kishen Dass Vakil, warning them at the same time that so long as they would not pay up the revenue tax (due to the Noble Sarkar) in entirety, his military camp would remain in the district of Bahawalpur and would only be called back after the payment would be actually made. They assured him that they were writing to their master, and that the revenue tax would actually be paid. The Noble Sarkar said to Diwan Moti Ram that the tax had been fixed at eighty five thousand rupees. He approved of the assessment. News came that Davende Khan and Dewan Singh, assisted by Sahibzadas of Nanakputra, had once again turned their attention towards Bhayia Ram Singh. The Noble Sarkar said that he would not accept it without finding out its truth. The Kotwal of the army stated that dry flour was selling at the rate of twenty-five seers a rupee (the English weight). The Noble Sarkar called upon Basant Ram, the provisions supplier of the battalions to supply rations and grain from the parganas of Chuna, etc., in the division of Kanwar Kharak Singh. He replied that that was not possible without a caravan. The Noble Sarkar said that he could send the sepoys of the battalions together with the requisition and get the rations. Later, he rode out for recreation on the river side, and entered his camp at nightfall. When the night had passed four hours, he took his meals and, afterwards, laid himself down to rest when the night had passed one quarter. It went on well otherwise during the night.

Thursday, dated 7th March, 1816 (7th Rabi-ul-Sani, 1213 A.H.); the Neighbourhood of Jalmer, on the Bank of river Beas.

The Noble Sarkar got up early in the morning and came out to the tent and held a durbar. The associates and employees presented themselves. He ordered Jodh Singh of Suriyan and other sirdars to march on and affix up their camps near Jalmer on the bank of the river Beas. Action was taken according to the order. Qazi Kamal-ud-Din, the Vakil of Nabha, stated that he wanted to say something in privacy, and was told that he would be allowed some other time. The Darogha of the Zanburkhana (swivels) requested for money to meet his expenses and the Noble Sarkar gave him five hundred rupees. A letter came from Raja Bhag Singh in reply to that of the Noble Sarkar, stating that he would personally come after a few days, but was sending his son Fateh Singh at that time. After considering it the Noble Sarkar had the reply despatched, that he must come to Amritsar at Bisakhi because the Noble Sarkar was going there after settlement of the revenues of Bahawalpur, Multan and other places. He ordered for the beat of drum to announce the march of the army, and after taking his meals, when the day had advanced by five hours, he himself also marched forward. After traversing a distance of fifteen kos when one quarter of the day was left, he entered his tent which was fixed with the camp in Jalmer on the bank of the river Beas and laid himself down to rest. When one hour of the day was left he got up, called in the dancing girls, enjoyed their dance, and rewarded them with one hundred rupees. Faqirullah Jamadar came and stated that the troops of the other side had also reached that side of the river, set up their camp but intended to advance for opposing the army of the Noble Sarkar. The latter asked all the commandants of the battalions and the special royal horsemen to state whether they would plunge into battle or not in case they were ordered to cross against the other party. They replied that that was their real desire, adding that if the Noble Sarkar ordered at that very moment, they would immediately march to oppose them. The Noble Sarkar called upon Kishen Dass Vakil to go to the troops of his master and to tell them that they must march backwards from the bank of the river, otherwise, the troops of the Noble Sarkar would oppose and put them to flight. He replied that he would go there and would make them march away. When the night had passed four hours the Noble Sarkar took his meals, all those who were present having walked out. Then he laid himself down to rest. All is well otherwise.

1816 (10)

News of the Deorhi of Sirdar Ranjit Singh Bahadur. Tuesday, dated 12th
March, 1816 (12th Rabi-ul-Sani 1231 A.H.), the same Village as
Previously.

The Noble Sarkar got up early in the morning and came out to the tent set apart for audience. The employees and the associates presented themselves. It was reported that fifty thousand rupees sent by Hukma Singh, Thanadar of Lahore, had arrived. The Noble Sarkar said that these must be made over to the Toshakhana. Action was taken according to the order. Sarab Dial of Patiala was called in and asked to state how many men he had with him. He replied that some six hundred men were with him. The Noble Sarkar asked Sarab Dial to prepare a list, containing the name of each of these persons in order. Bhai Sahj Singh came and stated that he had been to Muhammad Khan and Bikham Khan, the chieftains of the army of Bahawalpur, and had talked to them about the revenue tax for the Noble Sarkar. He added that they had informed him that they had sent a letter to the Nawab Sahib, the reply of which they expected in a day or two and that afterwards they would settle the revenue tax of the Noble Sarkar. The latter said that if they paid up the revenue within two or three days would be all right, otherwise he would have to march towards Bahawalpur and plunder the Nawab's country. Sujan Rai was ordered to prepare correctly a detailed account of the salaries for two months of all the battalions. One bejewelled plume was bestowed on Sham Singh, the son of Nihal Singh Attariwala. Fifty Sikhs were newly recruited. Dewa Singh the Vakil of Raja Jaswant Singh of Nabha, presenting two rupees as Nazar, submitted eleven rolls of long cloth on behalf of his master. The Noble Sarkar, turning to him, enquired after the health of that Raja, and kept on enquiring for two hours about the conditions in that district. At noon those who were accustomed to make obeisance having walked out, the Noble Sarkar laid himself down to rest after taking his meals. He got up again at about the third quarter of the day, and came out to the tent set apart for audience. His associates and employees presented themselves. Kishen Dass, the Vakil of Bahawalpur, came in and stated that Munshi Suba Rai had left the Nawab Sahib for the court of the Noble Sarkar with "Hundis" for the revenue tax, and some gifts, and was expected to be present in a day or two. Later, he went out for recreation along with some of his associates towards the river, and, on his return at nightfall, entered his own camp. Taking his meals, he laid himself down to rest when the night had passed four hours.

234

News of the Deorhi of Sirdar Ranjit Singh Bahadur. Thursday, dated 4th
April, 1816 (5th Jamadi-ul-Awwal, 1231, A.H.), a Stage on the Journey
to the Village of Ahmadpur.

The Noble Sarkar got up early in the morning, and announced his march through the beating of the drum. The luggage was sent ahead, while the Noble Sarkar himself came out to the tent and held a court. Bhai Gurbakhsh Singh, Diwans Moti Ram and Ganga Ram, Hakim Aziz-ud-Din Khan and several other sirdars came in and made obeisance. Nawab Ahmad Khan of Jhang came, paying his respects, presented five horses. The Noble Sarkar enquired after his health. A letter came from Phula Singh Akalia, mentioning that he had reached Sirdarpur in the neighbourhood of Multan where he had set up his camp, adding that he was awaiting orders of the Noble Sarkar. After considering it the Noble Sarkar sent him a reply that he must remain encamped there. Bahar Singh Nakka, having been granted a robe of honour, consisting of three garments was deputed to take charge of the fort of Talia and was warned, that as the Noble Sarkar was proceeding further, he must remain on the alert. In the afternoon he left the court, took his meals and laid himself down to rest. He got up again at about the third quarter of the day, and rode out from that place towards the next stage on his journey. After traversing a distance of ten kos, he reached the village of Ahmadpur at nightfall, entered his camp, took his meals and laid himself down to rest after giving an order for keeping strict watch and guard during the night.

Friday, dated 5th April, 1816 (6th Jamadi-ul-Awwal, 1231 A.H.), the
Terrace of Munshi Ram Jeo.

The Noble Sarkar got up early in the morning and announced his march by the beat of drum. The luggage having been sent ahead, he himself rode out on the next stage of the journey and reached the terrace of Munshi Ram Jeo on the bank of the river Ravi after traversing a distance of seven kos, and entered his camp. The servants and the staff presented themselves. Mohsin Shah, the Vakil of Multan, pleaded that the Noble Sarkar must not march further, because the revenue tax would be paid to him. At noon he took his meals and laid himself down to rest. He got up again at about the third quarter of the day, and came out to the tent set apart for audience. The officials and sirdars came in and made their customary bow. The Noble Sarkar said to Nawab Ahmad Khan that he must get ready to collect from his territories rations of grain and send the same to him. He replied that he would do so. He rode out for recreation to the river Ravi, and entered his camp on his return at nightfall. When the night had passed four hours, took his meals and laid himself down to rest during the night.

Saturday, dated 6th April, 1816 (7th Jamadi-ul-Awwal, 1231, A.H.), Sarai Siddhu.

The Noble Sarkar got up early in the morning and came out. The servants and the staff made their customary obeisance. He announced his march by the beat of drum. The luggage having been sent in advance, he rode from that place onwards and reached near Sarai Siddhu on the bank of the river Ravi at noon after traversing a distance of eight kos and entered the tent which was fixed in his presence. Mohsin Shah, the representative from Multan, came in and stated that the Noble Sarkar could take the half of the revenue tax immediately and take reliable hostages for the other half, assuring that the whole sum would be paid up shortly. The Noble Sarkar replied that without the settlement of the revenue tax their pursuit would never be given up. Mehr Chand, a representative of Raja Fateh Singh Ahluwalia, was ordered to write to his master to continue staying in the district of Multan. Letters were despatched to the zamindars of the division in the neighbourhood of (the estate of) Kanwar Kharak Singh to collect rations and grain and to send the same to the army without delay. Mohsin Shah, the Vakil of the Nawab of Multan, requested the Noble Sarkar that he might send Hakim Aziz-ud-Din Khan with him to Multan to realize and bring the large sums of the revenue tax. The Noble Sarkar ordered Hakim Sahib to go along with Mohsin Shah and to bring one lakh and fifty thousand rupees together with four horses, a sword and many other gifts, adding that if they showed negligence or procrastination, troops would be sent there. Accordingly they left for Multan at once. A note was sent to Sheikh Budha, Aziz Khan and the other commandants of the battalions, asking them to present themselves promptly. Diwan Bhawani Dass, Karam Singh Jahal, Jawala Singh and others came in and stated that, according to the orders, they had brought forty thousand rupees, after realizing the same from the tribe of Chhattas. The Noble Sarkar replied that they had done well. Robes of honour, consisting of three garments, were bestowed upon Mohan Singh and Sundar Singh, respectively, and they were sent to collect revenue tax from Nawab Muhammad Khan of Mankera. The Noble Sarkar emphatically ordered the maintenance of proper guard and watch, and, taking his meals, laid himself down to rest during the night. All's well otherwise.

Multan is at a distance of twenty kos from this place.

1816 (12)

Deorhi of Sirdar Ranjit Singh Bahadur. Sunday, dated 14th April, 1815 (15th Jamadi-ul-Awwal, 1231, A.H.), Lahore.

The Noble Sarkar got up early in the morning and came out to the tent. The sirdars made their customary bow. The Noble Sarkar sent word to the commandants of the battalions to march towards Multan. Mohsin Shah Vakil came in and stated that the Noble Sarkar could take fifty thousand rupees in cash immediately, and promised the payment of the remainder in two months. The Noble Sarkar said these terms were not acceptable, and insisted that the whole amount must be paid in a single instalment. Two horses and four thousand rupees in cash were distributed among the poor, etc. He rode out for recreation to the open land, and continued hunting until the evening when he returned to his tent. Taking his meals, he laid himself down to rest. All's well otherwise.

Monday, dated 15th April 1816 (16th Jamadi-ul-Awwal, 1231 A.H.)

The Noble Sarkar got up early in the morning and came to his scarlet tent. The sirdars presented themselves. A letter was sent to Sultan Mahmud, the Darogha of the Topkhana, ordering him to march from his station and cross the river. Letters were sent to Diwan Ram Dial and Dal Singh Bharania to march from their place and go over to the district of Ramgarhi without making any delay. Five thousand rupees were given for the rations and grain of the battalions of Sujan Rae Darogha. A letter came from Abd-us-Samad Khan from Dara-i-Din Panah, mentioning that he would soon be sending his Vakil to the Noble Sarkar, and that whatever he sending his Vakil to the Noble Sarkar, and that whatever he would state verbally, should be regarded as true and certain. Chaudhri Qadir Bakhsh stated that Diwan Jawahar Singh deserved being sent to Kapurthala. The Noble Sarkar replied that he would be allowed to go into the territories of the Raja. Ahmad Khan of Jhang was ordered to pay one lakh of rupees. He pleaded that something less might be taken from him. Bhai Gurbakhsh Singh stated that revenue tax be taken from him with some concession. The Noble Sarkar, taking his meals, laid himself down to rest. He got up again at about the third quarter of the day and rode out for recreation

237

towards the open land. He returned later one. When the night had passed one hour, he took his meals and laid himself down to rest. All's well otherwise.

Tuesday, dated 16th April (17th Jamadi-ul-Awwal)

The Noble Sarkar got up early in the morning and came out to the tent set apart for audience. The sirdars made their customary bow. Attar Singh of Faizullahpur presented a tray full of slabs of sugar and paid his respects. The Noble Sarkar enquired after his health. A note was sent to Sirdar Fateh Singh Ahluwalia, asking him to march from his place, to go over to the division of Ahmadpur, and to establish an entrenchment there. A note was sent to Phula Singh Akalia, asking him to march from his place and go and establish his camp near Multan. Ahmad Khan of Jhang was told that after the evacuation (of Multan) to be brought about with his help, etc., the country of Multan would be given to him. He welcomed the suggestion. In the afternoon, the Noble Sarkar took his meals and laid himself down to rest. At about the third quarter of the day he got up again and came out to the tent set apart for audience. His employees presented themselves. Later, he went to the other tent and began to drink wine. Nobody came to present himself after that. Taking his meals at nightfall, he laid himself down to rest. All's well otherwise.

1816 (13)

News of the Deorhi of Sirdar Ranjit Singh Bahadur. Monday, dated 22nd April, 1816 (23rd Jamadi-ul-Awwal, 1231 A.H.), the Place as Previously.

The Noble Sarkar got up early in the morning and came out to the tent set apart for audience. The sirdars came in, making obeisance. It was stated that dacoits had killed fifteen men of the army on the way. The Noble Sarkar heard this and kept quiet. The brother of Rajab Ali Khan Afghan of Maharajkot, having been granted a robe of honour consisting of five garments, was allowed to depart to assist in the management of the Taalluqa of Ahmadpur. Two horses and two camels and a letter sent by the ruler of Punchh, arrived. In reply the Noble Sarkar wrote him to send the revenue tax expeditiously, and paid twenty-five rupees to the bearer who had brought the letter, the horses and the camels. He was warned that, in case of delay, the amount of that revenue tax which had already been paid, would be forfeited. Mehr Chand, the Vakil of Ahluwalia, stated that his master, the Sirdar Bahadur, wanted a temporary loan of five thousand rupees, and the Noble Sarkar told him to take a "Hundi" from Sujan Rai

Darogha. Letters from Ram Dial and Dal Singh Bharania intimated that Muhammad Azim Khan of Kashmir had apologised for his faults. In reply the Noble Sarkar wrote that he had paid thirty thousand rupees as revenue tax to Sirdar Fateh Khan Wazir, and wanted to know why was the said Sirdar going towards Peshawar, adding that they also should march from that place and reach Lahore. Four horses were purchased from 'the merchants. A letter was sent to Diwan Bhawani Dass to present himself promptly after settling the revenue tax. At noon he went into the other tent, took his meals and laid himself down to rest. He got up again at about the third quarter of the day and came out. All the staff and servants made obeisance. He entered a boat for recreation and returned at nightfall. Entering the zenana, he took his meals when the night had passed one quarter and then laid himself down to rest.

Tuesday, dated 23rd April 1816 (24th Jamadi-us-Sani 1231, A.H.)

The Noble Sarkar got up early in the morning and came out to the tent set apart for audience. The officials and sirdars came in and made obeisance. When the day had advanced two hours, he went to the other side of the river Ravi along with his associates for a hunt, and returned and entered his camp at noon. Taking his meals, he laid himself down to rest. He got up again at about the third quarter of the day, and came out and held a court. The staff and the servants made their customary bow. A letter from Diwan Bhawani Dass came from Multan and stated that he had negotiated with the Nawab Sahib regarding the revenue tax according to the order of the Noble Sarkar, but that the Nawab offered horses and rolls of chintz instead of eighty thousand rupees in cash, and he requested to know the order of the Noble Sarkar in the matter. It was written to him in reply that the Noble Sarkar did not require horses and chintz, that he must take from him eighty thousand rupees in cash, or bring with him Munshi Jamait Rai or Atma Ram Sahu as hostages for fifty thousand rupees, and that failing these alternatives they should be asked to come out and fight. It was reported that Nawab Muhammad Khan of Mankera had died. The Noble Sarkar replied that he would not believe it without investigating the truth of the news. Himmat Singh Chillawala stated that Dal Singh Bharania had intimated that the Vakil of Raja Karam Singh of Patiala had reached Amritsar, and he (Dal Singh) wanted to know how he should treat him. In reply he was ordered to write to him that he should come and stay in Lahore. A letter was sent to Hukma Singh, Thanadar of Lahore, to accommodate Dal Sukh Rai on his arrival in Lahore. The associates stated that the troops felt greatly distressed and tired owing to the rigours of the heat of summer. He replied that it was quite true, but they could not be called back without the realization of the revenue tax from Mankera. It was represented that what the Sardar said was quite right, but that in the country of Mankera, water was not available at all up to a distance of twenty kos in all directions. The Noble Sarkar replied that the troops would move along the bank of the river. When the night had passed four hours, he, taking his meals, laid himself down to rest. All's well otherwise.

1816 (14)

Deorhi of Sirdar Ranjit Singh Bahadur. Friday, dated 10th May, 1816 (11th Jamadi-us-Sani, 1231, A.H.)

One hundred young men were newly recruited. A letter was sent to the garrison master of Attock to despatch the two hundred sepoys of Ramgarh, who were staying with him, to the court of the Noble Sarkar. The Darogha of the cannons driven by horses was ordered to go Shergarh together with Sujan Rai, the Darogha of the battalions. He replied that he would do so. The Noble Sarkar sent eleven garments, one bejewelled under-turban, a turban-gem, a plume and a horse for Nawab Sarfraz Khan of Multan through Sarab Dial. A messenger came and delivered a letter from Raja Fateh Singh Ahluwalia, mentioning that he had laid a siege around the fort of Mahmudkot in the division on Mankera, and felt sure that it would soon be evacuated. All's well otherwise.

1816 (15)

News of the Deorhi of Sirdar Ranjit Singh Bahadur. Saturday, dated 25th May, 1816 (26th Jamadi-us-Sani, 1231 A.H.), Lahore.

The Noble Sarkar got up early in the morning and rode out towards Balawal where he spent a few hours, and then entered into the fort. The sirdars presented themselves. Dal Sukh Rai, a Vakil of Patiala, presenting a Nazar of two rupees, paid his respects. The Noble Sarkar enquired after the health of his master. A letter was sent to Sahib Singh Malwai, asking him to present himself soon together with his troops. A note was sent to Kharak Singh, the eldest prince, to present himself together with Bhayia Ram Singh. A note was sent to Hakim Imam-ud-Din Khan, the garrison master of Gobindgarh, calling upon him to present himself. Diwan Moti Ram, the revenue collector, and Dal Sukh (?), the Darogha of the mint at Amritsar (داروغه دارالحرب امرت سر) and of the construction of work of the city wall and of the tank which lay in his Taaluqa, presented two rupees as

Nazar, and was told by the Noble Sarkar that in matters of the revenue tax he seemed to have committed an embezzlement. He replied that the Noble Sarkar could audit and take any balance from him. Sahib Singh, the Jamadar of the messengers, requested for money to meet his expenses. The Noble Sarkar gave him an order to realize two hundred rupees from the revenue collector of Suryian. Sarab Dial, Munshi Devi Dass and Bhawani Dass stood at the gate and were granted permission to enter it. During the night the Noble Sarkar took rest. All went on well otherwise.

Sunday, dated 26th May, 1816 (27th Jamadi-us-Sani)

The Noble Sarkar got up early in the morning and had a letter despatched to Desa Singh Granthi, asking him quickly to present himself. Bhawani Dass stated that Mohsin Shah and Hamiat Rai, the Vakils of Multan, were awaiting permission to leave. The Noble Sarkar replied that they would be called in on the following day. Jodh Singh Suryianwala submitted that the Noble Sarkar should get him two cannons after taking the same from Baba Sahib Singh Bedi. Diwan Ganga Ram stated that two or three accountants, who were very capable men, were looking for employment. The Noble Sarkar replied that he did not require any man. Jodh Singh Suryianwala was ordered to leave Qazi Sukh Dial in the fort of Nurpur, and was told that if it had been left in the charge of any other person he would have satisfactorily managed it. Narsingh Dass, the agent of Rama Nand Sahu, stated that it was no fault of Sukh Dial because he had come away from there according to the summons of the Noble Sarkar, adding that the Raja of that place had caused mischief and disturbance in his absence. Budh Singh was ordered to write to his father to send his troops towards Nurpur. Himmat Singh Chillawala stated that the fort of Nurpur and other places in the neighbourhood of that district should be entrusted to Desa Singh Majithia, adding that he would manage them very well. The Noble Sarkar replied it would certainly be done like that. Raja Sansar Chand came and stated that he had to say something in privacy. The Noble Sarkar ordered him to speak to Hakim Aziz-ud-Din Khan. Tej Ram intimated that the Vakil of Punchh had come. The Noble Sarkar replied that he should be brought in on the following day. He asked Hukma Singh Thanadar how many men had died in the explosion of gunpowder in the tower. He replied that the city wall had broken down near the tower of the Haveli through the shock of the gunpowder, and that some eight hundred men had died. Later, he rode out to the open and returned to his place in the fort after recreation. Then he went in, took his meals and laid himself down to rest.

1816 (16)

May, 1816 (13th Jamadi-us-Sani 1231 A.H.), the Place as Previously.

The Noble Sarkar got up early in the morning from his sleep and came out to the tent set apart for audience. The officials and sirdars came in and made their customary bow. Pindi Dass, the Vakil of the Nawab of Mankera, stated that although it was very hard for the Nawab Sahib to be asked to pay fifty thousand rupees, yet if the Noble Sarkar would depute a person to accompany him to Mankera, this amount either in cash or in "Hundi" payable at Amritsar, would be procured for him. Hence he was immediately allowed to go on the understanding that he would return and present himself again within seven days. The Noble Sarkar said to the Vakil of Bahawalpur to state how far the river Sind lay from Mahmudkot. He replied that it was five kos from there. Strong wind blow into a hurricane and all the tents were blown away. People came out of their tents and went to their own "Deras". The Noble Sarkar, taking his meals, laid himself down to rest. He got up again at about the third quarter of the day, and came out to the tent set apart for audience. His associates and attendants presented themselves. A letter from Nihal Singh Attariwala intimated that he had plundered the villages situated in the neighbourhood of Mahmudkot, and that his siege around the fort was so well laid that it was likely to be vacated within a very short time. In reply, he was urged to bring about its evacuation expeditiously. Later, the dancing girls were called and the Noble Sarkar watched their dance and continued talking with them jovially. When the night had passed four hours, he took his meals and laid himself down to rest, all others having walked out. Everything went on well otherwise.

1816 (17)

Deorhi of Sirdar Ranjit Singh Bahadur. Tuesday, dated the July, 1816 (13th Shaban, 1231 A.H.), Lahore.

Himmat Singh Jhallawala, Nihal Singh, Partap Singh, Jodh Singh and several others came in and made their customary obeisance. A robe of honour, consisting of five garments, was bestowed upon Vakil of Raja Laldev of Jasrota. Sixteen mortars were distributed among the special royal horsemen. The dancing girls of the town came in with a complaint that the sepoys of the battalions were creating disturbance and disorder in their Dera. The Noble Sarkar replied that they would be punished. Each of the zamindars of the village of Hamidpur, presenting one rupee as Nazar, submitted that the garrison master of Gobindgarh had seized five pairs of their oxen. The Noble Sarkar replied that he would be strictly ordered to return the same to them. Basakha Singh, the Darogha of the Adalat, was warned that he would be removed from his office, which would be bestowed on some other person, if he did not cease to be cruel in the administration of justice. Nihal Singh Attariwala stated that the zamindars of Chosa and Chatarpur

(از بیساکها سنگه داروغه عدالت فرمودند که شمارا برطرف کرده

دیگری را تعلق داده خواهد شد، لدرز عدالت ظلم نه کرده باشند)

had come with a complaint against the tyranny practised by the revenue collector under Kanwar Kharak Singh in demanding dues from them in excess of assessment. The Noble Sarkar replied that he would be stopped from doing so. Fifty Sikhs were newly recruited and made over to the battalion of Rae Sukh who was instructed to inspect their drill twice a day. Each of the zamindars of neighbourhood of the fort of Attock presenting one horse as Nazar, asked for honour and patronage to be shown to them. The Noble Sarkar, bestowing upon them a robe of honour and assuring them, sent them away. He rode a horse and went to the place known as that of Chhaju Bhagat where he made an offering of fifty one rupees. After spending four hours at that place he returned and entered the fort.

Dated the 14th Shaban, 1231 A.H.

The Noble Sarkar inspected the drill of Dhonkal Singh's battalion and saw the firing of the cannons. He distributed fifty rupees to the poor and the needy as charity. He ordered the son of Dharam Singh to take charge of a hundred horsemen. A small bag containing a letter from Sirdar Fateh Khan Wazir, expressing cordial sentiments, was delivered to the Noble Sarkar. Fifty horsemen were despatched for the protection of the passage at the Tawaifpul, so that the dacoits might not cause destruction or commit robbery there. A note was sent to the revenue collector of Gujrat, telling him that he as practicing great cruelty towards his subjects and misappropriating their property, warning him that he was likely to be punished. A letter was sent to Nand Singh, the Vakil of the Noble Sarkar, asking him to keep sending regularly full and authentic news of the glorious sahibs.

15th of the above-mentioned Month of the above-mentioned Year.

A letter from the garrison master of Kangra brought in the news of the events of that places. The Noble Sarkar, awarding ten rupees to the messenger, sent a reply that he must keep sending news about the rajas of the mountainous regions and of other affairs. The Noble Sarkar ordered Jaura Singh Munshi to post sixteen horsemen to guard and watch the Saman Burj day and night. He replied that his horsemen were away on his Jagir. Nihal Singh Attariwala was ordered to send one hundred of his horsemen, and he replied that he would do so. News from Delhi, sent by the grandson of Lakhpat Rai, was studied by the Noble Sarkar who awarded ten rupees to the bearer. Later, he told Garba Singh that he would be given charge of the fort of Maroogarh. All's well otherwise.

1816 (18)

News of the Deorhi of Sirdar Ranjit Singh Bahadur. Wednesday, dated 25th September, 1816 (2nd Ziqaad 1231 A.H.), Lahore.

The Noble Sarkar got up early in the morning and came out to Saman Burj. The sirdars came in and made their customary bow. After that .... (text torn) .... presented a detailed list of the salaries (?) for two months of the battalion of Dhonkal Singh commandant. The Noble Sarkar ordered that the money should be taken from the "Toshakhana" and distributed among them. He said to the Vakil of Raja Sansar Chand, that when he would go to their country three lakhs of rupees would be taken from his Raja as a fine because he had allowed Hazrat Shuja-ul-Mulk to go over to Ludhiana by travelling through his country. The Vakil replied that none of the rajas of the mountainous regions had any information about it, because the Shah was reported to have gone in disguise. The Noble Sarkar said to his associates that some one had told him that the Shah had gone there by traversing the roads and passes through the Taaluqa of the Raja of Chamba but that he did not believe it to be true. A letter was ordered to be despatched to Raja Sansar Chand, informing him that his camp was proceeding to that district and, therefore, he must keep his troops ready to be inspected by the Noble Sarkar on his arrival. Sukh Dial stated that his brother Kaida Mal had died in Nurpur and that, therefore, he wanted leave. The Noble Sarkar replied that he could go. He ordered Sultan Mahmud, the Darogha of the Topkhana, to arrange his departure, and Rama Nand Sahu to go the Bhayia Ram Singh and tell him

244

that, if he was willing to give something more as Nazrana, he would be set free and honoured once again. He replied that he would do so. Kanwar Kharak Singh came and the Noble Sarkar told him that he was bestowing the honour of receiving a robe upon Diwan Radha Ram instead of Bhayia Ram Singh. The Kanwar replied that he did not like the appointment of that Diwan and that it would give him great pleasure if Bhayia Ram Singh was honoured, adding that he would not at all be satisfied with any other person. The Noble Sarkar told him to explain to his mother all the facts, whereupon he replied that she did not accept his words. The Noble Sarkar then kept quiet. Rama Nand Sahu stated that he had gone to Bhayia Ram Singh according to the orders of the Noble Sarkar, and that the latter had said thus, "I have not a single penny with me. If the Noble Sarkar would honour me I will give some money as Nazrana after making collections from the country." The Noble Sarkar asked Hakim Aziz-ud-Din Khan that if Diwan Moti Ram was appointed to manage the affairs of Kanwar Kharak Singh, would he, in his opinion, be able to discharge his responsibilities satisfactorily. He replied that it required time to be able to manage things. At nightfall the Noble Sarkar went into the zenana, took his meals and laid himself down to rest when the night had passed one quarter. All went on well otherwise during the night.

Thursday, dated 26th September, 1816 (3rd Ziqaad, 1231 A.H.)

The Noble Sarkar got up early in the morning and came out to the Saman Burj. The officials and sirdars came in and made their customary bow. The Noble Sarkar ordered the staff in charge of the floorings to set up his camp near the Shalamar Gardens which he wanted to visit on the Dusehra day. Rama Nand Sahu mentioned that the brother of Sukh Dial had died in Nurpur, and while he was away there, his mother had passed away in his absence in Amritsar. The Noble Sarkar remarked that every one in this world had to go that way. A letter came from Sirdar Dewa Singh of Ropar, intimating that he had despatched ten thousand rupees regarding the revenue tax of Gujar Singh. The men of the battalion were ordered to get ready for the march, and the Darogha of the mules was ordered to send the same to Amritsar. Those who were present stated that the glorious sahibs had collected about ten or twelve thousand camels at various places for carrying water and all kinds of grain and stock, etc., but it could not be known to which direction they proposed to proceed. The Noble Sarkar remarked that nobody could know anything about their intentions and that it was only at the court of Khalsa Ji where all sorts of things were discussed openly and plainly. After .... (text torn) .... a robe of honour, consisting of three garments, was granted to Hukma Singh, the Thanadar of Lahore, who was ordered to realize the large sum of revenue tax of Shahdara from its revenue collector and to deposit it into the treasury. He replied that he would do so. A robe of honour, consisting of three garments and a pair of gold bangles, was granted to Besakha Singh of the court of Justice, and he was warned that he must administer strict justice in accordance with the principles of religion and the quality of the deed, so that no poor person should suffer the least unnecessary trouble.

از بیساکها سنگھ عدالت والہ ارشاد نمدند کہ عدل و انصاف از روئے

واحئی دھرم و کرم بکردہ باشند تاکہ بکنے غربا تکلیف نرسد۔

The mother of Kanwar Kharak Singh was asked to express her wish in the matter of release of Bahyia Ram Singh. She replied that she had no other wish besides the wish of the Noble Sarkar. The Noble Sarkar said that Kanwar Kharak Singh wanted to see him free, and she replied that the Noble Sarkar should do whatever he liked, as his authority was absolute. Then he asked her why was she accompanying the troops, and told her to stay at Sheikhupura. She replied that the work could go on without her remaining by their side, and that she could not feel at rest while not watching them. The Noble Sarkar heard this and went into the palace, and, after taking his meals, laid himself down to rest during the night.

Friday, dated 27th September, 1816 (4th Ziqaad, 1231 A.H.)

The Noble Sarkar got up early in the morning and came out. The staff and the servants made their usual bow. He went to the Saman Burj after inspecting the drill of the special orderly youth. The sirdars presented themselves. Kanwar Kharak Singh was granted a robe of honour consisting of eleven garments, one elephant with a silver howdah, a pearl necklace, a turban-gem and a plume, in honour of his appointment over his country. Diwan Bhawani Dass was allowed to depart with a grant of a robe of honour consisting of three garments and the rank of a paymaster in the troops of the said Kanwar. The Noble Sarkar made the battalions of Haryar Singh, Rasal Singh, Sheikh Basawan and Mian Singh march towards the gardens of Shalamar, and announced that his camp was proceeding towards Amritsar, within three or four days. He then rode out for recreation to the river Ravi, and distributed two hundred rupees as charity among poor. Later, he went into the zenana, and, taking his meals, laid himself down to rest during the night. All's well otherwise.

246

NORTHERN INDIA NEWS EXTRACTS

Deorhi of Sirdar Ranjit Singh Bahadur. Friday, dated 20th December 1816 (29th Muharram, 1231 A.H.); the Royal Fort, Lahore.

The Noble Sarkar came out to the Saman Burj. The sirdars who were usually present came in and made obeisance. Summons were sent to Sukh Dial in the mountainous regions. Those who were present stated that Raja Sultan Khan of Bhimbar wished to say that, if the Noble Sarkar would set him free, he would remain loyal and obedient to him for ever. The Noble Sarkar heard this and kept quiet. The gunners stated that they had purchased iron worth ten thousand rupees, and the Noble Sarkar replied that they had done well and must manufacture balls of it. Sant Ram Modi was ordered to send three hundred camels to Sri Gobind for bringing loads of gunpowder and ammunition. The commandants of the battalions were ordered that they should encamp inside the town in their cantonments. Besakha Singh, the Darogha of the Adalat, was ordered to pay five thousand rupees to the men posted at the gates of the city walls, and he replied that he would pay them gradually. Bhawani Dass stated that the troops of Kanwar Kharak Singh had been allowed to go on leave to their homes. The Noble Sarkar approved of it. At about the third quarter of the day, he rode out together with the Kanwar, went to the terrace of Chhaju Bhagat, made an offering of fifty-one rupees and returned riding from that place at nightfall. He entered the fort after making a trip, and engaged himself in watching the dance of the dancing girls.

Saturday, dated 21st December, 1816 (1st Safar, 1232 A.H.)

A letter came from the revenue collector of Sialkot, seeking permission to sell the fifty thousand maunds of grain. A reply was despatched that there was no need of selling it, and that he should send it to the sarai of Nowshera. A robe of honour consisting of five garments, one plume and an elephant was bestowed as a mark of favour on Hira Singh commandant. Narsing Dass was sent to Amritsar to bring Rama Nand Sahu. Mangal Singh Hindustani sought orders for himself. The Noble Sarkar replied that he should rest assured that he would be given some straw (?). Jahan Khan, the brother of Ahmad Khan of Jhang Sial, presenting one horse and paying his respects, submitted that if the Noble Sarkar would grant him an estate he would remain there, and that

247

otherwise he would leave for some other place. The Noble Sarkar replied that he should remain present, adding that he would be suitably favoured. The Noble Sarkar made the expert riders to test some horses. Sheikh Basawan stated that the battalion of the Sikhs wanted to leave to go to their homes, and the Noble Sarkar replied that they would be allowed to depart after the disbursement of their salaries. A horse was given to Ram Lal, the brother of Khushal Singh Jamadar. Bhawani Dass stated that Asa Nand, the Vakil of Mir Sohrab Khan, wanted to depart towards Talpur. The Noble Sarkar replied that he would be allowed to leave, after being entrusted with certain gifts. He ordered him to tell the Vakils of Multan that the instalment had not been remitted and to warn them that it would not be good for them.

Sunday, dated 22nd December, 1816 (2nd Safar, 1232 A.H.)

The Noble Sarkar rode out for a hunt and came back to the fort at nightfall after hunting two pigs. All's well otherwise.

1816 (20)
Deorhi of Sirdar Ranjit Singh Bahadur. Thursday, dated 26th December, 1816 (6th Safar, 1232 A.H.), Lahore.

The Noble Sarkar came out to the Saman Burj, and his associates and sirdars came in and made their customary bow. It was stated that Khushal Singh Jamadar had reached the Shalamar Gardens. The Noble Sarkar asked the Vakil of Ahmad Khan of Jhang Sialan as to how many lakhs of rupees were the income of the Taaluqa of Jhang Sultan. He was told that it might be five lakhs, and that Sujan Rai had been very cruel to the people there. The Noble Sarkar said that he knew all about it, and gave fifty rupees to him to meet his expenses. Sheo Dat Rai, the Vakil of Bilaspur, was given two hundred rupees to meet his expenses. The Vakil of Abdul Samad Khan stated that the Nawab of Mankera had taken possession of two places belonging to his master, and hoped the Noble Sarkar would appoint troops to help him in the matter. The Noble Sarkar replied that he must first pay his Nazrana and then his appointment would be made. He replied that he would do so. Sujan Rae was ordered to give Nazrana out of what he had earned in making embezzlements of the revenue tax of Jhang Sialan. He replied that he would do so as he would be ordered. Himmat Singh Chillawala submitted that the aforesaid person agreed to pay twenty thousand rupees, and the Noble Sarkar replied that he would be charged forty thousand. The Noble Sarkar went to the garden of Khushal Singh and inspected the drill of the battalion of the Sikhs, and later went out for recreation towards the river Ravi. He returned at nightfall to enter the fort where he continued enjoying the dance of the dancing girls afterwards.

Friday, dated 27th December, 1816 (7th Safar, 1232 A.H.)

The Noble Sarkar ordered Nihal Singh Attariwala to speak to Mahabir Singh and Diwan Singh of Ramgarh that they would shortly be honoured, and the Taaluqa of Dharamkot would be given to them as Jagir. The aforesaid person replied that they would not be able to maintain themselves on that Jagir. The Noble Sarkar said that, for the present, they would only be given that much. A letter from Diwan Moti Ram intimated that he had realized twenty-five thousand rupees as revenue tax of Mandi, and that procrastination went on with respect to the revenue tax of Kulu. He further added that the Raja of Mandi had offered himself as surety regarding the revenue tax of Kulu, and had requested him to march away from that place and leave only a small force there, and that he awaited the orders of the Noble Sarkar. Hakim Aziz-ud-Din was asked to state what answer should be given to that letter, and he replied that the Noble Sarkar was the master and could send any answer which he thought best. A letter was sent to Dal Singh Majithia, calling him to the Noble Sarkar. The Noble Sarkar went out of the Saman Burj to see the drill, and continually inspected it until the evening, when he got into a palanquin and came back to the fort.

Saturday, dated 28th December, 1816 (8th Safar, 1232 A.H.)

The Noble Sarkar granted, out of his kindness, a pair of gold bangles and a horse to Diwan Ganga Ram. It was reported that the Topkhana of Ghaus Khan, in charge of the swivels, had reached Lahore. After that Hakim Nur-ud-Din was granted a robe of honour consisting of seven garments and one horse with a letter of grant of the Taaluqa of Dharamkot as his estate, and was ordered further to remain with Nihal Singh Attariwala for a few days. The Noble Sarkar went out for a hunt to the open country at about the third quarter of the day, and returned at nightfall and entered the fort. All's well otherwise.

1817 (1)

Deorhi of Sirdar Ranjit Singh Bahadur. Wednesday and Thursday, dated 8th and 9th January, 1817 (19th and 20th Safar, 1232 A.H.), the place as before.

The Noble Sarkar came out of the Saman Burj, and the men accustomed to offer customary obeisance, did so. A letter was sent to Narain Dass, a Vakil from Ramgarh, calling him to the presence of the Noble Sarkar. Kanwar Kharak Singh stated that he had got ready two horse-driven cannons, and the Noble Sarkar replied that he had done well, adding that he must keep vigilant in all his affairs. Sada Sukh Bharania was ordered that he would very shortly be sent towards Jhang Sialan and he replied that he would go. Jodh Singh of Beego was granted villages in the division of Ramgarh and Shiam Singh Nakki was awarded one fine woolen garment. The Noble Sarkar ordered Diwan Chand accountant to show a parade of gunners, and he replied that he would. The Noble Sarkar reviewed the miscellaneous horsemen and gave the salaries for six months. He bought six articles of jewellery from Hazari Mal, and made Rama Nand to pay their price after bestowing upon him five garments. The Noble Sarkar ordered Hardas Singh, the broker, to call the sons of Bhai Gurbakhsh to the court and take up the definite work. He replied that he would do so. Dadu Mal and Harikishen Sahu came in, and each presented a tray full of slabs of sugar. A letter was sent to the revenue collector of Sahiwal together with several other letters for collecting grain, because the camp of the Noble Sarkar was shortly to go to that district. Another was sent to Hakim Nur-ud-Din to inform the Noble Sarkar what charities and alms had come to be regarded as religious convention through long usage in the country of Ramgarh, for he would let them continue in the future. Diwan Chand accountant was ordered to get prepared fresh planks for the cannons in the place of those which had broken down. One hundred uniform coats of "Banat" were distributed among the battalion of Sheikh Basawan. At about the third quarter of the day, the Noble Sarkar rode out for hunt and returned to enter the fort at nightfall with four pigs, which he had hunted. All's well otherwise.

1817 (2)

Deorhi of Sirdar Ranjit Singh Bahadur. Friday, dated 10th January, 1817 (21st Safar, 1232 A.H.), the place as heretofore.

The Noble Sarkar came to-day to the Saman Burj, and sent a word to Raja Fateh Singh Ahluwalia verbally through his representative, that he should go to Kapurthala, collect his troops and then return to the presence of the Noble Sarkar. The Noble Sarkar realized five thousand rupees as Nazrana from the sons of Bhai Gurbakhsh Singh, and granted out of his kindness one fine woolen shoulder mantle to Jassa Singh Misar, the Darogha of the Topkhana. A letter was sent to Bhayia Nand Singh Vakil, asking him to supply regularly news of Karnal. A note was sent to Rajab Ali of Alawalpur, asking him to present himself to the Noble Sarkar and assuring him of patronage and kindness. It was stated that the place of the "Beragis" had been robbed by Phula Singh Kirpalia. On learning this, a message was sent by the Noble Sarkar to the battalion of the Najibs and the Sikhs to keep ready, for they would be appointed to punish Phula Singh. Those who were present requested that troops should be despatched after investigating the truth of the report. Faiztalab Khan, the son of Sultan Khan, the Raja of Bhimbar, stated that his grandson was in prison since four years and sought his release, adding that he himself might be imprisoned instead. The Noble Sarkar said that he should wait for a few days. He very kindly granted that person one fine woolen shoulder mantle. He rode out to the "Chaubara" of Chhajju Bhagat, and, after distributing two hundred rupees among the poor and making an offering of fifty-one rupees at the "Chaubara," he returned at nightfall to enter the fort. All's well otherwise.

1817 (3)

Deorhi of Sirdar Ranjit Singh Bahadur. Saturday, dated 11th January, 1817 (22nd Safar, 1232, A.H.), the place as heretofore.

To-day Sarab Dial reported that four carts and fifty camels laden with gunpowder and shells, had come from the fort of Dasuha. The Noble Sarkar ordered for their delivery into the Topkhana of Ghaus Khan. Pindu Ratan Singh, the Vakil of Sirdar Jodh Singh of Kalsia, was allowed to depart with a robe of honour consisting of three garments and with a message for his master, that he must collect troops and come over to the Noble Sarkar. Two hundred and fifty uniform shirts and caps made of "Banat" material were distributed among the sepoys of the Battalion of Gurkhas.[91] A letter was sent to Sukh Dial, summoning him. Two horses,

251

sent by Kutb-ud-Din Khan of Kasur, were presented to the Noble Sarkar who awarded twenty five rupees to the person who had brought them. A letter was sent to the revenue collector of Haria to send five hundred maunds of lump sugar to the fort of Kangra. One fine woolen shoulder mantle was granted to the son of Jodh Singh of Surtian. Narain Dass, the Vakil from Ramgarh, came and presented a sword and a waste belt of Sirdar Jodh Singh Mastawfi. The Noble Sarkar liked and kept them. It was stated that a sepoy had made friendship with a loose woman and killed another of her friends but had himself been wounded by a gunshot. The Noble Sarkar ordered that he must be kept in prison. Sujan Rai stated that two hundred camels had come from Jhang Sialan, and the Noble Sarkar directed that they be distributed among the battalions. He rode to the "Chaubara" of Chhajju Bhagat, and making an offering of fifty-one rupees and distributing two hundred rupees among the poor, returned to the fort at nightfall. All's well otherwise.

1817 (4)

Deorhi of Sirdar Ranjit Singh Bahadur. Friday, dated 30th March, 1817 (11th Jamadi-ul-Awwal, 1232 A.H.), the same Place as Before.

To-day the Noble Sarkar ordered his special royal horsemen (سواران خاصگی) to cross the river Ravi and set up their camp at Shahdara. A letter was sent to Ram Dial, the son of Diwan Moti Ram, cautioning him that if the Nawab of Multan paid up the revenue tax it was all right, but otherwise his country should be devastated, that he should go afterwards to realize the tax from Dera Ghazi Khan, and that if he (its ruler) also refused to pay, his country should likewise be plundered. The Vakil of Rani Sada Kaur stated that she wanted troops from the Noble Sarkar who replied that troops would be sent to assist her after the receipt of fifteen thousand rupees from her as Nazrana. He replied that he would pay that sum. A letter arrived from Davind Singh and Amar Singh, intimating that they had reached near Tawabi at a distance of two kos from Phula Singh Akalia, had stopped the supply of grain to him from all sides, that he was sending messages that he would come to them personally, and that if he had come it would be all right but that otherwise they would fight him. The reply was sent that if he surrendered two cannons and one elephant and himself agreed to come over to Amritsar he should not be interfered with, but that in case he talked about anything else he should be punished and brought as a captive to the Noble Sarkar. The Vakil of the Raja of Patiala stated that the troops of his master had joined those of the Noble Sarkar who replied that they had done a very good thing, and ordered his associates to see that all the employees do set up their camp outside the town beside the camp of the Noble Sarkar, and that their failure to do so would be considered as an offense. Asa Nand, the Vakil of Mir Sohrab Khan, was given a letter expressing cordial sentiments for his master, and, having been given a robe of honour consisting of five garments as a farewell gift for himself, was permitted to leave.

Saturday, dated 31st March, 1817 (12th Jamadi-ul-Awwal, 1232 A.H.)

The Noble Sarkar came out to the Saman Burj, and inspected the drill of the special orderly youths. (جوانان اردئی خاص) He kept on inspecting the parade of the miscellaneous horsemen until the day had advanced one and a half quarter, and, afterwards, giving them two thousand rupees to meet their expenses, sent them to join the army of Hari Singh Nalwa. Kanwar Fateh Singh arrived and met the Noble Sarkar who enquired after his health. He replied that he was getting on well as usual. They kept on talking about the glorious sahibs for two hours, observing that they did not recede from any place where they once set their feet. Hardas Singh Doaba and Diwan Singh were ordered to go to Rani Sada Kaur and punish the zamindars of Badli. The revenue collector of Gujrat presented a Nazar of a tray full of slabs of sugar, and, paying his respects, stated that he had brought his revenue tax. He was ordered to pay it into the treasury. In the evening the Noble Sarkar rode out for a hunt, returning to the fort at nightfall.

Sunday, dated 1st April, 1817 (13th Jamadi-ul-Awwal, 1232 A.H.)

The Noble Sarkar went into the garden and kept on drinking wine along with Raja Fateh Singh Ahluwalia and watching the dance of the dancing girls until nightfall. Later, he returned from that place and went into the fort. All's well otherwise.

1817 (5)
Deorhi of Sirdar Ranjit Singh Bahadur. Friday, dated 10th April, 1817 (30th Jamadi-ul-Awwal, 1232 A.H.); Fatehgarh, in the Taaluqa of the late Mahan Singh Kanhya.

The Noble Sarkar rode out with his eldest son towards the next stage of his journey, and entered his tent near Fatehgarh after covering the distance of ten kos. His associates and others came in and presented themselves. Pindi Dass, the Vakil of the Nawab of Mankera, was

Ghazi Khan, warning him at the same time that in case of his making any excuses he would seize the boats carrying property belonging to the camp of Nawab Sadiq Khan and destroy the country of his master. The representative of Nawab Mohammad Sadiq Khan wrote all about the situation to his own master, and the Nawab replied that he regarded it a disgrace for him to surrender him the boats. The said Diwan heard this reply of Nawab Mohammad Sadiq Khan, and plundered *Keechar* territory in his dominions, and sent thousands of camels laden with grains from that place to Khanpur to be used there. That's all.

NEWS OF AMRITSAR

Dated 25ᵗʰ May, the Aforesaid year 1817 (8ᵗʰ Rajab, 1232 A. H.)

Khalsa Ranjit Singh Bahadur is staying at Adian Nagar and Hakim Aziz-ud-Din, Himmat Singh Chilla, Nihal Singh and Chaudhri Qadir Bakhsh are in attendance upon him. The Noble Sarkar made Sheikh Basawan fire canon balls against a target and three balls struck aright. That's all.

A letter from Hukma Singh of the fort of Attock intimated that Wazir Fateh Khan, being afraid of Shahzada Kamran, had sent his tribes of Kamar.

Chaudhri Qadir Bakhsh complained that the orderlies of the Noble Sarkar had used very rude words to his friends and wounded one of them. The Noble Sarkar calling upon them, sent them to prision. Later Chaudhri Qadir Bakhsh begged pardon for their faults and had them released. That's all.

A letter was sent to Diwan Bhawani Dass warning him that if he returned without realizing in full the revenue tax from Shahbaz Khan, he would be compelled to pay up the remainder from his own pocket. That's all.

NEWS OF RAWALPINDI
14ᵗʰ May, 1817 (26ᵗʰ Jamadi-ul-Akhir, 1232 A.H.)

It became known from the men who arrived from Peshawar that repeated invitations had reached the Wazir in Peshawar under the signatures of Hazrat Shah Mahmud, and that the said Wazir was keeping quite because he was awaiting the arrival of the treasurer from Kashmir. That's all.

The messengers (Jauri) had proceeded with a letter from the Noble Sarkar towards Fateh Khan Wazir who had left for Peshawar *via* Rawalpindi.

May you, the nourisher of the poor, continue to enjoy good health. Previous to this, on the 1st June, 1817, news about Peshawar and Amritsar was sent to you, and to-day when it is the third of the aforesaid month, news about Multan, Rawalpindi and Amritsar is being sent herewith and would before your eyes very shortly. That's all.

Yesterday the big Sahib Bahadur came from Shalamar and fell off his horse near the town and receive some injuries on the hand and the arm but nowhere else. Doctor Ladlo Sahib came and treated him.

Sender,

(Seal of Sayyad Azimullah inscribed, 1226)

1817. (7)
Deorhi of Sirdar Ranjit Singh Bahadur. Monday, dated 19th May, 1817 (2nd Rajab, 1232 A.H.)

The sirdars came in, making their courteous bow. Nihal Singh Atariwala stated that five or six villages belonging to him were situated in the Taaluqa of Ramgarh, and that the lease-holders of the district in which they lay were interfering with them in those days. The Noble Sarkar replied that they would be asked to desist. A letter from Divan Moti Ram intimated that, having marched from Sialkot, he had reached Gujrat. A letter from Sukh Dial stated that he had reached and stationed himself near the fort of Rehlu and that the news of the approach of Nathu, the Wazir of Chamba, was afloat. A reply was sent to him to induce Nathu Wazir to come to the Noble Sarkar by holding out to him some kind of temptation. Letters from Dewa Singh of Ropar and another chieftain intimated that, if the Noble Sarkar so ordered, they would manage to collect the revenue tax would be paid to them it would be all right, and that going across that river suddenly was not at all expedient. Letters from Desa Singh Majithia and Amar Singh intimated that they had negotiated with the zamindars of Dewa Batala according to the order of the Noble Sarkar, and that they had sent a reply regarding the payment of the revenue tax. They requested for further orders. The reply was sent that they should accept ten thousand rupees as revenue tax and establish the Thanas of the Noble Sarkar in the various places belonging to them. At about the third quarter of the day, the Noble Sarkar called in the dancing girls and watched their dance until nightfall.

Tuesday, dated 20th May, 1817 (3rd Rajab, 1232 A. H.)

Sayyad Imam Bakhsh, the Kotwal of the army, stated that he had brought ten thieves after effecting their arrest. He was ordered to mutilate their ears and noses and to turn them out of the army.[92] The Vakil of Bahawalpur was ordered to write to his master that if Ram Dial and Diwan Bhawani Dass should ask and require boats to cross the river Sind, he should tell his own employees to deliver the same to them. He replied that he would do so. The Noble Sarkar asked how many lakhs of rupees could be realized as income from Dera Ghazi Khan and was told that in the previous years the sum used to be seven or eight lakhs, but in that year it had been very little. Letters were despatched to the garrision master of Gobindgarh, Phillaur and Ramgarh to take out the old grain from the fort and sell it, and to store new grain in its place. A letter from the garrison master of Rohtasgarh intimated that property to the value of two thousand rupees, belonging to the traders, had been robbed in those days by the zamindars of Basan, also mentioning that, although the latter were closely pursued by horsemen, yet none had been captured. The reply was sent that it would be regarded as very good service on his part if he punished the evil-doers and restored the property to their owners. The Vakil of Raja Bhup Singh of Haripur, having been granted a robe of honour consisting of three garments was permitted to leave. A letter was despatched to the mother of Kanwar Kharak Singh, telling her to go to Lahore promptly as the camp of the Noble Sarkar was shortly going there.

Wednesday, dated 21st May, 1817 (4th Rajab, 1232 A. H.)

A letter from Mangal Singh Kalalwala intimated that he was encamped at that time in Jammu and had sent his men to Pandit Diwan Singh who was procrastinating in coming over to him, and that, as he was pitched on the top of a mountain, the troops could not capture him. The reply was sent that he must send his own men with those of Jammuwala to tell him that he would be granted a Jagir in Jammu, and that if he should thus be induced to come he should deal with him expediently.

258

Thursday, dated 22nd May, 1817 (5th Rajab, 1232 A.H.)

Rani Sada Kaur and Prince Sher Sing came and presented one tray full of slabs of sugar as Nazar and paid their respects to the Noble Sarkar who enquired after their health and asked them to send their troops to the mountainous regions. A messenger brought the news that a force of twenty thousand Durranis had reached the other side of the river Sind from the direction of Dera Ghazi Khan. The Noble Sarkar heard it and kept quiet. All's well otherwise.

1817 (8)

Deorhi of Sirdar Ranjit Singh Bahadur. Tuesday, dated 15th July, 1817(28th and 29th Shaban, 1232 A.H.)

To-day the Noble Sarkar rode out to the bank of the river Ravi and gave away in charity five buffaloes, five suits of clothes, five hundred rupees in cash and several other suitable things on the occasion of "Somti Amawas."[93] Later, he returned to his abode and distributed food to two hundred men who wore the sacred thread. A letter from General Ochterlony Sahib Bahadur arrived from his army with four horsemen, and intimated, "One, named Ram Dass, an employee of Alexendar Sahib, had taken some thousands of rupees from him and had run away to his own place. It is reported that he is staying with the Noble Sarkar. He has some papers of the government of the Company with him. I am sending herewith four horsemen, with whom the Noble Sarkar must send him back, because the relations existing between us and the Noble Sarkar are identical. In case this is not possible the Noble Sarkar must take possession of the money of the Company from him and send it to him (Ochterlony)." On hearing this the Noble Sarkar wrote to him in reply to send one of his accountants, so that he might realise his claims from that person after arriving at an agreed figure. It was reported that Ajit Singh Ladwawala had sent through his Vakil gifts to Muntazim-ud-Daula Bahadur. All's well otherwise.

1817 (9)

Deorhi of Sirdar Ranjit Singh Bahadur. Tuesday, dated 22nd July, 1817(7th Ramzan, 1232 A.H.), the Fort of Lahore.

To-day the Noble Sarkar came out to the Saman Burj, and Partap Singh, Arjan Singh Atariwala, Besakha Singh and several other sirdars came in and made their obeisance. A letter from Raja Akbar Khan of Rajauri intimated that he had practically arranged about the revenue tax which he would soon be sending. A reply was sent that he must expedite the payment, or troops would be asked to march upon his country. A letter was sent to summon Hardas Singh of Doaba for two months. The adjutant of the battalions of Dhonkal Singh commandant was ordered to grant two months' leave at a time to five men from each company to go to their homes, but they were warned that they must in their own interests stick to their promises to return. The news arrived that the Subedar of the battalion of Harnar Singh commandant had fled. An order was issued for his search. Ratan Chand Diwan was ordered to disburse salaries for six months among the horsemen of the late Jaimal Singh. He replied that so far the Noble Sarkar had paid nobody. The Noble Sarkar said that he must present their correct demands and all would be paid. Qaim Shah, the Vakil of Multan, stated that the ruler of Bahawalpur owns a country worth lakhs of rupees. Khuda Bakhsh of Chhatta, presenting a tray full of slabs of sugar as Nazar, paid his respects. The Noble Sarkar inspected the miscellaneous horsemen, (سواران متفرقه) and allowed them to depart after giving them five thousand rupees to meet their expenses. The Vakil of the Raja of Jammu, having been granted a robe of honour consisting of three garments, was allowed to depart. Later, the Noble Sarkar kept on enjoying the playing of fountains until nightfall.

Wednesday, dated 23rd July, 1817 (8th Ramzan, 1232 A.H.)

Besakha Singh prescribed five thousand rupees accruing from the administration of Justice. The Noble Sarkar sent a robe of honour, consisting of seven garments out of his kindness, to the camp of Nawab Abdul Samad Khan of Dera Din Panah. Diwan Bhawani Dass stated that the said Nawab would prove serviceable to the Noble Sarkar at some future time. The Noble Sarkar gave two hundred rupees for the cantonment of special horsemen. The zamindars of Uchh came and each presented one rupee as Nazar and said that the revenue collector of that place was tyrannising over them. The Noble Sarkar told them to stay on there adding what he would soon be called and punished in their very presence. The Noble Sarkar bestowed a robe of honour consisting of three garments out of his kindness on Hakim Alam Khan, a companion of Raja Bhag Singh. He next listened to a report, about the uniforms of the battalions from Hakim Aziz-ud-Din. Two thousand rupees were sent to the camp of Raja Bhag Singh, Harnar Singh, Chet Singh and other commandants were told that they would be granted robes of honour later on. One robe of honour consisting of five garments was sent to the camp of Nand Singh. Rama Nand Sahu was permitted to leave for his home, after being granted a robe of honour consisting of seven garments.

Thursday, dated 24th July, 1817 (9th Ramzan, 1232 A.H.)

To-day the Noble Sarkar ordered Diwan Bhawani Dass to state if he had received any news about Sirdar Fateh Khan Wazir. He replied that he had heard that the said Sirdar contemplated going to Qandhar, but that it remained to be seen. The Noble Sarkar, granting robes of three garments to Uttam Chand and Rup Chand, the Shahs (money-lenders), allowed them to go to their abodes. He watched the parade of the horsemen of Gurmukh Singh and Dial Singh until noon, and rode out at about the third quarter of the day for recreation to the open country, returning to the fort at nightfall. That's all.

1817 (11)

News of the Deorhi of Sirdar Ranjit Singh Bahadur. (Sunday, dated 3rd August, 1817 (19th Ramzan, 1232 A.H.), the Place of Writing as Before.

The Noble Sarkar got up early in the morning, and rode out for recreation through the open land. On his return he entered the fort, and, taking his meals, came out to the Saman Burj when the day had advanced one quarter and held a court. Dhana Singh Malwai, Dial Singh Bharania, Himmat Singh Chillawala, Karam Singh of Rangarnangal, Kutub-ud-Din Khan of Kasur, Dial Singh, Kirpal Singh Khamba, Diwans Moti Ram, Bhawani Dass, and Ganga Ram, Hakim Aziz-ud-Din Khan and several other sirdars came in, making their customary obeisance. Kutub-ud-Din Khan of Kasur stated that his nephew wanted some employment, and the Noble Sarkar told him to bring him on the following day. A letter came from the Thanadar of Amritsar, stating that a gunner in the fort of Gobindgarh had killed another with a swivel as the result of a dispute, so he wanted to know as to what to do in the matter. He was sent a reply that person should be sent to the Noble Sarkar. A letter was sent to the garrison master of Gobindgarh to store three thousand maunds of fuel in the fort of Gobindgarh by purchasing the same. Bhakar Mal stated that Diwan Chand had largerly embezzled the revenue tax of the Noble Sarkar, and was told in reply that he was quite wrong. The aforesaid person repeated once again that all the employees were of the same opinion as he was. A letter was sent to Sukh Dial to present himself, after dealing with matters regarding the revenue tax of the mountanous regions and allowing the troops of those regions to leave for their homes. Mangal Sian Hindustani asked for the lease of some place and the Noble Sarkar told him to produce some security. Tej Ram stated that two thousand rupees about the salaries had accumulated with Dewa Singh of Doaba, and that nothing out of it had yet been paid. The Noble Sarkar replied that he might be "shaken up" and the amount taken from him. The Noble Sarkar had a letter expressing cordial sentiments written in reply to the letters of Nawab Governor Sahib Bahadur and Muntazim-ud-Daula, which he entrusted to the messenger who was allowed to depart after being awarded one hundred rupees. A robe of honour consisting of five garments was bestowed upon Diwan Singh, a companion of Dewa Singh of Ropar, and he was then allowed to depart. Diwan Chand was ordered to purchase iron to the value of two thousand rupees, and to convert it into balls, (جولاها) for the cannons. A letter was sent to Bhupat Ram Bohra to purchase iron worth ten thousand rupees and send it over to the Noble Sarkar. Sultan Mahmood, the Darogha of the Topkhana, was awarded five hundred rupees out of kindness, and was told that a robe of honour as well would be bestowed on him. Mehr Singh Tariwala presented horse and paid his respects to the Noble Sarkar who enquired after his health and asked him to hold a parade of his horsemen. He replied that he would do so. The Noble Sarkar talked for two hours with Khairati Mal, the staff bearer of General Ochterlony Sahib Bahadur who had brought letters from Nawab Governor Sahib Bahadur and General Nasir-ud-Daula Bahadur. Ten Hindustani young men were recruited into the battalion of Aziz Khan. A letter from Ganda Singh intimated that Phula Singh Akalia had told him, that if he be given promise (of pardon) on oath, he would present himself to the Noble Sarkar. One basket of mangoes was sent to the camps of the Vakils of Mankera and Bahawalpur. He then laid himself down to rest after taking his meals. He got up again at about the third quarter of the day when it began to drizzle. He called in the dancing girls and engaged himself in listening to music and songs. Shiam Singh Nakka sought permission to leave and was ordered to wait patiently for the time being. Diwan Bhawani Dass was very angrily told that he was not doing well in not distributing salaries to the troops of Kanwar Kharak Singh. He replied that after checking and correcting their lists, the salaries would be distributed. A note was sent to Sirdar Sada Singh and Hardas Singh to go to Phula Singh Akalia and bring him to the Noble Sarkar. A letter came from the Raja of Jasrota. The Noble Sarkar listened to the music of Atar Khan, the flute player, and then laid himself down to rest during the night after taking his meals.

The Noble Sarkar got up early in the morning, and rode out for recreation to the open country. On his return, he entered the fort, took his meals, and came out afterwards to the Saman Burj when the day had advanced one quarter. He held a court where the sirdars presented themselves by making their customary bow. A letter from the garrison master of Manglan intimated that the zamindars had raised disturbance in those days at the instigation of the brother of Sultan Khan of Bhimbar, and that he had punished them by confronting them at the head of his troops. He was sent a reply that, if they ever made mischief again, troops would be sent immediately on receiving information. Himmat Singh Chillawala stated that there existed friction and dispute between Rattan Singh Garjaki and Gurmukh Singh Lamba, and asked the Noble Sarkar to bring about a settlement between those two. The Noble Sarkar replied that, calling them to his own presence, he would settle their dispute. Hukmi, the Vakil of Raja Sansar Chand, was allowed to depart after being granted a robe of honour consisting of three garments. Fateh Din, the nephew of Kutub-ud-Din Khan of Kasur, presenting a horse as Nazar, paid his respects and was told that he would be given charge of a Risala of horsemen. One basket of mangoes was sent to the camps of each of the commandants of the battalions. The Vakil of Ahluwalia, stated that his master had gone back to Kapurthala after making a trip through Rurbal. The Noble Sarkar replied that he had done well. He further reported that Diwan Ram Dial had caused a great deal of loss to the villages belonging to his master during his march towards Phillaur. Moti Ram was told that it was not a proper thing to do, whereupon he promised that such mistake would never be repeated. After inspecting the drill of the gunners of the battalion, the Noble Sarkar granted them salaries for two months. Ilahi Bakhsh Topkhanawala stated that six gunners had come from Delhi, and the Noble Sarkar told him to engage them. Panjab Singh Atariwala was granted a robe of honour of five garments. Ala Singh was ordered to make a present to the Noble Sarkar of the two mares which were with him. He replied that after sending for them from his villages he would present them. The Noble Sarkar asked Namdar Khan, the Vakil of the Raja of Jasrota, whether the men of his master were accompanying Sukh Dial or not. He replied that five hundred gunmen were ready with him there. Malik Muhammad Khan of Dalwana was granted a Jagir of ten thousand rupees in the Taaluqa of Khushab and was promised honour and patronage. A letter was sent to Jai Dit Singh Mokal to get the fort of Nurpur repaired wherever it had suffered a breach or decay and to demolish his other fort aitogether. Dal

Singh Bharania stated that Jiwand Singh Mokal had seized the cattle belonging to the Taaluqa of Mandera, and had not yet returned them. The Noble Sarkar said that he was a very bad man and did not give up his bad habits. Shiam Dass Adaltia was given a robe of honour, consisting of three garments, and sent towards Amritsar with instructions to administer justice with great care. (که از روئے واحد عدالت آنجا نموده باشند). He replied that he would do so. Man Singh commandant was ordered that he should call his (i) to Lahore and should keep them ready with himself. He replied that he would do so. Five hundred beams were given to Khushal Singh Jamadar for the buildings of a mansion. The Noble Sarkar laid himself down to rest and got up again at about the third quarter of the day. He then went out for hunting together with his associates. After hunting four pigs, he returned at nightfall, entered his fort, took his meals and laid himself down to rest.

Tuesday, dated 5th August, 1817 (21st Ramzan, 1232 A.H.)

The Noble Sarkar got up early in the morning and rode out for recreation to the open country. On his return, he went into the fort, took his meals and then came out to the Saman Burj when the day had advanced one quarter. He held a court which the sirdars attended, making their customary bow. For two hours he kept listening to the report about the battalion of the (i) and to Ilahi Bakhsh Topkhanawala. Hakim Aziz-ud-Din Khan was ordered to prepare and present a letter expressing cordial sentiments for Nawab Governor Sahib Bahadur and General Ochterlony Sahib Bahadur. He replied that he would do so. A letter from Sirdar Ajit Singh Ladwawala intimated that whatever villages belonging to him had been seized by the elder Mr. Fraser, were released at that time according to an order from Calcutta. Kutub-ud-Din Khan of Kasur was ordered to punish the dacoits who were reported to haunt his Taaluqa. He was further ordered to send his troops to his Taaluqa and himself to remain present before the Noble Sarkar. Sheikh Budha said that the battalion of Parmat Singh, a companion of Kanwar Kharak Singh, had raised disturbance about their salaries and had come and stationed itself near the Masti Gate with two cannons in their possession. On learning this, the Noble Sarkar called upon Diwan Bhawani Dass and other employees and peremptorily ordered them to settle their accounts and to distribute salaries to them. The Noble Sarkar distributed among those who were present two baskets of mangoes sent by the revenue collector of Shahdara. A letter was sent to Nawab of Bahawalpur, stating that twenty thousand rupees regarding the balance of the revenue tax had been received by the Noble Sarkar through his representative, Izzat Rai, that during the current year a reduction would be made in his tax at the time of payment, and that his Vakil would be shortly allowed to leave. The Vakil of Rani Sada Kaur stated that Rani Sahiba wanted to present herself. He was told that she would be invited on his arrival in Amritsar. Hira Singh commandant was ordered to permit his comrades to go on leave to their homes. He replied that he would do so. Jodh Singh Chakki was allowed to depart towards his home with a grant of a robe of honour consisting of three garments. Sarab Dial was ordered to go to the camp of Bhayia Ram Singh and to tell him that he would be honoured on the day after the following. After the adjournment of the court, the Noble Sarkar talked about domestic affairs to Hakim Aziz-ud-Din and Diwan Moti Ram. Later, he laid himself down to rest, but got up again at about the third quarter of the day. Nobody was admitted in. The Noble Sarkar allowed Khairati Mal, the staff bearer of the General Sahib Bahadur, to depart after a little talk with him and granting him a robe of honour consisting of four garments and one hundred rupees in cash together with a reply to his letters. After taking his meals, the Noble Sarkar laid himself down to rest during the night. It became known that Hazrat Mahmud Shah Badshah had made Sirdar Fateh Khan Wazir depart towards the province of Herat alongwith a company of troops and grant of a very valuable robe of honour, for Fateh Ali Shah Kachar had created great disturbance in that district. Shahzada Kamran was in Qandhar and had great ill-will for Sirdar Fateh Khan Wazir. The Nawab of Multan had started extortions in Multan, and the people were being put to great hardship and were praying that somehow the English Sahibs might come over and take over the administration of their country.

1817 (12)

Deorhi of Sirdar Ranjit Singh Bahadur. Wednesday, dated 6th August, 1817 (22nd Ramzan, 1232 A.H.)

To-day, the Noble Sarkar called in Sukha Singh of the long beard and asked him to go to the ruler of Multan together with his Vakils and to explain to him that he must send one lakh of rupees as revenue tax to the Noble Sarkar for the current year and to warn him that in case of delay a strong force would be deputed, after the rainy season, to conquer his country. He was allowed to go to the Nawab of Multan with a robe of honour consisting of eleven garments. The Noble Sarkar enquired about the condition of the Nawab Governor Sahib Bahadur from Kanwar Fateh

Singh. He replied that it was being heard all over that he would soon come to the district of Hindustan. The Noble Sarkar said to his associates that, as the lease-holders had made great profits, some tribute must be taken from them. The associates reported that the zamindars of Rohtasgarh had not abandoned their evil practices. The Noble Sarkar replied that he had several times sent orders to the garrison master for their suppression, that no control had been established over them, that he would send troops once again and that they would be punished. They replied that the garrison masters of the place took bribes from them. Later, he went to the river and got into the boat along with the dancing girls and returned to enter the fort at nightfall after a long recreation.

Dated 7th August, 1817 (23rd Ramzan, 1232 A.H.)

One, named Gulab Singh, being given a robe of honour consisting of three garments, was appointed to go and join the battalion of Hira Singh commandant, and to take training in drill vigorously. The Misteris (workmen) were ordered to manufacture strong guns which might not split on firing. A letter was sent to Hakim Nur-ud-Din Khan to distribute salaries for two months to the garrison of the fort of Sialkot. Sewa Singh, the brother of Himmat Singh Chillawala, presenting a tray full of slabs of sugar as Nazar, paid his respects. A letter was sent to the garrison master of Garh Dunala, asking him to get repaired the wheels of two cannons which lay there with him and to send them over to the Noble Sarkar. Ten mortars were given to one, named Mohan Singh, who was ordered to take drill from the men with him daily.

Dated 8th August, 1817 (24th Ramzan, 1232 A.H.)

The Noble Sarkar got up early in the morning and it began to rain. He busied himself in merry-making and enjoyment until the evening, nobody being admitted to offer his customary bow. He called in the dancing girls, inspected them and then allowed them to depart with grants of two hundred and fifty rupees and Benares Dupattas. All's well otherwise.

1817 (13)

News of Multan, dated 21st August, 1817.

On of the 15th of the aforesaid month Dilawar Khan Barakzai, a personal attendant of Wazir Fateh Khan, left Multan for Peshawar. At the time of his departure he asked the Nawab Sahib to send his Vakil alongwith him, but the Nawab Sahib replied that he would send him later. That's all.

The news reached Nawab Sahib that Mukahas of the Jini tribe had been appointed by Khalsa Ranjit Singh to devastate the country of Multan, and that having reached Jhang Sialan they had collected the horsemen of their own tribe and the Sikhs of Kot Kamalia and were planning to raid the belonging to Multan. On learning this the Nawab Sahib appointed Sirdar Khan, Sher Khan and Noor Khan Risaldars with three hundred horsemen to check the aforesaid horsemen and offer them battle in case they entered, even by a step his boundaries. That's all.

The employees of Nawab Muhammad Sadiq Khan Daudaputra seized about sixty agricultural wells from the Taaluqa of Khangarh which belonged to Nawab Haji Muzaffar Khan Bahadur. That's all.

News of Amritsar, dated 2nd September, 1817

Khalsa Ranjit Singh Bahadur is in Lahore and has ordered that six thousand rupees for the salary of Ilahi Bakhsh, the Darogha of the Topkhana, is to be realized from Diwan Bhawani Dass. Diwan Moti Ram was told that the Noble Sarkar had received the news just then that Nawab Governor Sahib had reached in close vicinity of Delhi, and he (the Diwan) was ordered immediately to leave for Phillaur. The Diwan was made to depart immediately with a grant of a robe of honour consisting of seven garments, a pair of gold·bangles and a fine woolen shoulder mantle. That's all.

Hakim Aziz-ud-Din stated that a "Hundi" of one lakh rupees, sent by the ruler of Jhang Sialan, had arrived, and the Noble Sarkar instructed him to hand it over to Diwan Chand, the superintendent of (text torn).

The Maharaja Bahadur spoke to Bhayia Ram Singh about the observance of formalities and ceremonies, and told him that the employees of Kanwar Kharak Singh were putting forth excuses and delaying or avoiding the payment of Nazrana to the Noble Sarkar. The latter directed that he (the Bhayia) was allowed henceforth to exercise the full authority of Kanwar Kharak Singh had remarked that on hearing this news they would certainly be prepared to pay up the Nazrana. He was further ordered to pay his fees to show his goodwill towards the Noble Sarkar, and it was whispered to him that he would be appointed as manager of the affairs of some sirdar as well. That's all.

The Noble Sarkar said to Shankar Dass and other employees of the Kanwar that Bhayia Ram Singh was offering the Noble Sarkar one lakh of rupees, adding that their independent authority could only be allowed to continue as before if they agreed to pay that amount. They replied that they were ready to do whatever would be the wish of their master. That's all.

It was stated that an accountant, a Risaldar and the messengers (Jauri) of Colonel Oscar Sahib Bahadur had come to take accounts from Jaisi Ram accountant who had fled from there and had come to the dominions of the Noble Sarkar. The Noble Sarkar ordered Munshi Hari Ram, an employee of his, to see the accounts being taken from that person in his own presence. That's all.

May the Nourisher of the Poor Remain Secure (غريب پرورسلامت)

The news about Amritsar was sent over to the Hazur on the ninth of September, 1817. To-day when it is the 13th of the aforesaid month of the aforesaid year, the news about Multan and Amritsar is being sent herewith, and it is hoped that it would soon be inspected by the Hazur. That's all.

Sender

Sayyad Azimullah.

(His seal given, inscribed 1226).

News about Multan reached the Hazur on the 3rd of October 1817 (22nd Ziqaad, 1232 A.H.)

News of Amritsar, dated 10th June, 1822 (20th Ramzan, 1237 A.H.).

Maharaja Ranjit Singh Bahadur entered Lahore. Some sirdars and Shahs presented themselves to him and offered Nazars according to their status. The Noble Sarkar inquired after the health of every one. The representative of Nawab Muhammad Sadiq Khan of Bahawalpur presented a small bag containing a letter from his master and three "Hundis" regarding the revenue tax, and also submitted a letter from the Nawab of Mankera. The Noble Sarkar listened to him in privacy and said that his master was treating his subjects very cruelly. He replied that his master had only punished them by way of warning, because the zamindars showed great avoidance in paying revenue. It was reported that the troops of the Noble Sarkar had reached a distance of five kos from Lahore, and would enter it on the following day. Khushwaqt Rae, the news writer in the service of the Noble Sarkar, presented himself, paid his respects and presented some papers. A letter from Jai Singh Attariwala and other from Sirdar Muhammad Azim Khan contained professions of their loyalty and obedience. The Noble Sarkar considered them and postponed their reply to some other time. The Rani of Jasrota related her own affairs and the Noble Sarkar replied that a "Risala" would be appointed to proceed with her for the management of her country. Rama Nand was ordered to show to the Noble Sarkar the account papers of the realization made from the country of Rani Sada Kaur.

When the troops of the Maharaja reached near the river Sind, Muhammad Azim Khan thought to come out for opposition. In the meantime, Muhammad Khan of the Khatak tribe, Bankro of the Mehmand tribe and Khalil and several other Afghans of the Yousafzai tribe wrote separate letters to the Maharaja Bahadur, stating that if the Noble Sarkar agreed to restore their Jagirs to them they would give up siding with Muhammad Azim Khan and come over to him. Muhammad Azim Khan marched towards Kabul alongwith his army with great haste on learning this news, and Yar Muhammad Khan, a brother of the said Khan, who was ruler of Peshawar, accepted to pay forty thousand rupees to the Noble Sarkar as a tribute of submission regarding Peshawar and promised to pay twenty thousand rupees in future. Some reliable persons from Russia came to the presence of Shah Ayyub through Muhammad Azim Khan and stated they were ready to give as much money he wanted to cover the expenses of his troops. Sirdar Muhammad Azim Khan stated that Ranjit Singh was his only enemy at that time and he was sure he would kill him with his own power and had no desire to get any assistance from them. He granted them robes of honour and made them depart. Shah Mahmud was in Herat and Shahzada Feroz-ud-Din was in the holy place of Mashad at that time.

NOTES AND EXPLANATIONS

1. The word is of Hindi origin, and is freely used in Urdu. It literally means the porch or some other structure, through which lies an entrance to the main buildings. Metaphorically, therefore, it stands for a mansion in which a notable person resides. Here it stands for the court of Ranjit Singh.

2. A road measure of about two and a half miles.

3. The word ﺟﺮ is used, which denotes a measure of time equal to three hours. "Pahr" is a Persian word meaning "fourth".

4. Jauri—The text establishes the fact that messages were carried to and from the court by a pair of messengers, each one of them being known as a Jauri messenger. These "Jauris" are being sent on all important missions and are distinct from other messengers who are not described as such.

5. In Sikh times, as in the time of the Mughals, a "Thana" was more in the nature of a military post than a police station and formed the most visible indication of the fact that the territory was in the occupation of the ruler on whose behalf the "Thana" was established.

6. *Hundi*–A document which, generally speaking, served the same purpose as do bills of exchange in modern times. It was negotiable.

7. Nasir-ud-Daula—A courtesy title given by the Mughal Emperor to Colonel Ochterlony. It literally means Defender or Helper of the State.

8. Darogha.—Superintendent, the man in charge of an organisation.

9. A fortress or a fortified place, such as provided a good defensive position against attack or obstruction in the path of an advancing force.

10. "Ghat" means a ferry, a place where the river is fordable and thus provides a passage.

11. "Gulbadan," literally means, with body like a rose. Here it means a kind of silken cloth.

12. A house, a dwelling, a habitation, a residence of a notability.

13. An executive officer of not a very high rank, such as a constable or a subordinate magistrate.

14. A justiciar or a judge.

15. An interesting statement indicating the institution of a regular news service, which, we also know from the Sikh official records recently recovered from the fort at Lahore, was maintained by Ranjit Singh in a systematic manner.

16. A lion-cloth. In some parts of this province the word is used for a variety of turbans made of silken materials.

17. A voluntary but conventional contribution in cash made on the occasion of the marriage of a relative or a friend.

18. Denotes a religious ceremony among the Hindus, according to which a person chooses to give in charity the equivalent of his own weight in cash or kind.

19. Refers to the sacred thread which all true Hindus must wear constantly after being formally initiated into Hinduism by the priests. This resembles the confirmation ceremony of the Christians.

20. The Muslim annual festival at which they offer prayers in the forenoon and sacrifice animals to commemorate the sacrifice of Abraham.

21. Refers to the Badshahi Mosque standing in front of the Lahore fort.

22. A religious mendicant. _____

23. The first day of the Hindu month of the Bikrmi era.

24. A gold necklace.

25. Col. Ochterlony.

26. Har Mandar Sahib is the name of the building situated in the center of the tank in the Golden Temple at Amritsar. It was founded by Guru Ram Dass, the fourth Guru of the Sikhs.

27. Bungas—are the various buildings which surround the tank of the Golden Temple at Amritsar. These were built at different times by Sikh chiefs and others to provide temporary shelter to the pilgrims.

28. Mehmoodi. A fine texture in muslin.

29. The Ganga Jamni style. A mixed design in cloth like check pattern used largely by orthodox Hindus.

30. Nazar. A present; an offering from an inferior to a superior; a voluntary gift offered to a king by his subjects. To Ranjit Singh, this was a large source of income, as such payments in cash or in kind were very often exacted by him from his subjects compulsorily.

31. A quarter consisting of a number of adjoining buildings with a spacious compound in the center of them.

32. Mir Munshi. The chief of the scribes. It was an old Mughal office which disappeared under the British regime in India, after surviving for many years in the Panjab as the Persian Secretariat.

33. Granth Baba Sahib. The most sacred scripture of the Sikhs containing the teachings of the ten Gurus, usually known as the Granth Sahib.

34. "Parshad Karah". Usually called "Karah Parshad". A kind of pudding; a sweet paste made of flour, sugar and butter. The Sikhs often associat. this preparation with their religious ceremonies and regard it as a sacred food.

35. Bara Dari. A room with twelve doors, so designed as to allow a free draught of air through it. Such places were largely used by notable persons for both formal and informal sittings particularly in the hot weather.

36. A big entrance divided into three doors.

37. Clarified butter which is largely used in cooking by Indians.

38. A variety of cloth.

39. An enclosure round a tent.

40. The word is used with regard to fruits and vegetables. A basket of fruits.

41. A well-known Hindu festival celebrated largely by sprinkling liquid colours on one another's clothes. Ranjit Singh observed this festival with great pomp, as is evidenced by various accounts of British visitors to his court.

42. The statement is significant as it provides positive internal evidence about the date of this important event of Ranjit Singh's reign.

43. The reference is to an important meeting which took place between Ranjit Singh and Fateh Khan at Rohtas in December, 1812, and the outcome of which was an arrangement arrived at between the two rulers regarding a joint expedition to Kashmir. This arrangement is repeatedly referred to in this text and provided scope for diplomatic negotiations and hostilities between the Sikhs and the Afghans in subsequent years. See Sohan Lal's *Umdat-ul-Tawarikh* and other contemporary works in connection with this episode.

44. Refers to the descriptive roll which is prepared at the time of enlistment of a recruit in the army to establish his identity.

45. Illustrates the feudal practice of assigning Jagirs or landed estates to various chiefs for maintaining fixed bodies of horsemen for service. Ranjit Singh maintained a large force of irregular horsemen known as the "Ghorcharas" on this basis.

46. General Lake.

47. This text provides valuable contemporary evidence about the extortion of Koh-i-Noor from Shah Shuja-ul-Mulk by Ranjit Singh. This account may profitably be compared with others given in other contemporary works.

48. This refers to a ceremony of exchanging turbans between two individuals who thereby formally proclaimed their brotherly regard and affection for each other.

49. Literally means determination to part with something. It denotes a Hindu ceremony marked by giving away cash or kind in charity as an act of propitiation.

50. The eleventh day of a Hindu month, counted from the day following the evening on which the moon makes its appearance.

51. A rich oriental dish prepared from rice, meat, butter, etc.

52. This represents a department of Ranjit Singh's artillery—the one which was concerned with the maintenance of swivel guns (Zamburaks).

53. See note 50 on "Sanklap" above. This refers to the Sikh practice of giving something in charity and also of offering a prayer to God.

54. Is a well constructed with steps to approach the surface of water.

55. Relates to one of the preliminary skirmishes that led to the battle of Haidaru which was fought between the Sikhs and the Afghans on 13th July, 1813.

56. This is interesting as it reveals the fact that there had started, even as early as 1813, diplomatic negotiations between Ranjit Singh and Shah Shuja-ul-Mulk—a fact which is usually ignored by writers of Sikh history.

57. Ranjit Singh charged specified sums from his chiefs who were in charge of his seals for their affixation. This was called "Moharana."

58. A "Kirpan" is a dagger and represents one of the five religious symbols of a true Sikh.

59. Dussehra represents, perhaps, the greatest and most popular religious festivals of the Hindus.

60. The 7th month of the Hindu (Bikrmi) era.

61. This is significant as it indicates the inauguration of a systematic organization of news service which was flung far and wide in all directions. See note 15 above.

62. A personal attendant.

63. It is said of Ranjit Singh by most of the contemporary European writers that he paid little attention to the proper administration of justice by his officials who acted tyrannically in most cases. This view has been controverted by Dr. G. L. Chopra in his "The Punjab as a Sovereign State." Here is further evidence of an indisputable nature to show that the Sikh ruler watched his judiciary vigilantly in their work and enjoined strict orders upon his "Adaltis" to be just and merciful in their decisions. This new evidence, indeed, is so positive and definite that we propose to offer it in original Persian in these notes:— به سجان رائے داروغه دعدالت ارشاد کردند که از داه دهرم عدالت کرده باشند

و هر کسی غربا ظلم و تعدی نسازند.

64. The original reads thus. لیکن دهرم و کرم عدالت کرده باشد.

65. We are told that Ranjit Singh never gave his name to any building, coin or monument or any other relic of a lasting nature. This is generally true, for we know of no one. Thus the name "Ranjit fort" used here is interesting as providing an exception to this general rule. The original reads:-

پروانه بنام حکما سنگه تهانه دار لاهور بدی مضمون نویساننده روانه کرد که امسال بارش باران

بسیار گر دیده است ضروری است , شجرت قلعه خوب نگه باید داشت. ذمه ایشان است.

66. Refers to the Hindu ceremony of propitiating goods by offering sacrificial food through fire.

67. Religious recreation by priests or theologians.

68. A form of charity according to which cash or kind is waived over the head of a person on whose behalf it is given in charity.

69. The king of Kabul is styled here as "Shahanshah," the Emperor.

70. Is the 14th day after the appearance of the moon according to Hindu computation.

71. The day on which the moon does not appear.

72. The 2nd today of the appearance of the moon.

73. The last month of the Hindu calendar.

74. A "Pacca" seer is equal to 1¼ seers of English weight.

75. See note No. 74 above. The English seer is "Kacha."

76. Shows to what extent the policy of westernizing the Sikh troops had progressed by 1814.

77. Mr. William Frazer Sahib (1784—1835), Commissioner of Delhi and a Major in Skinner's Horse. He was murdered on 22nd March, 1835, at the instigation of Shams-ud-Din Khan, the Nawab of Firozpur, who was hanged for the murder.

78. See note No. 76 above.

79. Is the name of a saint whose residence stands as a protected monument in the compound of the Mayo Hospital, Lahore.

80. A most interesting statement showing the deep-seated distrust of the English by Ranjit Singh. The original is quoted in full along with the text.

81. Another interesting statement of Ranjit's view about the Gurkhas and the English. Is quoted in the next in original.

82. This points to the approximate date of the flight of Shah Shuja from Lahore.

83. This is interesting as providing positive evidence about the fact that Ranjit Singh did inflict mutilation in certain cases. The original reads:-

فرمودند گوش و بینی آنها بریده از شهر بدر سازند.

84. The tracts lying between the Beas and the Ravi rivers.

85. The author of *Kitab-i-Tarikh-i-Punjab*—a valuable Persian Manuscript to be found in the British Museum, London. See the *Punjab as a Sovereign State* by Dr. G. L. Chopra, and also the last letter in the present collection.

86. This was the title of Mr. (afterwards) Sir Charles Metcalfe granted to him by the Mughal Emperor.

87. Ranjit Singh wanted Ram Lal to embrace Sikhism. Ram Lal fled from the Punjab but was brought back to Lahore by his brother, the Jamadar, on the insistence of the Maharajah. This incident is notable as it temporarily threw the Jamadar out of the royal favour and paved the way for the advancement of Dhian Singh.

88. It will be interesting to establish who this man was, as he was certainly one of the earliest among Englishmen who visited the Punjab in the lifetime of Ranjit Singh.

89. See note 76 above. The original reads:-

دوصد و پنجاه کرتی و علیائے یانات به سپاه در پلٹن گورکھا تقسیم شاکرده.

90. See note No. 83 above. The original reads:—

از غارشده که گوش و بینی تراشیده از لشکر بدر سازند.

91. See note No. 73 above. When the "Amavas" falls on a Monday it is so called and such Monday is regarded particularly auspicious for giving things in charity.